Learning to Teach
...not just for beginners

Revised and Expanded
3RD edition

The Essential Guide for All Teachers

BY LINDA SHALAWAY

NEW YORK • TORONTO • LONDON • AUCKLAND • SYDNEY
MEXICO CITY • NEW DELHI • HONG KONG • BUENOS AIRES

Teaching *Resources*

Acknowledgments

This third edition, just like the first two, results from the support, encouragement, and guidance of many people. It is the product of the wonderful experience I've had for more than 25 years working with dedicated professionals around the country.

Drs. Judith Lanier and Lee Shulman, former co-directors of the Institute for Research on Teaching at Michigan State University, greatly influenced my ideas and attitudes about teaching. Under their tutelage, I learned and wrote about many different aspects of teaching and research. The conversations we had as we pored over manuscripts—discussions of professionalism, the wisdom of practice, the growing knowledge base, and the never-ending challenge of learning to teach— are reflected throughout this edition and the first two. Their vision of professional teachers as thinkers and decision makers has inspired my efforts and the work of many others.

Dr. Maureen Mulvaney of Waynesburg College, who supervised my efforts to earn a teaching certificate, has also greatly influenced my professional attitudes and practices, as has Dr. Luise Savage of West Virginia University, director of my master's degree program in special education.

Leanna Landsmann, former editor-in-chief and publisher of Instructor Publications, was the impetus behind the first edition. Terry Cooper, who currently heads Scholastic Teaching Resources, initiated the book's subsequent revisions. I thank them both for their wisdom and their commitment to the book in general.

Editor Sarah Longhi skillfully and even cheerfully piloted this revision through the murky waters of major overhauls; much has changed in educational policy and practice since the last revision, and Sarah made sure the revision reflects these changes. Her editing and organizational skills made my job much easier! I am truly grateful for her expertise, commitment, and pleasant nature. It was wonderful working with her! Sarah organized a host of teacher reviewers from across the country who provided input and constructive criticism, and I thank all of them—Tim Bailey, Tamara Glupczynski, Cindy Gulisano, Alexis Ann Ludewig, Rhonda McGlinn, Bonnie Murray, Jon Runnalls, Debbie Smith, and Karen Vanek. Other teachers who provided a keen editorial eye and helped ready the manuscript in a number of ways include Rebecca Callan, Allyson Daley, Katie Lucarelle, and Rebecca Zerkin.

Thanks, too, to all the teachers and researchers I have ever worked with and learned from, especially the late Doris Dillon. Doris did not get to see this third edition, but her spirit lives on through the insightful comments and suggestions she offered at the book's inception; her deep practical knowledge continues to echo throughout this revision.

Thanks to my first (and best) teacher, my mother, Pearl Fulmer. And special thanks to my husband, Scott, who continues to be my constant support and inspiration. Balancing his own writing, consulting, and radio career with his wife's and children's overextended lives, he remains the anchor for all of us. And to Nora, now a college senior, and high-school sophomore Emma, who wasn't even born when I wrote the first edition—thanks for your patience and understanding with a project that took away many of our hours together. You are the reasons I care so much about good teaching.

Contents

Contents

Chapter Three
Motivating Students: Effective
Teaching Strategies

Contents

Contents

Chapter Six
Home-School-Community Connections

Chapter Seven
Teachers Helping Teachers

Contents

Chapter Eight
Reflective Teaching:
Thinking and Growing Professionally

Introduction

"Teachers can have the satisfactions of both scientists and artists in their professional lives. They can have the scientific approach in teaching: careful observations of their children, which is gathering evidence; experimental attitude in planning programs for their children, which is testing their data; flexibility in changing plans according to their findings. Teachers can function as artists in building a curriculum. They can be creative, not slavishly bound to a pattern, in thinking and planning for and with their children."

—Lucy Sprague Mitchell, educator and author

In her 1950 treatise *Our Children and Our Schools*, Lucy Sprague Mitchell gave voice to a concept of teaching that was years ahead of its time. Since then we have begun to fully embrace the notion that teaching is, indeed, both a science and an art. That's what makes it so attractive to creative, intelligent practitioners. And like the arts and sciences, teaching is a fluid, evolving process. Teachers meet new students, new situations, new knowledge, new challenges every year. Good teaching demands constant refinement and fine tuning. It's a lifelong process, and teachers are lifelong learners.

Learning to Teach is a celebration of this process of teacher learning. Teaching isn't a job; it's a lifestyle. As Stanford Professor Emeritus Lee Shulman, president of the Carnegie Foundation for the Advancement of Teaching, has said, "a school is a community of learners, and no one is entitled or obligated to learn more continuously, reflectively, and joyfully than teachers themselves." And as educator Willard Walter Waller wrote, "These recruits that face teaching as a life work are ready to learn to teach, and they are ready, though they know it not, to be formed by teaching."

Teaching in today's classrooms calls for reflective professionals set apart by special knowledge and skills. This is the "science" of teaching. We've learned a lot about "what works" because research is continually yielding a large and growing knowledge base. Research has documented the effects of various teaching strategies and identified different teaching and learning styles. The "art" of teaching occurs when skillful, caring professionals adapt this scientific knowledge to specific situations and students and to their own teaching styles and interests, exercising personal and professional judgment to decide what approach works and when to use it. This marriage of science and art contributes to one's "vision of teaching"—the vision that master teachers rely on to survive the pendulum swings as educational trends and fads play themselves out.

Like teaching itself, educational research is a fluid process. Teachers need to be aware of "the emerging character of educational research, the ways in which its findings and recommendations are always evolving and becoming reformulated," says Lee Shulman. This, in fact, is the reason for this new edition. We've learned a lot more about teaching—and learning—since *Learning to Teach* was first published in 1989. And we've acquired an awesome new partner: technology. Educational technology in the form of computers, the Internet, digital cameras, and multimedia in general has so revolutionized American classrooms that it now plays a lead role in teaching and learning. We've also witnessed the recent introduction of major federal education legislation featuring statewide standards and high-stakes testing; this legislation impacts all phases of teaching and learning in public schools.

Teachers contribute greatly to the knowledge base of education. Researchers refer to this as "the wisdom of practice." Teachers are not technicians implementing "teacher-proof" curricula but "artists" designing the curriculum to fit both the teacher and learner. Teachers plan with their students, not just for them. They understand the need students have to share ownership in what and how they learn.

However, contributing to the knowledge base about teaching is probably the farthest thing from the minds of beginners—the education major fresh out of college who has just received a first teaching assignment and begins work in three days, or the retired biologist embarking on a new career as a middle-school teacher, or the five-year veteran who has been reassigned to a different grade or subject area. These beginners are just trying to survive. Chances are that many of them, like others before them, will discover they are on their own to sink or swim.

Survival skills must come first: learning to manage a classroom, learning to organize standards-based instruction, learning to deal with colleagues and school policies. But it is not enough to simply "survive." Research shows that professional growth can be limited by teachers' reluctance to give up the very practices that helped them get through their first year.

So first you learn to survive. Then you begin to think about specific teaching strategies and developing your own style. Still later, you seek to refine and improve the strategies you adopt. It is this third step in the learning-to-teach process—striving to improve—that continues throughout the career of a good teacher.

This book is a guide and map through those first years of teaching and into a lifelong career. And like a map, it can point you in the right direction, but you have to

Special Note to Beginning Teachers

Welcome to the ranks of professional teachers. There's no easing into it, so just forge ahead. Right from the beginning you have the same duties and responsibilities as the most experienced veteran. As a beginner, you may have had four or more years of college, a one-year graduate course, or just six weeks of emergency training to prepare for this moment. No matter how long or how much, it's never enough.

Oh, you're familiar with classrooms, all right. For at least 16 years you've sat in them. Yet somehow, the scene is strangely unfamiliar from the other side of the teacher's desk. As all those eager faces stare back at you, the great expectations you held about teaching seem to melt away.

If this is your first year, you may suffer from a case of the beginner's blues. Whether you are fresh out of college, changing careers, or assigned to a radically different group or subject, you may experience such beginning symptoms as nervous apprehension, sweaty palms, sleeplessness, feelings of inadequacy, and nightmares about those 25 or 30 faces waiting for your words of wisdom—while you have nothing to say.

Take heart. Every teacher goes through this.

What can you do?

Take a deep breath, count to ten, and tackle each task one step at a time. Put your justifiable anxiety to work for you as a positive, creative force; it means you really care about doing well. And that says a lot for you as a professional educator and a dedicated teacher.

get there yourself. There are no direct transits; there are no signposts in teaching that guarantee specific results. Effective practice depends on skilled decision makers matching what to teach, and how, with different students in many different situations.

This book combines information about teaching with practical suggestions for how to apply that knowledge. It is a blending of the wisdom acquired by experienced teachers with insights gleaned from recent research. The voices of teachers nationwide echo throughout its pages. It represents the ideas, experiences, and contributions of numerous educators, including my own personal reflections as a teacher. It is a book of peers communicating with peers and lending support along the way.

Like knowledge in general, knowledge about teaching isn't linear but is interrelated. Thus, some topics in this book appear in more than one place. The first chapters concentrate on setting the stage for effective instruction. These chapters mirror the needs and concerns of all teachers, especially beginners: well-managed classrooms, interested and involved students, and organized days.

Subsequent chapters address the other major aspects of teaching: understanding children as learners, effective instructional practices, strategies for improving student behavior, special subject-matter concerns, assessing student learning, working with parents and the community, collaborating with colleagues, and professional development.

As a professional, you will combine the guidelines offered within these pages in a personal way to achieve your own special instructional approach. And you will renew and improve your teaching by continually examining its effect on student learning. I take tremendous comfort from the words of

teacher and author Mem Fox in her book *Radical Reflections:* "Teaching, like any art, is an endless cycle of trial and error. If you imagine you will one day have the whole game sewn up, think again and keep thinking."

And as you continually think and reflect about good teaching and strive to be the best teacher you possibly can be, know that your efforts really count for something. For as anthropologist Margaret Mead has pointed out: "Never doubt that a small group of thoughtful, committed citizens can change the world. Indeed, it's the only thing that ever has."

That's what good teaching is all about.

Chapter One

A Good Place to Start: Classroom Organization and Management

"Two children poke one another. Five or six others wander aimlessly around the room. I lean down to help a child with her writing, and she doesn't even know this is writing time. I hear a sudden noise at my back, and someone yells, 'Ouch!'"

—*Donald Graves*

Even though he's now retired from the classroom, Donald Graves has this recurring nightmare. "I suspect this is a common dream for anyone working in our profession," says Graves, a well-respected author and writing consultant. "Most teachers struggle with classroom organization throughout their professional lives."

To be a good teacher, it's simply not enough to know the subject matter or to like children. Effective teachers know how to manage and organize classrooms. An efficiently organized and managed classroom eliminates many potential behavior and learning problems and sets the stage for a productive year.

As veteran teachers know, a well-organized classroom doesn't just happen. It takes a lot of advance planning and hard work. Some of the most important work of teaching takes place before the first day of school. This is when teachers arrange the physical environment, decide upon the routines and procedures they'll use for daily life in their classrooms, plan curricula and activities consistent with state standards and benchmarks, and open lines of communication with parents.

It's important to get off to a good start before students even set foot in the classroom. Be ready for them on that first day of school. First impressions really do count. The attitudes and expectations students develop as early as the first few hours of school affect their behavior and learning all year. Even if you've received your teaching assignment late and have only a day or two to get ready, you can accomplish many of the most important preparations for creating a stimulating, effective environment that will motivate children, enhance learning, and reduce behavior problems. (If the school year begins *tomorrow*, proceed immediately to "The First Day" on page 46. Read the rest of the chapter when you have time.)

This chapter offers information and tips for creating an efficient, well-run classroom. It will help you organize a learning environment that fosters an atmosphere of community and collaboration, success and acceptance, joy and challenge. The emphasis here will be on the first few days and weeks of school, because this is when the most important management and organization work occurs.

❖ Important Beginnings for Beginners

If you are a new teacher or are new to a school, you need to get to know your colleagues before school starts. Perhaps the principal or someone else will introduce you to the building staff. If not, don't wait for people to come to you. Take the first step. Introduce yourself as a new teacher and explain that you are trying to learn the proper procedures. People will appreciate your effort and be much more inclined to help.

In addition to other classroom teachers, make sure you meet the custodians, secretaries, kitchen staff, librarians and media specialists, counselors, and special teachers (reading, math, gifted, Chapter 1, ELL, art, music, physical education, and so on). If time doesn't permit face-to-face encounters before school starts, ask for an organization chart that lists the staff in these positions.

Also, be sure to:

✔ read the school policy manual.

✔ learn the physical layout of the building.

✔ become familiar with schoolwide objectives.

✔ obtain a copy of your state curriculum standards—and READ it. (Find your state's standards and benchmarks on your state's Department of Education Web site. See Chapter Four for more information about standards and standards resources.)

✔ write out a detailed first-day schedule, keeping in mind that you must remain flexible enough to respond to the unexpected.

You'll also want to begin stockpiling materials. Long before the school year starts (or even before you have a permanent teaching position), you can develop an idea file and start collecting supplies. On page 14 you'll find great ideas for items to collect and what to do with them once you have them.

❖ The Physical Environment

Warm, well-run classrooms begin with the room's physical layout—the arrangement of desks and working space, the attractiveness and appeal of bulletin boards, and the storage of materials and supplies.

Arranging Space

The physical layout reflects your teaching style. If you want students to collaborate in small groups, for example, organize them around tables or clusters of desks. For frequent whole-group discussions, try a circle or U-shaped desk configuration. If you plan on an individualized, self-paced curriculum, you might set up learning stations.

The physical layout should also reflect you. Don't hesitate to give the room your personal touch with plants, art, rugs, posters, and maybe some cozy pillows for the reading corner.

"Creating a caring, child-centered environment takes lots of thought and planning," says fifth-grade teacher Frank Garcia. "Basic bulletin boards are not enough. I believe in a very colorful classroom with posters, functional bulletin boards, and other 'interesting' items to enhance the environment, such as a small refrigerator, TV, and a stereo system with CD player."

Materials to Save

Copy and post this list as a reminder of things to save for class projects—and ways to put these materials to work.

Save, stash, scrounge, tuck away:	To concoct, convert, invent, turn into, use for:
Paper bags	Costumes, masks, fold-away towns, wigs, puppets, forms for papier-mâché animals
Plastic lids	Coasters, frames, mobile parts, molds for plaster plaques
Buttons	Jewelry, mosaics, eyes for stuffed animals, decorations, collages, games
Panty hose/stockings	Weaving, braiding, knitting, crocheting, soft sculpture, doll or puppet heads
Cardboard fast-food containers	Unusual displays for class work or special projects
Nuts, cones, pods,	Mosaics, jewelry, decorated wreaths, candle rings, boxes, frames, flower and seed pictures
Stones, shells, and water-smoothed glass	Paperweights, sculptures, jewelry, mosaics
Pressed flowers, leaves, and grass	Place mats, window transparencies, collages
Rug and tile samples	Hot-dish mats, covers for small books, mosaics, fuzzy boxes, dioramas
Odd mittens, gloves, and socks	Finger and hand puppets, clothes for small dolls, loops for pot holders
Hangers	Simple mobiles, cloth banners, weavings, or masks
Scrap wood	Toys, carvings, construction, games, building blocks, printing blocks
Shredded paper	Stuffing for cloth dolls, animals, or pillows
Bits of string, yarn, and cord	Macramé, weaving, stitchery, knitting, crocheting, braiding, string painting, animal tails
Gift wrap paper	Collages, paper weaving, paper chains, origami, beads, dioramas
Old jewelry	New jewelry, accents in macramé or ceramics, holiday ornaments, collages
Wire	Armatures for papier-mâché or clay sculpture, flexible skeletons for cloth dolls, jewelry
Hair rollers	Armatures for cloth, clay, plaster, or papier-mâché sculpture, parts for doll furniture, jointed dolls, snakes, or marionettes
Plastic meal trays	Printmaking, necklaces, frames, dioramas
Plastic packing chips	Decorative chains, constructions
Foil pans and trays	Plaques, ornaments, jewelry, lanterns, rhythm instruments
Egg cartons	Containers, sculptures, animals, planters, sorting
Film canisters	Collecting and storing tiny items (such as beads)
Wallpaper samples	Frames, mats, crafts
Magazines and newspapers	Collages, math problems, compare/contrast writing

In Reggio Emilia, a northern Italian town that has internationally acclaimed early childhood programs, classrooms feature displays of children's work, collections of "found" objects, ample space for supplies (all aesthetically arranged), and clearly designated spaces for large- and small-group activities. Reggio Emilia educators stress the need for a classroom environment that informs and engages the child. They consider the physical space to be "another teacher." And in the sense that it can motivate children, enhance learning, and reduce behavior problems, the environment really is an extra teacher.

Author and educator Mike Hopkins points out that personal teaching style and specific educational needs should largely determine how you design your classroom space. Hopkins urges teachers to forget about the way things have always been done and to visit museums, libraries, other schools, and colleagues' classrooms to identify different ways of organizing learning space.

Many teachers prefer to create different areas within the classroom. For example, a classroom might feature a quiet reading corner, a music area where students can play soft music while completing work, a discussion/conversation center, a large table for cooperative projects, spaces for wet or messy projects, multimedia spaces, learning centers or stations, and individual work areas.

Easily accessible materials and supplies can eliminate delays, disruptions, and confusion as students prepare for activities. In poorly arranged classrooms, students spend a lot of time waiting— waiting in line, waiting for help, waiting to begin.

To eliminate some waiting, store frequently used items such as scissors and paste in several different areas.

Desk Placement
In many classrooms, the largest amount of space is devoted to the arrangement of individual student desks. Teachers' preferences for

Special-use spaces can be designated with something as simple as an area rug. Or you can get really imaginative, as one Greer, South Carolina, teacher did, and create a reading nook from an old rowboat lined with pillows!

DESIGNING CLASSROOM SPACE
The sky's the limit when it comes to designing classroom space. Here are three suggestions to spark creative ideas:

- Ask for material or time donations from friends and family members who have skills that may improve the design and function of your room. One teacher from Nevada asked her husband, a carpenter, to make a special desk with a recessed top. She used the desk to keep math manipulatives accessible and in one place.

- Collect clean food containers with lids and shoe boxes of different sizes to help organize materials. For example, pizza boxes stacked for storage can house finished projects, art supplies, manipulatives, and other long, flat materials.

- Make unique spaces in your room that serve special purposes. Teachers have placed comfy rocking chairs, giant rubber tires, and even old bathtubs in a quiet corner to serve as a special reading space. A fourth-grade teacher from New York built an eight-foot high loft (it can hold six children) in his classroom that functions as a puppet theater, quiet reading/writing space, teaching platform, private conference space, test make-up area, and place to stage skits, science experiments, and more.

desk arrangements vary greatly, but most teachers agree that the days of 30 desks lined in neat rows and facing the teacher's desk up front are long gone. Instead, some teachers like to arrange desks in cooperative groups of four, while many others prefer a U-shaped configuration, where everyone has a front-row seat.

"What's your purpose for your desk placement?" Mentor teacher Tim Bailey suggests teachers consider this question. "If all of your students need to see the chalkboard at one end of the room, then don't arrange the desks so that their backs are to it."

But no matter how you arrange desks, don't be afraid to make changes. Rearranging the furniture to support positive student interactions is essential from the first day of school through the rest of the year.

"Set your room up, and at the end of each unit

Safety Tips

As you design your space, keep basic safety precautions in mind. Use this checklist at the beginning of each school year.

- ☐ High-traffic areas (pencil sharpener, for example) are free of congestion.

- ☐ Students' desks are always visible.

- ☐ Art and science supplies—especially anything sharp or toxic—are stored safely.

- ☐ Breakable items are displayed or stored in safe places.

- ☐ Students can easily see instructional displays and presentations from their desks.

- ☐ Students have space to store their belongings.

- ☐ Electrical outlets are available, but frayed cords and other dangers are not.

- ☐ Window and door exits are unobstructed.

- ☐ Rugs are fastened down so no one trips.

- ☐ Fire drill procedures and exit routes are posted by the door.

- ☐ Your name, class, and room number are posted on the classroom door, where parents and students can easily see them.

16   Learning to Teach

or month, evaluate and make changes," advises fifth-grade teacher Laurie Borger. "Move students' desks on a regular basis so all children learn to cooperate with others."

Wisconsin teacher Alexis Ludewig offers this suggestion for managing seating changes: "Put each child's name on a small sticky note. You can arrange groupings and change seating assignments easily and yet maintain a current seating chart for substitute teachers." She explains that it's also easy to note any special seating considerations, such as vision or hearing, on the back of the sticky note.

Environmental Preferences

Other important environmental features include temperature, lighting, and noise level. These factors affect students in different ways and are directly related to individual learning styles. Studies suggest that when teachers adjust the environment to students' preferences, the students perform better academically and are better behaved.

How can you address environmental preferences in the classroom? Here are some tips from research and practice:

✔ **Create both well-lit and dimly lit areas** in the classroom by using bookcases, screens, plants, and other furniture. Some children learn best in bright light, but others do significantly better in low light. Bright light actually makes some students restless and hyperactive. Try allowing students to sit where they feel most comfortable, or try placing fidgety children in low-light areas and listless children in brighter areas.

✔ **Provide opportunities for children to move around** while visiting learning centers and other special classroom areas. Most of us have the mistaken impression that children learn best when sitting still, but research now proves that many children need extensive mobility while learning. These children learn significantly more if they move from one area to another as they acquire new information.

✔ **Establish informal furniture arrangements** where students can sit on soft chairs or pillows,

or lounge on the carpet. Another myth is that children learn best when sitting up straight in hard chairs. About 75 percent of the total body weight is supported on only four square inches of bone when humans sit up straight in a hard chair, so it is easy to understand how the resulting stress on the buttock tissues causes fatigue, discomfort, and the need for frequent changes in posture. Research supports the commonsense notion that many students pay better attention and achieve higher grades in more comfortable positions.

✔ **Set up listening stations with headsets** for children who need sound, and quiet study areas for those who work best in silence. Many children disprove another commonly held conception: that silence helps students concentrate better.

✔ **Help students become aware of their own temperature preferences** and encourage them to dress accordingly. Temperature preferences vary dramatically, and most children can't concentrate when they are either too cool or too warm. Ask students who tend to be chilly to keep an extra sweater at school.

❖ Learning Centers

One feature of many classroom environments is the learning center. A learning center is any part of the classroom designed for independent learning. Learning centers can offer individualized, curriculum-based instruction in exciting packages. For example:

✔ a full-length mirror where kindergartners try on costumes, masks, hats, or silly glasses. Here, they role-play and learn about themselves and their friends by observing and creating their own mirror games.

✔ a Book Box on a table filled with reading materials about a particular subject or theme, or organized by author or genre.

✔ an Art Cart with materials and instructions for making mobiles, puppets, dioramas, cartoon strips, crayon rubbings, and friendship cards— all tied to the curriculum.

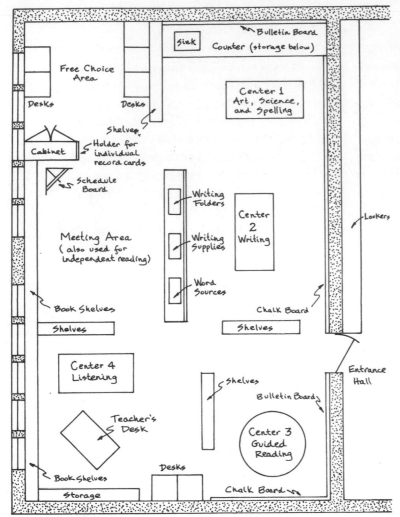

a sample layout of a classroom with effective learning centers

The following labels appear in the classroom layout:
- Sink
- Bulletin Board
- Counter (storage below)
- Free Choice Area
- Desks
- Center 1 Art, Science, and Spelling
- Desks
- Shelves
- Holder for individual record cards
- Cabinet
- Schedule Board
- Writing Folders
- Center 2 Writing
- Lockers
- Meeting Area (also used for independent reading)
- Writing Supplies
- Word Sources
- Book Shelves
- Shelves
- Chalk Board
- Shelves
- Center 4 Listening
- Shelves
- Entrance Hall
- Bulletin Board
- Teacher's Desk
- Center 3 Guided Reading
- Book Shelves
- Desks
- Storage
- Chalk Board

✔ a Math Path, where students find math games and activities stored in a large box.

✔ a Spare Chair, a comfy seat in a quiet corner designated for independent reading.

✔ a Writing Center, stocked with different types of paper, model fiction or nonfiction pieces, story starters, grammar tip sheets, word lists, and editing pencils.

Students of all ages love the challenge and the change of pace that working in a center promotes. Learning centers allow children to explore, apply newly learned skills, feel independent, be creative, and interact with peers.

You can use learning centers to supplement or enrich the curriculum, for "free-time" activities, and sometimes to deliver much of the curriculum. When you want to work with small groups or individual students, learning centers are an exciting alternative to seatwork. You can use centers as rewards or as places for extra help and practice. Use them to encourage students to cooperate or work independently. Learning centers are also a great way to involve parents as classroom helpers. One group of parents at Tinicum Elementary School in Pennsylvania meets regularly to design, implement, and monitor elaborate learning centers.

No matter how you use learning centers, the important thing is that you do use them, suggests author and educator Bonnie Murray. Learning centers "can provide reinforcement of newly learned skills as well as opportunities for children to discover new ideas for themselves," Murray writes. "They allow children to interact with other students and to manipulate learning materials."

Maintaining Effective Centers

Establishing and maintaining effective learning centers requires some advance planning and thought. Centers should be designed so that students can work independently. First, decide on the intent or purpose of your centers: enrichment, academically based free-time activities, or content instruction. Then, follow these suggestions offered by Mary Beth Spann, author of *Quick-and-Easy Learning Centers: Word Play*, and other mentor teachers:

✔ Begin with one learning center in an area of personal strength or in an area especially interesting to you and your students.

✔ Tie centers into your curriculum: the content or skills can change to match what you are studying in a particular subject area.

✔ Create a storage system of boxes, file folders, or large envelopes. Label all of the materials in each storage container.

✔ Include a variety of activities to engage different types of learners—avoid providing only paper-and-pencil tasks.

✔ Remember that children respond to inviting environments such as cozy corners, attractive decorations, and special touches from students (a mural painted on a cardboard room divider, for example). Area rugs and netting or sheer fabric also help set off an area and make it appealing.

✔ Account for the needs of second-language learners.

✔ Model expected behaviors and introduce learning objectives when you open the center and as needed throughout the year.

✔ Invite students to contribute to your centers with personal collections or related artifacts and items.

✔ Allow for some student choice. Simply rotating students doesn't allow them to practice self-direction and responsibility, Murray explains. "Keep in mind that choice doesn't mean a free-for-all," she cautions. To limit the number of children at individual centers, Murray suggests putting labeled clothespins or necklaces at each one. "When the labels for a center are gone, students know to select another center."

✔ Designate a special place to display student work.

✔ Invite donations and ideas from parents.

✔ Watch the centers in action to determine which seem most engaging and successful and which need fine-tuning.

✔ Periodically add new activities/centers to maintain student interest, but be realistic about how often to do so. Weekly is too often.

✔ Take photos of the centers to help you set them up the next time around. Alexis Ludewig suggests: "It is a great idea to take photos of learning centers, not only for your reference, but also for a volunteer to re-create for you in the future. I keep a mini photo album that I use as a reference when planning." Ludewig further notes that she puts a copy of the photo with the center's storage container and all its parts.

Arizona teacher Alice Rice points out that in learning centers, students learn decision-making skills, record keeping, filing, time management, and interpersonal skills. Rice has developed many learning centers herself and employs them extensively in her classroom. Each center generally has one theme with four activities. The purpose of an activity may be to teach, enrich, remediate, have children apply a new or previously learned skill, or test. Rice suggests that each learning center include these six features:

1. the objective

2. simple directions

3. a sample, when appropriate

4. materials in a self-contained box, folder, or area

5. a self-checking or proofreading system, if possible

6. follow-up or recognition by the teacher

Here are Rice's tips for organizing and maintaining learning centers:

✔ **Organize centers around subjects** such as art, creative writing, language, math, and independent reading.

✔ **Give centers catchy titles** such as Art Cart, Math Path, Think Tank, and Spare Chair.

✔ **Designate a monthly theme**, based on students' interests and grade-level standards, to tie together activities and learning centers. Rice uses the following schedule with third graders:
September—Friendship
October—Sports and Hobbies
November—The Five Senses/Thanksgiving
December—Celebrations Around the World
January—Jobs and Careers
February—Patriotism
March—Space
April—Ecology
May—Review

✔ **Plan the year with another teacher** who is interested in rotating themes and sharing materials.

✔ **Solicit help from volunteers.** Parents can help collect materials, make the activities, set up the centers, and assist students. (Make sure parents understand the purpose of the learning centers.)

✔ **Give students opportunities** to draw, color, cut, glue, match, list, write, play games, sequence items, talk, listen, fasten or connect, tie, select, compare, classify, outline, assemble, rearrange, and so on as they learn academic content.

✔ **Set a time schedule** for using the centers. (Rice and her team teacher schedule two 40-minute periods back-to-back each morning. During each period, half the students are in learning centers while the other half are in reading groups.)

✔ **Supply the necessary materials** for each activity. Usually, it doesn't work to have students sharing materials for different activities.

✔ **Provide a record sheet listing** the activities and have students record the ones they complete. They can keep the record sheet and the papers and products they produce in their own folders. By developing activities that are self-checking, you can pare down your paperwork and teach students to be responsible for their own learning.

✔ **Periodically review student folders** and decide how much catch-up or review is necessary, if any.

Be creative. Learning centers are limited only by your imagination. They are as simple or complex as you wish to make them.

A Sample Center

Here's an idea for an easy learning center that will motivate students all year long. This interdisciplinary center, developed by Lynne Kepler, author of *Quick-and-Easy Learning Centers: Science,* capitalizes on students' natural tendency to look out the window at the world around them. It can be adapted for any grade level.

Using your classroom window or one you have access to elsewhere in the school, begin by posting a topic and listing questions for a monthlong investigation. Have students keep a window-watch log to record their observations. At the end of each month, post a summary of students' discoveries. Here are the topics and questions Kepler suggests:

Seasons: (can be used for four different months): Look out the window. How can you tell it is autumn (winter, spring)? Record seasonal changes you see, such as leaf color, people's outerwear, precipitation, and plant life.

Temperature: What do you think the temperature outside is? Check the thermometer to find out. What are some words that tell about the temperature today? Keep a record of the temperature each time you visit. Work with a partner to create a temperature graph each week. Then make a graph to show the temperatures for the month. Did you notice any trends?

Clouds: What do clouds tell us about the weather? Illustrate types of clouds you see. Note weather conditions, too. (Be sure to record the date.) Try to find out the names of these cloud types. At the end of the month, look for connections between clouds and weather.

LEARNING CENTER RESOURCES

For more about learning centers, you might consult one of these books from Scholastic.

Quick-and-Easy Learning Centers: Writing, by Cynde Gregory (1995)

Quick-and-Easy Learning Centers: Word Play, by Mary Beth Spann (1995)

Quick-and-Easy Learning Centers: Science, by Lynne Kepler (1995)

Shoe Box Math Learning Centers, by Jacqueline Clark (2002)

For more resources on learning centers and other topics in this chapter, see page 49.

Ten Easy Art Centers

Art centers are a great idea if you don't have a separate art period in your daily curriculum, says art teacher Mary Parks of Naperville, Illinois. These centers also provide a good way to integrate arts throughout the curriculum. Here are ten centers, adapted from an article by Parks, that you can set up in any corner of your room.

1 The Easel: An easel, paints, paintbrushes, plastic containers for water, and paper (construction or newsprint) can help bring out students' natural creativity. Cover the floor with newspaper, position the easel near a sink, if possible, and have children get started by illustrating a story. One variation is to ask them to imitate the style of a certain children's book illustrator. If paint is too messy for your room, try colored chalk, pencils, pastels, crayons, or watercolors.

2 Masks and Puppets: Have students re-create the features of their favorite characters by gluing recycled scraps of fabric and paper to white paper plates for masks and brown paper bags for puppets. Then have them their own puppet show or mask-play about classroom rules.

3 Quick-Draw Station: Tips from how-to-draw books help children develop drawing skills. And since good drawings rely on basic geometric shapes, children also build math skills.

4 Stamp Prints: With rubber-stamp kits or stamps carved from potatoes, students can personalize their papers. Use tempera paint for ink.

5 Modeling Clay: Students can create three-dimensional representations of characters or objects that interest them. (Store modeling clay in airtight containers. For permanent sculptures, use inexpensive air-dry clays.)

6 Crayon Rubbings: Fill a shoe box with items such as leaves, scraps of textured fabric, coins, and small items students bring from home. Using thick crayons on thin paper—such as newsprint, typing paper, or tracing paper—students can make rubbings.

7 Theme-Oriented Murals: Set up a large roll of newsprint, paint, chalk, and crayons on one side of your room. Place the paper on the floor or tack it to a bulletin board. Have the class create a mural to go with the next science unit. Students can collaborate on an appropriate background, then add details and labels as their knowledge grows.

8 Paper Collages and Mosaics: Save and recycle scraps of construction paper, wallpaper, yarn, etc. Have students create fancy collages with the recycled scraps.

9 Tangram Kits: Integrate art and math with tangrams. Use either a premade kit or tangram pieces cut from construction paper. Challenge students to invent tangram challenges for one another involving symmetry and patterns.

10 Art and Music Appreciation: Display prints of famous paintings and set up a tape recorder and headphones with samples of different types of music. Then create sheets for students to fill in as personal responses. For example:
- The music made me feel
  _____.
- The artist is trying to say
  _____.
- This music (_____) seems to go best with this picture (_____) because _____.

Tip: To keep your art centers clean, assign two students per week to replace supplies, wipe up spills, and keep things in order.

From *Instructor,* September 1995.

Shapes: What shapes can you spot outside the window? Look for circles (squares, rectangles, ovals, and other shapes) in nature, in the structures you see, and in the sky. What shapes do you see most often? Why do you think this is so?

Birds (requires a bird feeder in view of the window): What kinds of birds live around our school? Observe birds at the feeder. Describe the birds you see, including behavior, markings, and size. Try to find out what they're called. At what times of day do you see them?

❖ Grouping

When we teachers organize students for instruction or activities, we are grouping them. First, they are grouped into classes, usually classes of children at the same grade level. Within classrooms, we further group students. Sometimes we use whole-group configurations (the whole class), and other times we divide the class into smaller working groups.

While grouping can often be an instructional strategy, as in the case of grouping for cooperative learning or grouping by ability in math or reading, it is also an organizational and management concern. Planning for groups sometimes occurs before students arrive on the first day, because group configurations can determine the classroom floor plan.

For example, many teachers organize their classrooms into groups of four to six students sitting together at tables or at desks pushed together. Students work in these groups to complete assignments and activities; they line up as groups; and they earn points and special privileges as groups.

Teachers and researchers alike stress the importance of keeping group membership fluid. Students need the opportunity to work with many different classmates in many different situations. Many teachers change their group seatings every month or every marking period. Others time the changes to coincide with major units.

Instructional Groups

When grouping students for instructional purposes in subjects such as reading, many educators make an important distinction between ability grouping and flexible grouping. *The Literacy Dictionary: The Vocabulary of Reading and Writing*, edited by Theodore Harris and Richard Hodges, offers these definitions:

Ability grouping: the placement of students according to similar levels of intelligence or achievement in some skill or subject, either within or among classes or schools; tracking; homogeneous grouping.

Flexible grouping: allowing students to work in differently mixed groups depending on the goal of the learning task at hand.

In his book *Flexible Grouping in Reading: Practical Ways to Help All Students Become Better Readers*, Michael Opitz says: "Most often, ability groups reflect children's overall reading achievement; those with similar achievement levels are placed together in one of three groups—high, medium, or low—to receive instruction.

"In contrast, flexible groups fulfill a variety of purposes. All children needing to learn a specific skill, for example, might be grouped to learn that skill. Once children have learned the skill, the group dissolves."

First-grade teacher Jim Henry uses ability grouping. "I have some kids coming into first grade reading at a third- or fourth-grade level and others who don't know all their letters yet," says Henry, explaining how he creates four reading groups based on ability. He purposely keeps the numbers small in the two lower groups and works with those groups every day. The other groups can work more independently.

Henry avoids naming the groups, calling them instead by the names of different group members (Jason's group, Jenny's group, and so on). He further blurs the distinction among groups by regularly inviting individuals from one group to join the activities of another group. Although students are grouped by ability, Henry moves them in and out of the groups as their progress dictates.

In her multiage first- and second-grade classroom, Laura Fendel groups children many different ways. For math skills instruction, she divides the class by ability, usually according to whether they are first or second graders. But frequently these groups overlap as first graders surge ahead or second graders' progress slows.

"I always explain these groupings to children," says Fendel. She tells them, "It's really important for you to learn what you need to learn. Don't think about it as first- or second-grade work."

Fendel also mixes and matches her first and second graders into ability groups for reading, and into interest groups for "Book Club" (where children group themselves according to which story they want to hear her read).

Middle-school educator and author Paula Naegle suggests grouping students randomly for short cooperative activities. "Part of your goal is to help students develop their social skills by working with students they may not ordinarily choose as partners," she writes.

Naegle describes how she quickly groups students by handing out items that can be sorted by color, shape, or type.

Benefits of Flexible Grouping

Educators such as Michael Opitz who use flexible grouping for reading instruction cite numerous benefits. These include helping all children to feel part of the learning community by sharing reading experiences, working cooperatively with a variety of peers, becoming more involved with learning, and avoiding the stigma of ability groups.

In flexible grouping, teachers employ a variety of grouping techniques to achieve specific goals in reading instruction. The table on page 24 shows eight ways to form groups and explains how and when you might use each. As Opitz stresses in his book, the groups dissolve once their purpose is met. Often, the groups break up after a few days, although they may last longer.

Balance in Groups

Adele Schroeter, principal at New York City's P.S. 59, remembers grouping her fourth graders when she taught at P.S. 321. She and her colleagues gathered before each new school year to group students into individual classes. They worked to achieve academic, racial, behavioral, and gender balance.

"Heterogeneously grouped classes become microcosms of the world children live in," Schroeter explains. "Our job is to build a sense of community, getting kids to know and appreciate each other as learners and individuals."

Within a heterogeneous class, students have many different chances to work in groups. Soon into the school year, after the students get to know each other, Schroeter suggests that teachers ask them to write letters describing who they think would be good learning partners— who would complement their own styles, strengths, and weaknesses. These student choices (surprisingly accurate, according to Schroeter) helped guide her successfully in regrouping the class.

For certain subjects, Schroeter recommends other types of grouping. In her math class (an ability-based class where students were drawn from the entire fourth grade), Schroeter regrouped her students every two weeks. She arranged children into seven cooperative groups by randomly handing them cards as they walked into class. (Unknown to the students, she reserved a few special cards to group those who need extra attention.) "Kids quickly learn that leadership qualities can be as valuable as discrete math skills," she explains. "The most sought-after workmates are not always the most skillful mathematicians."

In social studies, the students grouped themselves according to common interests. They then completed various group projects.

But perhaps the most exciting grouping occurred during reading. Here, the children formed book clubs of three or four individuals who chose their own books and assignments and conducted their own discussions. To select group members, the children first wrote letters to Schroeter commenting on the qualities they were looking for in other group members. Then they wrote "personal ads" modeled on classified ads.

Flexible Grouping Techniques

Grouping Technique	How	Use when . . .	Example
Random	This is completely arbitrary; have students group themselves by like book titles or by given colors.	your focus is on management and forming groups of equal size. Also use random grouping when you want students to get to know one another.	Students choose a book title from a bag you circulate and group themselves by like title. There are enough titles to form groups of equal size.
Achievement (Ability)	Use performance on a reading measure; students with similar scores are placed in the same group.	you want to have students read literature selections at their instructional levels as determined by the reading measure.	When completing a folktale unit, students are directed to read a folktale that corresponds to their general reading levels.
Social (Cooperative)	Group students according to specific social skills: leaders, followers; heterogeneous in that each group member has different skills.	students will need to function in different roles; students learn different roles from one another and work together to complete a group task.	Students read a script and glean important information to share with the rest of the class. When preparing, one person reads, another takes notes, another draws. One child is the group spokesperson.
Interest	Assign students to a group or have them assign themselves to a group based on interest in a topic. Grouping may be based on an interest survey.	student interest is the main motivating force for learning about a topic.	Students who are interested in a favorite author or illustrator come together to learn more about him/her.
Task	Group together students who are successful in completing given types of activities.	you want to enable students to use their strongest modality to show understanding.	Children who find drawing enjoyable are grouped together to construct scenery for the reenactment of a story.
Knowledge of Subject	Group together students with knowledge of a given subject or hobby.	you want students to see likenesses among one another and share information.	Students who are interested in baseball cards are grouped together to share the statistics of their favorite players.
Skill/Strategy	Group together students who need practice with a skill or strategy.	you want to teach the skill or strategy to those who need to learn it.	Children who need to learn specific print concepts are grouped to learn them.
Student Choice	Allow students to group themselves according to a like characteristic such as author or genre.	you want to use literature response groups in which students take the lead; also good to use when student success is not dependent on choice.	Several books are displayed and students are invited to choose the book they would like to read. Those with like titles are then put in the same group.

What About Gifted Students?

Teachers of academically gifted students sometimes claim that in heterogeneous groups, high-ability students are unchallenged by their less able peers, become resentful and/or bored with group members, and often end up doing most of the group work. Teachers of the gifted argue that these students need to have the same exposure to positive role models and challenges as other students do. Further, there is considerable evidence that constantly placing gifted students in heterogeneous groups where they are perceived by themselves and others as the "smartest" leads to arrogance, resentment, and negative consequences all around. Instead, many educators and researchers insist that high-ability students need the challenge (and humbling experience) of working with their intellectual peers.

Conversely, students with learning challenges need some group experiences in which they are the "smartest" or most able.

Despite the grouping controversy, most educators agree that group configurations should be kept flexible and that students need opportunities to work with many different classmates.

❖ Routines and Procedures

Consider these two classrooms: In the first, the teacher is trying to start a math lesson. She raises her voice for attention and gestures frantically as students jump out of their seats to sharpen pencils, retrieve math manipulatives, or ask friends for help. Cries of, "What are we supposed to be doing?" fill the air. The time this teacher has allotted for math is half over before the lesson begins.

Meanwhile, just across the hall, a writing workshop progresses smoothly. Circulating among small working groups, the teacher consults with some students while continuing to monitor the others. As they complete their writing, the students file their papers in their writing portfolios, then take out their library books, as previously instructed.

One teacher established routines and enforced them, the other did not. It's obvious which is which.

Routines Help Children

Routines are the backbone of daily classroom life. They facilitate teaching and learning. That's the bottom line. Routines don't just make your life easier, they save valuable classroom time. And what's most important, efficient routines make it easier for students to learn and achieve more. That's not to say teaching and learning can be made routine or formulaic. Never! But procedures for turning in assignments, talking in class, lining up for lunch, getting your assistance, using the pencil sharpener, and passing out materials must be.

"Routines are the most important thing," claims Deborah Charles of New Jersey. "It doesn't matter what the routine is, as long as it becomes routine."

"Children who often have trouble organizing their time benefit greatly from routines," adds Jane Kelling of Texas.

"Routine is good for the teacher and good for the students," concurs Pamela Shannon of San Diego. "Basically, kids feel secure with a routine. They know what's expected of them. You build on this security before you go on to something new and different."

Academic routines—lesson warm-ups, independent reading, weekly tests, homework collection and correction procedures, and other activities that structure learning—help children learn better, concludes researcher Gaea Leinhardt of the University of Pittsburgh's Learning Research and Development Center. In her studies of mathematics teaching in elementary classrooms, she found that the major difference between expert and novice teachers was in the use of well-practiced routines.

Leinhardt tells of an expert teacher who gave students guided practice after a lesson by assigning two problems and asking them to stand when they finished. Thus, the teacher could readily see who needed help, which she would offer during the next round of problems.

As Leinhardt explains, this routine enabled the teacher to pace the practice and give rapid feedback on performance to all the students.

"Academic routines are just as important as other routines," says Jane Kelling. "Starting lessons with warm-ups and ending lessons with reviews help children retain the material. And routines about homework and assignments are also extremely important for everyone to be successful."

Routines Help Teachers

Research documents the effectiveness of routines. Regents professor David Berliner of Arizona State University views teachers as executives who each day make more important decisions affecting the lives of others than some chief executive officers make in a month or a year. The only way teachers can do that, he explains, is to manage by routine. Many decisions become automatic as teachers transform patterns of activities into smooth routines.

Routines differ from teacher to teacher and class to class. Routines are an individual thing, says Barbara King-Shaver, adjunct professor at Rutgers Graduate School of Education and supervisor of English at South Brunswick High School in New Jersey. "You use what works best for you and your students."

Routines also eliminate many potential disruptions and problem situations, for example, the common problem of getting the teacher's attention and help.

Typically, students who need help must raise their hands, wait to be acknowledged by the teacher, state their needs, then receive an oral directive. This very public request for help not only may embarrass some children or be used as a

controlling mechanism by others, but it also disrupts the entire class every single time it occurs.

Many teachers list the daily routine, reminding students to sharpen pencils before school begins and directing them toward certain assignments and activities.

Especially important, say veterans, is the morning routine, or opening exercise. Effective teachers have an activity posted for students to start working on as soon as they enter the classroom. Their students know the procedure because they've been taught to follow it, and no time is wasted directing students on what to do. Not only does the morning routine establish an

---

ROUTINES FOR GETTING ATTENTION

What do you do when the decibel level is a little too high, or you want everyone's attention? Most teachers have a routine signal or strategy that students have been taught to recognize.

Texas teacher Jane Kelling holds her arm up in an L-shape, which her third graders know is the signal for everyone to be quiet. This technique works well with older children, too. Some teachers ask students to raise their arms in response, indicating that they've noticed the signal and are ready to listen.

Sixth-grade teacher Cindy Wong gets students' attention by saying, "Give me five." Her students then mentally review the five steps she's taught them, rehearsed with them, and posted on the wall: 1) eyes on speaker, 2) mouth quiet, 3) be still, 4) hands free (not holding anything), and 5) listen.

Laura Fendel makes a trumpet sound (da da-da daa)—an auditory cue that signals to students, "Let's get together for a minute."

Deborah Charles holds two fingers up like a peace sign and says, "Signal." Her students know that means to be quiet. Charles also turns the lights out briefly when she wants total attention. "The only classroom rule that's not negotiated in my class is the rule that when the lights are out, that's the signal for everyone to freeze."

Pamela Shannon, whose second graders sit at tables of six, gives each table five points at the start of an activity. If the children at a table become too noisy, the group loses a point. If a group loses all of its points, the children lose a privilege. Shannon says that the children do well in keeping each other quiet and on task.

Jim Henry also uses a point system. He lists the class teams (also arranged by table) on the chalkboard. "When I see a team that's doing what it needs to do, I give everyone on that team a point," he explains. "At the end of the day, whoever gets the most points gets a sticker." Henry adds that many days, all teams earn stickers.

"One thing that doesn't work is trying to talk over the kids," stresses Barbara King-Shaver. Teachers who continually demand that students "quiet down" are wasting their breath, she says.

orderly, efficient atmosphere, it forces students to take responsibility. They know it is their job to get right to work.

Routines Facilitate Transitions

One of the biggest payoffs of classroom routines is smooth transitions. Students following routines move quickly and efficiently from one activity or lesson to another, minimizing the time off-task.

Many teachers give children verbal warnings about how much time they have left to complete an activity. "You have five minutes to finish this science experiment," they say, or "Three minutes more and it's time to clean up your art projects."

Jim Henry's technique is a little more systematic. He winds down an independent activity by alerting students that in ten minutes, he'll ring a bell. When the bell sounds, students have learned that they should put their pencils down, put materials away, and look up at Henry to show him that they're ready.

Barbara King-Shaver refers to a kindergarten teacher who rings a soothing chime to signal to children that it's time to move from one activity group to another. The children work at stations and simply rotate from station to station.

"Effective transitions are effective routines," says Pamela Shannon. "For example, the children know that right after recess we read a story, so they are prepared and know just what to do."

Deborah Charles rings a bell to signal the beginning of sustained silent reading, times students for 15 minutes, then rings the bell again to signal the end.

"Everything is a routine," Charles claims. She describes the daily reading and writing workshop, where students gather together on a rug to hear a story, then receive a mini–writing lesson (using quotation marks, for example). Finally, Charles tells them that it's time to get out their writing folders, and they automatically know how to do this.

Practice Makes Perfect

Whatever procedures you decide to use in your classroom, remember to **practice** them numerous times with the whole class, giving children an opportunity to demonstrate that they know and understand them. This practice is critical. We can't assume that children know how we want them to behave until we've actually taught them the desired behavior, demonstrated how a child would look engaged in the behavior, and provided students the opportunity to practice.

"You have to teach the routines to the students," Pamela Shannon stresses. "If you don't, you suffer." Shannon and other experienced teachers spend the first several weeks of school teaching, modeling, and practicing classroom routines.

Your job as an effective classroom manager is to develop procedures for all major classroom activities, then teach and have students practice those procedures the first few days or weeks of school until they become established routines. For new and seasoned professionals alike, the beginning of the school year is the time to teach and reteach classroom

SIGNALING FOR HELP

Educators Harry K. Wong and Rosemary Tripi Wong, who also write for and instruct teachers, suggest several excellent procedures for students to signal when they need help.

- Give each student an index card folded and taped into a three-sided pyramid. One side is blank, one side reads, "Please help me," and the third side reads, "Please keep working." The blank side normally faces the student. But when the student needs help, she signals by turning the "Please help me" side toward the teacher. This, in turn, puts the "Please keep working" side toward the student as a reminder to continue quietly until the teacher can come. This silent procedure secures the necessary help without disrupting the entire class.

- Establish hand signals. Students raise their index finger if they wish to speak; they raise two fingers if they wish to leave their seats to sharpen pencils, get books, and so on; and they raise three fingers if they need the teacher's help. Again, the teacher can respond with a nod or hand gesture, and the class works on undisturbed.

The Wongs suggest it's a good idea to post this hand signal procedure on the wall as a reminder to students.

routines. It usually takes several weeks for these to become firmly entrenched, but the initial time invested pays huge dividends throughout the year.

Before a new school year, decide which procedures you need to help you operate the classroom most efficiently. You may wish to use the checklist on page 30. Circle several of the procedures you want to teach on the first day. Plan for students to practice those procedures until they become routines. You will probably want to designate signals to alert students to follow certain procedures. (For example, the T-sign could indicate that a student should get back on task, and a raised arm could signal that you want students' attention.)

❖ General Rules of Conduct

In addition to classroom procedures, you will need to establish general rules of classroom conduct. Students—especially the older ones—will respect rules more if they've had a hand in creating them. Many teachers develop a list of what they consider the bare essentials, then negotiate the remaining rules with their students.

The following list is a starting point. Use these rules as guidelines, adapting and expanding them to meet the needs of your individual class and grade level:

1. Treat others as you would like to be treated.
2. Respect other people's property and person (no stealing or hitting).
3. Laugh with anyone, but laugh at no one.
4. Be responsible for your own learning.
5. Come to class and hand in assignments on time.

6. Do not disturb people who are working.

Experienced teachers agree that it's best to select only a few rules—those that contribute to successful learning and an orderly environment. (No one can remember a long list.) Make your rules as clear and specific as possible. Then decide with students' help the consequences for breaking those rules.

Teach rules as you would a regular lesson. (Indeed, many veterans agree it should be your first lesson.) Discuss each rule individually, explaining the rationale behind it and asking for examples of how it could be broken. Explain that rules help make everyone's time in school more enjoyable; use examples to illustrate this point. It's a good idea to post the

OPENING EXERCISES

The opening exercises vary considerably in the primary classrooms featured here. But in each case, the exercise is a well-practiced routine. The children know exactly what to expect, and they start their day feeling safe and secure.

- The morning routine in Deborah Charles's multiage classroom revolves around students taking responsibility for all of the housekeeping details. Charles pairs a first and second grader together for each of the classroom jobs she assigns. The class secretaries take attendance, the librarians check in the books children return, the scientists record the temperature and tend to any pets, the class managers hand out student folders and lead the class in daily physical exercises.

- Jim Henry's opening exercises occur in the ten minutes between the morning bells. At 9:05, a bell signals for children to enter their classrooms. Henry's first graders know that this is the time to put their homework and notes from parents in a designated spot, put their lunches and book bags in the proper place, sharpen their pencils, and begin working on the morning's "fast math" problem. When the bell rings again at 9:15, students clear off their desks, stand for the Pledge of Allegiance, and listen to the morning announcements.

- Pamela Shannon views the opening exercise as a chance to make personal contact with each of her students. "When I call roll, I have each of the kids respond by saying 'Good morning,' then I ask them if they have anything they'd like to share—a good movie they saw the night before or something else," says Shannon. This way, she explains, each child gets her undivided attention at least once that day. The opening exercises vary considerably in the primary classrooms featured here. But in each case, the exercise is a well-practiced routine. The children know exactly what to expect, and they start their day feeling safe and secure.

rules as a reminder (many schools require this) and send a copy home with each student.

First-grade teacher Susie Davis suggests posting "picture" rules for kindergarten and first-grade students.

Kathy Wesley finds that with her primary-age students, it's best to "teach only the most important rules the first day, then add a few and review the following days. This is the most important time to be consistent with implementing rules. Often, a 'rule offender' will not have to be spoken to again about rule infractions. Fast, Firm, Fair really does work!"

Older students might write their own copies of the rules; just the act of writing the rules helps children remember them better.

It's also a good idea to have students help determine classroom rules. Experience shows that students who have "ownership" are much more likely to follow classroom rules. Deborah Charles can attest to that. Each year her primary students establish seven or eight rules revolving around two basic questions:

✔ What does it mean to be in a safe environment?

✔ What does it mean to get along together?

By teaching rules and routines and consistently enforcing them at the beginning of

ROUTINE COURTESY

When the class secretary (a rotating job) takes roll in Deborah Charles's multiage first-and-second-grade class, the children say, "Good morning" as their name is called, and the secretary replies, "Good morning."

"I insist at the beginning of the year that students exchange these pleasantries every morning," Charles explains. "It sets the tone for the whole day."

Every Friday, as Laura Fendel's first and second graders line up to leave, she turns to them and says, "At the end of the week, the children say to the teacher…" And students respond by bowing and replying, "Thank you for teaching me." Then Fendel responds with a bow, "And the teacher says, 'Thank you for teaching me.'"

This simple routine not only teaches common courtesy, it encourages the teacher and students to appreciate each other, and it reminds students that their teachers are learners, too, Fendel explains.

the year, you are establishing good discipline. After all, good discipline and student behavior start with good classroom management. The key is to prevent problems before they occur. (You'll find more on discipline and student behavior in Chapter Five.) Being a good manager does not mean ruling with an iron fist but, rather, providing leadership and a strong example of how to behave.

ONE TEACHER'S EXPERIENCE

After a five-year leave from teaching, Texas teacher Michelle Baker returned to the classroom to find that she felt like a beginner again—with all of a beginner's classroom-management problems.

"By Christmas I knew there was a problem in my room," said Baker. "The off-task behavior was getting out of control, and teaching effectively was becoming increasingly difficult. A slow change began within me. I started having tension headaches daily. Clockwatching became habitual. In the mornings I would lie in bed dreading going to school in fear of what the day would be like."

Baker characterizes that first year back as a "devastating failure." But the very next year was "a rewarding and enriching experience"—a complete success!

What happened? Baker learned to establish rules and routines. And more importantly, she took time to teach them to her students.

"I spent a great deal of time modeling what I expected from the children," she reports. "I used children to role-play each time a special direction was given. Those first two weeks of school resurrected me from a disastrous year and laid the foundation for a successful one. Always before, I took for granted that my students understood what I expected."

Procedures Checklist

Use these categories as guidelines to create your own checklist for classroom procedures.

Beginning Class
- ___ A. Roll call, absentees
- ___ B. Tardy students
- ___ C. Get-ready routines
- ___ D. Distributing materials
- ___ E. _____
- ___ F. _____

Work Requirements
- ___ A. Heading papers
- ___ B. Use of pen or pencil
- ___ C. Writing on back of paper
- ___ D. Neatness, legibility
- ___ E. Incomplete work
- ___ F. _____
- ___ G. _____

Instructional Activities
- ___ A. Signals for students' attention
- ___ B. Signals for teacher's attention
- ___ C. Student talk during seatwork
- ___ D. Activities to do when work is done
- ___ E. Student movement in and out of small group
- ___ F. Bringing materials to group
- ___ G. Expected behavior in group
- ___ H. Expected behavior of students not in group
- ___ I. _____
- ___ J. _____

Ending Class
- ___ A. Putting away supplies, equipment
- ___ B. Cleaning up
- ___ C. Dismissing class
- ___ D. Checking planners/agenda
- ___ E. _____
- ___ F. _____

Behavior Standards
- ___ A. Rules
- ___ B. Talk among students
- ___ C. Turning in work
- ___ D. _____
- ___ E. _____
- ___ F. _____

Other Procedures
- ___ A. Lunch procedures
- ___ B. Student helpers
- ___ C. Fire drills
- ___ D. Emergency procedures

Room/School Areas
- ___ A. Shared materials
- ___ B. Teacher's desk
- ___ C. Water fountain, bathroom, pencil sharpener
- ___ D. Student desks
- ___ E. Learning centers, stations
- ___ F. Playground
- ___ G. Lunchroom
- ___ H. _____
- ___ I. _____

Communicating Assignments
- ___ A. Returning assignments
- ___ B. Homework assignments
- ___ C. _____
- ___ D. _____

Checking Assignments in Class
- ___ A. Students exchanging papers
- ___ B. Marking and grading assignments
- ___ C. Turning in assignments
- ___ D. _____
- ___ E. _____

Grading Procedures
- ___ A. Recording grades
- ___ B. Grading criteria
- ___ C. Contracting with students for grades
- ___ D. _____
- ___ E. _____

Academic Feedback
- ___ A. Posting student work
- ___ B. Communicating with parents
- ___ C. Written comments on assignments
- ___ D. Handing back assignments

Excerpted from a list developed by the Mid-continent Regional Education Laboratory, 2550 S. Parker Rd., Ste. 500, Aurora, CO 80014.

❖ Paperwork (Making a Molehill Out of a Mountain)

Lisa Roe recalls her biggest shock during her first year of teaching: "When I was going to college, I was never told how much grading and record keeping there'd be. As a student teacher, I wrote the lesson plans and my supporting teacher did all the grading. I was just never exposed to all the paperwork. If you're not on top of it daily, you'll be swamped."

The late Doris Dillon reported that the first-year teachers working with her team of mentors in San Jose consistently ranked paperwork and grading as the most overwhelming aspects of teaching.

And they're not alone. New teachers and veterans alike are besieged daily with what seems like a never-ending stream of paper. There are daily attendance records, lunch counts, lesson plans, subject-area testing, report cards, homework and seatwork to check and record, information to gather for emergencies, records for parent conferences, students in special pull-out programs to keep track of, and much more.

These aren't tasks you can just ignore. But short of hiring a secretary or working 24 hours a day, what can you do?

Teacher educator Tamara Glupczynski recommends that novice teachers seek out the expertise of veteran teachers to figure out the best paperwork practices—their years of experience can save you hours of unnecessary paperwork.

"Teachers should work smarter, not harder," said the late educator Madeline Hunter, who suggested the following ways to cut paperwork to a minimum:

✔ Get help from students. Instead of developing and duplicating practice pages, have students make their own practice problems. Here are some samples:

1. List ten words in your reader that are objects you can touch (boy, ball) and ten words you cannot touch (in, new, the).

2. Using the same facts as those in the story problem in your text (or on the chalkboard), write one question that requires you to add to find the answer, one that requires you to subtract, one that requires you to multiply, and one that requires you to divide.

3. Make up five questions to test whether someone understood this chapter. Star the question you think is best. (This lets you examine just one question, reserving the others for verification if you doubt the student's understanding. Also, get double mileage here by choosing several of the best questions to give to the rest of the class.)

✔ Give quick and random quizzes. Instead of correcting every homework assignment, give quick quizzes to assess what's been learned. The quiz should include one or two questions from the assignment and one or two different questions of the same type. Collect and grade them on some days, and on others, give students the answers to evaluate their own quizzes. (Keep students guessing so they will always be motivated to learn from the homework.)

Testing and Diagnosis

✔ Measure student achievement formally by preparing short quizzes that test specific skills and concepts. These are easy to correct, and they give information you can use immediately.

WRITING ABOUT RULES

As an early-year activity, ask students to write and share their opinions about why rules are necessary. Here are two examples of student opinions.

Rules are important because they help keep us from having accidents.

Rules are important because then everyone gets a chance to talk and we all learn more.

✔ Informally diagnose by having students sign or signal answers. A simple head shake, raised hand, or hand signal can indicate answers to your questions. Deviant signals stand out. If you suspect they are copying, ask students to close their eyes and signal their answers.

✔ Verbal responses, individual or in chorus, are another way to diagnose learning. Tell Your Neighbor exercises (Think-Pair-Share, learning partners, reciprocal teaching, and other student-to-student methods of response) give each student the chance to respond, and a peer will usually correct wrong responses.

(You'll find more on evaluation and alternative assessments in Chapter Four.)

Checking Assignments

Homework and in-class assignments serve specific purposes. Students need practice with new skills or concepts, or they need to brush up on old ones. These are activities you want students to take seriously. And they will, if you do. Such work doesn't always have to be graded. But show students that you value their efforts. For example:

✔ On worksheets, mark a circle near each problem students answer incorrectly. When they correct their mistakes, simply add a K beside the original circle to give the children an OK on the end product.

✔ Use an all-purpose chart (see the sample on page 34) to keep track of completed assignments on a daily basis.

✔ Have students mark their own or each other's papers when possible. (Check your district's policy before you use this idea.)

✔ Have students help you collect papers.

✔ Use a pen of one color to record work that is handed in on time, and another for work that comes in late.

❖ Start Off Right With Parents

First impressions count with parents, too. Good public relations at the beginning of the school year can improve parental support. Experienced teachers suggest it is a good idea to contact parents even before school starts. You can set a positive tone for the whole year by mailing a back-to-school kit to each student's parents. Include such items as:

✔ a welcome letter to both child and parents or other caregivers. Tell parents they may make appointments to discuss special concerns or observe the classroom. (Explain that appointments will help you avoid interruptions during those critical first few days.) Also, ask parents to schedule children's medical appointments for after school or weekends whenever possible.

✔ a form to return that lists home and office contact information, emergency numbers, and the best times and ways to reach parents.

✔ a request for room parents and volunteers.

✔ a request for parents to write you a note detailing their child's strengths and accomplishments and any other information to help you make the child's year successful.

✔ a form for writing out special instructions regarding medical and other considerations.

✔ a copy of your policies, including late-work policies and the consequences for late work. (It's best to have parents and students sign off on these policies.)

✔ a list of supplies students should bring the first day. This demonstrates to both parents and students that you mean to get down to learning right away.

With her back-to-school letter, first-grade teacher Susie Davis suggests that students bring something personal to go along with the beginning-of-the-year theme, such as a teddy bear. It's a "security blanket" of sorts that helps new students feel more confident, Davis explains.

It's important to include non-English-speaking parents in your back-to-school communications. Check with your school's administration and your district for resources such as translators, forms in other languages, and policies for having documents translated.

(See Chapter Six for more ideas on fostering good home-school relations.)

❖ Planning

Planning is the most important aspect of organization and management. Your entire life as a teacher revolves around planning. Everything you do before the first day of school constitutes planning. Arranging the physical environment; deciding about rules and routines; collecting materials, supplies, and ideas; contacting parents—these and more are planning activities. You are planning for a productive school year.

The "other" side of planning, of course, is the actual preparation for teaching academic content. Planning lessons, weekly units, and an entire school year is a big task. Many of us find it the most intellectually intensive activity of teaching and a tremendous creative outlet.

Good planning takes practice. It's the key to professionalism. When you plan, you use your professional judgment to match ideas, activities, and materials with students' interests and abilities. Planning is not simply a matter of making a to-do list. Planning is deciding when, where, why, and how a certain lesson is taught.

Couldn't a good teacher just "wing it"? No way. A plan offers direction, confidence, and security. And plans help you use classroom time more efficiently by reducing confusion and wasted time. Generally, the more thoroughly you plan an activity, the less time it takes to complete.

What Experienced Planners Do

In studies at Michigan State University, researcher Christopher Clark and his colleagues found that experienced teachers generally use a four-step process when planning an activity:

1. Understand the total activity.

2. Imagine using it in the classroom.

3. Think of ways to avoid potential problems and modify accordingly.

4. Create a mental image of the revised version.

Effective teachers also:

✔ set aside a regular time for planning.

✔ make their daily and weekly plans fit into large units and yearly plans.

✔ correlate lesson objectives and activities to state standards.

✔ find out what students already know about a particular topic with formal or informal pretesting before planning lessons and units.

✔ overplan a lesson, because it's easier to cut than to stretch the lesson.

✔ plan for interruptions and unexpected events to maintain order and minimize disruptions.

✔ plan transitions from one activity to another. This minimizes wasted time, confusion, and behavior problems.

✔ clearly communicate the plan to students.

Teachable Moments

Clark advises teachers to think of their plans not as rigid scripts but as "flexible frameworks for action." Plans, he says, are devices for getting started in the right direction. Good teachers sometimes depart from their plans and often elaborate upon them as they proceed. They take advantage of those unplanned "teachable moments"—times when learning potential is high because student motivation and interest are high.

Veterans reflecting on their first few years of teaching often report that they were slaves to their plans. While it is important to develop and follow instructional plans, don't be so rigid that you pass up unexpected opportunities.

Suppose, for example, that a migrating flock of Canada geese lands briefly in a field outside your window. The students are excited and have lots of questions. Where are they going? Where did they come from? What are they eating? In response to the students' questions and enthusiasm, why not fly with a science unit on birds and migration?

One urban teacher turned the noisy disturbance of a nearby building demolition into an exciting class discussion about machines, building materials, and the people who had lived in the building. Another teacher used an incident of student littering on the playground to involve her students in an extended ecology, conservation, and recycling unit.

All-Purpose Chart

Must-Do List

Make a copy of this list to use before school starts each year.

___ Make bulletin-board decisions: where to post announcements, menu, and calendar; what kind of welcome-back display to make; which boards will be for subject-area work and which boards students will design; where to display students' original work.

___ Set up learning centers.

___ Make signs for room.

___ Prepare class rolls and permanent records.

___ Make class list to post on door.

___ Put your name outside the door.

___ Make student name tags for desks or have them make their own.

___ Find out schedules for lunch, gym, art, music, library.

___ Obtain supplies.

   __ textbooks and supplemental materials

   __ plan books

   __ storybooks for read-alouds

   __ attendance materials

   __ paper clips

   __ construction paper

   __ manila folders

   __ different kinds of tape

   __ extra writing paper

   __ grade book

   __ rubber bands

   __ stapler and staples

   __ handwriting paper

   __ spare pencils/pens

   __ tissues

   __ _____

   __ _____

   __ _____

   __ _____

   __ _____

___ Prepare packets for students to take home the first day. Include:

   __ emergency forms

   __ school rules

   __ supplies

   __ bus or transportation rules

   __ note to parents/request for room parents

   __ _____

   __ _____

   __ _____

___ Check which students may be going to special classes.

___ Check out library books and read-alouds.

___ Set up a folder for a substitute to use in case of emergency.

   __ daily schedule (fill in as soon as possible)

   __ seating chart (fill in as soon as possible)

   __ reproducible activities

   __ _____

   __ _____

   __ _____

___ Prepare a file for correspondence from parents.

___ Prepare a file for faculty bulletins.

___ Get a copy of state and district curriculum standards.

___ Write tentative lesson plans for the coming week.

___ Duplicate materials needed for the first few days.

___ Write your name and other important information on the board.

___ Make a checklist for returned forms (can be used later for report cards and other items).

   __ _____

   __ _____

Fourth-grade teacher Penny Strube relates an incident involving one student's biography on Ulysses S. Grant. Instead of flipping immediately to Grant in the encyclopedia he was using, the student began perusing. Suddenly, he asked Strube if she knew that there had been a gold rush in 1849. Failing to grasp the connection, Strube asked him what president he was working on. But he just continued excitedly, suggesting that that's where the 49ers football team must have gotten their name.

"The excitement of seeing that connection was felt all over the classroom," relates Strube. "I stopped what I was doing to grasp that teachable moment with the entire class. Ryan's comment started a discussion in which another student pointed out that the Pittsburgh Steelers got their name from a natural resource in that state, and another student mentioned the Oilers."

Teachable moments crop up often, especially if you stay alert for ways to build on students' interests, needs, and moods. In fact, it's a good idea to capitalize on student interests whenever possible. Effective teachers don't hesitate to solicit lesson ideas from students. Asking students what they would like to learn about can help you generate high-interest lessons. You can match their ideas to the concepts and skills you want to teach.

Three Types of Plans

Basically, there are three types of plans: 1) long-range (grading period, semester, or year), 2) the weekly schedule, and 3) daily lesson plans. In her book *The New Teacher's Complete Sourcebook: Grades K–4*, Bonnie Murray offers tips for each of the three types:

Long-Range Plans

✔ Referring to state and district standards, objectives, and benchmarks, determine an appropriate sequence for teaching required skills and concepts.

✔ With a blank calendar, mark in all holidays, grading periods, testing times (including time to practice test-taking skills), and schoolwide activities to determine actual instructional time.

✔ Determine the best time of year to study specific content. (You wouldn't schedule a unit on plants in January, for example.) Then write the corresponding objectives in appropriate places on your calendar.

✔ Use themes to integrate subject matter.

✔ Review long-range plans when you develop weekly lesson plans.

Weekly Schedule

✔ Find out what a schedule for instruction should look like according to your state or district.

✔ Have a copy of any recommendations or requirements for time to be spent on each subject.

✔ Make several copies of your weekly schedule planning form.

✔ Place lunch and recess, special classes, and pullout program times on one copy of the form.

✔ Think about how you would like to begin the day. (Journaling, singing, and independent or paired reading are among the many possibilities.)

✔ Think about what type of activity would be appropriate right after lunch. (Murray schedules independent writing to let students calm down and give her a chance to confer with individuals about their writing.)

✔ Think about how you would like to end the day. (Many teachers have students reflect on what they've learned that day.)

✔ Begin placing subjects at appropriate places in the schedule. (Murray suggests scattering "active" subjects such as science among "sedentary" subjects such as writing.)

✔ Recheck the minutes of instruction you have scheduled against any state or district requirements.

✔ Get feedback on your plan from colleagues and administrators. Adjust it as needed throughout the year.

✔ Use your weekly schedule to create a generic frame for your daily lesson plans.

Daily Lesson Plans

✔ Detail specific activities and content to be covered.

✔ Include objectives, instructional procedures, assessment procedures, student groupings, and materials.

✔ Check with your principal for planning guidelines or requirements. (Many principals check plans each week and ask to see lessons outlined in a specific format.)

✔ Balance grouping strategies, and include activities that meet the needs of all learning styles.

✔ Remember that effective planning is done in concert with assessment—knowing exactly where a student is on the learning continuum and how he or she learns best give your planning purpose and direction. (For information and resources on assessment, see Chapter Three.)

Planning for Substitutes and the Unexpected

Sometimes, even careful plans and well-designed lessons are not enough. What about the times when you are unexpectedly absent from the classroom or a situation demands your immediate time and attention?

With advance planning, you can be prepared for the unpredictable. Build a file of emergency activities and "sponges" to soak up time lost to interruptions or unexpected situations such as a child getting sick in class, a parent knocking on the door, or a school assembly starting ten minutes later than scheduled. By planning meaningful "instant" activities, you can turn lost time into learning time. (You might start your emergency activity file with the ten-minute think sessions suggested on page 39 by teacher Susan Petreshene.)

You can also plan for those times when you must be absent from the classroom.

"I never leave my classroom when the day is over without having the next day's plans and papers laid out on my desk, along with directions for the parent volunteers," says Washington teacher Kathy Wesley. "I don't want them to be without something to do if I end up with a sub the next day."

You can use the checklist on page 40 to prepare a file of information and ideas for substitutes.

"My school developed a schoolwide substitute procedure packet that every classroom has on hand," notes Utah teacher Tim Bailey. "In addition, I have a substitute folder on the wall behind my desk that has enough in it to get a substitute through a day if an emergency prevented me from preparing for a sub."

Don't forget to prepare students in advance for the possibility of a substitute. Discuss the conduct you expect from them when you are absent. Remind them how they can help the substitute and why their cooperation is important.

Washington teacher Judy Lee Dunn explains to her students that different teachers have different ways of doing things. Dunn suggests switching classes with another teacher for a day to allow children to experience different teaching styles and changes in routine. Dunn also suggests that you can reinforce the substitute's teaching by asking students to describe at least three new things they learned in your absence. She gives extra credit to students who can do so.

Florida veteran teacher, *Instructor* columnist, and author Mary Rose underscores the point that advance planning absences will make your day out of school, the students' day without you, and the substitute's experience much easier. In *The Substitute Teacher Resource Book*, she recommends, "As you plan for your absence, think through your substitute's day. . . . Picture your morning routine and how you automatically reach for lunch count forms and the attendance folder. Then think of the order of subjects that he or she will be expected to teach. Leave specific instructions about what students should and should not do, such as 'Use crayons or colored pencils to complete the graph, no markers please.' Let the substitute know where you keep supplies in case a student does not have his or her own." She also suggests these advance planning tips:

✔ Keep handy in your personal organizer or address book your district's substitute center phone number and the names and substitute ID numbers of preferred substitutes.

✔ Show one or two responsible students where you keep your materials for the substitute.

✔ Contact another teacher at your school and ask him or her to check on the substitute for you. In case of major emergencies, ask this trusted colleague to explain your absence to your students.

Finally, thank the substitutes who do a good job in your classroom. Call them or write a note. Let the principal know you were pleased, and ask for them again.

❖ Seatwork

Seatwork—the tasks and assignments students complete while working independently at their desks—can be an important classroom management tool. Children learn at different rates, and you can't help all of them at once. So seatwork—whether it is independent writing, silent reading, workbooks, or some other assignment—helps keep the class engaged in meaningful learning tasks while you work with individual students or small groups. At least, it's supposed to work that way.

Picture this scenario: The classroom fairly hums with concentration. Students pore over their reading workbooks. Pencils meet paper with a furious scratching sound as the children race to answer the questions on each page. Their teacher works quietly with a reading group in the back of the room.

No disruptions, no socializing, everybody's busy. There's a lot of learning going on in this classroom. Or is there?

JUST FOR SUBSTITUTES

If you are a substitute teacher yourself, you probably have already realized that you need your own "bag of tricks" to have a successful and satisfying school day. You'll pick up many ideas from other teachers, both substitute and full-time. "Keep a file folder of activities for each of the grades in which you substitute," suggests Wendy Buchberg, a substitute from Ithaca, New York. "This way you'll have backup material if the teacher left insufficient lesson plans."

Buchberg also keeps a pad of stick-on notes to place on students' desks, in case there is no seating chart. "Knowing everyone's name makes management easier."

Substitute teacher Amy Gotliffe from San Francisco has a list of "must-dos" for her teaching assignments. First, she establishes the class rules by asking students to restate them in their own words. Then, she tells students her own rules, if they are different from the class rules. Gotliffe also asks students how their teacher gets their attention (for example, raised fingers, flashing lights), then she chooses one method and practices it with them. Finally, she offers something of herself to her temporary charges.

"It's not often students have a guest," Gotliffe points out. "Tell them about your hobbies, bring an instrument, or tell a story. You are a wonderful new resource."

Veteran teacher Martine Wayman, currently teaching sixth grade, also has some advice for substitutes. When a student misbehaves, says Wayman, put your hand lightly on his or her shoulder. If the problem persists, send the child to an area away from the other children. "Then talk to the child and invite him or her to help you with something. It works," she insists.

Here's a behavior-management technique used by a substitute teacher in Baton Rouge, Louisiana: When she enters the classroom, this substitute puts a note on each child's desk saying, "I was good for the substitute teacher today." Then, throughout the day, she stamps the papers when children are behaving well or are on-task. She leaves the stamped notes on the desks for the teacher.

Dolores Choat, from Chickasha, Oklahoma, suggests giving students "Fast Five Problems" while you take roll and collect lunch money in the morning. The Fast Five might include fun math puzzles, riddles, geography or current affairs questions, or a short creative-writing assignment. Substitutes can then get to know students by reviewing their answers to the Fast Five.

There are many different strategies to take as a substitute teacher. The important point is that you have a strategy. Like any teacher, you must plan for a satisfying and productive day. The key to good teaching—even substitute teaching—is good planning.

Ten-Minute Think Sessions

These activities will help sharpen students' organizing, imagining, observing, patterning, questioning, and other thinking strategies. They'll also show children that you value original thinking.

More than one "right" answer!

Have students think of as many logical answers as possible to each of the following questions. Stress that there is no one right answer and encourage a variety of responses by showing that you value diverse and unusual thinking.

1. How could you know someone had a fire in a fireplace if you hadn't been there at the time? (fireplace still warm, wood pile lower . . .)
2. "It's important you don't lose these," said Kenny to Carl as they left on a weeklong backpacking trip. What might Kenny have handed Carl? (maps, matches, glasses . . .)
3. What sounds could you recognize without seeing what made the noise? (cat's meow, car horn, telephone ring . . .)
4. Some words name numbers, such as *three, ten,* or *twenty.* Other words do not directly tell you a number, but when you hear them, you often think of a number. For instance, *week* and the number seven go together. What other words make you think of numbers? (*duet, triangle, dozen, century, shutout...*)
5. "There must be an accident on the highway," said Mrs. West. What might cause her to say this? (traffic backed up, police car speeding by, flashing red lights ...)

Here's the answer; you give the question.

There are many possible questions to answers such as "the Dodgers." For example: Who won the game? What's your favorite baseball team? What's the name of the major league baseball team in Los Angeles? Help students think in "reverse" with these practice answers, then make up your own.

1. A: Under the bed. Q: Where are your shoes? Where did that sound come from? Where does the cat hide?
2. A: Fish. Q: What could you catch in a river? What swims in a bowl? What did you eat for dinner last night?
3. A: In the morning. Q: When is your house the busiest? When do you eat breakfast? When are you the grumpiest?
4. A: Yes! Q: Would you like to go to the movies with me? Would you like an ice-cream cone? Is she coming over?
5. A: My dad. Q: Who taught you to play the trumpet? Who drove you to school today? Who likes popcorn better than anyone you know?

"Adverbially" speaking

Name a verb and ask students to give you an adverb that "goes with" the verb. For example, if you said *cried,* a student might say *loudly.* Say the phrase back to students as a whole to emphasize a word picture. Ask for only one answer for each verb and specify that adverbs can't be repeated. (List the answers given so students can avoid repetition.) The activity becomes progressively more difficult as common adverbs are eliminated.
Suggested verbs: slept, dropped, tiptoed, played, stood, stopped, sailed, waved, touched, yelled, zigzagged, whispered, flew, carried, banged, disappeared, drove, wrote, walked, worked, paced, leaned, maneuvered, stared, coughed, floated, giggled. Ask students to suggest more possibilities.

1,001 uses for...

This activity allows students to practice divergent thinking by asking them to give practical, nonhumorous responses to the question: "How many ways can you use a . . . ?" Encourage students to think of uses they've never thought of before and ask them to explain their responses. How many ways can you think of to use a: cup, lightbulb, button, birdcage, plain piece of paper . . . ? Take turns suggesting new items.

Is that a fact?

Prepare a list of simple statements. Read a few to your class and discuss whether they are facts or opinions. After children understand the concept, tell them to stand if they think the statement is a fact, remain seated if it is an opinion, or cross their arms if they are uncertain. Allow time to think before you call for a response. Indicate with a hand signal when to begin.

How is a _____ like a _____?

Teach older children about similes and get them to practice divergent thinking at the same time by comparing unlike things. Make two lists of common nouns. Randomly choose one item from the first list and another item from the second list. Brainstorm to think of all the ways they are alike. For example: How is a tree like a child? (Both need water and sunshine to grow. Both grow taller every year. Both can be damaged by insects. Both need to put down roots. Both are important to society.)

Most of these activities were adapted by Susan Petreshene from *Mind Joggers: 5- to 15-Minute Activities That Make Kids Think!* Published by the Center for Applied Research, Inc., West Englewood, NJ 1985.

Preparing for Substitutes

Many teachers develop a file for substitute teachers. Use this checklist of teacher-tested ideas to prepare for substitutes in your classroom.

☐ Let your principal know the names of substitutes who work well with you and your classroom situation.

☐ Prepare a form letter to students explaining the situation and encouraging their good behavior.

☐ Draw up a sheet that familiarizes subs with daily procedures: lunch and attendance counts; other duties; classroom routines and discipline procedures; the schedule for aides, special-area teachers, and students in pull-out programs; and the names of helpful teachers, students, and staff members.

☐ Provide a building map with exits clearly marked and a list of emergency procedures (fire drill, tornado drill, etc.).

☐ Leave seating charts, including your arrangements for small-group activities.

☐ Prepare name tags for students to wear. This tends to reduce misbehavior.

☐ Include a daily schedule, indicating the times for lunch, recess, and school beginning and ending, as well as the academic schedule.

☐ Describe the special-needs children in your class and indicate the classroom-management strategies that work well for you.

☐ Leave detailed lesson plans. If your substitute has the proper credentials, give him or her the freedom to teach. Most substitutes can and want to undertake genuine teaching responsibilities.

☐ File away several books you know your students will love. Hearing a good story read aloud is an activity sure to please students, and it's a productive way to fill extra time.

☐ Include a few reproducibles and short activities to be used in spare moments.

☐ Develop a report form for the substitute to fill out on how the day went. Remind the sub to list both problems and positive outcomes.

Appearances can be deceiving. Students may be sitting quietly and working intently. But that doesn't mean they're learning. Researchers claim that many children complete seatwork assignments with little or no idea of what they're doing or why.

Critics charge that some teachers use workbooks, worksheets, and similar materials as busywork—something to "kill time" and keep students under control. Sadly, such abuse of instructional time does occur. But that doesn't mean we should just discard these potentially powerful teaching aids. Instead, we need to identify where it is that we go wrong and try to use seatwork more effectively.

What You Should Know

Researcher Linda Anderson and her colleagues in a Michigan State University study found that students care more about getting their work finished than doing it correctly. When assignments are too difficult or don't make sense, they complete them as best they can—by copying answers from friends, guessing at answers, leaving blanks, and so on. They're doing them, but they're doing them wrong. Yet teachers are fooled into thinking that students are working productively and learning.

Anderson suggests that the emphasis on staying busy, combined with assigning tasks that are too difficult, communicates to children that the important thing is simply completing the task, no matter how. The researchers found that some children just haven't learned to detect when they need help. Or worse, they've come to expect school tasks not to make sense, and so they give up trying to understand. Even many of the children who complete the assignments correctly have no real understanding of why they're doing them.

To use seatwork more effectively, it's important to examine and refine techniques for selecting, presenting, monitoring, and evaluating it. As with any tool, seatwork's effectiveness depends upon the skill of the user. Expert teachers know that children don't learn to read poems by filling in worksheets. But they can practice math skills effectively with worksheets, or use worksheets as reading guides for a textbook chapter in science or social studies.

Tips for Using Seatwork

Following are some tips experienced teachers and researchers suggest for using seatwork effectively:

✔ **Always match seatwork to the material already covered during a lesson.** Seatwork should never replace direct instruction of new material (except for enrichment activities).

✔ **Make sure students know the purpose of the assignment.** You can't assume children will figure it out; be specific. Give explanations such as, "This exercise will help you practice the new rules for sounding out words with *ou* in the middle so you can get faster at doing that and read more new words on your own."

✔ **Guide students through one or two think-aloud examples to model strategies they need to complete the assignment.** Guided practice should always precede independent practice, say researchers and expert teachers. Otherwise, children risk practicing their mistakes. Lower-ability students may need even more guided practice than other children.

✔ **Match seatwork with ability level.** Whole-class assignments are rarely effective; they're too difficult for some children and too easy for others. Instead, try to customize by offering high-ability students optional extension activities and lower-ability students extra practice in areas where they need it. It's not always possible to differentiate assignments, but some good examples include math worksheets that vary in difficulty and guided free choice on books to read.

✔ **Select seatwork that allows all students a 95-percent success rate.** In situations where students must progress independently, such as seatwork and homework, students need a very high success rate. As Michigan State University researcher Jere Brophy explains, skills must be "mastered to the point of overlearning" so they can be retained and applied to more complex material.

✔ **Limit the amount of time students spend working on seatwork.** Intersperse seatwork with opportunities to move around.

✔ **Carefully monitor seatwork.** Before you begin a group lesson or become occupied, circulate through the room for a few minutes to make sure that everyone has started, paying special attention to children who often have problems. Later, take additional time to circulate the room and offer help where it's needed. Get students to think about what they're doing by asking them how they got a certain answer. They'll soon realize that you value how they think, not just whether or not they have the right answers.

✔ **Teach students to recognize when they don't understand something.** Many students aren't aware that they need help, while others may seek unnecessary support. Make clear the difference between needing help and being overly dependent. Working independently is a skill children need to practice.

✔ **Establish routines or procedures for seeking help.** Hand signals, "help cards" propped on desks, and buddy systems are all effective procedures.

Seatwork is a tool designed for a specific purpose: helping to meet the individual needs of 25 or 30 students while providing them with important practice opportunities. Used properly, this tool really works.

❖ Time Management

Teaching takes time. And in school, as elsewhere, there's never enough of it. Like any executive responsible for the efforts of others, you will find that managing time—yours and the students'—is one of your biggest challenges.

Time management is the thread running through almost all aspects of teaching—organizing the day, organizing the classroom, deciding how long and how often to teach various subjects, recording student progress, or keeping time-consuming behavior problems to a minimum. Students have only so much time to learn in your classroom, and you have only so much time to teach them.

Effective use of school time begins with efficient classroom organization and management—and vice versa. Almost every topic covered up to this point has involved time management in some way:

✔ paring down paperwork
✔ planning
✔ establishing routines that eliminate wasted time and confusion
✔ using learning centers
✔ independent assignments and seatwork to give you time to work with small groups.
✔ classroom environments that allow students and activities to move smoothly from one activity to the next

Increasing Teaching Time

You may have less time to teach than you think. Lunch, recess, breaks, downtime between lessons and activities, moving from one classroom to another, interruptions, and other periods of noninstructional time account for at least 27 percent of an elementary school day. In many classrooms, that figure climbs beyond 40 percent. Incredible as those statistics may sound, they have been confirmed by separate studies at WestEd (formerly the Far West Laboratory for Educational Research and Development).

Sure, lunch, recess, and restroom breaks are important. But too much teaching time is lost. Add to that the time that slips away when students stare out the window or are otherwise disengaged during instruction, and you get the point.

Here are some ways beginners and veterans alike can substantially increase teaching time:

✔ **Decrease the time allotted for breaks** and social activities. Contrary to popular belief, students do not need a lot of break time to refresh themselves. In fact, research shows that long or frequent breaks may actually lower their involvement with academic work.

✔ **Find out which aspects of school time you can control.** In some schools, teachers discover they can change the scheduling of class periods, pull-out programs, lunch breaks, extracurricular activities, planning time, and outside interruptions. Ask your principal to help you control time-wasters such as unexpected visitors and frequent intercom announcements.

✔ **Schedule solid blocks of teaching time for each day.** You might hang a "Do Not Disturb" sign outside your door during those times. Also, secure your principal's help in scheduling pull-out programs around those blocks and ask parents not to schedule medical or dental appointments then.

✔ **Plan for smooth transitions** between lessons and always try to have materials ready for each lesson or activity.

✔ **Assign homework to extend practice time.** Homework should allow students to practice skills they have already learned.

✔ **Reconsider how you schedule restroom breaks.**

✔ **Improve student attendance.** Attendance has a big effect on teaching and learning time. Impress upon parents the importance of good attendance and teach an actual lesson on how it hurts to miss school. "At the end of each day, I try to tell kids what we will be doing the next day," notes first-grade teacher Susie Davis. "I emphasize the kinds of activities they look forward to, such as hands-on activities. This seems to encourage attendance."

Delegating Tasks

Good classroom managers know how to delegate. Aides, volunteers, and students can handle many classroom tasks and save you enormous amounts of time. Learn to use these valuable helpers.

If you are one of the lucky ones assigned a full- or part-time aide, draw on that person's special strengths and abilities. Aides can work with small groups or tutor individuals. They can make instructional games and resources, keep bulletin boards current, monitor seatwork and learning centers, read stories to the class, and assist you with assessments. They can also help with clerical and housekeeping duties (those the children can't do for themselves). And their assistance with field trips, special programs, and class parties is invaluable. Help your aide become increasingly responsible and involved in the classroom.

Volunteers are another valuable asset. Volunteers generally can take on any responsibilities you would assign to an aide—the amount of supervision and guidance you may need to provide depends on the individual, of course. (Make sure to check your district policies on the use of nonlicensed volunteers in the classroom.)

Volunteer programs can not only provide teachers with much-deserved help, they can also improve home and school relations. Parents, grandparents, businesspeople, and other volunteers become sympathetic to the problems facing schools and supportive of better budgets and improved opportunities. Also, they learn to play an active role in educating their children. It's a winning proposition for everyone. (See Chapter Six for more about school volunteers.)

Here are some ideas for securing volunteers:

✔ **Parents and relatives** of your students are your best bet. Send home a recruitment flyer on the first day of school. Be sure to mention that grandparents are welcome, too. Solicit volunteers at school functions and ask them to fill out a volunteer application. Also, ask your students' teachers from the previous year for the names of parent volunteers. Many parents like to move along with their children.

✔ **Senior citizens** organizations are good sources for volunteers. Service-minded groups such as the Retired Seniors Volunteer Program and the American Association of Retired Persons look for projects in which their members can participate. Take the initiative and contact these groups; ask to be included on a meeting agenda.

✔ **PTA members** and other parent clubs have lots of volunteer experience. Don't forget to recruit from their ranks.

✔ **High school and college students** can help, too. For college-age volunteers, get permission to post recruitment information around the campus. Check with the college's volunteer bureau, or talk to the instructors of education courses and ask them to nominate likely candidates. At your local high school, check with the guidance counselors, individual teachers, or service organizations. Many high schools now have a service component built into graduation requirements, and school volunteering would certainly qualify.

✔ **Employees in business and industry** have become an integral part of school volunteer programs in recent years. Many businesses actively encourage employees to help out in the community and give them the release time as well.

✔ **Your students** can also be effective classroom helpers. Students can accomplish many of the tasks that adult volunteers do, and teachers nationwide routinely employ students to take lunch count, run errands, manage the classroom library, take care of classroom pets, and even photocopy materials—so long as these jobs do not interfere with their participation during instructional time. Obviously, student assistants save us valuable teaching time. But the experience also gives students the chance to be responsible and to be depended upon. These are important confidence- and character-building opportunities.

Cross-Age Tutoring: Students Helping Students

The Teacher Assistance Program at New Hope Elementary School in New Hope, Minnesota, encourages students to apply for such "jobs" as stocking supplies or tutoring peers. They fill out applications, undergo an interview, and receive job training. Other school programs are less formal. But the intent is the same: to give students added responsibilities and participation in the daily working of schools while simultaneously increasing the time teachers have to teach.

It's important to note here that students can function as academic helpers, not just as clerical workers or "grunt" labor. For example, one valuable time-saver is the use of cross-age tutors. Here, older children help younger ones practice academic skills such as reading, writing, or math. Cross-age tutoring resembles a real-life or family situation in which older children help younger children.

Consider the experiences of resource teacher Jacki Lamb as she worked with low-achieving students. When her first and second graders were hard-pressed to finish their writing assignment, Lamb enlisted the help of her fifth graders. What happened?

"I listened to the fifth grader who had the worst handwriting and spelling of all the older students in the resource room encourage in a positive manner his young charge to write clearly and legibly, saying, 'You are doing a good job of keeping the words on the line, but look at your spacing. Use your finger between the words so they don't run together. I can't understand what you're saying otherwise. Check to see how you are holding your pencil. That's important, you know.'" A few minutes later, Lamb was amused to hear the boy say, "Let's look at this word. Do you really think this is how to spell 'because'?" Says Lamb, "This was the same boy who could not spell 'because' himself! He continued to tutor his student in the merits of good handwriting and correct spelling, and they both felt successful when the young writer was finished."

Lamb continues: "My attention was drawn to the shy fifth-grade boy who usually was reluctant to participate either in the resource room or in his classroom. In his gentle manner, he was involved with his student by reading aloud what the second grader had written. 'Tell me if you like what you hear.' Together they made the necessary changes until the second grader was satisfied.

"I was excited by what was happening," Lamb notes. "The fifth graders were moving from student to student, helping each one until the young author was pleased with the final product. The older students exhibited patience, motivation, and surprisingly, knowledge of writing skills. The primary students gave the older students an opportunity to share their individual writing skills, limited as those skills may seem."

Managing Your Own Time

Don't forget to make time for yourself, too. The following time-management tips are gleaned from several sources, including ideas shared by Michigan-based staff-development specialists Janice Hammond and Dennis Sparks, and Barbara Samuels of the University of Calgary in Canada:

TIPS ON CROSS-AGE TUTORING

Cross-age tutoring helps the tutor as well as the tutee. To initiate your own cross-age tutoring program in reading:

- work with a teacher from a different grade level, higher or lower, depending upon whether you want your students to be tutors or tutees.
- help the tutors communicate in a sympathetic and nonjudgmental way.
- when possible, select tutors who are low-achieving readers. They can benefit from what they learn about proper reading behavior, they are most likely to be sympathetic to others having difficulty, and the responsibility of helping others gives them much-needed confidence.
- use tutoring as an alternative to silent reading or enrichment activities, not to replace a student's free time or your instruction.
- celebrate each success, such as an advance in reading level.

You might also teach your tutors the three-step Pause, Prompt, Praise system. This method, developed by Kevin Wheldall of Macquarie University in Australia, and Paul Mettem of the University of Birmingham, England, helps students read at a higher level and with greater accuracy than students who read alone or with untrained tutors.

The first step, pause, requires the tutor to delay attention to a reader's error for at least five seconds, or until the end of a sentence. This encourages the reader to self-correct more often, which, in turn, increases overall accuracy and comprehension. If tutors correct errors immediately, readers may lose the meaning of what they've read. Also, they fail to learn self-correcting behavior.

Second, tutors should offer prompts or clues instead of correcting an error outright. If the reader still can't correct an error, the tutor must model the use of clues to predict words and meanings.

The third step is praise. Praise is important. Tutors should praise when readers correct their own mistakes. And they should praise for general effort and progress.

You can teach this system by modeling it yourself. Then let students practice it as you play the role of tutee. Later, students can practice on each other. In one study, a group of low-ability students learned the technique in just two 30-minute sessions. While many teachers can cite personal evidence of the effectiveness of tutoring, researchers have documented proof. Studies show that the tutors often make greater gains in achievement than do the students they tutor. Is this proof of the old adage, "You don't really know it until you can teach it"?

- ✔ Set goals, both professional and personal, and review them periodically.
- ✔ Make a to-do list every day, including only items that are not part of your daily routine.
- ✔ Do your toughest task early in the day, if possible, so you don't spend time and energy worrying about it.
- ✔ Work within your personal time needs and periods of highest productivity. Could you accomplish more by arriving at school a half hour earlier each day than by working an hour or two after school?
- ✔ Learn to say no to committee work, volunteer work, or social functions for which you don't have the time.
- ✔ Learn to concentrate. Establish a quiet work space and uninterrupted work time.
- ✔ Avoid procrastinating.
- ✔ Avoid perfectionism. The extra hours you spend making that slide show just a little better may not be worth it.
- ✔ Put to use the time you spend waiting—in the doctor's office, on the bus or train, for meetings to begin.
- ✔ Set time limits for tasks. Remember Parkinson's Law: Work expands to fill the time available for its completion.
- ✔ Set deadlines for yourself and your class, and stick to them.
- ✔ Never do anything a student can do just as well: taking lunch count, running errands, filing completed assignments.
- ✔ Decorate the classroom walls with students' work instead of your own time-consuming masterpieces.

✔ Team up with other teachers for special projects and events.

✔ Handle each piece of mail only once. As you pull it from your box, toss into the wastebasket (or recycling bin) those that require no response. Those that do, attend to immediately. This also applies to e-mail.

✔ Enhance your work space. Organize materials. Move your desk from view of the door and colleagues who may be prone to drop by for a chat.

✔ Make all your phone calls in a set block of time.

✔ Energize during break periods. A brief change of pace (walking, reading the newspaper, or chatting) can increase concentration and efficiency.

✔ Take time to play. Everyone needs regular exercise, recreational activities, and social events. Renewal increases your effectiveness.

Time can be your enemy or your ally. If you learn to use it effectively, the payoffs will be big—for you and your students. Time management is not an easy skill to master. It takes time. But it's time well spent.

❖ The First Day

Your advance preparations are completed, and now you're ready to put your plan into action. Or maybe you've had only a day or two to prepare for your new teaching assignment. In either case, get off to a great start by making the first day much more than a chance to recount summer vacations or to get acquainted.

The first day is the most critical point in the critical first few weeks. This is the first time students will see you in action. And what they see will color their perceptions for the whole year. Your role as teacher and classroom manager will be much easier if you create a positive first impression.

Students can detect your attitude, expectations, and demands within the first few hours. If classroom activities flow smoothly, students will expect that's how things should

go; if activities are disorganized, they will think chaos is the norm—and will behave accordingly.

From the first minute of the first day, make sure students have an assignment. And from the first, post the assignments in the same place every day so students know exactly where to find them. It is important to get students to work as soon as class begins. This means planning in advance for legitimate activities—not handing out busywork or irrelevant worksheets—that contribute to the day's lessons. Don't take roll, do lunch count, or do anything else until you have students productively engaged.

Educational consultant Adele Fiderer describes one primary-grade teacher who begins each day by writing a message on the board. She leaves out some letters, asking children to use context and phonetic cues to figure out the missing letters and interpret the message.

An important part of learning to teach is striving to achieve that level of productive engagement throughout the day: A master teacher sets goals for transitions, lunch, recess, and dismissal as well as allotted instructional time. For example, on the first day you might incorporate a community-building activity during lunch in which student partners must discover one unique thing about the other person and one thing they share in common. Pairs may present their unique and different traits when they return to the classroom.

Providing meaningful activities right from the start is a form of role modeling. Be organized and prepared if you expect the same from your students. And be work-oriented and businesslike if you expect students to be serious about learning.

Tips for the First Day

The following list represents the accumulated wisdom of many different practicing teachers. These are the strategies the experts use:

1. **Arrive early.**
2. **Write your name on the board** so students can learn it immediately.

3. **Have an activity laid out** on each child's desk so children can be productively engaged from the start and you can take care of "housekeeping" details. Try a simple drawing or writing activity. First-grade teacher Susie Davis uses dot-to-dot or word-search activities. "These are things the children already know how to do."

4. **Greet students at the door** with a smile and a pleasant "Good morning!"

5. **Ask students to sit when they arrive.** They can wait to sharpen pencils, recount their summer, or ask questions. This helps you create a good working climate right away.

6. **Conduct a get-acquainted exercise.** (This could be combined with roll call.) For older children, Judith Rio suggests creating a class dictionary. Children write a three-part definition of themselves that includes physical characteristics, personality traits, and favorite hobbies or interests. Definitions could also include a pronunciation key to last names. Make sure to do one for yourself and compile the definitions into a book.

7. **Enjoy a good story and a good laugh together** to create a pleasant mood and ease students' fears and anxieties.

8. **Introduce the important features** of the room and the school.

9. **Present the most important classroom routines** in a positive way, as you would a regular lesson. Explain, discuss, and give students a chance to practice such routines as opening-of-day exercises.

10. **Work with students to develop classroom rules.** Discuss the consequences for disobeying the rules. Post the rules. (Have older students copy them.)

11. **Post a general schedule** for lunch, music, physical education, recess, and class work. Emphasize and teach the routines that will help students move into these periods quickly and efficiently. (Remember, they won't learn it all in a day. Continue to emphasize and practice classroom routines for the first few weeks.)

12. **Post a daily schedule** stating academic goals for the day. Note interruptions in the daily schedule, such as class pictures, programs, or speakers.

13. **Begin simple academic activities**—short reviews that guarantee a high success rate. These will boost confidence and ease fears. And they can serve as trial runs for practicing such routines as turning in completed work or asking for assistance.

14. **Monitor and maintain constant contact** with students. Don't spend time on clerical work the first day. And never leave students unattended. In an emergency, get another teacher or school adult to monitor students.

15. **Deal promptly with behavior problems.** Offer a lot of positive reinforcement to students picking up on routines quickly.

16. **Generate interest and enthusiasm** by hinting at exciting new topics you plan to begin later in the week.

17. **Issue books and discuss their care.** (Making book covers is a useful first-day activity.)

18. **Take students on a tour of the classroom** and explain what is in all the cupboards and drawers. Show them what is accessible and what is off-limits. Areas in which students will work independently, such as a listening center, should remain off-limits until you've had a chance to fully explain the purpose of the area and model how students will use it.

In general, make a good impression and keep enthusiasm high with first-day activities that involve students, provide success for all, create a working climate, maintain a whole-group focus, establish you as leader, focus on content, and communicate something about you and your positive expectations.

Tips for the First Few Weeks

1. Make a list of important rules and routines. Post the list prominently and make sure parents have a copy.

2. Be fast, firm, fair, and predictable in enforcing rules.

3. Make sure students understand the consequences of breaking rules.

4. Always have materials and activities ready.

5. Reinforce good behavior by acknowledging it.

6. Use student helpers.

7. Closely monitor students, giving clear instructions and directions.

8. Be calm.

9. Make sure students know what to bring to class.

10. Teach academic routines as well as "housekeeping" routines.

11. Hold students accountable for their work.

12. Eat lunch with students during the first few weeks.

13. Do not leave students unsupervised. If you must leave the classroom when students are there, make sure a colleague or qualified aide can watch your class.

14. Communicate instructional objectives and the minimum standards you expect.

15. Make sure parents understand your goals and objectives.

❖ In Summary

Effective teachers get the year off to a good start before students ever enter the classroom. These teachers know that certain factors will set the tone for the entire school year: the way the classroom looks, the routines and procedures established, the learning centers prepared, the steps taken to ensure students' comfort, the contact made with parents and colleagues. Well-organized classrooms set the stage for teaching and learning. They help to motivate children, enhance learning, prevent behavior problems, and create a stimulating classroom environment. And they help teachers make that important positive first impression.

❖ Works Cited

Anderson, Linda, et al. "A Qualitative Study of Seatwork in First-Grade Classrooms." *Elementary School Journal* 86, no. 2 (1985): 123–140.

Brophy, J. "Classroom Management Techniques." *Education and Urban Society* (1986): 18, 182–194.

Brophy, J., and J. Putnam. "Classroom Organization and Management." *Elementary School Journal* 83, no. 4 (1983): 265–285.

Cruickshank, Donald and Associates. *Teaching Is Tough.* Englewood Cliffs, NJ: Prentice Hall, 1980.

Cruz, Carol S., and John Mahaffty. *Classroom Management Training.* Portland, OR: Northwest Regional Educational Laboratory, 1985.

Duke, Daniel, ed. *Classroom Management: The National Society for the Study of Education, 1978 Yearbook, Part II.* Chicago: University of Chicago Press, 1979.

Harris, Theodore, and Richard Hodges, eds. *The Literacy Dictionary: The Vocabulary of Reading and Writing.* Newark, DE: International Reading Association, 1995.

Kaback, Suzanne, Constance Perry, and Brenda Power. *The Back-to-School Book: Everything You Need to Organize the Classroom, Establish Routines, and Kick Off the Best Year Yet!* New York: Scholastic, 2003.

Kanter, Patsy. *Quick-and-Easy Learning Centers: Math.* New York: Scholastic, 1995.

Murray, Bonnie. *The New Teacher's Complete Sourcebook: Grades K–4.* New York: Scholastic, 2002.

Naegle, Paula. *The New Teacher's Complete Sourcebook: Middle School*. New York: Scholastic, 2002.

Kepler, Lynne. *Quick-and-Easy Learning Centers: Science*. New York: Scholastic, 1995.

Leinhardt, Gaea, and James G. Greeno. "The Cognitive Skill of Teaching." *Journal of Educational Psychology* 78, no. 2 (1986): 75–95.

Mitchell, Lucy Sprague. *Our Children and Our Schools*. New York: Simon and Schuster, 1950.

New, Rebecca S. "Reggio Emilia: Some Lessons for U.S. Educators." Urbana, IL: ERIC Clearinghouse on Early Education and Parenting. (EDO-PS-93-3).

Opitz, Michael. *Flexible Grouping in Reading: Practical Ways to Help All Students Become Better Readers*. New York: Scholastic, 1998.

Opitz, Michael. *Learning Centers: Getting Them Started, Keeping Them Going*. New York: Scholastic, 1994.

Perlmutter, Jane, and Louise Burrell. *The First Weeks of School: Laying a Quality Foundation*. Portsmouth, NH: Heinemann, 2001.

Ryan, Kevin. *Induction of New Teachers*. Bloomington, IN: Phi Delta Kappa Educational Foundation, 1986.

Spann, Mary Beth. *Quick-and-Easy Learning Centers: Word Play*. New York: Scholastic, 1995.

Wong, Harry K., and Rosemary Tripi Wong. *The First Days of School: How to Be an Effective Teacher*. Mountainview, CA: Harry K. Wong Publications, 1998.

❖ Resources

General
Instructor New Teacher magazine. Scholastic.

Classroom Environment and Organization
Clayton, Marlynn K., and Mary Beth Forton. *Classroom Spaces That Work*. Greenfield, MA: Northeast Foundation for Children, 2001.

Grouping
Cohen, Elizabeth G., and John I. Goodlad. *Designing Groupwork: Strategies for the Heterogeneous Classroom*. 2nd ed. New York: Teachers College Press, 1994.

Wrubel, Ronit M. *Great Grouping Strategies* (Grades 1–5). New York: Scholastic, 2002.

Learning Centers
Incorporated Creative Teaching Press. *The Complete Guide to Classroom Centers*. Redding, CA: Creative Teaching Press, 2004.

Nations, Susan, and Mellissa Alonso. *Primary Literacy Centers: Making Reading and Writing Stick!* Gainesville, FL: Maupin House, 2001.

Management
Chang, Maria. *Classroom Management in Photographs: Full-Color Photographs with Teacher Descriptions and Insights About What Really Works*. New York: Scholastic, 2004.

Diffily, Deborah, and Charlotte Sassman. *Teaching Effective Classroom Routines* (Grades K–2). New York: Scholastic, 2004.

Evertson, Carolyn M., Edmund T. Emmer, and Murray E. Worsham. *Classroom Management for Elementary Teachers*. 6th ed. Boston: Allyn & Bacon, 2003.

Planning for a Substitute
Rose, Mary. *The Substitute Teacher Resource Book: Grades K–2*. New York: Scholastic, 2005.

Rose, Mary. *The Substitute Teacher Resource Book: Grades 3–5*. New York: Scholastic, 2005.

Chapter Two

Children as Learners

"Meeting the diverse needs of students is foremost on my mind. In my class I have limited-English proficient students . . . I have kids with allergies, physical disabilities, and a host of other challenges. I have kids who are just learning their letters and another kid who said to me, 'Mrs. Peden, I'm reading the book Treasure Island at home, too.'"

—*Cheryl Peden*

Cheryl Peden, 1994 Disney Teacher of the Year, describes a teaching situation that feels familiar to many of us. Perhaps the only characteristic that most of our students share is their uniqueness as human beings and as learners.

Who *are* these children in your classroom? Where do they come from? What are their interests and abilities? Are there features of their home lives that negatively impact their school lives? We can't expect to match instruction to students' needs until we know who these children are.

Children come in different sizes, shapes, colors, genders, and personalities. They have different preferences, interests, learning styles, backgrounds, strengths, and weaknesses, and they have reached different levels of ability and development. Often they speak different languages and come from different cultures. But each one is capable of learning. Each has special strengths and abilities. Each needs to experience success and security in the classroom. And each needs to feel valued and loved and accepted.

This chapter presents information to help you identify and understand different learner characteristics. These characteristics interact and overlap to form the whole child. Not until you understand the whole child can you begin to plan your instruction to meet the special needs of each student. As Thomas Jefferson pointed out more than 200 years ago, "There is nothing more unequal than the equal treatment of unequal people."

❖ Age and Developmental Levels

Any teacher or parent knows that children develop physically, emotionally, and intellectually at different rates. These rates often don't correspond to chronological age. Yet schools organize students into groups based on chronological age. Obviously, children respond very differently to schooling depending on their developmental levels. This is one of the most important considerations in matching students and instruction. Yet it's a consideration frequently missing in our nation's schools and classrooms.

Developmental Stages

To plan and offer the most developmentally appropriate education for students, it is essential to pay attention to developmental stages.

"Each child's temperament and rate of development is unique, but there are characteristics that children of the same age have in common," explains child-development specialist Clarice Kestenbaum, professor of child and adolescent psychiatry at Columbia University.

Dr. Kestenbaum describes two stages of normal development for children ages 5 through 10. (Keep in mind these are only guidelines. Children develop at different rates.) For example, **typical 5- to 7-year-olds:**

- ✔ are attached to the primary caretaker and can extend these warm feelings to teachers and friends.
- ✔ may have some separation anxieties (particularly the 5-year-olds).
- ✔ are ready to work and play in a group setting and learn how to share.
- ✔ are learning to sit and listen to the teacher, follow directions, concentrate, and quiet down at the appropriate time.

- ✔ feel good about themselves.
- ✔ can play imaginatively, are artistic, and have a "whimsical way of thinking."
- ✔ have a clear sense of gender identity.
- ✔ have acquired certain values and a beginning sense of right and wrong, and can be rigid in dealing with others.
- ✔ are egocentric and frequently can't empathize with others.
- ✔ are concerned about bodily harm. They may fear, for example, that if they get a cut, their blood will all flow out.
- ✔ have active imaginations and employ magical thinking, frequently acting as if "wishing will make it so." Teachers and parents often misinterpret this magical thinking as lying, but Dr. Kestenbaum cautions that this is unfair to children of this age. They really do believe that someone else knocked over the paints or spilled the milk. And yet these "wish-fulfilling fantasies exist side by side with concrete logic," Kestenbaum explains.
- ✔ have excellent memories.
- ✔ are ready to learn the 3 R's, but don't yet possess the ability for abstract thought.

THE ORIGIN OF KINDERGARTEN

German schoolteacher and philosopher Friedrich Froebel envisioned "kindergarten" as a place full of plants, flowers, and other natural objects, which children instinctively love. Hence the name kindergarten, or children garden. Froebel believed that children should be nurtured in nature. The teacher's function, he believed, was to present children with lofty ideals and "make intelligible the inner spiritual nature of things" in the natural world. Quite simply, he advocated the education of very young children through guided exploration of the natural world—a world to which they were instinctively drawn.

✔ possess the motor skills that enable them to tie their shoes, ride tricycles or bicycles, throw balls, skip, jump, and clap in rhythm.

Warning signs at this age include:

✔ playing in a repetitive and stereotyped way or only playing alone

✔ listless and apathetic behavior

✔ trouble expressing themselves in the classroom

One major developmental change children of this age undergo is their ability to work in the presence of the teacher without needing the teacher actually to work with them. The kindergarten student often needs to work directly with the teacher; the 7-year-old second grader can work alone.

Kestenbaum refers to the years from 5 to 7 as "The Wonder Years," explaining that the world is an exciting place for normal 5- to 7-year-olds. "Incredible growth and development occurs during this period, as every teacher who has taught kindergarten and then first or second grade knows."

Not everyone agrees on what is appropriate education for these early developmental stages. While some experts reject formal academic instruction in kindergarten, others feel that the problems lie not with academic learning, but with the teaching methods used. As Marie Sloane, a teacher in Des Plaines, Illinois, points out, it is almost impossible to find an academic skill that all primary-school students are ready to learn at the same time in the same way. Says Sloane, "Nowhere is this more obvious than with my kindergarteners. Some are struggling to learn the alphabet; others can read."

The next major developmental stage, **7 to 10 years old**, features characteristics and abilities very different from those of younger children. These **middle-grade children**:

✔ enter the "age of reason," as logical thought replaces intuitive thinking. This is when major cognitive growth takes place. These children are ready for formal learning.

✔ experience incredible growth in both fine- and gross-motor skills.

✔ improve listening skills markedly.

✔ develop the ability to form close friendships using their new abilities to compromise and cooperate.

✔ can now lose a game without falling to pieces.

✔ welcome rules and take them literally.

✔ respond to concrete rewards such as stickers, grades, or teacher praise.

✔ fear (more than anything else) not being liked or accepted.

ONE EXPERT'S VIEW

One of the most balanced and informed discussions of developmental appropriateness can be found in *Developmentally Appropriate Programs in Early Childhood Education: A Practical Guide* by Marjorie J. Kostelnik, et al. The authors say that using children's interests and ways of learning as guides, effective teachers do the following three things to promote appropriate academic learning among young children:

- **They understand the broad nature of literacy and mathematics**, and the concepts, processes, and content of each. They know, for example, that reading is not reciting the alphabet or making letter-sound associations; that writing is not penmanship; that mathematics is not rote memorization of number facts.

- **They recognize the expressions of academic interest and exploratory behavior** in their students. Children who are asking, "What does this say?" or "How many do we need?" are naturally involved with academics.

- **They provide concrete materials and relevant experiences to enhance children's academic learning.** Kostelnik suggests reading to children and inviting them to respond to and interpret the story; singing songs and reading poems; playing rhyming games that feature sound associations; giving children materials to count, sort, sequence, estimate; and offering children many ways to express themselves orally and in writing.

Warning signs at this age include:

✔ isolation and exclusion from the peer group

✔ chronic fear of not doing well and a constant need for rewards and compliments

✔ the need always to be first or win

A third development stage, **11 to 14 years old**, encompasses **children in middle school or junior high**. Since the work of Jean Piaget in the 1950s, educators, psychologists, and developmental biologists have been working to identify the characteristics and educational concerns of these preteens and early adolescents. Caught between the worlds of childhood and adulthood, thrust into the throes of puberty, the typical student this age is "highly distractible, peer-centered, confused by abstract concepts, unable to sit still or stay quiet, and full of insecurities from living inside a body that is not fully formed," says middle school expert and author Bruce Hammond.

Sound familiar? Teachers and parents of early adolescents know these characteristics only too well. Here's a list of specific intellectual and social-emotional characteristics offered by Hammond and also the Palo Alto Medical Foundation (using information from the American Medical Association).

Intellectually, these upper-elementary to middle-school-age children:

✔ are still largely concrete thinkers, perceiving things as good or bad, right or wrong.

✔ begin to imagine possibilities, recognize consequences of their actions, anticipate what others are thinking.

✔ begin to question family and school rules, challenging adults.

✔ believe that bad things won't happen to them, which leads to risk-taking behavior.

✔ believe they are the center of attention, which makes them painfully self-conscious and sensitive to criticism.

Hammond expresses a special concern for female students, noting that "girls seem to lose self-confidence and self-esteem in middle school after outperforming boys by a significant margin in the earlier grades."

Socially and emotionally, preteens and early teens:

✔ spend more time with peers and less time with family or adults.

✔ explore different clothes, hairstyles, friends, and music in the attempt to form an identity.

✔ exhibit frequent moodiness and mood swings.

✔ push adult-set limits to assert independence.

✔ may act out to express emotional pain.

What do these characteristics mean for teachers and schooling? A lot, says Hammond. "The first day of middle school is the biggest transition in a student's K–12 education," he claims. "Fresh from the child-centered classrooms of the elementary grades, middle schoolers plunge into a world designed to mimic the high school model." Hammond and others contend that middle schools (or junior highs) need to balance academic challenges with the developmental needs of early adolescents.

In an online article for parentsoup.com, Hammond notes that good middle schools share these traits:

✔ **A Curriculum That Connects**. As they transition from concrete to abstract thinking, students at this age need materials and activities that are directly related to their daily lives. Hammond offers the example of a lesson on the American Revolution that begins with a discussion of how students feel when their parents make decisions without consulting them.

✔ **Variety in the School Day**. The high school model of lecturing leaves middle school students cold. Hormonal changes make these students restless and fatigued, so asking them to sit for long periods of time is unreasonable. They need active learning experiences and frequent opportunities to move around. The best classrooms feature hands-on active creation rather than passive absorption of information, says Hammond. "A good middle school teacher rarely asks kids to sit in one place for more than 20 minutes," he notes.

✔ **Good Guidance**. Young adolescents have so many daily conflicts and misunderstandings that overworked guidance counselors need teachers to help with guidance and advising. (My school and many others include as part of the required curriculum an actual class focusing on social and emotional issues.)

Multiage Grouping

Because children do develop at different rates, many educators advocate the grouping of students by developmental level, not by chronological age. Such grouping is best achieved in multiage classrooms or settings. In a combined first- and second-grade classroom, for example, children can work with their intellectual and developmental peers.

Many experts, including child development specialist David Elkind, believe that multiage grouping is the most effective way to compensate for the natural variability among young children. Elkind identifies three advantages of this type of grouping. First, he says, advanced younger students can be grouped with older students at the same level for certain activities and lessons. Second, older students can be used to tutor their younger classmates, "an important and beneficial learning experience for both sides." And third, teachers have their students for a longer period of time and get to know them better, thus they are better able to determine when students should move on to more complex activities.

Like most strategies, multiage grouping also has its disadvantages: Teachers must master the curricula for two or three developmental levels; poor personality matches between teachers and students are prolonged; and parents of older students may wonder if their children receive enough intellectual stimulation. "None of these problems are insurmountable," says Elkind, "and the benefits of multiage grouping considerably outweigh them."

Teacher Testimonials

Many teachers confirm the benefits of multiage groupings.

"In multiage classrooms, **children are given**

ONLINE RESOURCES FOR CHILD DEVELOPMENT

Child Development Institute
(www.cdipage.com) Although geared primarily to parents, this site offers a wealth of information and practical suggestions for all levels and aspects of child development. It also includes extensive information on childhood disorders and learning disabilities, including specific tips for teaching children with these disorders.

Children, Youth, and Family Consortium
(www.cyfc.umn.edu) This site from the University of Minnesota connects research, teaching, policy, and community practice. There is a "Search for Experts" option that allows site visitors to search for an expert on an extensive array of child development topics. Contact information is given, so teachers can ask an expert for advice on a particular child or situation.

Foundation for Child Development (FCD)
(www.ffcd.org) Information and publications are featured on the major areas of FCD work: studying the alignments between preschool and the K–12 years in school systems; looking at the unique educational needs of immigrant children; and measuring the well-being of American children and youth.

Society for Research in Child Development
(www.srcd.org/public.html) Here the society makes available free summaries of articles in its subscription journal *Child Development*. Viewers need *Adobe Acrobat Reader* (available for download) to access the summaries.

RESOURCES & ORGANIZATIONS ON MULTIAGE CLASSROOMS

• **Enhancing Learning Through Multiage Grouping** is a not-to-be-missed online resource sponsored by the North Central Regional Educational Laboratory. It includes a treasure trove of research-based information, audio interviews of classroom teachers describing their multiage classrooms and methods, specific recommendations and "Action Options," extensive links to related topics or additional information, illustrative cases of successful multiage programs (with direct links), personal contacts, and a thorough list of references. This excellent resource was written by multiage teacher Debra Johnson and curriculum director Cheryl Fox and is available at www.ncrel.org/sdrs/areas/issues/methods/instrctn/in500.htm.

• **Staff Development for Educators** (formerly the Society for Developmental Education) sponsors a National Looping and Multiage Conference each July, and it presents other multiage workshops and conferences throughout the year for elementary educators. Phone or write for information to SDE at 10 Sharon Rd., P.O.B. 577, Peterborough, NH 03458; (800) 924-9621; www.sde.com.

• The **National Alliance of Multiage Educators** (NAME) facilitates the sharing of ideas, information, resources, and experiences among multiage educators. Write or call the Alliance at 10 Sharon Road, Peterborough, NH 03458; (800) 924-9621; www.sde.com.

• The **National Multiage Institute** is an internationally renowned program at the College of Education at Northern Arizona University. It hosts several summer institutes on multiage instruction for teachers seeking graduate course credits. It also offers other multiage education seminars at other locations throughout the year. For more information, write or call the Center for Excellence in Education at Northern Arizona University, P.O.B 5774, Flagstaff, AZ 86011-5774; (520) 523-4280. For course descriptions and online registration, visit the College of Education Website at http://coe.nau.edu.

enough time to mature," says Laura Fendel, who teaches a combination first and second grade. The wide range in ages helps her group students appropriately for reading and mathematics, and keep the groupings fluid. Students move in and out of groups as their development dictates.

Deborah Charles of New Jersey praises the benefits of peer tutoring in her class of first and second graders. Not only does she ask the second graders to help the first graders academically, she also pairs them to complete classroom chores and practice good citizenship.

"The multiage classroom is a 'natural' for building a learning community," Charles notes. She reports that her **classes become an extended family**, and the first graders sometimes cry at the end of the year because they don't want to "lose" the second graders. But by the following fall, the new second graders settle into their role as leaders and tutors.

"We all teach and learn from each other," says Arizona teacher Becky Stahlman of her second-/third-grade class. "**Students can progress at their own rate of learning**— regardless of age."

Adds her colleague Bobbie Faulkner, "The range of abilities in most multiage classes is no greater than in a single grade class."

Peggy Timbrooks, also from Arizona, teaches a combination fifth-/sixth-grade class. She talks about the social and emotional benefits of multiage grouping. "Sixth graders tend to be rulers of the roost whenever they're alone," she says. But when they are **working with the younger children, they learn to be a little more patient** and more considerate."

Vermont teacher Meg Kenny says that one of the biggest benefits of teaching her grades 6–8 class is the **extended time spent with each student**. "When you work with a student for more than one year, you know what strategies work best with that child, and you can just pick that up when the school year starts."

Susan Padilla, who teaches a K–1–2 class in Austin, Texas, stresses that both the **curriculum and assessment must focus on the individual child**. She and other multiage teachers suggest portfolios, narratives, and other alternative assessments.

❖ Multiple Abilities/ Multiple Intelligences

The traditional concept of "intelligence" has limited our capacity for adequately providing for children. In schools, we typically focus on verbal and mathematical abilities as the hallmarks of intelligence.

But psychologists and educational researchers now offer convincing evidence that ability and intelligence are broad concepts encompassing many human traits and activities. We all have talents and intelligence. As a classroom teacher, think of yourself as a "talent scout" working to identify each student's unique strengths and abilities and using those strengths to help students improve less-developed abilities. "Every child is special if we create conditions in which that child can be a specialist within a specialty group," says Joseph Renzulli, director of the National Research Center on the Gifted and Talented.

Reading Ability Rules

Retired Stanford University researcher Elizabeth Cohen claims that our entire education system is misguidedly based on the notion of reading ability as the sole indicator of intelligence. Cohen has shown through extensive research that teachers assume good readers will be competent in any content area, and those who read poorly will do poorly on any task.

Classrooms create and maintain a whole status order based on reading abilities, says Cohen. The order is understood and accepted by teacher and students, and their expectations and actions are influenced accordingly. Unfortunately, this order ignores the fact that there are many types of abilities, and each child "shines" in his or her own way.

Some other abilities Cohen has identified include (but are not limited to):

✔ creativity

✔ suggesting new ideas

✔ helping a group reach a decision

✔ visualizing problems and solutions

✔ physical skills, such as strength and dexterity

✔ reasoning (identifying relationships and patterns, categorizing, and so on)

✔ problem solving

✔ curiosity and inventiveness

✔ persistence

Eight (and More) Different Intelligences

Perhaps the strongest support for the idea of multiple intelligences and abilities comes from the long-term and widely recognized work of Harvard psychologist Dr. Howard Gardner.

"Human beings have evolved over a long period of time to think in at least seven ways, which I call intelligences," Gardner explained when he first developed definitions of intelligence in the mid-1980s. Since then, he has added an eighth intelligence to the list, and he is examining a ninth possibility, acknowledging that as understanding about the human brain increases, other intelligences will likely be identified.

The intelligences, as Gardner defines them, and as his colleagues Noel White and Tina Blythe describe them, are:

✔ **Logical-mathematical:** the ability to reason deductively or inductively and to recognize and manipulate abstract patterns and relationships. People exhibiting this intelligence include scientists, mathematicians, philosophers, individuals who thrive on sports statistics, and those who systematically analyze problems and test solutions.

✔ **Linguistic:** the ability to apply reading and writing skills with ease, and to be sensitive to the nuances, order, and rhythm of words. Poets exemplify linguistic intelligence. Those who always tell stories, easily learn other languages, enjoy rhymes and puns, and make sense of the world through language also display this intelligence.

✔ **Musical:** the ability to discern pitch, timbre, and rhythm and to be responsive to music. Composers, musicians, those attracted to birds singing, and those who tap out rhythms with pencils or pens display this intelligence.

- **Spatial:** the ability to create visual-spatial representations of the world and to transfer those representations mentally or concretely—to think in pictures and to create them. Architects, sculptors, and engineers exhibit this intelligence, as do students who like to "web" ideas before writing, or gravitate to the graphics in a textbook.

- **Bodily-kinesthetic:** the ability to use the body to solve problems, create products, and convey ideas and emotions. This intelligence is used by dancers, athletes, surgeons, craftspeople, and students who prefer to make models rather than write reports.

- **Interpersonal:** the ability to work effectively with and understand others, and to notice their goals, motivations, and intentions. Teachers, politicians, psychologists, salespeople, and students who enjoy group work and interacting with friends and classmates exhibit this one. These are the students who work well with others and use tact as a tool.

- **Intrapersonal:** the ability to work well alone at one's own pace. People with this intelligence "know themselves"—understand their strengths and weaknesses—and make well-thought-out choices and decisions.

- **Naturalist:** the ability to distinguish among, classify, and use features of the environment. Plant and wildlife biologists, farmers and hunters, archaeologists, geologists, gardeners, and students who know the features of every make of car exhibit this intelligence.

The first two, linguistic and logical-mathematical, are the intelligences most valued and emphasized in school. But equally important, Gardner stresses, are the other types. He explains that everyone has strengths and weaknesses among the various intelligences.

"Strength in one intelligence does not have predictive value for strength in another intelligence," he stresses. "Psychologists who claim that intelligence is a single entity—educators who think of students as either smart or dumb—are wrong. A person can be smart in one area and dumb in others." The "Student Strengths" table on page 109 presents a description of the intelligences through learning preferences, famous examples, and common misbehaviors.

Biological Basis for Intelligence

Gardner has also examined other "intelligence" candidates, but none have yet completely met the criteria. (He expects some will in the future.) These criteria include biological and psychometric evidence, among other things.

"There was powerful evidence from the study of neuropsychology for the existence of different mental faculties," Gardner wrote in a recent paper. "That evidence constituted the strongest leg on which to justify MI [Multiple Intelligence] theory." (For more on brain research, see Chapter Three.)

An ability judged to be an intelligence can be isolated by brain damage, identified with a core set of information-processing mechanisms, has a plausible evolutionary history and produces definite "end-state" performances, and meets other criteria as well.

Theory Into Practice

These intelligences can be nurtured, or developed over time, says Gardner. This has major implications for the way we design and present curriculum.

Gardner and his colleagues have developed practical classroom applications for multiple intelligences (see the resource list at the end of this chapter). But Gardner is concerned about the misuse of his theory. Multiple intelligences are not learning styles and cannot be reduced to arts-and-crafts activities.

"Much work needs to be done on the question of how the intelligences can best be mobilized to achieve specific pedagogical goals," he claims, adding that one way MI approaches are particularly useful is when a student is trying to master a challenging new concept.

Many educators have used the theory successfully to design instruction and classroom activities. In Indianapolis, teachers founded the Key School—the first school organized around MI theory. (For a look at this school, which includes both an elementary and a middle school, see the detailed information at www.ncrel.org/sdrs/areas/issues/students/atrisk/at6lk69.htm.)

I teach a unit on multiple intelligences to my seventh- and eighth-grade gifted students. Many of these students rely on their strong linguistic and logical-mathematical intelligences to succeed in school, and this unit helps them see their peers in a new light. Through activities and demonstrations that require the application of intelligences outside the linguistic and logical-mathematical areas, they learn that the school's athletes, artists, musicians, peer leaders, mechanics, and outdoorsmen are also intelligent. It confirms what most of them already suspected: There are many intelligent students who don't necessarily earn good grades or win the respect of teachers.

Naturalist intelligence became a key theme in my unit on Marjorie Rawlings' *The Yearling*. Jody's father, Penny, is a wonderful example of an individual perfectly in tune with his environment. His knowledge of the natural world serves as inspiration and a source of pride to the students in my small, rural school, many of whom are avid hunters and woodsmen. They clamor to contribute their own naturalist wisdom. To learn that a Harvard scholar and educators around the country value this type of knowledge builds self-esteem in these children.

Karen Vanek teaches a formal lesson on multiple intelligences that involves students evaluating their own strengths and weaknesses and making a human graph of the results. "I'm always amazed at the inferences and generalizations that come out of this tangible graphing activity," notes Vanek. "Many times students notice a pattern about who is together in the different categories and why some categories have so few or no students in them."

Students then write a response to the question "How am I smart?" The final result of this lesson is a list of classroom experts in different areas—experts who can be consulted during the year as necessary. "This brings pride to everyone, as everyone is smart in different ways," Vanek concludes.

Intellectual Capacity Is Fluid

In a discussion of IQ and intellectual capacity, educator and author Barbara Clark concurs that intellect is a fluid quality, changing over time. "Our [intellectual] capacity will change," she writes, "depending on the opportunities we are given to develop." As Clark demonstrates, students often lose ground in school, due to practices and activities that stifle rather than enhance intellectual capacity. She claims that this is particularly true of gifted students.

More than 60 years ago, Piaget discussed stages of intellectual development and claimed that the age at which children pass from one stage to the next depended not only on their genetic makeup but also on the quality of their environment.

Piaget's view of intelligence as educable did not become prominent among scholars until well into the 1960s, however. And it still hasn't reached many teachers, administrators, and parents. Many of us, including students, hold the notion that intelligence is fixed. One has a little or a lot, but the amount never varies. It's easy to see how this misconception leads to the commonly held belief that some students are good in everything while others excel in nothing.

Researchers suggest that it's helpful to view ability as the expression of experience and opportunity, and that limited ability should more accurately be seen as limited experience. Think about the differences separating higher- and lower-ability students. Factors such as enriching home environments and out-of-school experiences frequently characterize the higher-ability students.

The HOTS

Putting this "lack of opportunity and experience" idea into practice, Dr. Stanley Pogrow at the University of Arizona has developed a successful program to teach low-achieving students how to think. His HOTS (Higher Order Thinking Skills) Project challenges some basic assumptions about "low-ability" students and demonstrates that these students have far greater intellectual capacity than most teachers expect. In the hundreds of elementary schools nationwide where HOTS is used, it completely replaces remedial programs for at-risk and Chapter 1 students.

Pogrow says that traditional remedial programs targeted for "discouraged learners" (he dislikes the term "low-ability") treat the symptoms (poor basic skills and lack of factual knowledge) and not the cause. The "cause," he explains, is that "discouraged learners do not understand 'understanding.'" They cannot deal with more than one concept at a time, cannot converse about ideas, and cannot think ideas through. They never learn how discrete facts and bits of information fit together to form connections. Traditional remedial methods and teachers' questioning strategies calling for simple recall answers contribute to students' lack of understanding.

Thinking processes must be modeled for students through sophisticated conversation, Pogrow claims. Some children hear such conversation at home, but many do not. And they don't hear it in school, either. Studies show that most teachers' questioning strategies call for only one- or two-word answers.

"The most underused technology in American education is not computers—it's conversation," Pogrow asserts. "How are students supposed to know the conventions of thinking about ideas, if they have not had any experience with them?"

As Pogrow explains, "Recalling facts is probably the only learning experience that these students have had, so they equate learning with acquiring discrete facts." But those facts are easily forgotten. "The mind retains information by linking new information with existing knowledge. If students do not make such linkages and associations, it is unlikely that they will retain or apply what they are learning."

HOTS teaches them to make those links. A specially designated HOTS teacher receives intensive training in Socratic teaching methods,

Socratic teaching, based on the ideas and practices of the Greek philosopher Socrates, focuses on teaching by asking rather than telling. Using the format of classroom discussions (Socrates used "dialogues," as recorded by his pupil Plato), teachers ask students questions rather than give them answers. The idea is that true knowledge is based on understanding, not memorizing or regurgitating facts. Thus, if students know the "why's" behind the facts, can explain their thinking, and critically judge and react to the thinking of others, they truly understand.

Stanford professor Rob Reich offers tips for Socratic teaching in the classroom:

1. Set down conversational guidelines. (Students must participate fully, not just offer a single comment. Also first-person anecdotes are less effective than articulating concepts or principles.)
2. Learn to be comfortable with prolonged silence. Reich suggests waiting at least ten seconds for a student response before "nudging" the discussion.
3. Produce an atmosphere of "productive discomfort." Socratic method frequently involves cognitive dissonance, where students discover that their

beliefs or intuitions don't withstand scrutiny.
4. Be open to learning something new and discarding the lesson plan. Often, unexpected or interesting ideas will arise that students need to pursue.
5. Be sensitive to welcoming "the totally crazy idea" while discouraging comments that are attempts to avoid serious discussion.
6. Encourage honest comments, and discourage those designed to give you what the student thinks you want.
7. Find a classroom arrangement that facilities face-to-face discussion.

Adapted from "Scholar [Rob Reich] Discusses Educational Benefits of Socratic Method" by John Sanford. Stanford University News Service, May 2003.

A HOTS Dialogue

The following sample of a HOTS unit illustrates the "thinking environment" created by the HOTS Project. The unit is titled "Figuring Out Rules," and students use a HOTS computer game called SNAP to practice their thinking skills. Below is part of a script that presents a typical dialogue between teacher and students on Day 2 of the unit. The **boldface** text suggests what the teacher says (the teacher can paraphrase). The words in parentheses are the hoped-for student answers. Underlined words in the parentheses indicate a key idea, which must be elicited to indicate that the student truly understands the concept. The regular text without parentheses is directions to the teacher. HOTS program developers stress that teachers do not need to follow the text literally, except for key linkage questions. The printed words are just a starting point. Teachers are trained to respond to unexpected answers and improvise their own questions. Lesson plans also include suggested follow-up questions.

In this game you have to match words that are exactly the same. What does that mean? (The words have to be the same in <u>every</u> way.)

What else have we worked with this year that have been exactly the same? (Yuppies or Gruppies) **To be exactly the same they had to be the same for what traits?** (Height, color, width, nose, or tail) **What do we call babies who are exactly the same?** (<u>Identical</u> twins) **Regular twin is the wrong answer!**

Am I the same person I was yesterday? (Yes) **Am I exactly the same as I was yesterday?** (No) **Why not? What traits are different?** (Wearing different clothing, feel different, and so on)

Does anyone remember what we call it when we try to figure out the meaning of a word from the surrounding words in sentences? (Context or setting)

Good. I am going to read two sentences from the instructions for the SNAP game. SNAP is a reaction game. If you react correctly, you score a point. Then ask:

What do you think *react* or *reaction* means? How do you know from the words I read? Keep probing until students respond that it is something you do <u>in response to</u> <u>something else</u>.

If students say only that it is something you do quickly, type some words quickly into the computer and say: **This is not reacting, even though I am typing quickly. What is the difference between what I am doing now and what you did in SNAP?** (Yesterday we were typing fast in response to what the computer was doing.)

What were we reacting to? (What the computer was doing) **Do people react to medicine?** (Yes) **How?** (Some medicine might make you sleepy, and so on.)

Now I am going to get tricky and more general. Are you ready? If *react* means something we do in response to what the computer did, what would *react* mean if there was no computer—only people? (It's something we do in response to something someone else does.)

Can anyone give me an example of a situation in which you react to another person? (Laugh when someone tells a joke, duck when someone throws a ball at you, and so on)

and the curriculum focuses on the thinking process rather than specific content.

Thinking skills develop from how we question children and how we respond to their responses, says Pogrow. "Everything a kid says must be responded to."

The HOTS teachers learn to maintain a proper level of ambiguity in discussions so students learn to resolve ambiguity, construct meaning,

and articulate ideas and strategies. One of their most important challenges is to guide students without simplifying a problem or telling students what to do. And the students struggle for a while. "We call it controlled floundering," says Pogrow. "And you know what? We don't see kids giving up. They love to solve problems. And by making them experience the problem and solve it themselves, they realize how smart they are."

All student achievement, discipline, and attitude improve dramatically.

"Fascinated students are not 'tough' or discipline problems," says Pogrow. And who can measure the increases in self-esteem and positive attitude gained by children who realize for the first time in their lives that they are smart?

For more information on the HOTS program and to order curriculum materials, visit their Web site at www.hots.org, or call or write The HOTS Project, P.O.B. 42620, Tucson, AZ 85733; (800) 999-0153.

❖ Learning Styles

Just as students differ in their capacity to learn, they differ in **how they learn**. This well-accepted fact has enormous implications for classroom teaching. As Dr. Rita Dunn and colleagues at the Center for the Study of Learning and Teaching Styles, St. John's University, explain, "Learning style is a biologically and developmentally imposed set of personal characteristics that make the same teaching method effective for some and ineffective for others. Every person has a learning style—it's as individual as a signature." If we accept the idea of learning styles, then we must also accept an approach to teaching that helps students develop skills through their strengths.

Sensory Preferences

The most familiar learning-style categories involve students' sensory preferences and how those preferences affect their learning. We label such preferences visual, auditory, kinesthetic, and tactile. In the simplest sense, visual learners are those who best acquire new information through sight. For example, the visual learner would prefer the teacher demonstrate an assignment rather than just describe it. This student sometimes seems to ignore oral directions. The auditory learner, on the other hand, needs to hear an explanation of the content. The tactile learner learns best by manipulating materials (writing is not tactile enough for children below fourth grade, according to Dunn). A kinesthetic learner prefers to use the whole body, favoring such

activities as dramatization and pantomime, field trips, and interviewing.

These sensory preferences or modalities are familiar to most teachers, but attempts to accommodate them are often shallow, says learning styles expert Pat Guild.

For example, teachers may know that visual learners need visual information. "But if the visual is words on an overhead projector repeating the words spoken out loud, this is a superficial accommodation of the learner's style," Guild claims. Far better, she says, would be the information presented through an image, a symbol, or visual representation.

Presenting literature to my junior high school students, I often project paintings representing such literary ideas as tone or symbolism. Cartoons or caricatures help communicate the concepts of hyperbole or satire. A colleague in the history department uses a poster of Leutze's *George Washington Crossing the Delaware* to supplement a written description of the event.

Guild offers another example, involving the kinesthetic learner. "Many teachers know that the active, kinesthetic learner needs hands-on experiences," she writes. But this learner's "impatience to get started sometimes causes teachers to demand that they explain what they will do before they start. This is difficult for these students, since the doing leads to the understanding and the explaining."

There are many examples from research of appropriate activities for different learning styles. Several resources are listed on page 92.

Other Individual Preferences

Sensory preference is just one aspect of learning style. Dunn and other researchers have found many other aspects, including preferences for sound levels, light levels, temperature, seating arrangements, mobility, group size, type of learning activity, eating and drinking while concentrating, and chronobiology (time preferences). Dunn claims there are even connections between learning style and hemisphericity—left- and right-brain functions.

Learning Styles Test for Teachers

To find out the learning style or styles you prefer, respond to the following statements. Check the statements you agree with. Then use the scoring instructions on page 63.

❏ 1. I prefer to hear a book on tape rather than reading it.

❏ 2. When I put something together, I always read the directions first.

❏ 3. I prefer reading to hearing a lecture.

❏ 4. When I am alone, I usually have music playing or hum or sing.

❏ 5. I like playing sports more than reading books.

❏ 6. I can always tell directions such as north and south no matter where I am.

❏ 7. I love to write letters or in a journal.

❏ 8. When I talk, I like to say things like "I hear ya, that sounds good" or "that rings a bell."

❏ 9. My room, desk, car, or house is usually disorganized.

❏ 10. I love working with my hands and building or making things.

❏ 11. I know most of the words to the songs I listen to.

❏ 12. When others are talking, I usually am creating images in my mind of what they are saying.

❏ 13. I like sports and think I am a pretty good athlete.

❏ 14. It's easy to talk for long periods of time on the phone with my friends.

❏ 15. Without music, life isn't any fun.

❏ 16. I am very comfortable in social groups and can usually strike up a conversation with most anyone.

❏ 17. When looking at objects on paper, I can easily tell whether they are the same no matter which way they are turned.

❏ 18. I usually say things like "I feel," "I need to get a handle on it," or "get a grip."

❏ 19. When I recall an experience, I mostly see a picture of it in my mind.

❏ 20. When I recall an experience, I mostly hear the sounds and talk to myself about it.

❏ 21. When I recall an experience, I mostly remember how I felt about it.

❏ 22. I like music more than art.

❏ 23. I often doodle when I am on the phone or in a meeting.

❏ 24. I prefer to act things out rather than write a report on them.

❏ 25. I like reading stories more than listening to stories.

❏ 26. I usually speak slowly.

❏ 27. I like talking better than writing.

❏ 28. My handwriting is not usually neat.

❏ 29. I generally use my finger to point when I read.

❏ 30. I can multiply and add quickly in my head.

❏ 31. I like spelling and think I am a good speller.

❏ 32. I get very distracted if someone talks to me when the TV is on.

❏ 33. I like to write down instructions that people give me.

❏ 34. I can easily remember what people say.

❏ 35. I learn best by doing.

❏ 36. It is hard for me to sit still for very long.

Learning Styles Inventory developed by Pat Wyman, M.A. The Center for New Discoveries in Learning, P.O.B. 1019, Windsor, CA 95492-1019; (707) 837-8180. Web sites: www.howtolearn.com and www.discoveries.org.

Scoring for Learning Styles

The scoring for the learning styles test on page 62 is as follows:

Visual Questions: 2, 3, 6, 7, 12, 17, 19, 23, 25, 30, 31, 33
Auditory Questions: 1, 4, 8, 11, 14, 15, 16, 20, 22, 27, 32, 34
Kinesthetic Questions: 5, 9, 10, 13, 18, 21, 24, 26, 28, 29, 35, 36

Fill in the chart.

Question #	Visual	Auditory	Kinesthetic
1.			
2.			
3.			
4.			
5.			
6.			
7.			
8.			
9.			
10.			
11.			
12.			
13.			
14.			
15.			
16.			
17.			
18.			
19.			
20.			
21.			
22.			
23.			
24.			
25.			
26.			
27.			
28.			
29.			
30.			
31.			
32.			
33.			
34.			
35.			
36.			
	Total____	Total____	Total____

To get the percentage of each learning style, total the number checked in each column. Divide by the total checked in all three columns. Multiply this number by 100.

Persons oriented more to left-brain functions (analysis and induction) seem to "learn successively, in small steps leading to understanding," she explains. Those with right-brain orientation (global apprehension and deduction), on the other hand, appear to "learn by obtaining meaning from a broad concept and then focusing on details."

As brain research continues and knowledge about how the brain works expands, hemisphericity has received renewed interest. Researcher Pat Wolfe claims that the terms "right-brained" and "left-brained" are inaccurate. "While each hemisphere does have specialized functions, they work in concert with one another at all times," says Wolfe. "To explain a person's personality by stating that it is a preference for one hemisphere over the other is inaccurate and misleading."

Bruce Morton of the University of Hawaii School of Medicine has expanded on earlier research with a more specific and quantifiable definition. "Hemisphericity," says Morton, "is the bias in thinking orientation, behavioral style, and personality resulting from the inherent laterality of the individual's sole executive system within the bilateral brain." In other words, thinking and behaving are affected by the way a person routinely accesses both sides of the brain. Morton writes that a left-brain bias is a "top-down, self-survival, important details view," while the right-brain bias moves "toward the bottom-up, group-survival, global orientation" preference.

Learning-styles research also documents the effectiveness of small-group learning. Dunn reports that except among the gifted, students in grades 3 through 8 will learn better if they can work in small, well-organized groups, as opposed to working alone or with the teacher.

Research undertaken by the National Association of Secondary School Principals showed that many students have intake preferences—differences in their need to eat and drink while concentrating. Think about your own cognitive activities as an adult—the times you've curled up with a novel or textbook and a good apple, or the pretzels you munch on as you evaluate student papers. Teachers who understand intake preferences may allow for small snacks or water sippers to be used in class. (Keep in mind that some students are severely allergic to certain foods. Make sure you obtain allergy information from parents at the beginning of the year. Know which students must avoid certain foods before serving any food in class.)

Common Myths

Learning-styles research also exposes many of the myths educators have held dear:

Myth: Physical activity prevents learning. Children who are up out of their seats, touching things, tapping their feet or pencils, and constantly moving are typically viewed and sometimes labeled as hyperactive or learning-impaired. But psychologists report that most children referred by schools are not clinically hyperactive. They are simply normal children who need to move. And the less interested children are in the lesson being presented, the more they need to move. Simply reassigning these children to classrooms where less passivity is required results in positive gains.

Myth: Children are most alert in the morning. One of the more startling research findings is that most students are not "morning alert." That is, they concentrate much better in the late morning or early afternoon. Many teachers firmly believe that the most serious instruction should take place before lunch. But only about one-third of the more than a million schoolchildren tested by Dunn and associates preferred early-morning learning. Conversely, the researchers found that "most teachers are early-morning, high-energy people but often experience lows after 1 P.M."—just the time when the majority of students are most alert.

Myth: Classrooms should be well lit, slightly cool, generally quiet places where noises and movements are sharply curtailed. Most teachers can't tolerate gum chewing, foot tapping, and other "bothersome" noises and movements. Yet Dunn points out there are students who actually need such activities to help them concentrate and learn. It's well documented that many early adolescents (junior-high age) need sound or "background noise" to work. Also, younger children need less

Aspects or Dimensions of Individual Learning Style

Biological Preferences and Sensitivities
- sound
- light
- temperature
- texture
- design (e.g., seating arrangements)
- intake (need to eat and drink while concentrating)
- mobility
- duration
- chronobiological highs and lows (alert in the morning vs. alert in the evening)

Developmental and Sociological Preferences and Sensitivities
- motivation
- responsibility (conformity)
- need for structure

light than older children. "However," Dunn writes, "teachers often view negatively the children who squirm in their seats, tap their pencils, complain about the temperature, or become restless (in some cases because of too much illumination)."

What Does It All Mean?

The research shows that when instruction is matched with students' learning preferences, whether they be social, sensory (perceptual), environmental, hemispheric, or related to mobility or time of day, achievement increases and behavior improves. Teachers have learning styles, too, which contribute to their teaching styles. Instinctively, we know that we work better with some students than others. Now we know why. The closer our own personal learning style matches a student's, the more that student will achieve in our classroom.

In a perfect world, we could establish a learning style profile for each student in every school and offer learning environments and experiences exactly suited to each. But until then, there are several important changes teachers can make.

First, we need to change our attitudes and understand that **one learning style is neither superior nor inferior to others; they're simply different.** Each style exhibits similar intelligence ranges. Some components of learning style are developed through experience, but most are biological in nature and extremely resistant to change. It is unreasonable and unproductive to expect students to alter their learning styles to match the teacher's. Differences among diverse cultures tend to be developmental aspects of style. Yet Dunn and others have found as many style differences within cultural groups as between them. Even within nuclear families, style differences are considerable. Once teachers understand these differences, they can respond to them. Some students, often those who are low-achieving or misbehaving, are actually physically uncomfortable with their teacher's style. How well could you, as an adult, work in discomfort?

Next, we can alter our instruction to **provide many different types of strategies, activities, and experiences**—something for everyone. Different group configurations, opportunities to move and interact with learning materials (for example, learning centers), structured and unstructured activities, verbal explanations, and visual resources are all ways to engage the variety of learners in our classrooms.

Finally, we can organize our classrooms to provide different types of lighting, sound, and seating arrangements, allowing students frequent choices about where they want to be. The cozy reading corners set up in some classrooms are a good example. These areas feature softer lighting, informal seating (often pillows on the floor), and sometimes low music for background noise. It's a lot more difficult to provide areas of different temperatures, but students can adjust their clothing according to their preferences.

Try to educate your students about learning styles and **help students discover their own preferences.** They, in turn, can help you discover the activities and experiences that will be most meaningful for them.

Think variety! Variety may be the spice of life, but for meeting students' unique learning styles and needs, it's an essential ingredient.

❖ Cultural Differences

Cultural background figures prominently in the portrait of the individual student. Culture relates directly to individual learning style and to the preferences and values each student holds. Teachers have to be aware of these cultural differences and consider them in attempting to reach the whole child. America is a multiracial and multiethnic society. Further, minority students are already the majority in the nation's largest city school systems. Understanding, valuing, and nurturing this cultural diversity should be a national priority.

"As America's classrooms become increasingly diverse, many teachers face a culture gap that can hinder positive relationships with students and their families," notes Linda Ross, a diversity trainer in schools.

Too often, we don't understand people who are different from us. And what we don't understand, we tend to view as negative. "We're all biased in one way or another," Ross writes. The key, she suggests, is to notice the value judgments we make about people and try to figure out where those judgments come from. Minority students currently comprise almost 40 percent of the public school students in this country, according to the National Center for Education Statistics. Many predict that by 2025, more than half the U.S. school population will be students of color.

Discussions of culture must also acknowledge the fact that there are cultures beyond race, ethnicity, and geography.

"One culture that is often overlooked is the culture of poverty," teacher Tim Bailey points out. "It has definite cultural aspects of its own, and a number of studies and books have pointed out its impact." (See the resources list at the end of the chapter for three excellent treatments of poverty's effects on learners and for Tyrone Howard's article on overcoming teacher biases.)

One Size Doesn't Fit All

Despite cultural and individual differences, schooling tends toward uniformity.

"Sameness is always easier to accommodate than difference," writes Guild, "and education practices often have been developed to consciously promote the same education for all students."

But Guild adds that "the emphasis on uniformity is a serious disadvantage for students whose culture has taught them behaviors and beliefs that are different from the norms of the majority culture most often emphasized in schools."

Cultural differences are often viewed through a "deficit paradigm," notes Lois Weiner, professor of education at New Jersey City University. That is, lack of school success is thought to be "due to problems in students, their families, their culture, or their communities," Weiner explains.

"Underachievement is viewed as stemming from deficiencies in the students, so policies and practices to help students succeed attempt to correct their deficiencies."

Guild notes important philosophical questions in the uniformity vs. diversity debate: "Is equality of instruction synonymous with equity of educational opportunity for all? Is the purpose of public schooling to create a 'melting pot' or a 'salad bowl'?"

Guild, Weiner, and many others argue that we need to structure successful school experiences for all students by capitalizing on their natural styles and cultural patterns. Cultural differences are areas of individual strength, just as learning styles and special abilities are. By knowing and understanding a student's cultural background, we can structure successful school experiences for that student.

Culturally Relevant Teaching

To break away from the idea of students being "culturally disadvantaged," Gloria Ladson-Billings, a professor at the University of Wisconsin–Madison, urges teachers to ask "What's right?" with their diverse student populations, not "What's wrong?" Ladson-Billings suggests that teachers must embrace and incorporate diverse cultures in their teaching, not just understand them.

Multicultural education is not a once-a-year celebration of diversity. Rather, it includes a range of cultural perspectives throughout the curriculum. Ladson-Billings cites the example of an elementary classroom in which the teacher reads different versions of the Cinderella tale: the European version by Perrault, and versions from China, Egypt, and Zimbabwe. Students compare and contrast the versions along these lines: story structure, plot development, moral and ethical dilemmas, use of magic, standards of beauty, settings, use of language, and specific characters. Along the way, students learn the importance of understanding cultural differences and similarities.

To teach in a culturally relevant way, teachers need to be more aware and respectful of cultural differences, and more sensitive and responsive to them. Ladson-Billings has found that teachers who practice culturally relevant teaching share three important characteristics:

✔ They focus on academic achievement.

✔ They value students' cultural competence, allowing them to be who they are without forcing them to give up their language or behaviors.

✔ They cultivate a sociopolitical consciousness in students—a sense of community that accommodates difference.

In addition to these characteristics, successful teachers of minority children must understand that they, too, have a culture that affects their outlooks and responses to others, Ladson-Billings explains. For example,

---

IDENTIFYING OUR BIASES

Diversity trainer Linda Ross offers the following self-assessment tool to help teachers get a handle on the assumptions they make about students and parents who are "different." She suggests that you ask yourself:

1. What are the different cultures in my school? (Include such "cultures" as various ethnic groups, students with disabilities, new immigrants, residents of public housing.)
2. What characteristics first come to mind when I think of each group?
3. Where do these impressions come from? (peers, family, media, religion, other)
4. How do I treat people based on these assumptions?
5. Can I remember a time when someone made assumptions about me based on a group I belong to? How did it make me feel?

From *Instructor*, July/August 1995.

European-American monolingual women who comprise the majority of teachers in this country have a distinct culture that may be invisible to them as members of the mainstream culture. Ladson-Billings stresses that all teachers need to understand that "the kinds of decisions they make, the way they think, the way they see the world, is culturally mediated." She adds that teachers will never learn all the cultures there are to learn. "But if you learn your own, it's one of the things that I think will help you understand that culture functions in particular ways."

Teach All Students

The student population in this country is becoming increasingly diverse, while the teaching population remains predominantly white. Can students of color be taught effectively by white teachers? Yes, asserts Ladson-Billings. And black teachers can be "incredibly successful" with white kids, she adds.

To be effective, we must be prepared to teach all types of students. Ladson-Billings concludes, "If we teach our kids in ways that respect who they are, that have intellectual and academic integrity, and help develop in them a sort of critical consciousness, it doesn't matter so much if the kids in the classroom are Latina/Latino, Asian, European, Native, or African American."

The Whole Child

Despite these observed and reported differences among cultures, however, researchers are quick to point out that **there are as many differences as similarities among individual members of the same cultural group.** Pat Guild cautions, "Even as we acknowledge that culture affects learning styles, we know that distinct learning-style patterns don't fit a specific cultural group." She and others urge educators to use information about culture and learning styles as ways to focus their instruction and assessment, not to label or stereotype students. Cultural patterns should simply be one consideration in our attempts to match instruction with individual students. Add to that a student's personal learning style, special abilities, and unique challenges, and you begin to have a picture of the whole child.

"Diversity means all diversity, not just color," says Martine Wayman, sixth-grade teacher from Washington state. "It means abilities, disabilities, physical handicaps, learning styles, religious affiliations, and more. In my room there is a huge sign that says, "Accepting Differences," and that is the theme of my classroom all year. I spend much, much time talking about it and designing activities that promote it."

❖ English Language Learners

One special aspect of student diversity is the different languages children bring to the classroom. The National Center for Education Statistics reports that as of 2002, public schools served 3.8 million students whose primary language was not English. In California alone, 1.5 million students labeled "LEP" (Limited English Proficient)—one-quarter of the state's elementary and secondary students—received support services for learning English. In Texas, one child in seven received LEP services. Considering that not all schools offer these support services, the number of students who are English Language Learners (ELL) is even higher than the statistics indicate and increasing rapidly. These students represent both unique opportunities and unique challenges.

Specific teaching strategies for reaching ELL students are described in Chapter Five. But first it's important to understand who these students are.

ELL students in American classrooms represented literally all corners of the globe. The late Doris Dillon, a noted language arts resource teacher in San Jose, California, reported in 1998 that her elementary school represent children speaking 39 different languages and dialects! This, of course, is an extreme, but many schools include students from at least two or three different language backgrounds.

Stages of Language Acquisition

Despite their diversity, these multinational children all pass through several distinct stages as they acquire proficiency in English. Andrea Hernandez, principal of the Bilingual Bicultural Mini School in New York City, lists these stages:

1. **Preproduction**. Students are starting to understand the new language, but they cannot yet engage in conversations or respond to questions. Appropriate activities include listening, pointing to things, selecting, and drawing.
2. **Early Production**. Gaining better comprehension, ELL students can now respond to questions with one- or two-word answers.
3. **Speech Emergence**. Comprehension continues to increase, and students can now respond with simple sentences. Expect errors at this stage, but encourage children to retell, define, describe, and explain.
4. **Intermediate Fluency**. Acquiring very good comprehension, students can now construct complex sentences and engage in higher-order thinking in the new language.

The Teacher's Role

We tread a fine line between giving ELL students challenging opportunities to exhibit their emerging knowledge and skills, and frustrating or defeating them with expectations that are too

high. Experienced ELL teachers suggest that we carefully include students by capitalizing on their strengths in their native language. As they interact with other students, their new skills will emerge.

Your patience and sensitivity will go a long way with these young learners. So will a bilingual aide, peer tutor, or volunteer.

❖ Exceptionalities

Much preservice and in-service teacher education today focuses on students who are different in ways we label "exceptional." The label, of course, implies that most students fit some standard mold, which is a shaky concept at best. Nevertheless, in our well-intentioned attempts to provide students with opportunities to realize their full potential, we can identify individuals who could benefit from modified instruction.

Public Law 94-142 calls for the identification of children "in need of special services" by their school. These individuals range from the severely mentally impaired to the physically disabled, learning disabled, and gifted. Typically, the "special services" offered are pullout programs where these children work with specialists for all or part of their school day.

Inclusion

In the 1990s, however, the trend moved toward placing exceptional children in "the least restrictive environment," frequently interpreted as the regular classroom. Thus regular classroom teachers increasingly find themselves working with students of a much wider range of physical and mental abilities. It's an awesome task—one for which teachers are frequently unprepared.

In theory, this inclusion of exceptional students in regular education involves the specialist coming into the classroom to co-teach with the regular teacher. Advocates argue that inclusion results in less fragmented learning for special-education students and less stigmatization, which pull-out programs increase; critics charge that classroom teachers rarely get adequate help from the specialists, who are spread too thin, and the extra time spent helping one or two exceptional students in a classroom is time lost by other students.

Whatever your position on the matter, the fact remains that exceptional students continue to be full- or part-time classroom members. It is possible to enhance their learning and weave them into the classroom fabric only when the nature of their exceptionalities is clearly understood. Many service agencies exist to help teachers with exceptional children. You'll find a list on page 76.

Learning Disabilities

Learning disabilities are neurobiological disorders that interfere with a person's ability to store, process, and retrieve information. Most often, these disabilities affect students' reading and language skills (including writing and speaking). They can also impair math computation skills and social skills.

Learning disabilities are widely misunderstood, even by teachers. **Students with learning disabilities have average or above-average intelligence, and many are gifted**. Yet many people associate learning disabilities with mental retardation. Learning disabilities are not related to mental retardation, emotional disturbance, blindness, deafness, or autism. Nor are they a result of economic or environmental factors or cultural differences, according to the National Center for Learning Disabilities. Yet these disabilities can be compensated for and even overcome through instructional modifications and learning-environment accommodations.

Ability vs. Performance A learning disability creates a gap between ability and performance because the mind processes words and information differently. This, in turn, makes it difficult to learn—especially in school, where learning experiences are typically structured in ways unsuited to the learning-disabled student.

Because many LD students exhibit high intelligence and creativity in some areas, their teachers and parents assume they are being lazy

or obstinate when they don't do well in others. Pediatrician Mel Levine, author of *The Myth of Laziness*, explains that the academic performance of LD students is unbelievably inconsistent. They might have one good week in school followed by another that is disastrous, or be able to perform a math problem one day and not know how to the next day. "Because they've been caught doing something well once in a while, people accuse them of not really trying the rest of the time," Levine notes.

Discrimination Is Widespread As a result, children and adults with learning disabilities typically face discrimination, misunderstanding, and emotional and psychological abuse. Instead of being helped to develop their strengths and compensate for their weaknesses, they are humiliated at every turn.

The National Center for Learning Disabilities (NCLD) reports that almost 3 million public school children in the United States have been diagnosed with learning disabilities and are receiving some form of special education services. In the U.S. population, an estimated 15 percent suffer from learning disabilities, and many probably go undiagnosed. Learning disabilities seem to run in families.

Dyslexia Is Most Common The most common learning disability is dyslexia. As defined by the International Dyslexia Association (IDA), "Dyslexia is a specific learning disability that is neurological in origin. It is characterized by difficulties with accurate and/or fluent word recognition and by poor spelling and decoding abilities." People with dyslexia have a deficit in their ability to process sounds and distinguish among the sound units or phonemes that make up words. This difficulty often results in delays in reading comprehension, vocabulary acquisition, and the building of background knowledge. The IDA estimates that 15 to 20 percent of American students have a language-related disability, and of those, 85 percent have dyslexia. This disability runs in families, and it cuts across all socioeconomic and educational levels.

Following are some of the major types of learning disabilities, as identified and defined by the National Center for Learning Disabilities:

1. Apraxia (Dyspraxia): the inability to motor-plan or to make an appropriate body response.
2. Dysgraphia: difficulty writing, both in the mechanical and expressive sense, and difficulty with spelling.
3. Dyslexia: difficulty with language in its various uses, not just reading.
4. Dyssemia: difficulty with social cues and signals.
5. Auditory Discrimination: trouble perceiving the differences between sounds and the sequences of sounds.
6. Visual Perception: difficulty understanding and putting meaning to what one sees.

Arnold Wilkins, professor of psychology at the University of Essex, England, takes a different approach to dyslexia. He and others have found that some dyslexics have extreme sensitivity to light, especially the fluorescent lighting found in schools. For them, black words on white pages disappear, blur together, flicker, and cause eyestrain and physical pain. Some call this condition the Meares-Irlen syndrome or scotopic sensitivity syndrome.

"Visual perceptual distortion," as Wilkins calls this condition, "should be suspected in children who have trouble learning to read, particularly if they report headaches and eyestrain from prolonged exposure to the page. If the child reports any illusory movement of the letters or words, or glare from the white paper, then treatment with colored overlays or filters should be considered."

Wilkins and others have developed a process of testing dyslexics for light sensitivity, determining what color is most beneficial to them, then fitting them with specially tinted glasses. The results are impressive. Students fitted with the tinted glasses can read and write much better than they can without them.

Experts point out that even though we label dyslexia a disability, it is not a disease to have and be cured of, but a kind of mind. Very often it is a gifted mind. Every one of us is unique, and how people come to terms with language contributes to that uniqueness.

Specific Strategies Sally Smith, professor and head of special education at the American University in Washington, DC, offers some helpful tips. Actually, these tips represent good teaching strategies for *all* students, which brings us back to the point (again and again!) that good teaching is good teaching—for LD students, gifted students, or "average" students. The more we teachers use these effective strategies, the greater our chances of meeting all children's needs.

1. **Help students apply what they've learned**. Smith suggests that teachers ask these students (and others) to draw pictures, reenact events, collect relevant magazine photos, and construct models, always discussing and verbalizing what they're attempting to do and what they've learned.
2. **Break tasks down into many smaller steps** and complete each step successfully before moving on. This includes directions and instructions for task completion. Since many LD students have trouble with oral directions, it is important to speak slowly, loudly, clearly, and precisely. Try writing the steps as directions to which students can refer back. Ask them to repeat each step aloud.
3. **Provide a predictable structure**, even something as basic as a list of topics to be covered on a certain day.
4. **Help students understand abstract concepts**. Smith suggests asking students to illustrate a concept with their bodies, other concrete objects, or pictures.
5. **Assure students that it's okay to make mistakes**. Teachers make mistakes and students make mistakes. The important thing is to learn from your mistakes. Here, humor is a good tool. Smith adds, "Teachers who laugh at themselves in an easy, accepting way are important models for children who tend to see themselves with

RECOGNIZING LEARNING DISABILITIES

The Learning Disability Association of America describes difficulties in the following areas as signs of learning disabilities at various ages:

Preschool
- pronunciation
- finding the right word
- making rhymes
- learning numbers, the alphabet, days of the week, colors, and shapes
- concentrating
- interacting with peers
- following directions or learning routines
- controlling pencils, crayons, scissors
- buttoning, zipping, typing

Grades K–4
- learning the connection between letters and sounds
- distinguishing basic words (run, eat, want)
- reading and spelling, including consistent errors such as letter reversals (b/d), inversions (m/w), transpositions (felt/left), and substitutions (house/home)
- learning basic math concepts
- learning about time
- learning new skills
- remembering facts

Grades 5–8
- comprehending reading or learning math skills
- writing letters in the correct sequence (soiled for solid)
- recognizing prefixes, suffixes, root words and learning spelling strategies
- organizing bedroom, notebook, papers, and desk
- keeping up with papers or assignments
- handwriting
- managing time
- understanding discussions and expressing thoughts aloud

High School and Adults
- spelling the same word consistently in a single document
- accomplishing basic reading or writing tasks
- answering open-ended questions on tests
- recalling and using other memory skills
- adapting skills from one setting to another
- working at a fast pace
- grasping abstract concepts
- focusing on details
- reading information correctly

despair or as a source of worry to others." When LD students feel depressed or overwhelmed, as they frequently do, have them make a list of their strengths. These children—and all of us—need frequent reminders of what it is they do well.

ADD/ADHD The NCLD also includes attention-deficit (hyperactivity) disorder in its list of learning disabilities, although technically it is not one. It is a behavioral disorder. But as experts point out, inattention, distractibility, impulsivity, disorganization, and overactivity, the major characteristics of ADD or ADHD, all interfere with learning. Attention deficits and learning disabilities frequently occur simultaneously.

Attention deficit—the inability to keep attention focused—is by far the most frequently diagnosed disability. Many psychologists think that it is overdiagnosed and students who just naturally need to move a lot are mislabeled as hyperactive. Many educators and specialists agree that we must first ensure that our classrooms and instruction match students' developmental levels before we attach labels. Sometimes the classroom demands are inappropriate, not the student's behavior.

ADD/ADHD Resource Page

Recognizing Signs of ADD/ADHD

Here is a list, from Children and Adults with Attention Deficit Disorder (CHADD), of symptoms that students with ADHD commonly exhibit.

ADHD predominantly inattentive type:

✔ fails to give close attention to details or makes careless mistakes

✔ has difficulty sustaining attention

✔ does not appear to listen

✔ struggles to follow through on instructions

✔ has difficulty with organization

✔ avoids or dislikes tasks requiring sustained mental effort

✔ loses things

✔ is easily distracted

✔ is forgetful in daily activities

ADHD predominantly hyperactive/impulsive type:

✔ fidgets with hands or feet or squirms in chair

✔ has difficulty remaining seated

✔ runs about or climbs excessively

✔ has difficulty engaging in activities quietly

✔ acts as if driven by a motor

✔ talks excessively

✔ blurts out answers before questions have been completed

✔ has difficulty waiting or taking turns

✔ interrupts or intrudes upon others

ADHD combined type:

✔ Individual meets both sets of inattention and hyperactive/impulsive criteria

Further, notes CHADD, children with ADHD often experience a two- to four-year developmental delay that makes them seem less mature and responsible than their peers. In addition, ADHD frequently occurs with other conditions such as depression, anxiety, or learning disabilities.

Excerpts from "Fact Sheet 1," July, 2001. © CHADD. CHADD National Resource Center on AD/HD. 8181 Professional Place, Ste. 150, Landover, MD 20785; (800) 233-4050. www.chadd.org/fs/fs1.pdf.

Tips for Behavior Management with ADHD

The Attention Deficit Disorder Association offers these tips to teachers and parents for helping the ADHD child learn adaptive behaviors.

Parents can:

✔ Provide structure and a consistent schedule—help the child learn routines around daily activities such as getting dressed, turning in homework, or going to bed. Use a picture calendar or schedule for the young child. Make sure that the child gets enough sleep.

✔ Work out cleanup routines and organize and label areas used for storage (toys or school supplies) and clothing. Make picture labels for a young child and word labels for a child who can read.

✔ On a daily basis, supervise the school-age child in reviewing homework assignments, organizing the backpack, and filing papers (but don't do it *for* the child).

Teachers can:

✔ Model and monitor organizational routines and stay in close communication with parents so parents know what is going on at school.

✔ Allow hyperactive children to take movement breaks.

Both can:

✔ Provide consistent low-key reminders, prompts, and cues when needed.

✔ Be consistent about rewards and consequences so that the child knows what to expect.

✔ Be generous with praise when the child performs well, but avoid being overly critical when things are not going well.

✔ Teach the child to use organizational strategies such as color-coded folders for different subjects, labeling, checklists and to-do lists, setting goals, and breaking projects into small, manageable chunks.

Learning to Teach   73

Children who do have the disorder face difficult obstacles, including peer rejection and achievement problems.

While there are varying degrees of severity with each type of ADHD, the NCLD reports that "Children with the **inattentive** type avoid putting the attention and effort into their school work that is required. They have difficulty keeping track of assignments and homework papers. Organizational difficulties become increasingly apparent when the child must assume responsibility for school work." Individuals with the second type of ADHD, **hyperactive/impulsive**, are constantly moving and fidgeting. They have difficulty taking turns in activities, and they often speak out of turn. Some have difficulty controlling their tempers, and many act without thinking or considering the consequences. Many children have a combination of both types. (See page 73 for a list of characteristic behaviors of students with ADD/ADHD and tips for behavior management.)

But attention deficit disorder can have a much more subtle expression, according to Sari Solden, who writes about the disorder in women. "It can be a quieter, less obvious kind of impulsivity, with excessive shifting of tasks or life directions." Whereas ADHD has primarily been diagnosed in males, Solden reports that more recently this "quieter" form (without hyperactivity) is seen in girls.

Everyone suffers. The ADHD student underachieves, and teachers spend more time responding to inattention and misbehavior and less time teaching and interacting with other students. And ADHD students themselves continually receive negative messages from teachers and peers.

What can be done to help these students and improve the situation for everyone? The most effective approach involves combining proper medication with therapy or counseling to learn coping skills and adaptive behaviors, says Peter Jaksa of the Attention Deficit Disorder Centers of America. According to the Attention Deficit Disorder Association (ADDA), clinical experience and studies suggest that students make "the most significant, long-lasting gains" when behavioral and emotional counseling supplement their medications.

Many ADHD children take Ritalin (Dexedrine or Aderall) to stimulate the central nervous system and make them more responsive to feedback from the social and physical environment. These stimulants, in either short-term or longer, sustained-release dosages, help children control hyperactivity, inattention, distractibility, and impulsive behavior. In short, when they are medicated, ADHD students can pay better attention, complete their work, increase achievement, and improve relations with peers and adults.

"Nine out of ten children improve on one of the stimulant drugs," reports the ADDA. But the drugs stimulate controversy as well as nervous systems. Some argue that stimulant drugs are prescribed unnecessarily to control disruptive behaviors of students who don't have ADHD. The ADDA points out that "many things, including anxiety, depression, allergies, seizures, or problems with the home or school environment can make children seem overactive, impulsive, or inattentive."

At any rate, medicine alone is not enough. "These medicines don't cure the disorder, they only temporarily control the symptoms." The experts stress that medicine can do its job only when accompanied by long-term behavioral therapy and emotional support. The ADHA child needs to learn appropriate behavior and improve self-esteem.

One strategy that works for my junior high school ADHD students (and would for middle and upper elementary students, as well) is the consistent use of a daily planner. Each day, students write all in-class and homework assignments in the planner. I sign off after checking the planner, and parents sign off at home after homework is completed.

We still have the challenge of making sure the completed work gets to class, but parents can help by providing homework folders and backpacks. This strategy allows for continual home-school communication, which is critical to helping these children succeed.

Experts at the ADDA suggest that teachers and parents praising the child and not the medication when improvements are seen can bolster children's self-esteem. They also suggest making children feel comfortable about their daily medication by comparing the pills to eyeglasses, braces, and allergy medicines that help other children.

Also, make sure children understand the "bright side" of ADHD. As author Sari Solden notes, "There are many positives with ADD, including a surplus of ideas, creativity, excitement, and interest, which accompany this kind of mind."

Despite appropriate teaching practices and behavioral and medical interventions, however, serious classroom problems sometimes continue. At this point, it is important to realize that you, the classroom teacher, cannot do it all alone. Successful treatment requires the collaboration of many professionals. Teachers must have assistance in dealing with children with ADHD, says psychologist Adele Brodkin. There are some behaviors and situations that teachers simply shouldn't be expected to deal with, she claims. School psychologists and parents must play a critical role, and administrators must be supportive. You can also consult the organizations listed on page 76.

General Guidelines While there are specific strategies for dealing with each type of learning disability, experts agree on these general guidelines:

✔ Acquire the broadest training and knowledge possible. Take advantage of courses and in-services offered.

✔ Develop effective teaching techniques and modify curricula to meet students' needs. LD students' brains work differently from those of other students, so simply slowing down your traditional teaching techniques will not work.

✔ Know the warning signs; watch for students who may have a learning disability.

✔ Understand that LD children can learn and become successful students, given fair opportunities.

✔ Provide structure. LD students need to learn to monitor their own progress and regulate the time and effort they spend on assignments.

✔ Collaborate with parents to develop coping approaches, both at home and at school.

✔ Become an advocate for your LD students, protecting them from discriminatory practices.

You can also use "bypass strategies" to circumvent a child's weak areas. For example, word processors can greatly aid children who cannot recall how letters are formed because they lack "motor memory." Tape recorders help those who can't take notes or have trouble remembering directions.

Most importantly, avoid humiliating the LD child. Suggests Dr. Adele Brodkin, take an honest, optimistic approach, saying something like, "You seem to find some things easy and some hard to do in school. But you and I are going to work together on helping you with that."

Learning disabilities affect us all. Studies show that children with undetected or untreated learning disabilities are far more likely to face school failure, increased incidence of drug and alcohol abuse, criminal activities, and unemployment. How many of our social problems could be improved or solved if we could just identify and meet the learning needs of all our students?

Giftedness

Like learning-disabled students, gifted students are those whose minds work in ways different from most children. They use their brains more effectively and more efficiently. Research on the human brain has demonstrated that gifted children are biologically different; there are cellular changes and biochemical processes setting these individuals apart. As a result of these differences, gifted students:

✔ think faster.

✔ can identify and solve more complex problems.

ORGANIZATIONS DEVOTED TO EXCEPTIONAL CHILDREN

ADD Centers of America
www.addcenters.com

ADD Warehouse
(distributes materials)
(800) 233-9273
http://addwarehouse.com

**Alexander Graham Bell Association
for the Deaf and Hard of Hearing**
(202) 337-5220 or (866) 337-5220
www.agbell.org

American Foundation for the Blind
(800) 232-5463
www.afb.org

**Children and Adults With Attention
Deficit Disorder**
8181 Professional Pl., Ste. 150
Landover, MD 20785
(800) 233-4050
www.chadd.org

Council for Exceptional Children
110 North Glebe Rd., Ste. 300
Arlington, VA 22201
(888) CEC-SPED
www.cec.sped.org

Emily Hall Tremaine Foundation
290 Pratt St.
Meriden, CT 06450
(203) 639-5542
www.tremainefoundation.org

**Federation for Children
With Special Needs**
1135 Tremont St., Ste. 420
Boston, MA 02120
(617) 236-7210
www.fcsn.org

The International Dyslexia Association
(formerly the Orton Dyslexia Society)
Chester Building, Ste. 382
8600 Lasalle Rd.
Baltimore, MD 21204-6020
(410) 296-0232
www.interdys.org

LD Online
www.ldonline.org.

**Learning Disabilities Association of
America**
4156 Library Rd.
Pittsburgh, PA 15234
(412) 341-1515
www.ldanatl.org

**National Center for Learning
Disabilities**
381 Park Ave. S., Ste. 1401
New York, NY 10016
(212) 545-7510 or (888) 575-7373
www.ld.org

**National Information Center for
Children and Youth With Disabilities**
P.O.B. 1492
Washington, DC 20013
(800) 695-0285
http://nichcy.org

**National Rehabilitation Information
Center**
4200 Forbes Blvd., Ste. 202
Lanham, MD 20706
(800) 346-2742
www.naric.com

**National Research Center on the
Gifted and Talented**
University of Connecticut
2131 Hillside Rd., U-3007
Storrs, CT 06269-3007
(860) 486-4676
www.gifted.uconn.edu

**Office of Special Education and
Rehabilitation Services**
U.S. Dept. of Education
400 Maryland Ave., SW
Washington, DC 20202
(202) 205-5465
www.ed.gov/about/offices/list/osers/
index.html

✔ think in unusual and diverse ways.

✔ exhibit profound insights.

Controversy and Disagreements Almost
everyone agrees that advanced brain function
results from *both* genetic inheritance and

environmental opportunities. But that's where
agreement in gifted education ends.

Gifted programs are nothing if not
controversial. There's controversy surrounding
the concept of giftedness, controversy
surrounding types of programs and the selection

HELPING GIFTED STUDENTS SUCCEED

One good source of information on gifted children is Ellen Winner's *Gifted Children: Myths and Realities*. Winner, a psychologist, points out how American schools harm gifted children. Such children, she notes, are always outsiders in a society suspicious of intellect and a schooling system fond of lumping kids together rather than treating them as individuals. Winner suggests that gifted children need mentors, advanced instruction, and other specialized programs.

of participants, and disagreements about how giftedness should be defined. Schools embracing the philosophy of inclusion are moving toward eliminating gifted programs completely, arguing that gifted students' needs can be met in the regular classroom.

Perhaps. But that would require extensive individualization, considering experts' claims that students with IQs of 140 or above know 90 percent of the content before ever walking into class.

Also, what are extracurricular sports programs if not gifted programs? We have no qualms about investing huge portions of school budgets in exclusionary programs for students gifted in athletic ability. Yet comparable academic programs are constantly under fire.

Definitions of Giftedness The federal government offers a broad definition of giftedness. According to **Public Law 97-35 (the Education Consolidation and Improvement Act of 1981)**, gifted children "give evidence of high performance capability in areas such as intellectual, creative, artistic, leadership capacity or specific academic fields, and . . . require services or activities not ordinarily provided by the school in order to fully develop such capabilities."

Individual states plan gifted programs based on all or parts of this federal definition. Traditionally, gifted programs have focused on the intellectual and academic aspects, using intelligence and achievement tests to select program participants. More difficult, perhaps, and certainly less common, are programs that seek to develop students' artistic, creative, and leadership abilities.

Author and educator Barbara Clark defines intelligence and giftedness as the aggregate of an individual's cognitive, affective, intuitive, and physical functioning. Those who are more intelligent, says Clark, tend to have more integrated use of these functions.

Gifted Programs Basically, there are three types of programs, or interventions, currently used with gifted students:

1. **Enrichment:** extending classroom work, either by using more in-depth material or by adding topics or areas of study not typically found in schools. Enrichment frequently builds on the student's own interests and involves individual or small-group projects. Joseph Renzulli, director of the National Research Center on the Gifted and Talented, University of Connecticut, has developed the Schoolwide Enrichment Model, which serves gifted students on three levels:
   a) in the regular curriculum, with enrichment activities integrated into it
   b) in enrichment clusters, where nongraded groups of students sharing common interests work together in designated blocks of time with adults who have expertise in the area of interest
   c) in a continuum of special supplementary services that challenge students at the highest levels of their interest and ability (such as mentorships, advanced coursework, and out-of-school experiences). Renzulli writes that his model is a "practical plan for total school improvement."

2. **Acceleration:** offering content at an earlier age so a student can complete schooling in less time. This is accomplished by early entrance to school, grade skipping, advanced placement, or moving rapidly through the curriculum. Despite teachers' traditional reluctance to accelerate students and fears about social maladjustment, research consistently supports the effectiveness of acceleration and its positive impact on gifted students.

3. **Affective Programs:** These address gifted students' social and emotional needs. Advocated by educators such as Jim Delisle, director of gifted education at Kent State University and strong proponent of serving gifted students' social and emotional needs, affective programs focus on the special problems and concerns of gifted children: career choices, values, and coping strategies.

Which of these interventions is best? Measures of student satisfaction and achievement point to acceleration. Yet most educators specializing in gifted students recognize the need for a balance of all three approaches. The best overall approach is a combination of enrichment, acceleration, and affective programs.

Specific Strategies As for meeting the unique needs of the gifted students in your own classroom, several strategies are effective:

1. **Give gifted children many opportunities to make choices** about what they learn, how they learn, and how they demonstrate their learning. Encourage the natural self-directed behavior most of these students possess. And capitalize on their interests.

2. **Allow gifted children the opportunity to work with other high-ability children.** All too often we use (or misuse) gifted children as tutors for others. Cooperative-learning situations that continually group gifted children with slower or more average learners can build resentment and frustration.

3. **Offer gifted students opportunities to struggle with complex material.** Without regular encounters with challenging material, say researchers, gifted children have trouble developing good study skills and learning how to learn.

4. **Practice "curriculum compacting"** by giving students credit for what they already know and modifying the curriculum to allow them to learn something new. If they've mastered all the concepts of a reading series, for example, let them test out of the series and work on more challenging material or individual projects.

5. **Allow for independent study projects, mentorships, and thematic instruction.**

6. **Provide opportunities to practice divergent thinking and critical thinking.** Sandra Kaplan of the University of Southern California urges teachers to teach even the standard curriculum at a greater depth and complexity through divergent and critical thinking.

Dr. Carol Ann Tomlinson, University of Virginia, reports research that shows teachers make more adjustments for struggling learners than for advanced ones. Too often, teachers and the general public think gifted kids can get by on their own.

But if we are dedicated to the notion that all children deserve an education that challenges them to reach their full potential, then how can we leave gifted students out? If we agree (and most experts do) that intelligence is influenced by both genetics and environment, then how can we deny gifted children (or any children) an educational environment suitable to their needs?

From his synthesis of research on gifted youth, Dr. John Feldhusen concludes, "To provide for the gifted, we must upgrade the level and pace of instruction to fit their abilities, achievement levels, and interests. The only suitable enrichment is instruction on special enriching topics at a high level and a fast pace. We must also provide them with highly competent teachers and with opportunities to work with other gifted and talented youth."

In reality, the teaching strategies and practices advocated for gifted students constitute good practice in general: capitalizing on students' natural interests, giving lots of choice about what and how to learn, functioning as the "guide on the side," rather than the "sage on the stage," compacting curriculum and not forcing students to endure endless repetition, and holding high expectations.

All students benefit from personalized teaching, and gifted education offers teachers a strategy for such individualization. Learn as much as you can about gifted education and the practices of teachers who work with the gifted. The payoffs could be tremendous for all your students.

Other Exceptionalities

There are many other less common exceptionalities that most teachers deal with at least occasionally, such as mental retardation, visual and hearing impairment, other physical disabilities, emotional disturbances, behavioral disorders, autism, Down syndrome, and specialized health-care needs.

Fortunately, information on these and all types of exceptionalities is readily available. For a start, see the list of Organizations Devoted to Exceptional Children on page 76. A simple Web search also can reveal numerous information sources, including full journal articles, for the specific exceptionality you seek to learn about.

❖ Gender Differences

Ethnic and ability differences aside, teachers deal with two distinct types of students: males and females. And although girls and boys often do exhibit different behavior and learning styles, both groups are still entitled to the same chance to participate and learn.

It is easy to discriminate unknowingly—in the questions we ask, the praise we offer, the tasks we assign, the attention we give. Largely unaware of the implications and consequences of our actions, we act on ingrained attitudes and behaviors. With actions that speak louder than words we are telling some children that they are not as capable

as others simply because of their gender.

Low expectations, poor self-concepts, low self-confidence, low achievement, fewer opportunities and options, conflict, behavior problems—these are the consequences of discrimination based on gender. Even when teachers know they are being observed for gender bias, they unconsciously exhibit discriminatory behaviors.

Discriminatory Behaviors

That's where research can help make us aware of our discriminatory actions. The following documented behaviors show ways that teachers treat boys and girls differently. Are these behaviors discriminatory? Do they result in unequal opportunities to learn? You decide. Research shows that teachers:

✔ give boys more direct instruction, approval, disapproval, and attention.

✔ ask boys more factual, abstract, and open-ended questions.

✔ give more teaching attention to boys during mathematics instruction and to girls during reading instruction.

✔ expect boys to be more assertive and active, and girls to be more quiet and passive.

✔ ask boys to assume leadership roles, repair equipment, run VCRs and computers, move furniture, and carry books.

✔ reprimand boys more frequently and more harshly and punish them more severely, even when girls and boys are misbehaving equally.

✔ praise boys more for the intellectual quality of their work and girls more for neatness, following directions, and other matters of form.

✔ criticize girls more for skill deficiencies and boys more for behavior.

Are your classroom actions and attitudes based on underlying stereotypes? Find out with the consciousness-raising scale for teachers on page 80 and for students on page 81. And give students a chance to say whether they think teachers treat boys and girls fairly by asking

How Raised Is Your Consciousness?

Teachers, it's your turn to take a test today. Let's see how you rate yourself on the following consciousness-raising scale.

YES NO

1 When assigning reading material to my class, I carefully check to see whether the characters have been cast in stereotypical roles. ☐ ☐

2 When disciplining the children in my class, I tend to be easier on the girls than on the boys because girls are more emotional. ☐ ☐

3 For a class party I tend to ask the girls to bring baked goods and the boys to bring games and CDs. ☐ ☐

4 I would be more inclined to leave a group of girls unsupervised than a group of boys because girls are generally better behaved and less rowdy. ☐ ☐

5 When I need audiovisual equipment brought into the class, I always ask the boys to bring it in or set it up. ☐ ☐

6 In my experience, girls appear to have a better understanding of the feelings of others than boys do. ☐ ☐

7 When discussing career education with my class, I usually include examples of male secretaries, nurses, and teachers as well as female lawyers, truckers, and those in other nontraditional roles. ☐ ☐

8 A student tutor is needed for the kindergarten. I would probably send a girl because girls relate better to smaller children than boys do. ☐ ☐

9 I am preparing a social studies lesson and must complete a large wall map by shading it with color. I will probably ask some boys in my class to work with me. ☐ ☐

YES NO

10 I have been asked to organize the school sports day. I will probably separate the girls from the boys in most events. ☐ ☐

11 I would much rather work for a male principal than a female one. ☐ ☐

12 I'm addressing a newsletter to parents. I will probably ask a group of girls to help address the envelopes because they have neater handwriting than boys. ☐ ☐

13 When the principal comes to my door asking for two students to help in the gym, I send boys because they are stronger. ☐ ☐

14 The boys in my classes need to be challenged through competition in order for them to achieve the motivation that the girls already have. ☐ ☐

15 I think the girls in my classes are more easily persuaded than the boys. ☐ ☐

16 The school is having a concert next week, and a student host is required to help greet parents. I will probably choose a girl because girls are generally more polite and have better manners. ☐ ☐

ANSWERS
Give yourself one point for each answer indicated here. The closer your score is to 16 points, the less you stereotype. 1) yes 2) no 3) no 4) no 5) no 6) no 7) yes 8) no 9) yes 10) no 11) no 12) no 13) no 14) no 15) no 16) no

Developed by Dr. Barbara Samuels. Originally appeared in *Instructor*, February 1980.

Values Voting

Check an answer for each statement. Then compare and discuss answers with your class. Decide how you might rewrite the statements.

YES NO

☐ ☐   1. It's all right for boys to cry.

☐ ☐   2. It's all right for girls to cry.

☐ ☐   3. Being a nurse is a good job for a woman.

☐ ☐   4. Being a nurse is a good job for a man.

☐ ☐   5. Boys can be baby-sitters.

☐ ☐   6. Girls can be baby-sitters.

☐ ☐   7. Women can be firefighters.

☐ ☐   8. It's all right for boys to play with dolls.

☐ ☐   9. It's all right for girls to play with dolls.

☐ ☐   10. Girls are smarter than boys.

☐ ☐   11. Boys are afraid of spiders.

☐ ☐   12. Girls are afraid of spiders.

☐ ☐   13. I like to help out cooking in the kitchen.

☐ ☐   14. I like to help out fixing things around the house.

☐ ☐   15. Boys are better in math than girls are.

☐ ☐   16. Girls behave better than boys do.

☐ ☐   17. Boys can be secretaries.

☐ ☐   18. Girls have more patience than boys do.

☐ ☐   19. Boys are stronger than girls are.

☐ ☐   20. Girls are better cooks than boys are.

☐ ☐   21. A woman can be president.

☐ ☐   22. Men are better drivers than women are.

"Values Voting" developed by Gordon Tokushige, Waiahole Elementary School, Hawaii. From *Oceans of Options: Sex Equity Lessons for the Classroom.* Published by Far West Laboratory for Educational Research and Development, 730 Harrison St., San Francisco, CA 94107.

Are Teachers Fair?

Do teachers treat boys and girls the same in the classroom? Make an X in the box to answer each question. You don't need to put your name on the paper.

	Boys	Girls	Both
1. When heavy things must be carried to the office, library, or car, who gets the job?			
2. When the boards need erasing, who gets the job?			
3. When there are errands to run, who gets the job?			
4. Who is praised the most in the class?			
5. Who is scolded the most?			
6. When there are papers to pass out, who gets the job?			
7. When it is time to line up for lunch, recess, gym, or to go home, who lines up first?			
8. Who gets the most help from the teacher during class time?			
9. Who is reminded to be quiet the most?			
10. Who gets to write on the board the most?			
11. Who gets the special favors and fun things to do?			
12. Who does the cleaning-up jobs?			
13. Who gets picked the most to answer questions?			
14. Who gets the hardest questions to answer?			
15. Who does your teacher think are better readers?			
16. Who does your teacher think are better in math?			
17. Who do you think your teacher likes most?			
18. Who gets punished the most in your class?			
19. Who seems to get in trouble the most?			
20. Who talks to the teacher the most?			
21. Who is chosen for leader or captain the most?			

Total Score _____ _____ _____

"Are Teachers Fair?" developed by Carol Hankinson, Waiahole Elementary School, Hawaii. From *Oceans of Options: Sex Equity Lessons for the Classroom.* Published by Far West Laboratory for Educational Research and Development, 730 Harrison St., San Francisco, CA 94107.

Watch Cartoons!

Cartoons are more than just fun entertainment. They influence how we think and behave. For example, they tell us how good people and bad people act. But these messages are often stereotypes. They may limit what we think we can and cannot do. Watch cartoons on Saturday morning or after school, and the commercials in between. Then write what you see the characters doing. Discuss your observations with your class.

Name of cartoons:

Name of characters: (male or female?)

What do characters do in the cartoon?

Select one commercial. Name the product advertised.

What are the boys doing in this commercial?

What are the girls doing in this commercial?

How are the actions of the boys and girls different?

With what types of toys do girls play in this commercial?

With what types of toys do boys play in this commercial?

Ten Quick Ways to Detect Sexism and Racism in Children's Books

Both in school and out, young children are exposed to racist and sexist attitudes. These attitudes—expressed over and over in books and in other media—gradually distort their perceptions until stereotypes and myths about minorities and women are accepted as reality. It is difficult for a librarian or teacher to prompt children to question society's attitudes. But if a child can be shown how to detect racism and sexism in a book, the child can proceed to transfer the perception to wider areas. The following ten guidelines are offered as a starting point in evaluating children's books from this perspective.

1. Check the Illustrations

Look for Stereotypes. A stereotype is an oversimplified generalization about a particular group, race, or sex that usually carries derogatory implications. The following are some infamous overt stereotypes: blacks: happy-go-lucky, watermelon-eating Sambo, and the fat, eye-rolling "mammy"; Chicanos: sombrero-wearing or fiesta-loving, and the macho bandito; Asian Americans: the inscrutable, slant-eyed "Oriental"; Native Americans: the naked savage or "primitive brave" and his "squaw"; Puerto Ricans: the switchblade-toting teenage gang member; women: the completely domestic mother, the demure and doll-loving little girl, and the wicked stepmother. While you may not always find stereotypes in the blatant forms described, look for variations that in any way demean or ridicule characters because of their race or sex.

Look for Tokenism. If there are racial minority characters in the illustrations, do they look just like whites except for being tinted or colored in? Do all minority faces look stereotypically alike, or are they depicted as genuine individuals with distinctive features?

Who's Doing What. Do the illustrations depict minorities in subservient and passive roles, or in leadership and action roles? Are males the active "doers" and females the inactive observers?

2. Check the Story Line

Liberation movements have led publishers to weed out many insulting passages; however, racist and sexist attitudes still find expression in less obvious ways. The following list suggests some of the subtle (covert) forms of bias to watch for.

Standard for Success. Is "making it" in the dominant white society projected as the only ideal? To gain acceptance and approval, do persons of color have to exhibit extraordinary qualities—excel in sports, get A's, and so on? In friendships between white and nonwhite children, is it the child of color who does most of the understanding and forgiving?

Resolution of Problems. How are problems presented, conceived, and resolved in the story? Are minority people considered to be "the problem"? Are the oppressions faced by minorities and women represented as related to social injustice? Are the reasons accepted as inevitable? Does the story line encourage passive acceptance or active resistance? Is a particular problem that is faced by a member of a racial minority or female resolved through the benevolent intervention of a white person or male?

Role of Women. Are the achievements of girls and women based on their own initiative and intelligence, or are they due to their good looks or relationship with boys? Are sex roles incidental or critical to characterization and plot? Could the same story be told if the sex roles were reversed?

3. Look at the Lifestyles

Are minority persons and their setting depicted in such a way that they contrast unfavorably with the unstated norm of white, middle-class suburbia? If the minority group in question is depicted as "different," are negative value judgments implied? Are minorities depicted exclusively in ghettos, barrios, or migrant camps? If the illustrations and text attempt to depict another culture, do they go beyond oversimplifications and offer genuine insights into another lifestyle? Look for inaccuracy and inappropriateness in the depiction of other cultures. Watch for instances of the "quaint-natives-in-costume" syndrome (most noticeable in areas like clothing and custom, but extending to behavior and personality traits as well).

4. Weigh the Relationships Between People

Do the whites in the story possess the power, take the leadership, and make the important decisions? Do racial minorities and females of all races function in essentially supporting roles?

How are family relationships depicted? In black families, is the mother always dominant? In Hispanic families, are there always lots of children? If the family is separated, are societal conditions—unemployment and poverty, for example—cited among the reasons for the separation?

Ten Quick Ways to Detect
Sexism and Racism (continued)

5. Note the Heroes

For many years, books showed only "safe" minority heroes—those who avoided serious conflict with the white establishment of their time. Minority groups today are insisting on the right to define their own heroes (of both sexes) based on their own concepts and struggles for justice.

When minority heroes do appear, are they admired for the same qualities that have made white heroes famous or because what they have done has benefited white people? Ask this question: Whose interest is a particular hero really serving?

6. Consider the Effects
on a Student's Self-Image

Are norms established that limit any child's aspirations and self-concept? What effect can it have on black children to be bombarded continuously with images of the color white as the ultimate in beauty, cleanliness, virtue, and so on, and the color black as evil, dirty, menacing, and so on? Does the book counteract or reinforce this positive association with the color white and negative association with black?

What happens to a girl's self-image when she reads that boys perform all of the brave and important deeds? What about a girl's self-esteem if she is not "fair" of skin, not to mention slim of body?

In a particular story, are there one or more persons with whom a minority child can readily identify to a positive and constructive end?

7. Consider the Author's
or Illustrator's Background

Analyze the biographical material on the jacket flap or the back of the book. If a story deals with a minority theme, what qualifies the author or illustrator to deal with the subject? If the author and illustrator are not members of the minority being written about, is there anything in their backgrounds that would specifically recommend them as the creators of the book?

8. Check Out the Author's Perspective

No author can be wholly objective. All authors write out of a cultural as well as a personal context. Children's books in the past have traditionally come from authors who were white and who were members of the middle class, with one result being that a single ethnocentric perspective has dominated children's literature in the United States. With any book in question, read carefully to determine whether the direction of the author's perspective substantially weakens or strengthens the value of the written work. Is the perspective patriarchal or feminist? Is it solely Eurocentric, or do minority cultural perspectives also receive respect?

9. Watch for Loaded Words

A word is loaded when it has insulting overtones. Examples of loaded adjectives (usually racist) are *savage, primitive, conniving, lazy, superstitious, treacherous, wily, crafty, inscrutable, docile,* and *backward.*

Look for sexist language and adjectives that exclude or ridicule women. Look for use of the male pronoun to refer to both males and females. The following examples show how sexist language can be avoided: *ancestors* instead of *forefathers; community* instead of *brotherhood; firefighters* instead of *firemen;* the *human* family instead of the family of *man.*

10. Look at the Copyright Date

Books on minority themes—usually hastily conceived—suddenly began appearing in the mid-1960s. There followed a growing number of "minority experience" books to meet the new market demand, but most of these were still written by white authors, edited by white editors, and published by white publishers. They therefore reflected a white point of view. Not until the early 1970s did the children's book world begin even remotely to reflect the realities of a multiracial society. The new direction resulted from the emergence of minority authors writing about their own experiences. Nonsexist books, with rare exceptions, were not published before 1973.

them to complete the questionnaire on page 82. Their evaluations could initiate an enlightening class discussion. These stereotypes and discriminatory behaviors harm girls and boys equally.

Nonbiased Teaching

There are many ways to make the classroom a more equitable place for girls and boys of all races and ethnic origins. In addition to avoiding discriminatory practices, try these suggestions:

✔ Direct lower-order and higher-order questions to both boys and girls.

✔ Assign leadership and support roles equitably.

✔ Eliminate segregated play areas and discourage students from segregating themselves.

✔ Avoid grouping on the basis of gender. (Conversely, some educators have suggested that grouping boys and girls separately in math and science classes would force some girls to participate more when they would otherwise have deferred to the boys.)

✔ Encourage boys and girls to participate in nontraditional activities.

✔ Avoid stereotyping girls as compliant and obedient and boys as disruptive and aggressive.

✔ Reinforce boys and girls who are working and playing together.

✔ Avoid thinking of girls only as being "neat" and boys as being "intellectually competent."

Teachers can also present activities that teach valuable lessons about gender bias and stereotyping, such as the questionnaire on page 82.

Subtle Messages

Some types of bias are quite subtle, such as the messages we give children about their abilities and efforts. Researchers Del Siegle and Sally Reis, of the University of Connecticut, cite studies showing that as early as first grade, teachers tend to attribute boys' successes and failures to ability and girls' successes and failures to effort. Apparently, students get the message loud and clear. When asked themselves, boys usually attribute academic success to ability and failure to lack of effort; girls attribute success to effort or luck and failure to lack of ability.

Siegle and Reis further cite evidence that "successful students who received feedback complimenting their ability, rather than focusing on their effort, developed higher self-efficacy and learned more than students who received feedback complimenting their effort."

No wonder so many girls doubt their own abilities. Paradoxically, their self-doubts are increased when they receive higher grades than boys. As Siegle and Reis explain, gifted adolescent girls believe that high ability means achieving good grades effortlessly; they reason that if they must work hard, they obviously lack ability.

Middle school expert Bruce Hammond reports that "girls seem to lose self-confidence and self-esteem in middle school after outperforming boys by a significant margin in the earlier grades."

Challenges of Gender

Researchers today talk about gender differences and teaching practices that affect the academic performance of both sexes. In addition, a plethora of studies point to the disabling effects society has on boys and girls as they develop their identities and concepts of self. Several landmark studies and books address these issues. (See the resource list at the end of this chapter for complete publishing details.)

In *Real Boys: Rescuing Our Sons from the Myths of Boyhood*, Harvard psychiatrist William Pollack talks about the "Boy Code"—society's image of boys as tough, physical, and obsessed with cars, sex, and sports. The many boys who don't fit this stereotype suffer in school and elsewhere as they try to pretend they do or lash out against it. Pollack claims that new research shows boys are faring less well than before. And further, "the rates of both depression and suicide in boys are frighteningly on the rise." Dan Kindlon and colleagues in *Raising Cain: Protecting the Emotional Lives of Boys*, echo the sentiment that boys suffer from a too-narrow definition of masculinity.

Mary Pipher writes about the "girl-poisoning" society that causes many adolescent females to lose enthusiasm, interest, and even IQ in *Reviving Ophelia: Saving the Selves of Adolescent Girls*. We teachers, as purveyors of culture, need to understand these seemingly insurmountable challenges facing children. We need to recognize gender bias and stereotyping (we've experienced it, too!) and avoid it in our teaching. Again, it all boils down to treating learners as individuals and accommodating as best we can the unique interests, backgrounds, personalities, and styles they bring to the classroom.

❖ Children in Crisis

Chronic poverty; absence of mother, father, or both; emotional or physical abuse; serious mental or physical health problems in a family member; racial prejudice; death or major loss; exposure to violence and drug or alcohol abuse; homelessness; fear of random violence; and terrorist attacks—the problems affecting today's children take a huge toll on learning. When children suffer, says Dr. Adele Brodkin, their development suffers. The stress in their young lives often leads to behavioral and learning problems. Yet some students in crisis manage to overcome the odds. How?

Protective Factors

There are certain "protective factors," explains Brodkin, a child psychologist, professor, and long-time consultant to schools and hospitals. "High on the list is the reliable presence of at least one nurturant individual who has a close bond with a child and believes in the child." A parent is the ideal nurturant individual, she says, but teachers can fill the role, too. "A teacher may be the first person outside of the home, or anywhere at all, who has been consistently caring and trustworthy."

Helping Stressed Students

To help students burdened by stressful lives, Brodkin suggests you identify the most caring and reliable adult in the student's life and support that individual. Meet regularly with that individual, sharing information about the student's strengths in school. Encourage that individual to play a special role in the classroom, and if possible or appropriate, try to facilitate community support for the individual or family.

In class, build on the student's strengths and interests. Encourage him or her to express feelings in drawing, writing, dramatic play, and role-play. These techniques provide an important outlet for all types of situations, including those in which students have witnessed violence. "Don't make the mistake of thinking that Mary will forget it if she is distracted and discouraged from discussing it," Brodkin cautions.

Getting Extra Help

Sometimes, says Brodkin, crises are too great for children to handle, even with your help. At this point, ask for help from administrators and professionals in your school. Warning signs include overwhelming sadness, withdrawal, lack of interest, repetitive play, unusual aggressiveness, indifference to caretakers and other children, chronic irritability, poor concentration and decrease in cognitive functioning, fearfulness or dangerous fearlessness, and rocking or head banging.

Students' personal tragedies intrude on their school experiences and successes, and teachers cannot help but get involved. Following are some resources for students in crisis:

NEA Health Information Network
1201 16th St. NW, Ste. 521
Washington, DC 20036
Free publication hotline: (202) 822-7570
www.neahealthinfo.org

KidsPeace: National Center for Kids in Crisis
✔ educational materials: (800) 25-PEACE
✔ 24-hour Helpline for kids, parents, professionals: (800) 334-4KID
✔ www.kidspeace.org

OSDFS: Office of Safe and Drug-Free Schools
U.S. Dept. of Education
(202) 260-3954

National Association for Children of Alcoholics
(888) 55-4COAS
www.childrennotalcoholics.org

Families Anonymous (for children with drug abuse and related problems)
(800) 736-9805
www.familiesanonymous.org

Kids Help Phone (child abuse)
(800) 668-6868
http://kidshelp.sympatico.ca

Childhelp USA (counseling for victims of child abuse and neglect)
(800) 4-A-CHILD
www.childhelpusa.org

National Runaway Switchboard Metro-Help, Inc. (serves runaway and homeless youths and families)
(800) 621-4000
www.nrscrisisline.org

National Youth Suicide Hotline (800) 621-4000

National Center on Child Abuse and Neglect
Children, Youth, and Families
U.S. Dept. of Health and Human Services
P.O.B. 1182, Washington, DC 20013-1182
(800) FYI-3366

Prevent Child Abuse America
200 S. Michigan Ave., 17th Floor
Chicago, IL 60604
(312) 663-3520
www.preventchildabuse.org

American Humane Association
63 Inverness Drive E.
Englewood, CO 80112-5117
(303) 792-9900
www.americanhumane.org

American Academy of Child and Adolescent Psychiatry
3615 Wisconsin Ave. NW
Washington, DC 20016
(202) 966-7300
(Ask for the "Facts for Teachers" publication.)
www.aacap.org

❖ In Summary

With so much information on student characteristics that directly affect learning, it's easy to feel overwhelmed and doubtful that you can meet the needs of each individual student. What about the gifted minority student who speaks English as a second language? The learning-disabled student who's being emotionally abused at home? The important point is to recognize that these children are individuals. Understanding the unique characteristics that make them individuals can only help us to improve and tailor the instruction we offer them.

Cheryl Peden sums it up nicely: "How do I address the diverse needs of my students—and my school, too? I meet this challenge, like many of my colleagues across the country, with lots of hard work, hours, thought, and a deep commitment. I strive to create a classroom climate of caring, individualization, and high expectations. I advocate a belief in and a recognition of the talents and joyful discoveries of children. Together, children, parents, and I develop a strong, consistent foundation from which we launch explorations."

❖ Works Cited

American Association of University Women. *How Schools Shortchange Girls*. Washington, DC: National Education Association, 1992.

Attention Deficit Disorder Association
http://add.org

Clark, Barbara. *Growing Up Gifted: Developing the Potential of Children at Home and at School*. 6th ed. Upper Saddle River, NJ: Merrill/Prentice Hall, 2002.

Cohen, Elizabeth. *Designing Groupwork: Strategies for the Heterogeneous Classroom.* New York: Teachers College Press, 1994.

Dunn, Rita, Jeffrey Beaudry, and Angela Klavas. "Survey of Research on Learning Styles." *Educational Leadership* 46, no. 6 (March 1989): 50–58. Available: www.ascd.org.

Dunn, Rita, and Shirley A. Griggs. *Multiculturalism and Learning Style: Teaching and Counseling Adolescents.* Westport, CT: Praeger, 1998.

Elkind, David. "Developmentally Appropriate Education for 4-Year-Olds." *Theory Into Practice* 28, no. 1 (Winter 1989): 47–52.

Elkind, David. "Formal Education and Early Childhood Education: An Essential Difference." *Phi Delta Kappan* 67, no. 9 (May 1986): 631–636.

Feldhusen, John F. "Synthesis of Research on Gifted Youth." *Educational Leadership* (March 1989): 6–11.

Gardner, Howard. *Frames of Mind.* New York: Basic Books, 1983.

Gardner, Howard. *Intelligence Reframed: Multiple Intelligences for the 21st Century.* New York: Basic Books, 1999.

Gardner, Howard. *Multiple Intelligences: The Theory in Practice.* New York: Basic Books, 1993.

Gardner, Howard. "Multiple Intelligences After 20 Years." Paper presented at the American Educational Research Association, Chicago, IL, April 21, 2003.

Garlikov, Rick. "The Socratic Method: Teaching by Asking Instead of Telling." Available: www.garlikov.com/Soc_Meth.html.

Guild, Pat. "The Culture/Learning Style Connection." *Educational Leadership* 51, no.8 (May 1994): 16–21.

Guild, Pat. "Diversity, Learning Style and Culture." New Horizons for Learning, 2001. www.newhorizons.org. Adapted from *Marching to Different Drummers*, 2nd ed., by Pat Burke Guild and Stephen Garger. Alexandria, VA: Association for Supervision and Curriculum Development, 1998.

Haggerty, Brian. *Nurturing Intelligences: A Guide to Multiple Intelligences Theory and Teaching.* Menlo Park, CA: Addison-Wesley, 1995.

Hammond, Bruce. "Middle School Crisis." Available: www.parentsoup.com (biweekly newsletter of ivillage.com). July 10, 2002.

International Dyslexia Association www.interdys.org

Jaska, Peter. "Fact Sheet on Attention Deficit Hyperactivity Disorder (ADHD/ADD)." Attention Deficit Disorder Association, 1998. Available: http://add.org/content.htm.

Kostelnik, Marjorie J. "Myths Associated with Developmentally Appropriate Programs." *Young Children* (May 1992): 17–23.

Kostelnik, Marjorie J., A. P. Whiren, and A. K. Soderman. *Developmentally Appropriate Programs for Early Education:* New York: Macmillan: 1994.

Kindlon, Daniel J., and Michael Thompson with Teresa Barker. *Raising Cain: Protecting the Emotional Lives of Boys.* New York: Balantine Books, 1999.

Learning Disabilities Association of America www.ldanatl.org

Learning Styles Network www.learningstyles.net

McDiarmid, G. W. "What Do Prospective Teachers Need to Know About Culturally Different Children?" In M. M. Kennedy, ed., *Teaching Academic Subjects to Diverse Learners.* New York: Teachers College Press, 1991.

McDiarmid, G. W. "What to Do About Differences? A Study of Multicultural Education for Teacher Trainees in the Los Angeles Unified School District." *Journal of Teacher Education* 43, no. 2 (1992): 83–93.

Morton, Bruce. "The Reconstitution of Hemisphericity." University of Hawaii. Available: www2.hawaii.edu/~bemorton/Hemisphericity.

"Multi-Age Teaching: Is It for You?" *NEA Today* (May 1996): 4–5.

National Center for Educational Statistics http://nces.ed.gov

National Center for Learning Disabilities www.ld.org

National Center for Research on Teacher Learning. "Findings on Learning to Teach." Michigan State University, East Lansing, MI, 1993.

O'Dell, S., and M. O'Hair, eds. *Diversity and Teaching: Teacher Education Yearbook I.* Fort Worth: Harcourt, 1993.

Piaget, Jean. *The Origins of Intelligence in Children.* M. Cook, trans. New York: International Universities Press, 1952.

Piaget, Jean. *The Psychology of Intelligence.* New York: Routledge, 2001.

Pipher, Mary. *Reviving Ophelia: Saving the Selves of Adolescent Girls.* New York: Putnam, 1994.

Pollack, William. *Real Boys: Rescuing Our Sons from the Myths of Boyhood.* New York: Random House, 1998.

"Preparing Teachers for Diversity." (Description of work by Gloria Ladson-Billings.) *WCER Research Highlights.* University of Wisconsin–Madison, Winter 2003–2004. Available: www.wcer.wisc.edu.

Renzulli, Joseph. "Teachers as Talent Scouts." *Educational Leadership* 52, no. 4 (1994/1995): 75–81.

Rothenberg, Dianne. "Full-Day Kindergarten Programs." ERIC Digest (EDO-PS-95-4). Urbana, IL: ERIC Clearinghouse on Elementary and Early Childhood Education, May 1995.

Ruenzel, David. "Paradise Lost." *Teacher Magazine* (May/June 1996): 26–34.

Sadker, Myra, and David Sadker. *Failing at Fairness: How America's Schools Cheat Girls.* New York: Scribner, 1994.

Sanford, John. "Scholar [Rob Reich] Discusses Educational Benefits of Socratic Method." Stanford University News Service, May 27, 2003. Available: www.stanford.edu/dept/news/pr/03/socratic 528.html.

Siegle, Del, and Sally M. Reis. "Gender Differences in Student and Teacher Perceptions of Gifted Students' Ability and Effort." *Gifted Child Quarterly* 42, no. 1, (Winter 1998).

Smith, Sally. "Enabling the Learning Disabled." *Instructor,* July/August 1993, 88–91.

Smith, Sally. *Succeeding Against the Odds: How the Learning Disabled Can Realize Their Promise.* Los Angeles: J. P. Tarcher, 1993.

Solden, Sari. *Women With ADD.* Grass Valley, CA: Underwood Books, 1995.

"Some Basic Facts About ADD Medications." Attention Deficit Disorder Association, http://add.org/content/treatment/meds1.htm.

"Teenage Growth & Development: 11–14 Years." Palo Alto Medical Foundation. Available: www.pamf.org/teen/parents/health/growth-11-14.html.

"Theory of Multiple Intelligences." Project SUMIT. Available: www.pz.harvard.edu/sumit/misumit.htm.

Weiner, Lois. "Why Is Classroom Management So Vexing to Urban Teachers?" *Theory Into Practice* 42, no. 4 (Autumn 2003).

Wilkins, Arnold. "Coloured Overlays and Coloured Lenses: Frequently Asked Questions." Available at www.essex.ac.uk/psychology/overlays.

Willis, Arlette, and Lewis, Karla. "Focus on Research: A Conversation With Gloria Ladson-Billings." *Language Arts* 75, no. 1 (January 1998).

Winebrenner, Susan. *Teaching Gifted Kids in the Regular Classroom: Strategies and Techniques Every Teacher Can Use to Meet the Academic Needs of the Gifted and Talented*. Minneapolis: Free Spirit Publishing, 2000.

Winner, Ellen. *Gifted Children: Myths and Realities*. New York: Basic Books, 1996.

Wolfe, Pat. *Brain Research and Education: Fad or Foundation?* Mind Matters, Inc., 2003. Available www.patwolfe.com.

❖ Resources

Behavioral Issues and Learning Disabilities

Brodkin, Adele M. *Fresh Approaches to Working With Problematic Behaviors*. New York: Scholastic, 2001.

Child Development Institute
www.cdipage.com
Includes information on developmental stages, classroom interventions, and strategies for ADD and other developmental challenges.

Children and Adults with Attention Deficit Disorder.
www.chadd.org
The nation's leading nonprofit organization for ADHD offers a free online newsletter, fact sheets, and information on everything from legal rights to products and services that help.

DuPaul, George J., and Stoner, Gary. *ADHD in the Schools: Assessment and Intervention Strategies*. New York: Guilford Press, 2003.

Identifying and Treating Attention Deficit/Hyperactivity Disorder: A Resource for Home and School. U.S. Dept. of Education, 2003. Available: www.ed.gov/teachers/needs/speced/adhd.

Levine, Mel. *The Myth of Laziness*. New York: Simon and Schuster, 2003.

Pfiffner, Linda J. *All About ADHD: The Complete Practical Guide for Classroom Teachers*. New York: Scholastic, 1999.

Culture and Education

Delpit, Lisa. *Other People's Children: Cultural Conflict in the Classroom*. New York: New Press, 1995.

Esquith, Rafe. *There Are No Shortcuts*. New York: Pantheon, 2003.
A story of one teacher's determination to help impoverished children overcome the limitations of poverty.

Howard, Tyrone C. "Culturally Relevant Pedagogy: Ingredients for Critical Teacher Reflection." *Theory Into Practice* 42, no. 3 (Summer 2003). A reflective process for preservice teachers, and specific questions and strategies for reflection.

Kugler, Eileen Gale. *Debunking the Middle-Class Myth: Why Diverse Schools Are Good for All Kids*. Lanham, MD: Scarecrow Press, 2002.

Ladson-Billings, Gloria. *Crossing Over to Canaan: The Journey of New Teachers in Diverse Classrooms*. San Francisco: Jossey-Bass, 2001.

"Multicultural Education." *New Horizons for Learning Online Journal* IX, no. 2 (Spring 2003). Available: www.newhorizons.org/journal/journal38.htm.

Payne, Ruby K. *A Framework for Understanding Poverty*. Baytown, TX: RFT Pub., 1998. Available: www.ahaprocess.com.

Weinstein, Carol, et al. "Culturally Responsive Classroom Management: Awareness into Action." *Theory Into Practice* 42, no. 4 (Autumn 2003). Weinstein urges teachers to create caring, inclusive classrooms and practice equitable classroom management by recognizing and respecting cultural differences. She includes many instructive examples from real classrooms.

Gifted Education
Delisle, Jim, and Judith Galbraith. *When Gifted Kids Don't Have All the Answers*. Minneapolis: Free Spirit Publishing, 2002.

Learning Styles
All Kinds of Minds Institute
www.allkindsofminds.org
A nonprofit organization for the understanding of differences among learners. Founded by Dr. Mel Levine.

Dunn, Rita, and Shirley A. *Griggs Synthesis of the Dunn and Dunn Learning-Style Model Research: Who, What, When, Where, and So What?* New York: St. John's University Center for the Study of Learning and Teaching Styles, 2003.

Learning Styles Network
www.learningstyles.net

Tomlinson, Carol Ann. *How to Differentiate Instruction in Mixed-Ability Classrooms*. 2nd ed. Alexandria, VA: Association for Supervision and Curriculum Development, 2001.

Multiple Intelligences
Armstrong, Thomas. *Multiple Intelligences in the Classroom*. 2nd ed. Alexandria, VA: Association for Supervision and Curriculum Development, 2000.

Gardner, Howard. "Reflections on Multiple Intelligences: Myths and Messages." *Phi Delta Kappan* 77, no. 3 (2003): 206–09.

Kornhaber, Mindy, et al. *Multiple Intelligences: Best Ideas from Research and Practice*. Boston: Pearson, 2004.
Includes detailed case studies, investigation of more than 40 schools, and suggestions for how educators everywhere can integrate multiple intelligences in curriculum.

Nelson, Kristen. *Developing Students' Multiple Intelligences* (Grades K–8). New York: Scholastic, 1999.

Project Zero. Harvard University
www.pzweb.harvard.edu
The site features research projects on thinking and learning, including Howard Gardner's work on multiple intelligences.

Chapter Three

Motivating Students: Effective Teaching Strategies

"Do not train children to learn by force and harshness, but direct them to it by what amuses their minds, so that you may be better able to discover with accuracy the peculiar bent of the genius of each."

—Plato

Motivation is the key to learning . . . and teaching.

As novelist Richard Bach describes a character in his well-known allegory *Jonathan Livingston Seagull*, "Fletcher Gull was very nearly a perfect flight student. He was strong and light and quick in the air, but far and away more important, he had a blazing drive to learn to fly." Fletcher and Jonathan come to realize, and Bach himself gently teaches us, that it's not ability that dictates how well we'll learn to fly, but rather the intense drive to want to fly higher and faster and better. Such desire is the flame that ignites a passion for learning.

The story offers important reminders to teachers: the idea that personal desire or motivation underlies any successful attempt to learn, and that learners must be encouraged to take risks and to understand that sometimes failing is part of succeeding. Jonathan endured many mishaps as he learned to fly, but he never gave up.

Further, successful teachers capitalize on students' interests and curiosity as they model the learning process. When Jonathan finally succeeds in overcoming his limitations and soaring to incredible heights, the first thing he wants to do is share his new knowledge with the rest of the flock. When the others won't listen, he simply demonstrates his techniques tirelessly, winning converts slowly but surely and inspiring them by his example.

We can help our students soar. With effective instructional strategies, we can motivate students and foster their desire to learn. Their quest for knowledge and curiosity about the world are natural human attributes. We can feed that curiosity and facilitate that quest.

Motivation Comes Naturally

When asked about how good teachers can inspire passion for learning in their students, national activist for educational reform Deborah Meier responded, "It isn't something you have to inspire them with; it's something you have to keep from extinguishing. Human beings are by nature passionate, curious, intrigued. We are by nature theorists. We seek to connect, find patterns, make sense of things. . . . Unfortunately, kids stop expecting school to be a place where they use their curiosity and theoretical abilities. They think of school as a place to find out what someone else wants from you or how to appear to conform. That's true of our successful students and our failures both."

Teachers need to model passion for learning. "It's not enough for teachers to be interested in the subjects they're teaching," says Meier. "It's imperative that they be intellectually curious about the world around them."

Meier, principal of Mission Hills School in Boston and founder of the Central Park East Schools, knows that properly structured learning experiences foster motivation naturally. Teachers don't have to dangle tangible rewards in front of students' eyes if they provide them with opportunities to ask and seek answers to their own questions about topics they've selected, help them see the connections between schoolwork and their lives, allow them ownership of their own learning and accomplishments, and account for their individual styles and preferences. Under these conditions, students will be motivated to succeed. And success itself is highly motivating.

❖ The "Science" of Teaching

This chapter presents motivating instructional strategies that work, as attested by expert teachers and research. Scholars refer to these strategies as the professional knowledge base—knowledge unique and essential to good teaching. These are teaching behaviors that make a predictable difference—the science of teaching. (See the Introduction on page 8 for a discussion of the art and science of teaching.)

More specifically, these are the strategies over which teachers have some control. We usually can't determine the size of our classes or create multiage classrooms where administrative policy precludes them, but we can use our professional judgment and practice in these areas (many of which are covered in this chapter):

✔ organizing instruction into **integrated, thematic units**

✔ using **cooperative learning** and group approaches

✔ recognizing and teaching to **multiple intelligences**

✔ accommodating **individual learning styles**

✔ stressing **thinking skills** over rote memorization

✔ harnessing the power of **technology**

✔ practicing **authentic assessment** of students' learning

✔ **praising and encouraging** students effectively

✔ **motivating** students to value learning

✔ acknowledging the importance of **active teaching, engaged time,** and **academic learning time**

✔ using wise **grouping practices**

The list is long and growing. Most importantly, the strategies and ideas presented here assume a certain philosophy of education: that a teacher's most important job is teaching students how to learn and how to become independent thinkers. The most effective instructional strategies, generally, are those that foster this independence. "I believe that the primary goal of schooling is intellectual, not academic," asserted Meier in an interview on public television. "Academic has to do with what people study. Intellectual means using your mind." Meier explains that fostering the intellect means helping students develop their capacity to play with ideas and to take ideas seriously. The goal of schooling, then, "is to develop the capacities for intellectual behavior, rather than turning it off."

The Research Base

Researchers observe, interview, and study successful teachers to identify effective instructional strategies. They look for key behaviors and what it is these teachers do differently from others. Strategies identified can then be tested in experimental studies. That is, other teachers learn to use the strategies in their classrooms, and researchers document the effects.

But research offers only guidelines. Theory and research inform teachers' thinking—they don't replace professional experience and judgment.

In his foreword to the first edition of this book, Stanford University professor Lee Shulman described "the emerging character of educational research, the ways in which its findings and recommendations are always evolving and becoming reformulated." Shulman cautioned that teachers must understand that "[r]esearch on teaching is not a laboratory science, not a program of inquiry that conducts its investigations in isolated hothouses and then attempts to plant its seedlings in the real world of classrooms and schools. Indeed, research on teaching takes place in the vibrant, busy and complex arena of those real classrooms themselves. The scholar's laboratory is the classroom, not the test tube or isolation chamber. Researchers on teaching gain their understanding through the study of practice. They observe and interview able teachers, attempting to discern the insights and accomplishments of veterans and novices alike. Research thereby becomes a vehicle for detecting the wisdoms of practice, refining and elaborating those insights, and then sharing those understandings with practitioners from whose work they derive."

Teacher Judgment Is Critical

Ultimately, it is you, the professional, who decides what, where, when, and how to teach, keeping in mind state standards and how the particular needs of your students direct the delivery of your standards-based teaching. Research provides information to help you make those decisions. It increases your repertoire of options.

Teachers sometimes criticize educational research for not being more specific—for failing to offer "recipes" for practice. But teaching isn't cooking. You can't mix together a specific list of ingredients and produce a product that looks the same every time. Teaching is a complex human endeavor that can be guided, but not prescribed, by research. A key word here is *human*—human variation among teachers and students. No two teachers, students, or situations are the same. That's why your judgment calls are so important.

Judgment calls and decision making, constant challenges, variety and change—these are the factors drawing many talented and multifaceted people into teaching. These are the reasons why good teaching invigorates and extends us.

What's Our Basic Role?

The instructional strategies we employ depend, of course, on our basic beliefs about what our roles should be as instructors. Are you the "sage on the stage" or the "guide on the side"?

Many different educators and scholars have reflected on the basic aim of teaching and education. The novelist Edith Wharton perhaps stated it most eloquently when she remarked that "[t]here are two ways of spreading light: to be the candle or the mirror that reflects it."

Today, most experienced teachers and experts agree that the teacher's role must change from being primarily a provider of information to someone who guides students through discovery and exploration. This basic premise underlies the strategies and discussion that follow.

BRAIN-BASED COMPUTER PROGRAM FOR READING IMPROVEMENT

While most of the science of teaching still emanates from behavioral psychology, and true brain-based teaching is still in its infancy, some neuroscience is already reaching the classroom. Eric Jensen offers the example of a practical classroom application developed by two neuroscientists. Stanford's Dr. Michael Merzenich and Dr. Paula Tallal from Rutgers developed a phonological processing improvement product called Fast ForWord. This computer program, already found in hundreds of classrooms, uses discoveries in neural plasticity to change the brain's auditory processing ability; it turns out that many students who struggle with reading and writing actually "hear" some sounds at different frequencies than their more successful peers. As students move through different levels of picture-sound matching activities in the Fast ForWord program, the auditory cues speed up and students' brains learn to respond to increasingly faster processing speeds, eventually distinguishing sounds delivered at the speed of a normal conversation. The program has seen promising results for improvement of across-the-board reading skills for underachieving readers. For more information, visit the Scientific Learning Web site at www.ScientificLearning.com.

❖ The "Science" of Learning

Just as we need to consider the scientific research base in our teaching—proven strategies that make a predictable difference—we must also consider the research on how learners learn—"brain-based research."

Advances in neuroscience have yielded tremendous insights into the inner workings of the human brain, says expert David Sousa. He points out that medical instruments can now show the human brain in action.

And what do we see?

The student brain of today is quite different from the one of 20 years ago. "The rapidly changing, multimedia-based culture and the stresses from an ever-increasing pace of living have a dramatic impact on how the developing brain interprets and interacts with its world," explains Sousa. "Today's children spend much more time with television and other electronic media than with their parents. They have become accustomed to rapid sensory and emotional changes, and they respond more readily to the unique and different—what we might now call novelty."

Obviously, teaching practices must keep pace with these changes. What we're coming to understand is that many of our most "sacred" practices work at odds with the way children learn and how their brains retain knowledge.

No Magic Bullet

Despite its tremendous potential for teaching and learning, brain research is still in its infancy. Sousa, along with experts Pat Wolfe, Eric Jensen, John Bruer, and others, cautions that educators who link brain science with teaching and learning must be cautious about how they proceed. Many of the contemporary claims and models of "brain-based teaching" are developed from research about the psychology of the mind rather than the biology of the brain. There's a tremendous difference. What's needed is more research in the practical application of neuroscience—more science of teaching based on the science of learning. Still, there's much we already know about the human brain that we can use in our teaching.

"Windows of Opportunity"

One thing neurobiologists have discovered is that the human brain has "critical periods," or "windows of opportunity" for acquiring skills and knowledge. These are the times when the brain is being "wired" or primed—the times during which environmental influences have the greatest impact on development or learning, explains Michele Rogers, executive director of the Early Learning Institute.

Neurobiologists have suggested that a child's learning window for math and logic is from birth to 4 years of age; for language, from birth to 10 years; for music, from 3 to 9 years. "Fortunately, there are relatively few critical periods in which experience, or the lack thereof, cannot be ameliorated by interventions at a later date," Rogers notes. Still, it is important for teachers and other caregivers to understand these developmental windows of opportunity— "especially as they relate to neural plasticity— the reciprocal phenomenon whereby activities are incorporated into the structures of the developing brain," Rogers explains, adding that, "A later experience may change the mature brain, but an early experience helps organize the brain systems."

Sousa concurs: "These so-called 'windows of opportunity' represent critical periods when the brain demands certain types of input to create or consolidate neural networks, especially for acquiring language, emotional control, and learning to play music." Sousa explains that one can learn new information and skills at any age. "But what the child learned during that window period will strongly influence what is learned after the window closes."

Sousa suggests that if teachers of the primary and intermediate grades understand these different times and areas of brain growth, "they can decide how best to approach the content and skills in their curriculum, and provide an enriched, brain-friendly classroom environment."

"Early experiences are so powerful, they can completely change the way a person turns out," claims pediatric neurobiologist Harry Chugani of Wayne State University, quoted in a *Newsweek* article by Sharon Begley.

The implications for education are enormous. For example, language development occurs best before the age of 9, yet foreign-language instruction typically begins in middle or high school. Begley suggests that intensive instruction in some areas begins too late to fundamentally rewire the brain.

Music, Art, Phys. Ed.

Brain research also shows that music and art train the brain for higher thinking and reasoning skills. And physical exercise nourishes the brain with glucose and increases nerve connections, making it easier to learn. Yet music, phys. ed., and art classes are frequently sacrificed to budget cuts.

Many researchers suggest that if school administrators understood brain biology, schooling would look drastically different. Foreign languages and geometry would be offered much sooner, and music and physical education would be daily classes.

Brain Is a "Jungle"

University of Oregon emeritus professor Robert Sylwester, who writes a monthly column for the online magazine *Brain Connection*, talks about other implications of brain research.

Based on current studies and research models, Sylwester suggests that the brain may operate less like a computer and more like a jungle ecosystem.

Referring to work by Nobel Prize winner Gerald Edelman, Sylwester explains: "Think of the vast number of highly interconnected neural networks that make up our brain as the neural equivalent of the complex set of jungle organisms responding variously to environmental challenges. The natural selection processes that shape a jungle over long periods of time also shape our brain and its neural networks within our lifetime."

This and other new theories seem to support much current thinking and practice among expert teachers.

For example, Sylwester points out that Edelman's "model of our brain as a rich, layered, unplanned jungle ecosystem is especially intriguing because it suggests that a jungle-like brain might thrive best in a jungle-like classroom that includes many sensory, cultural, and problem layers that are closely related to the real-world environment—an environment that best stimulates the neural networks genetically tuned to it."

Activities enhancing multiple intelligences and learning styles, cultural diversity, real-world problems and connections—these current practices would all contribute to such a "jungle-like classroom."

"The classroom of tomorrow," Sylwester adds, "might focus more on drawing out existing abilities than on precisely measuring a student's success with imposed skills; encourage the personal construction of categories rather than impose existing categorical systems; and emphasize the individual, personal solutions of an environmental challenge. . . . The curriculum might increase the importance of such subjects as the arts and humanities, which expand and integrate complex environmental stimuli, and de-emphasize basic skills and forms of evaluation that merely compress complexity."

Children Need Activity

Further, researchers claim that children need to be physically active in the classroom, and that children retain knowledge longer if they connect physically and emotionally to the material.

For example, acting out a play or battle scene can be much more effective than reading about it. Building complex models to scale can be much more effective than computing angles and dimensions on worksheets. Activities such as these give students a multisensory, multidimensional mental model that's easier t o retain and retrieve. In other words, they experience the material more thoroughly.

Yet despite an abundance of recent research on the brain and learning, little makes its way to the school or classroom. Too often, school decisions such as cutting music and gym classes are made for economic and not educational reasons.

❖ Internal vs. External Motivation

Motivation is an elusive concept. Generally, we define motivation as processes or behaviors that initiate, direct, and sustain goal-oriented behavior. Sometimes these processes are nurtured by drives and needs within ourselves (internal motivation) and sometimes outside forces direct them (external motivation).

"People learn when they have a reason," says Ron Brandt, former executive editor of *Educational Leadership*. "An essential part of teaching is helping students find their own good reasons to learn."

External Motivation

When we expect external rewards for completing an activity or behaving a certain way, we are externally motivated. These external or extrinsic motivators—good grades, a teacher or parent's praise, extra privileges and free time, public recognition, competition, even material goods such as stickers or candy—are expected or relied on by many students. Too often, these motivators get in the way of real learning.

But while they are sometimes overused or abused, many experts believe that extrinsic motivators can be very effective in helping students develop intrinsic motivation to learn or behave. Perhaps the most important role of extrinsic motivators is to make students aware of the powerful social reinforcement given to those who try hard, learn, and succeed.

Alfie Kohn disagrees. He argues that rewards, just like punishments, are only ways to manipulate behavior, and that students know they're being manipulated. Further, "Rewards are most damaging to interest when the task is already intrinsically motivating," Kohn asserts.

In his landmark book, *Punished by Rewards*, Kohn cites numerous studies showing that extrinsic motivators—including good grades, some types of praise, and other rewards—are not merely ineffective over the long haul but also counterproductive to such things as creativity, task quality, desire to learn, and commitment to good values.

Instead, "What kids deserve is an engaging curriculum and a caring atmosphere so they can act on their natural desire to find out about stuff," Kohn believes. "No kid deserves to be manipulated with extrinsics so as to comply with what someone else wants."

Kohn's ideas may be hard to swallow for those of us who believe that praise and rewards will motivate students. And indeed some researchers and educators argue that external rewards even encourage students to become more efficient learners. He argues that rewards simply motivate people to get more rewards.

But one thing we can all agree upon is that students are often not as deeply engaged in learning as we'd like them to be. With interesting, relevant curriculum and connections to kids' lives, maybe we won't have to worry about external rewards and other motivational gimmicks.

Internal Motivation

Most important, and certainly most long-lasting, is internal motivation. Internal, or intrinsic, motivation is fueled by curiosity, the desire for mastery, success, a sense of accomplishment, confidence in ability, a sense of ownership (choice), and other factors inside us. It's the motivation we are born with—a quality as basic as the urge to breathe. Intrinsic motivation is expressed as the love of learning for learning's sake. And sadly, it's a quality that many students have lost by the upper elementary grades.

"As both a parent and an educational psychologist, I have watched my two children start out with boundless love of learning, natural curiosity and motivation to learn and explore their worlds, and an initial excitement about school," writes Barbara McCombs. "What happened to their natural motivation to learn and the motivation of a growing number of our nation's schoolchildren?"

With that question in mind, McCombs has reviewed extensive studies of students' motivation to learn. She concludes that "it is necessary for teachers to see learners as naturally motivated to learn and learning as a psychological event that flourishes in fun, exciting, personally meaningful, and supportive environments." She stresses that teachers' understanding of this natural motivation is "key to promoting a depth and joy of learning for a lifetime."

Further, McCombs found that "[t]he support is overwhelmingly on the side of learner-centered practices that honor individual learner

---

EFFORT EQUALS OUTCOME

One way to cultivate internal motivation is to teach students to recognize the relationship between effort and outcome. Just spell it out. And model the effort-outcome link in your own actions. Don't assume students already understand the relationship.

Researcher Jere Brophy suggests portraying effort as investment rather than risk (for example, "Learning spelling words helps us read and write better"); portraying skill development as incremental ("We must learn several different skills that, together, enable us to do long division"); and focusing on mastery rather than normative comparisons ("We learn to read to enjoy a lifelong pleasure, not to be better than someone else").

---

perspectives and needs for competence, control, and belonging." She concludes, "We need to move beyond the perspective of 'motivating students' to fostering and enhancing the natural learning and motivation that exist in all of us."

Educational psychologist Jere Brophy of Michigan State University takes a different approach to internal motivation. Students who are internally motivated to learn approach learning tasks seriously, do them carefully, and expect to benefit from them, he says. This does not mean that they will always find learning tasks interesting or enjoyable, Brophy explains. Rather, they are convinced of the value of learning and believe it will directly benefit them.

Brophy points out that students can find academic activities pleasing and rewarding without being motivated to learn. For example, they can play a learning game in class and thoroughly enjoy its social or competitive aspects without thinking at all about what they are supposed to be learning. But teachers and

---

FROM THE STUDENT'S PERSPECTIVE

Researchers concerned with enhancing students' motivation to learn advocate listening to the advice of students themselves. Barbara McCombs reports that when students are asked what makes school a place where they want to learn, they list, among other things, learning activities that are relevant and fun, learning experiences that offer choice and require action, and opportunities to discuss personal meanings and values.

schools have obligations to teach specified content, says Brophy. His research on motivation currently focuses on helping students develop an appreciation for particular content areas and learning activities, independent of achievement or assessment goals (grades, for example).

The point is that you can design lessons and activities to capitalize on student interests, but that's not enough. The main goal of your motivational strategies must be to nurture students' motivation to learn. Students properly motivated are students who value knowledge and skills for their own sake. Such students become lifelong learners. As teachers, we can facilitate the process.

Leading by Example

Teachers can serve as important role models. If you let students see and hear your interest and motivation and communicate your expectations that students will enjoy learning, they'll pick up on the idea that learning is a pleasant activity, not a competitive or high-pressure one.

Presenting learning tasks in a positive way (and not by threatening that "You'll need this on the test" or "Your grade depends on this") capitalizes on students' innate motivation to learn. Here are some suggestions:

✔ Stress the value of the task by pointing out how knowledge and skills can bring pleasure and satisfaction.

✔ Personalize by expressing your beliefs, attitudes, or own experiences that illustrate the task's importance.

✔ Be enthusiastic by stating your liking for this type of task.

✔ State positive expectations by telling students you know they will enjoy the task and do well.

✔ Explain personal relevance by tying the task to students' lives and interests.

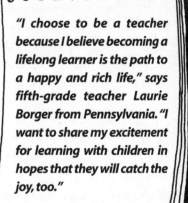

"I choose to be a teacher because I believe becoming a lifelong learner is the path to a happy and rich life," says fifth-grade teacher Laurie Borger from Pennsylvania. "I want to share my excitement for learning with children in hopes that they will catch the joy, too."

A Few Words on Praise

One external reward that many of us overuse is praise. We think we are building self-esteem or motivating students through encouragement when we praise. But the fact is, verbal praise is not often effective as a reward. It may even seem more like punishment to a child who is embarrassed or threatened by special attention. Delivered insincerely or inappropriately, praise does more harm than good.

Some ways of praising hide negative messages. Even if these messages are unintended, students can usually hear them loud and clear.

Suppose, for example, that you praise a child who has just stumbled her way through reading a passage out loud. You are trying to encourage the child, but she feels humiliated and wonders why you have just called attention to her poor performance.

Or you praise a student for completing an easy assignment. The student reasons that "any dummy could do this, so Teacher must really think I'm stupid." You're only trying to be kind. But you've just shot down the student's self-esteem another notch.

Further, there are hidden messages in the ways we praise girls and boys.

Studies show that we tend to praise girls more for matters of form (neatness, following directions, speaking clearly) and praise boys more for substance (academic performance and intellectual responses). The messages received from these types of praise are that boys are more capable than girls when it comes to academic tasks. Clearly, this is not the message we intend to send.

So user beware: Praise can undermine efforts to encourage or motivate if it's used inappropriately.

Based on extensive analyses, Jere Brophy concludes that praise is most effective when it is:

✔ sincere (spontaneous)

✔ delivered privately

✔ directed to noteworthy accomplishments

✔ specific

✔ focused on individual improvement and not compared to the accomplishments of others

✔ phrased to emphasize the accomplishment, not the teacher's role as authority or expert

Author and educator Bonnie Murray offers her own suggestion about praise. "I've discovered that it sometimes works well for students to have it written down," comments the Las Vegas teacher and author. "Sticky notes are great for that. I've had students who have kept certain notes I've written to them for the full year," Murray comments, adding that students occasionally pull out the written notes as "reminders that they have accomplished other difficult things and therefore can work through this problem, too."

Praise vs. Encouragement

Some prominent psychologists and educators make a distinction between praise and encouragement. It may seem to be a question of semantics, but those advocating "encouragement" make some strong points.

Whereas praise "always contains an element of judgment and evaluation," writes Timothy Evans, encouragement is positive feedback that focuses on effort or improvement rather than outcomes. Encouragement also focuses on strengths and assets, rather than a student's weaknesses or disabilities. "Encouragement is desperately needed

MOTIVATIONAL AND AFFECTIVE FACTORS AFFECTING LEARNING

Washington teacher Kathy Wesley expects all of her kindergartners to feel good about participating in class. To ensure that they do, she calls on all her students and makes no indication if their responses are correct or not. She simply thanks them and then says, "This is how you can get the answer . . . "

"By this time," Wesley reports, "everyone feels good because they have responded, but no one feels badly about not having been correct."

Wesley also asks a lot of open-ended, opinion-type questions and stresses that all of their answers are "right."

"I insist that I would rather have an incorrect answer than no answer," she says. "And it works. I have watched the most timid child eagerly wave her hand for a chance to give an answer."

Instructional practices like Wesley's create an encouraging learning environment where students are motivated to participate. The American Psychological Association has identified these additional factors affecting students' motivation to learn and achieve:

Motivational and emotional influences on learning

What and how much is learned is influenced by the learner's motivation. Motivation to learn, in turn, is influenced by the individual's emotional states, beliefs, interests and goals, and habits of thinking.

Intrinsic motivation to learn

The learner's creativity, higher-order thinking, and natural curiosity all contribute to motivation to learn. Intrinsic motivation is stimulated by tasks of optimal novelty and difficulty, relevant to personal interests, and providing for personal choice and control.

Effects of motivation on effort

Acquisition of complex knowledge and skills requires extended learner effort and guided practice. Without learners' motivation to learn, the willingness to exert this effort is unlikely without coercion.

Principles 6–9, "Learner-Centered Psychological Principles," summarized from the APA (American Psychological Association) Work Group of the Board of Educational Affairs, November 1997.

WHAT DO THEY SOUND LIKE?

Timothy Evans offers examples of encouragement, discouragement, and praise.

Encouragement vs.	Discouragement
"I think you can do it."	"Here, let me do that for you."
"You have what it takes."	"Be careful; it's dangerous."
"You're a hard worker."	"Don't forget your assignment."
"What do you think?"	"Let me give you some advice."
"I could use your help."	"When you're older, you can help."
"It looks like a problem occurred."	"I told you to be careful."

Encouragement vs.	Praise
"You put a lot of effort into your work."	"I'm proud of you when you do well."
"I know you did your best."	"Next time, if you work harder, I know you can get an A."

today," Evans asserts. "Children and teachers need encouragement like plants need water."

Based on his studies and the work of experts such as Don Dinkmeyer and Rudolf Dreikers, Evans notes five ways that teachers unintentionally discourage students:

✔ setting overambitious expectations or standards that overwhelm students

✔ focusing on mistakes to motivate

✔ comparing one student to another

✔ making pessimistic interpretations

✔ dominating students' learning experiences by helping too much

Karen Stephens, professor at Illinois State University and director of the university's child care center, also talks about the differences between praise and encouragement. "Sometimes children are so dependent on praise they won't perform without it," whereas encouragement helps children develop self-pride and internal motivation, she writes. Stephens says that encouragement, as opposed to praise, acknowledges effort toward an accomplishment, highlights ongoing efforts and self-discipline, and communicates faith in a child's abilities. Also, encouragement should be specific to the behavior or task. For example, encouragement could be, "You put all your books away. Now they won't get stepped on and torn. Way to be organized." Praise, on the other hand, tends to be general and value-laden: "You are such a good girl. You are a nice person."

Praise is important, but only in small, specific quantities, says Stephens. By encouraging children more than we praise them, she adds, we can shift the focus from "the need to please others to the importance of meeting personal goals and expectations."

Evans concludes that encouragement, "based on mutual respect and dignity and on focusing on a person's strengths," is "essential for creating a stimulating learning environment."

❖ Expectations

Teacher expectations can influence motivation, too. Our expectations about people influence our actions and attitudes toward those individuals, and they respond in kind. That's why expectations tend to become self-fulfilling prophecies.

It is easy to communicate the message that some students are winners and others are losers. Whom we call on, how long we wait for responses, and how we group students can all reveal our expectations.

"A careless remark, a misphrased question, or a facial expression unchallenged can result in negative expectations about self and learning," notes author Loyce Caruthers. "Through socialization in the home and the community, children learn of expectations for their lives." She adds that what children come to believe about themselves results from the messages from parents and other adults. "During the past two decades we have learned that teachers do, indeed, form expectations for student performance and that teacher expectations influence student performance."

If your expectations for students are high, chances are very good they will perform well. Unfortunately, the reverse is also true.

The Effect of Expectations

How are expectations translated into actions, either beneficial or harmful? How do we treat students unequally, based on our expectations? Try to avoid the following pitfalls, revealed by research:

✔ Teachers call more on those they think are most capable and give them more time to respond.

✔ Some teachers actually "shun" students labeled low achievers, offering little or no eye contact, praise, interaction, or opportunity to answer in class.

✔ Students perceived as low achievers receive less praise and more criticism.

✔ Teachers tend to stress conduct more than learning with low achievers.

✔ Attempting to encourage, teachers may praise low achievers for insignificant accomplishments or simple tasks; this may be interpreted by students as further proof the teacher thinks they're "dumb."

✔ Low achievers experience more rudeness, lack of interest, and inattentiveness from teachers.

✔ Low achievers are often physically separated from the rest of the class.

BUILDING GREAT EXPECTATIONS

Individual differences in ability certainly do exist, and these differences must be addressed. However, research has documented ways to communicate higher expectations, encourage better performance, and increase all students' opportunities to learn. Here are some suggestions:

- Ask yourself whether you are unfairly judging a student's ability based on reports from previous years, grades or test scores, or others' opinions.
- Consciously try to call on every student.
- Give students at least five seconds to respond.
- Rephrase questions or give clues to help a student respond.
- React positively to students' answers, either affirming them or correcting them.
- When students speak, make eye contact and listen to what they say.
- Try to give all students equal attention and opportunities for success.
- Downplay ability grouping by grouping students differently for various activities.
- Offer praise that is specific and sincere.
- Model the respect and courtesy you expect students to return.
- Show an interest in the lives and experiences of all your students, and be sensitive to their emotional needs.
- Encourage students to set goals for learning.

Students' Expectations

The effect of teacher expectations is magnified by students' expectations—for themselves and for their classmates. Students take their cues from teachers. If the teacher expects a student to do poorly, the student expects as much. So do his or her classmates. It is this mirroring effect that magnifies the power of expectations.

Students form expectations for classmates as early as kindergarten, where children of high ability can be heard making unkind remarks about the drawings and work of children with lower ability. In kindergarten, students first perceive others' expectations for them. They use these perceptions to develop a self-image.

How Expectations Develop

To break the vicious cycle of low expectations, it is important to understand how they develop.

Expectations are frequently associated with a student's cultural or racial background, gender, or socioeconomic status. Teachers and parents "know," for example, that girls are more verbal than boys, or that boys are more aggressive than girls.

Our expectations are also influenced by the labels assigned to students, comments from previous teachers, and grades or standardized test scores.

Reading ability is another critical factor. Stanford University professor emerita Elizabeth Cohen claims that our entire education system is misguidedly based on the notion of reading ability as the sole indicator of intelligence. Cohen explains that teachers assume good readers will be competent in any content area, and that those with poor reading ability will do poorly on any task. Cohen's ideas certainly apply in the case of gifted students who can't read or read poorly due to learning disabilities. Before these students' special gifts are discovered (if they ever are!), they are placed in remedial classes and are expected to be low achieving.

To counteract negative expectations, Cohen and others advocate cooperative learning and small group work designed to highlight the talents and abilities of all children. Using each other as resources, students in small groups work on tasks that require multiple abilities and ensure that each student makes an important intellectual contribution. Expectations increase when students realize that everyone has something important to contribute—something vital to group success.

❖ Differentiated Instruction

Among teaching strategies that foster and nurture students' motivation to learn, differentiated instruction heads the list.

"Differentiation is about meeting individual needs in the context of best-practice instruction," explains Carol Ann Tomlinson, guru of differentiated instruction from the University of Virginia.

In a world of diverse learners, differentiation is an approach that makes sense, an approach that facilitates learning and motivates children to become lifelong learners, regardless of ability level, learning style, or interests. Differentiation is less a "strategy" than a philosophy of meeting kids where they are and taking them where they need to go. It's the philosophy behind other strategies described later in this chapter, such as teaching to multiple intelligences, group work, using a project approach, integrating subjects, giving students choices, and so on. Students learn the same essential skills and content, just in different ways and degrees.

"Students can take different roads to the same destination," says Tomlinson. And that, in a nutshell, is differentiation.

How do effective teachers differentiate instruction?

First, says Tomlinson, they must have solid curriculum in place. "Differentiation is not so much the 'stuff' as the 'how,'" she explains. That's why differentiation can fit well with standards-based instruction. The standards are the "stuff," and the differentiation is the "how."

"A lot of the standards-based teaching is dreadful stuff—cramming lists of skills and facts into kids so that maybe they can burp them back on a test," says Tomlinson. "But if you organize the standards as concept umbrellas, if you can help kids discover patterns, answer essential questions, and organize their thinking, then it's more likely that the standards will be useful instead of defeating," she continues. "Concepts, as contrasted with facts, give us a much sounder footing on which to differentiate."

Tomlinson notes that differentiation provides students with options in exploring the curricular content—options such as multiple texts, supplementary materials, learning and interest centers, independent learning contracts, group investigations, computer programs, assignments with varying levels of complexity, and evaluations accounting for a range of abilities.

Differentiation can take many different forms, as the following sections illustrate. But the goal is always the same: meeting the unique needs of diverse learners. Another constant, Tomlinson stresses, is "teacher clarity about what students should know, understand, and be able to do" as a result of the instruction. (See the resources section at the end of this chapter for more on differentiated instruction.)

❖ Framing Group Work: Complex Instruction

One way to differentiate instruction effectively for students is to make sure they have opportunities to each participate fully as a member of a learning group. To help teachers design meaningful group work in heterogeneous classrooms where students vary so much in achievement, proficiency in the language of instruction, and social status, Elizabeth Cohen and her colleagues at Stanford University developed a strategy called Complex Instruction. This strategy helps students develop higher-order thinking skills and group problem-solving skills, Cohen explains, and it gives diverse students equal access to learning opportunities.

Complex Instruction (CI) has three major components:

1. **A multiple-ability curriculum** that organizes group work around a central concept or big idea. Students work interdependently to solve open-ended tasks. The tasks require a wide array of intellectual abilities so that each student can make a meaningful contribution.
2. **Student-managed groups.** Teachers train students to use cooperative strategies and play specific roles. Teachers observe groups carefully, and they provide feedback.
3. **Treating status problems** that cause unequal participation. Some students who are "social isolates" or are perceived by others as less able participate less, and

thus, learn less. To remedy this, teachers use strategies to broaden perceptions of what it means to be smart. It is the teacher's role to convince students that they each have important intellectual contributions to make to the multiple-ability task.

Group Work Works

According to Cohen, the more students talk and work together in CI, the more they learn. She notes that research documents significant achievement gains in classrooms using this approach.

There are other benefits, too, as Vancouver teacher Helen Hait discovered.

"Group work is a key structure in supporting and building a community in the process of learning and growing together," says Hait. After carefully observing group work in action with her fifth and sixth graders, Hait is absolutely sold on the idea. She points out, however, that students must be taught how to work together.

"Although group work with this class resulted in more altercations, rudeness with each other, arguing, and other inappropriate interactions," Hait notes, "it was through these social situations that training in proper responses to each other was facilitated. The students worked very hard at learning polite and respectful ways of interacting." She, adds how thrilled she was with their progress in helping each other more, using respectful words and voice tones, demonstrating care toward each other, and monitoring their own tendencies to criticize each other.

Just as Hait worked hard to establish an equitable situation in which each student made valued intellectual contributions, Cohen stresses this need for teachers to intervene to overcome "status differences" among children that impede learning. It's not easy, but it's certainly worth it! (For more information on Complex Instruction and the schools using it, visit www.stanford.edu/group/pci.)

❖ Teaching to Multiple Intelligences

Just as we now recognize that people learn in different ways and employ different learning styles, we also know that there are different ways of being smart. Harvard psychologist Howard Gardner has identified at least eight intelligences: bodily-kinesthetic, interpersonal, intrapersonal, logical-mathematical, musical, linguistic, spatial, and naturalist. Other scholars label these intelligences somewhat differently, but most agree on the concept of multiple intelligences. Further, most agree that while we are "naturally" good in some areas, we can learn to be better in others.

The implications for schools are enormous.

First, by focusing so heavily on the verbal and mathematical intelligences, schools have failed to recognize the abilities of many students. These are the students typically earning the "average" or "below average" or even "learning-disabled" labels.

Second, schooling that ignores these other important types of intelligence denies all students the chance to increase their abilities and develop their weaker areas. As Gardner and others point out, children possess a combination of intelligences, and they are capable of growth in all areas.

What does this mean for practice?

Many teachers are restructuring the curriculum and putting the intelligences to work in their classrooms. For example, sixth-grade teacher Kristen Nelson has developed a unit that introduces the concept of multiple abilities and has created learning centers (she calls them "flow areas") that allow students to explore the different intelligences.

"The biggest impact that the Multiple Intelligences Theory has had in my classroom is that it has helped me create an individualized learning environment," writes Nelson. "I no longer expect students to think exactly alike in order to be right. . . . I am more comfortable with my students' individualistic thinking—and my own. In personalizing each student's education experience, I find that an increasing percentage of students discover their own strengths, put more effort into improving their weaker areas, and feel better about themselves."

As a mentor teacher on multiple intelligences in her California district, Nelson works with teachers and students grades K through 6 and claims that even the youngest children understand that there are different ways of being smart.

In structuring her introductory unit on the eight intelligences, Nelson first brainstorms with students about what it means to be smart. She points out that reading, writing, and math skills certainly help them succeed in school, but that these skills aren't the only important ones. She talks about famous people who did poorly in school but used their "other" intelligences to become highly successful (Albert Einstein and Pablo Picasso, for example). She also gives the students many examples of skills, activities, and professions in each of the intelligences. (See the reproducible on page 109 for examples.)

After this lesson introducing the various intelligences, Nelson spends a separate day on each one. Students undertake activities in each area and spend time discussing famous people, historical figures, and book characters who exemplify each intelligence. (You could invite guest speakers—parents and community members—representing each intelligence area to describe various professions and provide a personal testimonial to the importance of each area.)

To give her students the chance actually to explore and develop their eight areas of intelligence, Nelson sets up flow areas (or learning centers). Ideas for these flow areas are as limitless as your imagination. Here are a few that Nelson finds successful:

1. **Linguistic**: Set up a language lab with cassette player and tapes, earphones, and talking books. After students write a poem or story, encourage them to tape it and share it with others.

2. **Logical-Mathematical**: Set up a math lab with manipulatives, calculators, and objects to measure and graph. You could also include 3-D puzzles and brainteasers.

3. **Spatial**: Include art activities of any kind. Or create an architecture center where kids can draw floor plans with the aid of rulers, pencils, and large sheets of paper.

4. **Bodily-Kinesthetic**: Create an open space for juggling, learning dances, or staging dramatic performances.

5. **Musical**: Set up a music lab where students can compare and contrast different musical styles and periods. Or encourage students to compose their own music.

6. **Interpersonal**: Provide a round table to encourage student discussions. You can suggest topics, or they can come up with their own. Another idea is to give a group of students a common school-related problem that they must discuss to come up with solutions.

7. **Intrapersonal**: Ask students to draw a picture that expresses their current mood or feeling. Encourage them to express themselves in journals. Ask children to list ten strengths or ten ways that they are a good friend.

8. **Naturalist**: Ask children to observe a bird feeder or feeding station set up outside a classroom window. They could identify and record the types and numbers of birds visiting the feeder. They could also track the growth of classroom plants, or identify the types of rocks found outside the school.

All year long, Nelson incorporates multiple-intelligence activities into her lesson plans, allowing students to build on their strengths and improve in their weak areas. For example, she might encourage a student who is a visual learner and strong in spatial intelligence to draw a picture about a story before attempting to write about it. She suggests that students choose an intelligence area and complete a one- to two-week project in that area.

To get a better handle on your students' multiple intelligences, take a look at your own. What are your strengths and weaknesses, and how does your teaching reflect them? You can answer this by looking at the activities in your

Student Strengths

You may wish to make note of students who fit these descriptions. Most students will fall into more than one category so you'll want to avoid rigid categorizing.

Intelligence Area	Is Strong In	Likes To	Learns Best Through	Famous Examples	Common Misbehaviors
Linguistic	Reading, writing, telling stories, memorizing dates, thinking in words	Read, write, tell stories, talk, memorize, do word puzzles	Reading, hearing, and seeing words; speaking; writing; discussions	T. S. Eliot, Maya Angelou, Abraham Lincoln	Passing notes, reading during lessons
Logical/Mathematical	Math, reasoning, logic, problem solving, patterns	Solve problems, question, reason, experiment, use computers	Working with patterns classifying, abstract thinking	Albert Einstein, John Dewey	Working on math or building things during lessons
Spatial	Reading, maps, charts, drawing, puzzles, imagining things, visualization	Design, draw, build, create, daydream, look at pictures	Working with pictures and colors, visualizing, drawing	Pablo Picasso, Frank Lloyd Wright, Georgia O'Keeffe, Bobby Fischer	Doodling, drawing, daydreaming
Bodily/Kinesthetic	Athletics, dancing, acting, crafts, using tools	Play sports, dance, move around, touch and talk, use body language	Touching, moving, processing knowledge through bodily sensations	Charlie Chaplin, Michael Jordan, Martha Graham	Fidgeting, wandering around the room
Musical	Singing, picking up sounds, remembering melodies, rhythms	Sing, hum, play an instrument, listen to music	Rhythm, melody, singing, listening to music and melodies	Leonard Bernstein, Wolfgang Amadeus Mozart, Ella Fitzgerald	Tapping pencil or feet
Interpersonal	Leading, organizing, communicating, resolving conflicts	Have friends, talk to people, join groups	Sharing, comparing, relating, interviewing, cooperating	Mohandas Gandhi, Ronald Reagan, Mother Teresa	Talking, passing notes
Intrapersonal	Understanding self, recognizing strengths and weaknesses, setting goals	Work alone, reflect, pursue interests	Working alone, self-paced projects, reflecting	Eleanor Roosevelt, Sigmund Freud, Thomas Merton	Conflicting with others
Naturalist	Distinguishing, classifying, using features of the environment	Name and describe things, identify relationships among things such as human actions and effects on the environment	Understanding where items or ideas fit in a hierarchy or schema, observing the natural world	John James Audubon, Roger Tory Peterson, Charles Darwin	Staring out the window, skipping school to go fishing or hunting

Adapted from *Developing Students' Multiple Intelligences* by Kristen Nicholson-Nelson. © 1998 by Kristen Nicholson-Nelson. Used by permission of Scholastic Inc.

lesson plans and writing the name of the corresponding intelligence type beside each. You can also take the learning styles test on page 62. Try teaming up with teachers who have different strengths from yours. They can offer ideas and strategies in areas that you have yet to develop.

This idea of multiple intelligences is really not all that radical or new. Haven't you known teachers, maybe yourself included, who have claimed for years that every child is gifted in some way? And doesn't this sound like a great way to individualize learning? Gardner's Theory of Multiple Intelligences simply supports what wise practitioners have known all along: A teacher's job is to recognize the strengths of each student and provide opportunities to improve weaknesses.

❖ Giving Children Choices

In classrooms from preschool to college, teachers are discovering an obvious but revolutionary idea: Students who are given choices in what and how they learn will learn more and have a better attitude about it. Without choices, children "burn out" just as adults do, says writer and consultant Alfie Kohn. They perceive themselves as powerless and respond with apathy or aggression.

"What is disturbing about students' attitudes and behavior may be a function of the fact that they have little to say about what happens to them all day long," Kohn asserts. "They are compelled to follow someone else's rules, study someone else's curriculum, and submit continually to someone else's evaluation.

"Deprive them of self-determination," Kohn writes, "and you have likely deprived them of motivation."

Student choice is a key component of learner-centered approaches to education. It's the hallmark of authentic assessment. And it's a strategy that works, according to experienced teachers, researchers, and other experts.

It's a question of control. When we feel that we have control over our lives, we feel happier, produce more, and even live longer. Research shows that this need for self-determination is as important for children as it is for adults.

Achievement improves, too. Kohn reports that second graders in Pittsburgh completed more learning tasks in less time when given choices such as which tasks they would work on at which time. Preschoolers in Massachusetts worked more creatively than others when they were permitted to select the materials they wanted to use in making a collage. Second graders developed more sophisticated reasoning and thinking skills when they worked in groups to figure out their own solutions to problems and had the freedom to choose the materials they needed.

Other studies show that students who are given choices about their schoolwork score higher on achievement tests and persist longer on difficult or uninteresting tasks.

"There is no question about it," Kohn concludes. "Even if our only criterion is academic performance, choice works."

> *"As a general rule, it is more important for children to have the chance to generate different possibilities than merely to select one possibility from among those that have been set before them."*
>
> **Alfie Kohn**

LITERATURE CIRCLES

Literature circles provide an excellent opportunity for student choice. As expert Harvey Daniels explains, literature circles are small, temporary discussion groups organized by students' choice of reading material, not ability levels. Although the strategy varies from classroom to classroom, all literature circles share three basic elements: diversity, self-choice, and student initiative. Literature circles give students the power to select what they will read and discuss. They also provide opportunities for students to interpret what they read in cooperative groups. (Read more about literature circles in Chapter Four).

Four Types of Choices

There are four aspects to academic decisions that students can make, according to Kohn: *what* to learn, *how* to learn it, *how well*, and *why*.

The *what* is anything from choices about literature to choices about which mammal to study in a science unit. Individual research projects are another perfect opportunity for student choices. Even when you select the unit of study, says Kohn, give students choices within the general topic to be studied. He suggests beginning any unit by inviting students to discuss what they already know about the topic and then what they would like to learn more about. This is a great opportunity to use graphic organizers, descriptions and examples of which are included later in this chapter (see page 129).

How a student learns includes decisions about individual or group work, whether information is obtained from print sources or through interviews, whether the student sits at a desk or lies on the floor to work, and so on.

The *how well* aspect involves assessment and evaluation. "Students ought to help determine the criteria by which their work will be judged and then play a role in weighing their work against those criteria," Kohn claims. "Students can derive enormous intellectual benefits from thinking about what makes a story interesting, a mathematical proof elegant, or an argument convincing," he continues. Even with traditional tests, we can give students choices about what the test should cover and when they should take it.

Finally, students need to talk about *why* they are learning something. How is it connected to their lives? What will their new knowledge contribute? "There may be no better use of classroom time than a sustained conversation following someone's challenge: 'Why do we gotta do this stuff?'"

Barriers to Choice

Giving students choices can be a little bit intimidating, and many of us resist. After all, shouldn't we be in control of the classroom? How can students possibly know what's best for

TEACHING TIP

Try to give your students at least one opportunity each day to decide what to do. The choices might include reading a book, creating artwork, writing in a journal, asking for special help on something they don't understand, going to the library, or using the classroom computers.

them or do the "right" thing? Kohn argues that teacher control undermines academic motivation. It replaces the natural excitement learners experience when they can be self-directed. Only when student participation is valued above adult control, says Kohn, do students have the chance to learn self-control.

Our job is to teach students to make responsible choices and take control of their own learning and behavior. And the choices students make must be real ones. "More than once," says Kohn, "I have heard teachers pride themselves on letting students choose 'when I don't really care what they end up with'—which is, of course, a far cry from a democratic process that helps students to become responsible decision makers."

Ironically, students often resist the relinquishing of teacher control even more than teachers do. After years of being conditioned to play a passive role, students who are suddenly expected to make academic decisions may simply refuse to do so, may offer outrageous or inappropriate suggestions just to see if the teacher is really serious, or may simply offer suggestions they think teachers want to hear. At this point, it may be tempting to give up or conclude that students just can't handle responsibility for their own learning. "But our challenge is to persevere," says Kohn.

"Specifically, the comment 'That's your job' provides a teachable moment, a chance to engage students in conversations about their experiences with being controlled and about when they have found learning to be most exciting."

Special Considerations

As experts concur, children need adult guidance as they learn to make good choices. Certainly children need limits and rules, but who sets them? In classrooms where student choices and opinions are valued, children and adults determine the rules (behavioral or academic) *together*.

Of course, we must make allowances for age. Very young children need more guidance and practice than older children in making good choices. But *all* children need to learn to make decisions, and if we wait until they are "mature enough," we will deprive them of the experiences that help them develop good decision-making skills.

Further, children must learn to account for how their decisions affect others. "What must occasionally be restricted," says Kohn, "is not choice, but *individual* choice." Children must learn the importance of community when they make their choices, and that "it is the integration of these two values, community and choice, that defines democracy."

What Will *You* Choose?

Ask yourself some tough questions when you plan for a new school year: Do you respect children as individuals with specific preferences and points of view? Do you believe that students have the right to express their points of view? Are you trying to foster independence? Do you want your students to take risks and make good decisions?

If your answer to these questions is yes, then make student choices a major aspect of your classroom and curriculum.

❖ The Project Approach

Student choice is a main component of an instructional and motivational strategy known as the Project Approach.

Early-childhood expert Lilian Katz, former professor at the University of Illinois, defines a true project as "an in-depth investigation of a topic worth learning more about." Working individually, in small groups, or as a whole class, students ask questions that guide the project, and they make decisions about activities that will help them find the answers to their questions.

While younger students may need more teacher guidance than those able to read and write independently, "Project work provides a context for taking initiative and assuming responsibility, making decisions and choices, and pursuing interests," Katz writes.

Katz describes three distinct phases of a project: getting started, fieldwork, and culminating and debriefing events.

Getting Started

Here, a topic is proposed (by students or teacher), and the class spends several brainstorming sessions selecting and refining the topic. Students recall their previous knowledge about the topic, pose questions, and

---

Here are some of the benefits of student-driven project work and those of teacher-driven systematic instruction. It is important to keep the learning outcomes you want in focus as you select an approach to each component of your instruction.

PROJECT WORK

1. Provides opportunities to apply skills
2. Addresses students' proficiencies
3. Stresses intrinsic motivation
4. Encourages students to determine what to work on and accepts them as experts about their needs

SYSTEMATIC INSTRUCTION

1. Helps students acquire skills
2. Addresses learning deficiencies
2. Stresses extrinsic motivation
4. Allows teachers to direct students' work, use their expertise, and specify learning tasks

---

identify subtopics. A web or concept map helps to organize and record these brainstorming sessions.

Katz suggests that a project topic should meet several important criteria:

✔ The topic should be closely related to everyday experience. Students should know enough about the topic to be able to raise good questions about it.

✔ The topic should allow for integrating such subjects as science, social studies, math, and language arts.

✔ The topic should be "rich" enough to allow at least a week's worth of exploration.

✔ The topic should be more suitable for examination in school than at home.

Fieldwork

After the first phase of the project, the fieldwork or direct investigation begins. Here students can explore, observe, draw, write, construct models, take field trips, predict, test predictions, interview experts, record findings, present findings, discuss, and sometimes, dramatize findings or new knowledge.

Culminating and Debriefing Events

In the final phase, students prepare and present the knowledge they've gained. These presentations might be visual displays of findings and artifacts, dramatic presentations, discussions and talks, or explanations of models.

Lilian Katz stresses that project work complements the formal, systematic aspects of the curriculum, and that both project work and systematic instruction have an important role to play in the classroom. She compares the major features of both in the chart on page 112.

The project approach combines the best of effective teaching practices: student choice, subject matter integration, inquiry-based learning, authentic assessment, cooperative learning, real-world connections, accommodating multiple intelligences and

"ALL ABOUT BALLS"

Lilian Katz offers the example of a project undertaken by a kindergarten class on a common object: balls. Students brought to school as many balls as they could find—31 kinds in all, including gumballs, cotton balls, globes, and an American football (is it really a ball?).

The teacher recorded what the students wanted to find out about balls, and the children then formed subgroups to examine questions they had identified, including: surface texture, circumference, and material composition. Each group displayed and reported its findings.

Next, the students made predictions about the balls and tested their predictions, based on these questions:

• Which balls would be the heaviest and which the lightest?
• How was weight related to circumference?
• Which balls would bounce the highest?
• After rolling down an inclined plane, which balls would roll the farthest on grass or gravel surfaces?

After these scientific investigations, the class discussed various types of ball games and how balls are thrown or struck by hands, feet, bats, clubs, mallets, racquets.

Katz points out that this compelling project motivated the kindergarten students to apply and practice such skills as drawing, measuring, writing, reading, listening, and discussing. Also, their vocabulary expanded as they thoroughly explored these familiar objects.

learning styles, and more. It also ties curriculum more closely to recent research on the brain, which reveals that our brains are most stimulated and most effective in a rich, varied, multisensory "jungle-like" environment.

A Project on Rocks

From Dot Schuler and 21 second graders at Grafton Elementary in Grafton, Illinois, and Dr. Eileen Borgia of Illinois State University

1 PHASE

Starting Out To begin the project on rocks, Dot made a web to become aware of her own knowledge of rocks and to brainstorm the different avenues of investigation that the children might pursue in their study of rocks.

A letter was sent to parents, explaining the project and requesting that each child bring in a collection of rocks in an egg carton or ice-cube tray. The letter included an invitation to families, relatives, and friends to share their expertise on rocks.

On the first day, Dot told three personal stories about rocks and invited students to think of personal events that involved rocks. She suggested thinking about famous rocks that they had visited, games played with rocks, jewelry or other things made of rocks, a special rock that they like, or a special place they like to go to look for rocks.

The children shared, discussed, and wrote about their previous experiences with rocks.

2 PHASE

Experimentation and Investigation Phase 2 began with planning a field trip to the hills adjacent to the school. For about a week after the trip, students investigated the rocks they had collected in activity centers. They painted memories; dictated stories; graphed the number of rocks in each student's collection; categorized rocks; and made Venn diagrams, comparing and contrasting the lower hill to the upper hill.

Three experts visited: an environmental educator, a geologist, and a garden hobbyist who helped the children make a rock garden in a transparent sphere.

Later, the children conducted experiments to determine various properties of rocks. They used balance scales and gram weights for weighing; magnifying glasses to determine luster and finer detail; water for buoyancy and absorption; magnets to test for metals; plastic, pennies, and nails to test for hardness; and vinegar to test for calcite. They recorded their findings on rock and mineral charts.

This formal experimentation was followed by other investigations. Two different groups interviewed people in the school. One group asked what rocks are made of; the other asked what rocks are used for. These interviews were documented with photographs and displayed on posters.

Josh wanted to find out how rocks change, and froze a rock in a cup of water. He also froze plain water in a vial with a lid. He observed that the water in the vial "higher-upped." His discovery was recorded in a flow chart. Actually, the rock made no changes, so he speculated that it takes much time for changes to occur. He also changed the shape and size of two pieces of sandstone by rubbing them together.

Another group planted lima bean seeds in a clear glass and then poured plaster of paris over the top. The question was, Can the seed grow through the rock? Another group made a papier-

A Project on Rocks (continued)

mâché model of a volcano. They also made a diagram to represent the ground underneath the volcano. Another team made a papier-mâché model of Devil's Tower, a National Monument in Wyoming that one of the children had visited. Sue and Kim created a puppet show. Others made a rock from plaster of paris mixed with other small rocks.

Two children were in charge of transforming our wall into a bluff, with the assistance of one of their fathers! Cinquain poems were mounted on papier-mâché rocks to be placed at the bottom of the bluff.

Throughout the project, reading, writing, dialogue through journals, and discussions about the investigations helped the children share their knowledge and experiences. Children often chose to stay and work in lieu of afternoon recess. Parents and members of the community were hearing about the project from the children, and occasionally sent in an object, a picture, or an offer to help.

PHASE 3 **In Closing** By early April, after almost two months, we sensed that the children were growing tired of their study of rocks and it was time to enter Phase 3 and bring the project to a close. The beautiful three-dimensional bluff, complete with paper vines, trees, small rocks, an occasional bird, a cave at the bottom, and houses on top, was the focal point of their final display. In Nicky's words, "It was something for people to remember." Invitations were sent to parents,

colleagues, and the community. Parents volunteered to provide refreshments.

Posters explained each experiment. Each team kept a "boulder folder" during the project, and all of our representations (stories, poems, activities) were stored there. Each team selected work samples for the display, making sure that each child contributed at least two finished products. Children's paintings and writings adorned all the walls. The class produced a puppet show on rocks. The volcano "erupted" many times, to the delight of the guests. With "rock" and roll music softly playing in the background, students heard many positive comments.

"A Project on Rocks" by Dot Schuler and her class of second-graders at Grafton Elementary School, Grafton, Illinois and Eileen Borgia, Illinois State University. Reprinted by permission of the authors.

The Iditarod Project

From Kim Bierly and 28 fourth graders in Oak Harbor, Washington

1 PHASE

Preliminary Planning This topic emerged from a read-aloud I shared with the class. I was reading *Woodsong* by Gary Paulsen. The class was studying the Midwest, and this autobiographical story took place in Minnesota. The author primarily wrote about his Northwoods dog-sledding experiences and his participation in Alaska's Iditarod race. In my classroom observation/reflection journal I wrote:

"The Iditarod! I absolutely love reading aloud Gary Paulsen's book *Woodsong*. I love his frank and descriptive style; I relate to his perspectives on nature. And, I love his relationships with his dogs and dogsledding. The dog stories have really captured the kids. We, the kids and I, are experiencing a mutual passion for this book. I want to go deeper with the dogs and the Iditarod. I asked how many kids knew what the Iditarod was, and more than two-thirds of them raised their hands. I was surprised. But, how much do they know? I truly am curious . . .

"Something is feeling different here for me . . . my excitement about this topic is charged and deep. The class has been infected with my enthusiasm, and I want to go somewhere with it."

The next day I asked students to brainstorm in their journals what they knew about the Iditarod. While most had heard of the race,

few really knew anything about it. As students shared what they knew, questions started to come up. We created a topic web.

At home I found photo slides of friends who used to dogsled in northern Minnesota (where *Woodsong* took place). I found the Iditarod home page on the Internet and discovered we could cover the race with current updates on a daily basis. I discovered I could order an "Iditarod for the Classroom" packet that included background information on the race, musher biographies, a video, a dog bootie, a map of Alaska with the race trail, and sample letter envelopes the mushers traveled with. I also contacted some friends in Anchorage who said they would send newspapers when the race started. I let parents know about our study in a weekly letter home.

As we waited for materials to arrive, we continued to read *Woodsong*, getting some of our questions answered by the author. I shared my photo slides with the class and told Minnesota and dog stories.

Concerns addressed during phase 1

- What were the students' prior experiences with the Iditarod and dogsledding?
- What did the kids know about the Iditarod and dogsledding?
- What resources could I locate for the classroom?

- How could I inform parents about our study?

2 PHASE

Tapping Into Resources About one week prior to the actual race, we watched a video about the previous year's race. This brought a real-life sense to the race as well as visuals. The students could see and hear from mushers. They could see actual dogsled teams and dogs. They could hear the discussion of dog types, sled types, and racing strategies. Questions on our topic web were answered, and new questions were generated. Books arrived, and students started reading and sharing aloud. Students studied musher biographies and started selecting mushers they wanted to root for. Posters were made, and debates occurred over who was most likely to win and why. We followed the different racers with pins on a map.

Then the race began! An Internet team went up to the one Internet computer at our school on a daily basis to pull up race

The Iditarod Project (continued)

results. These results were used to fill out information on a race statistics chart on our bulletin board. Math problems were generated from race statistics and information.

Each day students eagerly awaited race updates. I also taped TV news and radio news updates. Newspapers were also arriving from my friends in Alaska, and students pored over articles.

One racer favored by many students was disqualified because one of his dogs died. This led to in-depth and heated discussions on whether the death was the racer's fault, the importance of making wise decisions and the resulting consequences, humane animal treatment, animal rights, and rule fairness. As the race was nearing its end, I asked the class to reflect on what we did and learned during this study.

We generated a list, constantly referring to our web to see what questions we could answer. I then asked how could we share this with parents at conference time. One student suggested that each student take part of the list (as we did for a novel study—a prior experience she was drawing on), write about it, and draw pictures or make a model to go with the writing. We adopted this format.

Concerns addressed during phase 2

• How can the children visually experience the Iditarod when it is happening in Alaska?

• How can the children keep updated on the actual race and experience it in real time?
• What resources can be introduced into the classroom for the kids to learn more from?
• What, and how, can they represent what we did and learned?
• How to assess their learning and what is important to assess?

 **Closing the Study** Student projects and what we learned were displayed on a bulletin board during an open-house night just prior to third-quarter conferences. Projects were primarily written reports and illustrations that reflected answers to questions raised during our brainstorm sessions. Some student-generated questions included:

• How do we cover the Iditarod?
• Where does the Iditarod take place in Alaska?
• How did the Iditarod get started?
• What does the word *Iditarod* mean?
• What happens if a dog gets hurt or dies?
• Who are the mushers?
• What kinds of dogs are sled dogs?

Besides written reports and illustrations, some students chose to share musher information in the form of large sports-type cards that included background information as well as race statistic information about their musher. One group shared what students learned about different types of sled dogs in a "television" documentary presentation. Some students drew maps tracing out and labeling the race route.

Along with student work, I posted photographs showing students engaged in various phases of the study. During the open house, students shared the bulletin-board display with their parents.

Concerns addressed during phase 3
• How can we bring this study to a close?
• How do we share our study with parents?

Excerpts from "The Iditarod Project" reprinted by permission of Kim L. Bierly.

❖ Theme Studies

One technique that Missouri teacher Penny Strube employs to motivate her fourth-grade students is theme studies.

Using a project approach, Strube has her students conduct independent studies on topics of their choice.

"Children have a choice in every aspect of the study," Strube explains. They choose what they want to know about a topic, activities and methods of gathering information, the nature and contents of the finished product, and deadlines for completing the study.

With theme studies, the students' roles change, and so does the teacher's. The teacher no longer acts as the provider of information to students, who are passive recipients. Instead, "The classroom becomes one big research laboratory with the teacher as head researcher," Strube explains. Of course, teachers need to align study topics and activities with state standards and objectives, as they do with any curricular strategy.

A Close-Up Look

Penny Strube shares the theme study she and her students developed on the topic of oceans. In planning the unit, she developed a "web of possibilities." Careful planning is necessary, but "be ready to handle the unexpected avenues that the children wish to pursue in their learning process," Strube cautions.

Next, she developed learning centers focusing on the theme of oceans, including the Columbus bulletin board, the whale center, the ship center, the shell center, and the living nature (aquarium) center. "Learning centers need to cater to the children's senses in order to motivate their learning," Strube suggests. These centers, which are constantly changing and evolving with the students' contributions, allow students to touch, observe, research, and discover.

After the students have experienced the learning centers and explored the various resources Strube collects for them, the class brainstorms to develop a list of "What We Want to Know" questions. This is where the students take charge of their learning and identify the topics that motivate and interest

---

ONE VETERAN'S PERSONAL PHILOSOPHY

After many years of experience, Penny Strube has fine-tuned her beliefs about how students learn best. This philosophy has led her to replace a standard text-driven curriculum with theme studies. Here's what experience has taught her:

1. Students learn by doing.
2. They learn through the help of their peers.
3. They are motivated to learn when they are given a choice.
4. Learning takes place when there is a purpose.
5. Students increase their knowledge when they share it.
6. They are ultimately responsible for their own learning.

---

them. Of course, as a member of the learning community, the teacher contributes ideas and questions, too. (See list of possible ocean topics to explore on page 119.)

This list, which continues to grow and evolve throughout the study, becomes the impetus for the individual choices the students make about which particular area they want to focus on. In the ocean study, for example, a child could choose to research a particular marine animal, investigate how pollution is affecting oceans, focus on sunken treasure, or discover how ancient sailors navigated the seas.

After they've made their individual choices, the students decide which activities they'll undertake in their investigations—how to collect and later present the information they're seeking. Strube stresses that it's also important at this point to agree upon deadlines and due dates. "Along with the privilege of choice," she notes, "comes the awesome responsibility of meeting the common goals."

The Benefits of Theme Study

In addition to its role as a natural motivator, building on students' interests and choices, theme study offers other important benefits.

One is the chance to individualize learning and opportunities for each student. Few would dispute the effectiveness of interacting one-on-one with students on a project geared to their abilities and interests.

Further, theme studies cut across curricular areas and activities, so they provide opportunities for students to discover relationships and connections. Strube relates the incident of one of her students making the accidental discovery that the San Francisco 49ers football team got their name from the gold rush of 1849. "That one connection stimulated many new connections among the students that had never crossed their minds," she explains. "The class had identified a new key to understanding the world around them. They had a new perspective on unlocking the mysteries of knowledge through the idea of making connections."

Student choice is involved in every aspect of Penny Strube's theme studies, including this one on oceans. After brainstorming topics and deciding how they will demonstrate new knowledge, students develop a chart like this one to guide the study.

OCEANS

THINGS WE WANT TO KNOW ABOUT

1. Movement—waves, tides, currents
2. Description—how many, how deep, size, location, type of water
3. Sailors—Vikings, Columbus
4. Maps—different kinds, mapmakers, symbols, continents
5. Sea life—food, enemies, level they live on, habits, how they move, protection
6. Pollution—causes, effects
7. Storms—kinds, how formed, damage they cause
8. Sunken ships—famous, treasure, divers, reasons for sinking

THINGS I WILL PUT IN MY REPORT

1. Title page
2. Table of contents
3. Maps—oceans, continents, explorers' routes, ancient maps
4. Illustrations—ships, people, treasure, sea life
5. Cover

HOW I WILL DO MY REPORT

1. Use three sources—encyclopedia, magazine, trade book
2. Make a web of my notes
3. Write sentences for each bubble of my web
4. Put my sentences in paragraphs (ROUGH DRAFT)
5. Conference with my teacher
6. Write my final draft

And perhaps most importantly, theme studies can lead to a passion for lifelong learning.

"I believe that the most important thing I can instill in my students is the idea that learning is exciting, enjoyable, and something they can possess and cherish throughout an entire lifetime," writes Strube. "Theme study makes learning synonymous with 'exciting,' 'enjoyable,' 'interesting,' and 'lifelong.'"

❖ Integrating Subjects

Combining different subjects into multipurpose lessons is not a new idea. But there is renewed interest in this instructional strategy as teachers struggle to cover a wide range of academic content, meet state standards, teach writing and thinking processes, and meet the individual needs of each learner.

There are many good reasons to integrate subject matter into multipurpose lessons:

✔ Through integrated lessons, students learn the interrelatedness and interdependence of knowledge. Math skills help them solve science problems. Reading and listening skills keep them informed of current events.

✔ Subject-matter integration saves time, allowing teachers to cover two or three subjects in less time than it would take to teach them separately.

✔ Multipurpose lessons make instruction more meaningful. For example, students learn that writing serves a real purpose when they write letters expressing their views on a local environmental issue.

✔ Subject integration increases learning and achievement. More time spent on more subjects, more meaningful instruction, more awareness of how different types of knowledge and skills are related—it all adds up to more learning for students.

What to Integrate

While virtually any combination of subjects is possible, most integrated lessons—including many of the examples in this book—involve the language arts. "Reading and writing should be taught all day, every day, in all subject areas," asserts Utah teacher Tim Bailey. This view is gaining currency as researchers and teachers realize their students must be proficient in all subject areas at gathering, analyzing, and communicating information.

In fact, the language arts are tools that must be applied to something. As teachers, we choose, or encourage our students to choose, which topics they will write, read, or speak about, listen to, view, or represent visually. If we make these choices wisely, we give students many more opportunities to practice their language arts skills.

You can get more mileage from reading selections that expose students to different types of content, compared to those that are "content-neutral." Even if your mandated reading text is content deficient, you can supplement it with newspapers, magazines, storybooks, electronic text, and other sources.

Also, recognize that reading materials vary not only in the amount of content, but also in the type of content. Some content focuses on specific subject matter; some "how-to" selections teach skills such as problem solving, reasoning, and persistence; and some feature characters modeling virtues such as humility, patience, courage, kindness, honesty, or hope. All three types are useful for creating multipurpose lessons.

Social studies is another subject ripe with possibilities for integration. I can't imagine teaching literature without including the people, places, and time periods various works represent.

Science, too, lends itself well to multipurpose lessons. Science and social studies, for example, overlap in many topics, including energy and food production, population and other environmental problems, weather and climate, natural resources, and national defense. Science and mathematics team up nicely, too, as mathematics is the language of science.

What about subject combinations that aren't so obvious? In integrated science and music lessons, for example, students might study vibrating systems. They could observe the physical and musical vibrating systems of simple instruments they make from straws, rubber bands, string, or soda bottles. In integrated science and art lessons, children might focus on techniques common to both areas—concentration, careful observation, and detail. They could learn to appreciate the beauty in science and the natural world, and be exposed to the art of biological illustration and nature painting.

Planning Integrated Lessons

An integrated unit is easier to plan and visualize with a useful tool called a graphic organizer, especially a webbing graphic organizer. Webbing is a graphic illustration of how a single topic (whales, for example) becomes the focus for spin-off lessons in various subjects. See the example on page 131.

INTEGRATE WITH NOVELS

Carefully selected novels and reading materials help teachers extend the amount of material and topics they can cover. My middle-school language-arts classes love the novel *Julie of the Wolves* by Jean Craighead George. Not only do they get an exciting story about a brave young girl whose intelligence and knowledge of her Inuit heritage keep her alive on her own in the Arctic wilderness, they get a healthy dose of biology and anthropology in the process. After reading how the story's protagonist gets a wolf pack to "adopt" her, students can't wait to dig for more information about wolves and Inuit culture. Integrative units such as this one lend themselves well to meeting state standards. Here, for example, I've addressed the following West Virginia standards and objectives: use the writing process to compose various types of writing; use technology to locate, evaluate, and collect information from a variety of sources; and identify historical, cultural, and biographical influences of literary works.

Try making separate webs for resources, activities, and skills covered. Create webs, or brainstorm with a colleague. You might even try making it a classroom activity; let students participate in the planning process and give them a choice about what they'll study next.

You will undoubtedly integrate subjects without even trying. But make the most of integrated instruction by consciously planning multipurpose lessons and following state standards for each subject covered. Help students see how these subjects intertwine.

To read more about Basic Schools, visit the Basic School Network Web site at www.boyercenter.org/basicschool or obtain Boyer's *The Basic School: A Community for Learning*, available from the Carnegie Foundation for the Advancement of Teaching. To order, call 650-566-5147 or visit www.carnegiefoundation.org.

The "Basic School"

Subject-matter integration plays a major role in a concept of education proposed by the Basic School Network. Founded by the late Ernest Boyer, president of the Carnegie Foundation for the Advancement of Teaching and U.S. Commissioner of Education, the ever-growing network originated in 1994 with 12 demonstration schools and today includes more than 100 participating schools nationwide.

Basic Schools connect subject matters with eight integrative themes, or "commonalities." In a 1995 *Instructor* magazine interview, Boyer called the core commonalities "those universal human experiences . . . those essential conditions that give meaning to our lives." The core commonalities include:

1. **The Life Cycle**, including humans.
2. **The Use of Symbols**, including the history of language and the way animals send signals.
3. **Response to the Aesthetic**, including a formal study of the arts.
4. **Membership in Groups**, including an examination of the family unit and of community and social groups.
5. **A Sense of Time and Space**, including the construction of students' own histories.
6. **Producing and Consuming**, including the learning of a craft or skill and learning about the exchange of goods and services.
7. **Connections to Nature**, including the use of scientific method.
8. **Living with Purpose**, including the examination of issues such as personal happiness, hero worship, and pro-social behaviors.

Boyer explains that these Core Commonalities apply from kindergarten through twelfth grade, and that every area of knowledge expected by state departments or standardized tests can be integrated into this overall framework for organizing the curriculum. In addition, it solves the problem many schools have of confusing, fragmented courses of study where each grade level is disconnected from the others.

The Basic School concept centers on the notion that all knowledge is interrelated, and only by making this interrelatedness obvious to students can we help them make the connections that are critical to learning. When students understand how everything fits together, individual content areas become much more meaningful.

❖ Teaching Thinking Skills

Knowing how to think—to extend the mind beyond the obvious and develop creative solutions to problems—should be the outcome of a good education. Our thinking skills affect how well we can receive and process new information. Yet American children often fall far short in this critical skill. Educational researcher John Goodlad of the University of Washington estimates that we spend less than 1 percent of class time asking students to reason and think, not simply recall. Researcher Stanley Pogrow from the University of Arizona argues convincingly that under- and low-achieving students need extra practice in developing their thinking skills, not the rote skill and drill practice featured in most remedial programs. (See the description of Pogrow's Higher Order Thinking Skills (HOTS) Program in Chapter Two).

Creating a Thinking Atmosphere

Like everything else worth doing, thinking takes practice. Authors Edwin Kiester Jr. and Sally Valente Kiester suggest ways to create a "thinking

---

SAMPLE INTERDISCIPLINARY UNITS

The Regional Educational Laboratory at AEL and the Virginia Education Association have teamed up to produce 15 teacher-developed and tested interdisciplinary units and alternative assessments. Each unit also includes criteria and guidelines for scoring the alternative assessments. The units, ranging from 1 to 12 weeks, cover all grade levels. Teachers can use the units as they are, adapt them for their own purposes, or use them as models for developing their own integrated units. In a solar system unit for first through third graders, for example, students make a sundial, read folktales, and develop board games to acquire and demonstrate knowledge of the sun, moon, and Earth.

To order Interdisciplinary Units with Alternative Assessments: A Teacher-Developed Compendium, write to the Regional Educational Laboratory at AEL at P.O.B. 1348, Charleston, WV 25325. Call (800) 624-9120 or log on to www.ael.org.

---

atmosphere" and teach children how to be critical thinkers. Their suggestions, geared toward parents, work equally well in the classroom:

✔ **Examine your own thinking about thinking.** Don't accept the mistaken belief that intelligent students are automatically good thinkers. Too often these children haven't developed a thinking habit because they've been able to succeed with quick answers. Also, realize that academic skills (knowing how to read, memorize math facts, and so on) are not the same as thinking skills.

✔ **Start early.** Even preschoolers can be challenged to think and stretch their imaginations.

✔ **Give children something to think about.** Expose children to art or museum exhibitions or music and then challenge them to think about what they've seen or heard. Ask lots of "What if . . . " questions.

✔ **Tell jokes.** Jokes and puns often revolve around looking at words or situations from a different perspective.

✔ **Teach children to look at all sides.** The obvious answer is not always the best one. For example, children might readily respond yes to the question of whether they want an increase in allowance—until they consider the pros and cons and realize that such an increase could involve more chores at home or an increase in responsibility for paying for clothes or entertainment.

✔ **Encourage students to find threads and patterns and make connections.** "How does this relate to what I learned last week?" The ability to make connections is key to learning.

✔ **Encourage students to question "the way it's always been done."** Human progress has been one long succession of overturning accepted ideas.

✔ **Ask unconventional questions.** "What if all cars were painted yellow?" "What if we could extract dinosaur DNA from blood-sucking insects preserved in amber and clone real dinosaurs?" These interesting, open-ended, problematic questions are the ones that elicit thought, not those that require only single-answer factual recall.

✔ **Teach children to say what they mean.** Precise words sharpen ideas, say Kiester and Kiester. How do the terms *acquaintance* and *friend* differ? When you call someone *weird*, what do you mean? "Defining terms is tough mental discipline that can help your child clarify what she really thinks," say the authors.

✔ **Encourage students to consider other points of view.** When we listen to different points of view, we frequently broaden our outlook. Show them how different news reports or different history books give different interpretations of the same event.

✔ **Ask children to "wear another person's shoes."** Cultivate the habit of trying to understand how others think and feel. One good way to practice this skill is to write something from someone else's perspective or to take the perspective of a character in a story in explaining an incident or idea.

✔ **Write it down.** Writing is a good intellectual activity. In fact, as most scholars readily agree, writing is thinking. Often our thoughts are unformed and fuzzy until we clarify them on paper. Teachers can encourage students to keep journals and learning logs, write their responses to various types of literature, and write "explanations" of what they are learning to each other and to their teachers.

Asking Good Questions

Ever since Socrates asked questions to provoke his students into thinking and analyzing their thoughts approximately 2,400 years ago, educators have recognized the value of good questioning strategies. The "right" questions can stimulate higher-order thinking skills and give students the practice they need to develop creativity and insight.

We teachers ask a lot of questions, all right—probably hundreds every day. But far too often, our questions simply require factual recall and only a literal level of comprehension—the lowest level of cognitive functioning.

Questions serve many purposes, including assessing what students already know, setting the stage for a new lesson by piquing students' curiosity, determining what factual information students have absorbed, and stimulating higher-order thinking so students can apply what they've learned to new situations.

Researchers and experienced teachers offer these tips for asking good questions in the classroom:

✔ Ask knowledge-level questions (see Bloom's taxonomy, Level One, page 125) to assess whether or not students can recall information. Such questions help assess both what students already know before a lesson or unit and what they have learned as a result of that lesson or unit.

✔ To elicit thought, ask questions such as *Why? What if . . . ? How do you know that? Are there other ways of looking at this? Is it possible that . . . ? What makes you say that?*

✔ Prepare questions in advance but be alert for ways to spontaneously follow up on comments and insights students share.

✔ Ask questions that students can sometimes answer silently or in writing, not just aloud.

✔ Call on students randomly to respond to questions.

✔ Often it's helpful to have students repeat a question before they attempt to answer it.

✔ Give students adequate time to respond to your questions. In a landmark study, the late Mary Budd Rowe suggested a "wait-time" of three to five seconds after asking a question. She found that with this amount of time, more students answer questions and answer them better.

Ask better questions and help students become better thinkers by converting simple questions into more challenging ones. See pages 127 to 128 for eight strategies offered by Hilarie Bryce Davis.

Students' Questions

Sometimes the role is reversed and students are the ones asking the questions. Students can gain information from the questions they ask, and frequently they can help other students gain valuable insights and information. Further, students' questions help teachers to detect misunderstanding or confusion.

But asking questions is risky business. One could be ridiculed by classmates or chastised by a teacher who views questions as disruptive. Only in a safe, secure environment will students be confident enough to raise important questions that not only give us a window on their thinking but also provide good models and intellectual stimulation for other students.

Encouraging Creativity

One important aspect of higher-order thinking and intelligence in general is creativity. Scholar Barbara Clark defines *creativity* as the synthesis of all human functions, including cognition, emotion, action, and intuition. Truly creative people have a different way of "seeing." Daydreaming, imagining different worlds and new situations, looking at problems from a new perspective, wondering how things could be, as opposed to how they are—these are outlets for, and evidence of, creativity.

There is much we can do to "liberate" the creativity that scholars claim resides in all children. A few of the best techniques include:

✔ **role-playing**—asking students to take the perspective of someone else in debating an issue, acting out a part, or writing something (a personal essay, letter, journal entry, poem).

✔ **posing "What if . . . " questions**—What if children wrote the rules for society? What if there was no gravity on Earth? What if there were no different races among humans? What if we could communicate with whales?

✔ **practicing divergent thinking**—How is a school like a tree? How is a person like a book?

✔ **solving open-ended problems**—How might you create a model building out of toothpicks and marshmallows? How can you use discarded packaging and other "trash" to create art?

ENCOURAGING BETTER THINKING

Francis Hunkins offers three questioning techniques for helping students become better thinkers:

1. Probe for answers, leading students to appropriate responses. For example, encourage students to explain why leaves change color with questions such as: What do you know about autumn? Are days longer or shorter in the fall? What does sunlight have to do with the color of leaves?

2. Ask students to clarify or elaborate on their answers: Why do you say that? Can you explain your answer?

3. Use questions that elicit different opinions or more than one correct response: What risks did the colonists face in declaring independence? Do you think *The Wizard of Oz* is a good movie?

Nurturing Imagination

"Imagination is a delicate thing. It can be killed with a sneer or a yawn. It can be stabbed to death by a quip or worried to death by a frown. It can also be encouraged by a kind word or a clap." Lou Kassem, author of *Middle School Blues*, recalls an incident in her childhood when her teacher had asked students to write a few paragraphs about the Ice Age. Kassem's creative response was to write a story about an Ice Age family frozen solid in a glacier who thawed and came back to life years later. Her wise teacher recognized her divergent thinking and creative talent, and instead of making fun of her or dismissing her ideas, as classmates did, her teacher acknowledged her effort and involved the class in a discussion of "What if such a family did come to life today?"

Imagination is the tool that enables us to create. It enables us to adapt to a rapidly changing world and to improve the world we have. Where would our inventors and scientists and artists and great thinkers be without imagination?

Yet too often, in attempting to teach students the "right" answers, it's easy to squelch their imaginations. Don't forget to give them the room they need to develop that important intellectual tool—their imaginations.

Levels of Thinking: Bloom's Taxonomy

Bloom's taxonomy, developed in 1956, remains the standard for describing various levels of thinking skills. Following are the six levels of the taxonomy, from lowest to highest, with a few examples of questions or activities at each level. Levels four, five, and six represent what we commonly call **higher-order thinking skills**:

1. **Level One: Knowledge**. This level of thinking involves memorization of material. Questions and activities at the Knowledge Level are factual recall, such as "Name the major parts of speech" or "Recite the multiplication tables."
2. **Level Two: Comprehension**. An example of a question at this level would be, "Paraphrase the opinions expressed by the character in this story."

LEVELS-OF-THINKING VERBS

Using precise language when you plan your lessons or phrase questions can help you target all levels of thinking.

Knowledge	Analysis
Memorize	Survey
Define	Compare or contrast
Label	Examine

Comprehension	Synthesis
Explain	Design
Predict	Rewrite
Summarize	Construct

Application	Evaluation
Show	Defend
Illustrate	Choose
Sequence	Prioritize

---

3. **Level Three: Application**. Here, students use principles, concepts, or generalizations and apply them in new situations. For example, "Knowing what you know about fractions and division, how can you share these three candy bars equally among five children?" or "How can we use what we've learned about sentence fragments to improve our own writing?"
4. **Level Four: Analysis**. Here, students need to detect elements or see relationships among the parts. For example, "How do these two stories differ, and how are they the same?"
5. **Level Five: Synthesis**. Here, students combine ideas, concepts, or information into new patterns or structures. For example, "Write a story about life in the year 2050, using current trends and technology as clues" or "Draw a picture that uses the Impressionists' views and ideas."
6. **Level Six: Evaluation**. At this level, students make judgments using standards or criteria. For example, "Write a review explaining why next year's class should or should not read this book" or "Compare the writing techniques of poets Shel Silverstein and Emily Dickinson."

A Questioning Quiz

The first step to asking better questions is understanding the difference in questions. Take this quiz to check your questioning IQ. These are questions you might ask students after reading *The Three Little Pigs*. Write L for the lower-level questions that require just factual recall and H for those that involve higher-order thinking skills.

_____ 1. What were the pigs building?

_____ 2. What is straw?

_____ 3. Why is brick better than straw for building?

_____ 4. Who was trying to blow down the pigs' houses?

_____ 5. Which pig was the first to lose his house?

_____ 6. Why do you think the third little pig let the other two stay in his house?

_____ 7. What happened to the wolf at the end of the story?

_____ 8. Do you think the first two little pigs will be building new houses?

_____ 9. Is this story like another pig story you've read? How?

_____ 10. Why do you think a wolf is the "bad" character and not some other animal?

Answers: 1. L 2. L 3. H 4. L 5. L 6. H 7. L 8. H 9. H 10. H

Asking Good Questions

Ask better questions and help your students become better thinkers with these eight strategies that convert simple questions into more challenging ones.

1 Yes, but why?

Ask students why an answer is correct. For example, *Why is 6 x (9 – 4) equal to 30 and not 50?* or *Why does Columbus get credit for discovering America?* In each of these converted questions, it's easy to tell if students know the basic information. And the bonus is that these questions also require the processing of that information.

2 What's the use?

Ask questions that focus on the use of information. So, to the question *Why do you need to know the effect of light on plant growth?*, more students might answer: To do landscaping, know where to plant a garden, or decide which houseplants to buy for the light exposure available. Such questions increase the likelihood that students will remember facts because they apply them.

A natural outgrowth of using "why" questions is that students soon begin to ask them as well as answer them.

3 What's different now?

Asking about the implication of a change is also worthwhile. To use this conversion strategy, first change something about the information you want the students to know. Alex Osborn in *Applied Imagination* suggests eight tactics for change:

1. **Adapt**—borrow an idea from somewhere else. *How would our lives be different if we hibernated all winter long as some animals do?*
2. **Modify**—make a small change for the better. *If Hansel and Gretel had brought a map with them into the forest, what might have happened?*
3. **Substitute**—use something for something else. *How would a blueberry sandwich taste?*
4. **Magnify**—add, multiply, or extend. *What would Newton's Fourth Law be?*
5. **Minify**—make it smaller, omit something, divide it. *Can you imagine a world without gravity?*
6. **Rearrange**—revise the order of things. *What would be the consequences if A was the last letter in the alphabet, and Z the first?*
7. **Reverse**—turn things completely around. *How would you like to go to bed in the morning and get up at night?*
8. **Combine**—add two or more things together. *How would the world be different if each continent was only one country?*

4 Can you prove it?

Asking for the proof of an answer requires that the student both formulate the answer and offer support for it. The question *How do we find the area of a triangle?* becomes *Does the formula you are using to find the area of a triangle always work? Why?* This strategy works especially well for literature assignments. Questions about character actions, plot events, and author style may be answered only with support from the text.

5 Right, wrong, or neither?

Too often, higher-level questions become lower-level ones because the questioner has a predetermined answer. One way to avoid this is to consciously suspend judgment on an issue and another is to ask a question that has no right or wrong answer.

Finding this kind of open-ended question requires the questioner to do some real exploration on the subject. For instance, a factual question about the names of the 13 colonies might become—after some thought—one of the following higher-level questions: *Why do people name places instead of using another identification system such as*

Asking Good Questions (continued)

numbers? *How important was communication among the colonies in moving toward independence?* The higher-level thinking question you choose will depend on the direction you have chosen for your unit and your students' interests.

6 All of the above? Asking questions that have more than one answer calls for careful analysis and multiple answers from the students. This strategy has wide application for teaching basic skills. Instead of asking for the definition of a noun, for example, ask *How many words can you think of that fit this sentence: "The exhausted _____ raced around the corner?"* Obviously, only nouns may be used to complete the sentence. In addition, the question has changed from asking for the recall of a definition to an active search for words that meet a certain set of conditions.

7 Alike or different? The questions *How are Jefferson and Lincoln alike? How are they different?* and *What do the formulas for finding the areas of the following figures have in common?* use comparison and contrast—another effective strategy. A good way to introduce students to this concept is to compare and contrast concrete objects. Give small groups of students two similar objects to compare—forks of different patterns, coins, or hats. Ask them to list similarities and differences. When all the groups' lists have been combined on the chalkboard, ask students to identify the categories they used as the basis for their comparisons, such as texture, color, size, and so on.

With a little practice, students quickly get in the habit of searching for categories and characteristics. The next step is to compare and contrast on a more abstract level: a story and poem about the same event, multiplication and division, or mammals and birds.

8 Square peg and round hole? Formulating questions using unusual relationships requires creativity on the part of the teacher as well as the student. When studying verbs, for example, relate them to the actions and habits of people: *What would a helping verb say to an action verb if they happened to meet?* or *If we think of the parts of speech as a family, who would the family members be, and how do you see their family roles?*

You could also proceed by placing any event or topic in an entirely remote context. The more remote the association, the more effectively it will stretch your students' thinking. The ability to break out of familiar ways of thinking is an important element in creativity.

By Hilarie Bryce Davis, from *Instructor*, November 1980.

❖ Graphic Organizers

Imagine this situation: A fourth-grade teacher wants to assess how much his students know about whales before he begins an integrated unit on the subject. He asks the students to brainstorm in groups and list everything they can think of involving whales. Then he asks the group leaders to present their lists while he writes the items on the chalkboard. Next, he asks the entire class to think of ways to group the individual items—categories or subheads under the main heading "Whales." The web below shows what they come up with.

The "picture" is a graphic organizer. There are many different kinds of graphic organizers—semantic maps, webs, story maps, Venn diagrams, and so on—but they all function as a visual "picture" of knowledge.

Powerful Tools

Graphic organizers are powerful teaching and learning tools. They encourage active learning, demonstrate that knowledge is interconnected, facilitate group work, accommodate individual learning styles, and engage students in higher-order thinking.

When or how could you use them? In many different contexts for many different purposes. In the example below, the web allows the teacher to assess what the students already know, and it gives the students a framework of knowledge upon which to build. This activity also serves as an exciting introduction and cues students about the lessons and activities to come.

Further, graphic organizers can be used as prereading or prewriting strategies to activate background knowledge or generate interest. Or they can help students organize the material in a textbook, story or novel, film or video, or class discussion. After a lesson or unit, a graphic organizer helps students assimilate and reflect upon new knowledge, and it can even be used as an assessment tool. After the integrated unit on whales, students reflected upon what they learned by revising and expanding their original graphic organizer (see page 130).

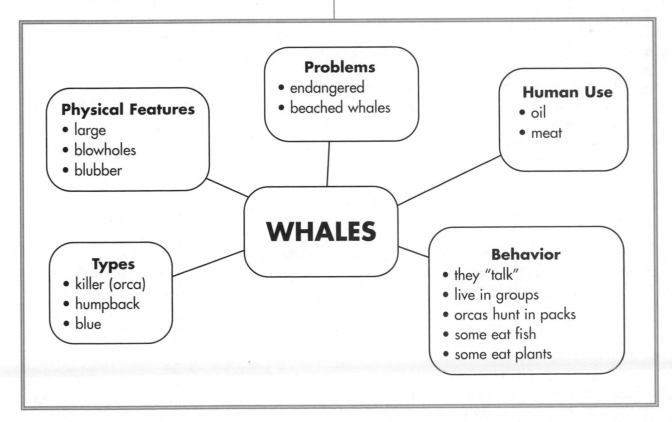

WHALES

Types
- orca
- humpback
- blues
- gray
- sperm/finback
- right
- narwhal
- dolphins
- porpoises

Physical Features
- largest animals on Earth
- blowholes/lungs
- blubber
- baleen
- sonar
- mammals (live birth, nurse young)

Social Issues
- "Save the whales"
- hunting bans (international)
- boycotting
- whale watching
- native cultures dependent on whales

Behavior
- whale songs and communication
- migration
- social groups called "pods"
- filter food through baleen
- orcas are predators; hunt in packs like wolves
- echolocation

Human Uses/Products
- oil
- meat
- perfume
- scrimshaw

Problems
- endangered
- beached whale
- water pollution

Miscellaneous
- cetaceans
- cows, calves, bulls

Why are graphic organizers effective? They help retrieve and retain information. As research demonstrates, the brain stores information in orderly categories. These categories create a framework called a **schema**. When prior knowledge is activated or retrieved, as in the whale brainstorming session, the existing schema becomes a framework upon which students can attach new knowledge. New knowledge is retained and makes sense only when it relates to something we already know.

Besides their obvious benefits to learners, graphic organizers can also facilitate teaching. Many teachers use them for instructional planning. The organizer on page 131 might be used to plan an integrated unit on whales.

Ways to Organize Knowledge

Karen Bromley, Linda Irwin-DeVitis, and Marcia Modlo suggest that knowledge can be organized in four ways: conceptually, hierarchically, cyclically, and sequentially. Different types of graphic organizers support each way.

Conceptual. A conceptual approach includes one main idea or category with supporting characteristics or examples. The webs on whales are one example. Another good one is a Venn diagram, used to compare and contrast topics or concepts.

Hierarchical. This linear approach includes a main concept with subconcepts under it. For example, students could list the ways that humans use their environment, or they could outline a main idea and its supporting details.

Cyclical. This approach presents information or events that have no beginning or end. A butterfly's life cycle, the cycle of water on the planet, or the cyclical nature of history or some stories can be effectively illustrated with a cyclical graphic organizer. Cyclical graphic organizers are effective with prereaders simply by substituting pictures for words.

Sequential. A sequential organizer, such as a time line, is linear in nature. It arranges events in chronological order. One of the most frequent uses of a sequential organizer is for delineating a story plot or a set of historical events.

Teaching How to Use Graphic Organizers

"Students who understand how to create a graphic organizer have a new and valuable tool for planning, understanding, remembering, and assessing knowledge," say Bromley, Irwin-DeVitis, and Modlo. But they point out that first we must explicitly teach students how to use them.

Try modeling the process by thinking aloud as you create an organizer. "Discuss the way in which you determine the central concept and the key relationships," the authors suggest. "It helps students tremendously when you show the 'mistakes' and 'alterations' you make as you generate and revise your organizer. Through this candid demonstration students can better understand the thinking, rethinking, hypothesizing, and decision making that go into creating a graphic organizer."

Lead students gradually from depending on graphic organizers that you provide (see the reproducible organizers on pages 133 to 136) to creating their own organizers. Also, teach them that the process of creating and sharing a graphic organizer is more important than the product and that there is no single best way to create a graphic organizer or represent certain information.

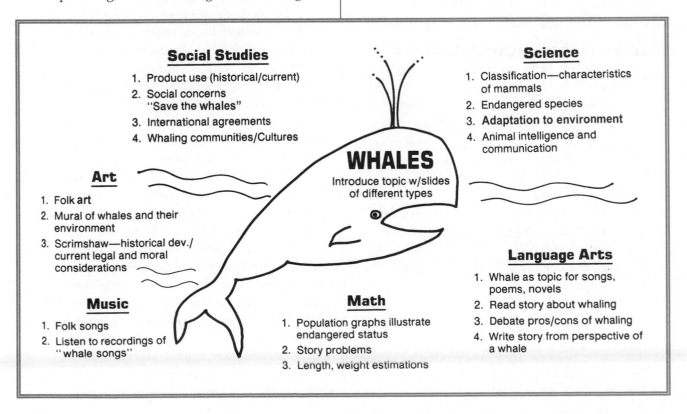

Social Studies
1. Product use (historical/current)
2. Social concerns "Save the whales"
3. International agreements
4. Whaling communities/Cultures

Science
1. Classification—characteristics of mammals
2. Endangered species
3. Adaptation to environment
4. Animal intelligence and communication

Art
1. Folk art
2. Mural of whales and their environment
3. Scrimshaw—historical dev./ current legal and moral considerations

WHALES
Introduce topic w/slides of different types

Language Arts
1. Whale as topic for songs, poems, novels
2. Read story about whaling
3. Debate pros/cons of whaling
4. Write story from perspective of a whale

Music
1. Folk songs
2. Listen to recordings of "whale songs"

Math
1. Population graphs illustrate endangered status
2. Story problems
3. Length, weight estimations

❖ Keep Them Actively Engaged

Active teaching helps students learn because it keeps them motivated and attentive by allowing them to succeed at academic tasks. No matter what your instructional style or how much experience you have, you must actively engage students and allow them plenty of chances to succeed.

Active Teaching

Call it direct instruction, explicit instruction, active teaching, structured learning, or any other phrase. But when it means teachers organizing and clearly leading learning activities, it works. In direct instruction, teachers carefully structure academic tasks. They tell students how to accomplish these tasks, and they guide them through exercises leading to mastery. They give students frequent opportunities for practice, and they assess whether reteaching or more practice is needed.

First-grade teachers directly instructing reading groups, for example, introduce new words to students, pointing out important phonetic features. They talk about what a word means and give examples of how it is used. They let students practice words in oral reading and ask questions to make sure students understand what they read and are able to analyze the words.

To actively teach fractions, a teacher introduces the topic, explains what fractions are, gives concrete examples, works problems on the board, guides the class in working problems together, makes sure students understand the lesson, and then gives them opportunities to practice independently with problems they can handle.

While the current thinking favors more student-centered, individualized approaches, most researchers and experienced teachers agree that there is a time and a place for active teaching. Certain topics, concepts, and skills are better taught directly by the teacher. Researchers also caution that many of the individualized or student-discovery approaches rely on high degrees of learner independence, concentration, and self-motivation that must be cultivated. Further, the research suggests that students even need explicit instruction in becoming independent learners (how to work alone, how and when to seek help, seeking solutions to problems that might arise, knowing what resources are needed).

Active teaching clearly works. But like other strategies, it works best when adapted to particular students and situations. For example, many teachers describe the mini-lessons they give on English usage or mechanics as problems occur while students are writing. These **mini-lessons** are examples of active teaching—succinct five- to ten-minute presentations focused on a specific topic that students can integrate into their work, such as using quotation marks to punctuate dialogue

Idea Web

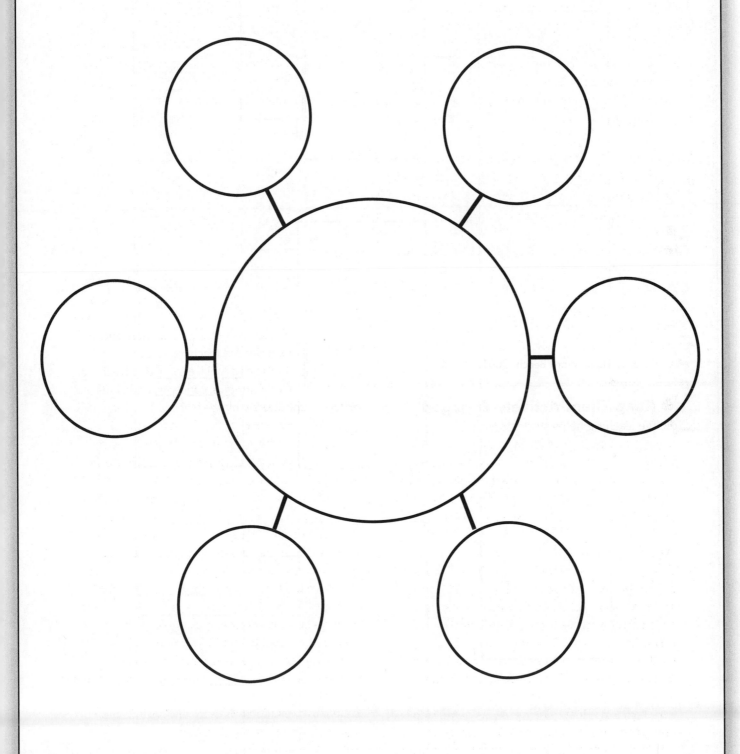

Idea Organizer

Cycle of Ideas

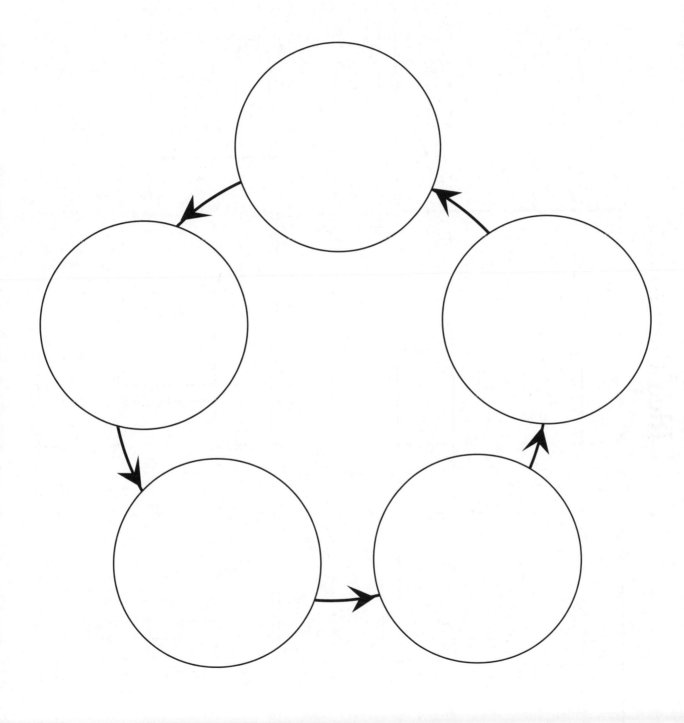

Ideas in Sequence

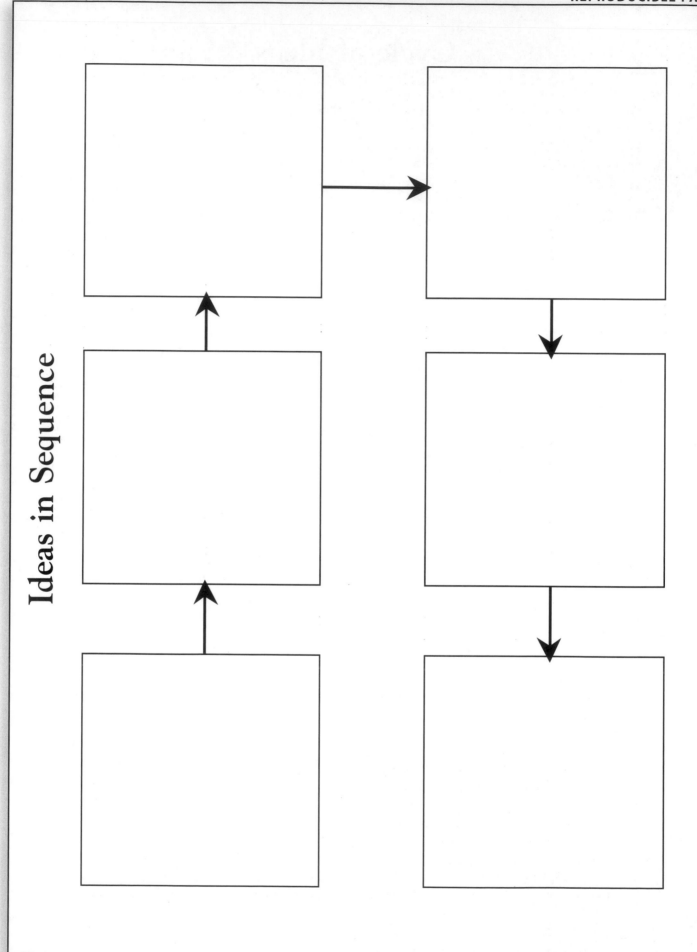

during a narrative writing unit. The need for active teaching also varies with grade level. In the upper grades, teachers can spend more time teaching and less time directing practice.

Active teaching also works best when cognitive achievement (as measured by standardized tests) is the goal. Other approaches, researchers suggest, may be more appropriate for growth in noncognitive areas, such as attitudes, emotions, interests, and social development.

It's your judgment call. Use your professional knowledge of students and situations to decide when and where you'll actively teach.

Time to Learn

Time is opportunity to learn. And some students have more opportunity than others.

Researchers recognize three different aspects of classroom time.

✔ **Allocated time**—the amount of time allotted to various subjects and topics within a subject. Teachers also allocate different types of time: whole-group or small-group teaching, individual work, and tutorial or cooperative activities.

✔ **Instructional time**—the time you actually have to teach. This is the time allocated to a lesson, less disruptions (inside or outside the classroom), transitions from one activity to another, and other time wasters.

✔ **Engaged time**—the time students are paying attention or are busily involved. This is often referred to as time on-task. Instruction does not automatically translate to learning. Students learn only when they're engaged—successfully.

On a typical school day, a child in one classroom might spend 84 minutes on reading instruction, while a child in another spends only 24 minutes. Add to this the variations in time students spend concentrating on the instruction (and not daydreaming or using the restroom) and you have some idea of the tremendous differences in opportunities to learn.

Effective teaching strategies won't help if you don't have time to teach and students don't have time to learn. Studies nationwide have documented huge differences in teaching and learning time among classrooms. For example, there are great variations on the time students actually spend working or paying attention, in the amount of time they are successfully engaged—actually succeeding at their work— and in the amount of time they spend doing seatwork as opposed to receiving direct instruction. Also, teachers differ in the amounts of time they devote to certain subjects, often depending on personal likes or dislikes.

Even small differences in teaching and learning time add up to big ones. Just 25 minutes more (or less) instruction a day amounts to two hours a week or 80 hours a year.

Fortunately, there are ways to increase students' opportunities to learn. First, give yourself more time to teach by establishing a learning environment and good classroom management. For example, reduce transition times with efficient routines. Save time with careful planning and preparation. (See Chapter One for more ideas.) Another good time-saver is integrating different subject matters into one lesson. (See page 120.)

Engaged Time

Engaged time is the major concern in this chapter. Whereas effective management can increase teaching time, effective instructional strategies increase the time students spend attending to lessons. And no matter how much time you spend teaching, students won't learn unless they're paying attention. Here's how to ensure they do:

✔ Offer enough direct instruction. Have a focus and purpose each time you ask for students' attention. Make sure students understand the material and what it is you are asking them to do.

✔ Strive for eye contact from all students while you give directions or offer an explanation.

✔ Make sure students have plenty of opportunities for success. (The strategies suggested in this chapter and Chapter Five will help.) Learning occurs during that portion of engaged time when students are actually succeeding at a task. Researchers call this "academic learning time."

✔ Pace lessons as briskly as possible.

✔ Establish efficient classroom management. Do you monitor independent work? Have you established routines to reduce the amount of time students spend waiting for you, for supplies, or for each other? Do your management practices prevent time-consuming behavior problems? Not surprisingly, there's a strong correlation between good management and good instruction. Both require efficient organization and careful planning.

❖ Technology in the Classroom

By the 1840s, a bold new technology had invaded American classrooms: the chalkboard. Teachers were confused about how to use this newfangled device, and experts wrote books instructing teachers in its use.

Obviously, we've moved way beyond chalkboards—and ditto machines, overhead projectors, filmstrips, and cassette players, for that matter. Today's classrooms boast computers, the Internet, CDs and DVDs, virtual reality, e-mail and instant messaging, digital cameras, Smart Boards, data projectors, and many more high-tech innovations that have changed our world. And like their 19th-century counterparts, many teachers today find the new technology daunting.

Author David Dockterman, technology expert and former history teacher, notes that computers abound in classrooms, but many teachers aren't using them. In fact, less than 10 percent of today's teachers use computers for instruction at least once a week, and more than 50 percent never use them at all. That's because too many people perceive computers as replacing teachers, rather than assisting them, he explains.

"Teachers won't begin to use this tool regularly until they find software and hardware that are designed to work in concert with them," says Dockterman. "We need to respect the incredible insights, intuitions, and knowledge good teachers bring to the learning process already, and which no technology can replace."

Computers hold tremendous promise, but only if they are woven into the regular classroom curriculum, rather than used as an independent event where students spend time "blowing up adverbs with diphthong bombs or shooting improper fractions from the sky," says Dockterman. He stresses that technology is a tool. It can help us meet instructional standards and objectives if it is integrated into everyday teaching and learning.

How Technology Can Help

The most powerful role technology can play is in helping students and teachers obtain, organize, and present information. Technology is the vehicle for theme studies and the project approach. It offers the opportunity for students to control their own learning, which enhances a student's motivation and facilitates learning.

Technology allows us to create learner-centered classrooms, says Barbara McCombs, senior researcher at the University of Denver. McCombs explains that technology can be used in ways that learners perceive as interesting, fun, meaningful, and relevant. And that, in turn, motivates students to learn.

McCombs offers the example of the Generation WHY program in the Olympia, Washington, school district. In this program, students in grades 6 through 12 collaborate with teachers, the local community, higher education, and corporate sponsors to assist in restructuring education with technology. After an 18-week training course, the students actually mentor teachers in using technology to improve teaching and learning.

"This approach has not only led to greater student engagement in learning, but has also led to increased school attendance and reduced discipline problems," McCombs reports. "New school cultures of mutual respect and caring have emerged. Students who indicated they would have dropped out of school or been involved in gangs are now making plans to go on to college and/or enter high-tech careers." She adds, "This and other examples of involving youth in meaningful partnerships are effective strategies for integrating technology to enhance learning and motivation."

Continues McCombs: "We need to consider technology-supported teaching and learning strategies for sharing knowledge, expertise, power, and control among learners—students as well as teachers—building true learning communities. This will not all be easy but will move us toward the goal of every student learning at his or her highest potential inside and outside of school—and loving it."

As the experts agree, technology is a potent tool. Dockterman identifies four ways that technology can help teachers and learners meet educational objectives:

✔ **content acquisition**—information we want children to know and remember, such as the multiplication tables, spelling rules, grammar, or the order of mathematical operations.

✔ **skill mastery**—practicing skills necessary for problem solving, reading, and writing.

✔ **concept understanding**—understanding that allows students to create new information. For example, the child who understands science concepts can infer and draw conclusions from new data.

✔ **"other good stuff"**—a catchall category for intangibles such as teamwork, empathy, citizenship, civility, and the ability to listen and communicate.

TECHNOLOGY'S CONTRIBUTIONS

As researchers Barbara Means and Kerry Olson see it, the new technology makes five major contributions to education. Technology:

- **makes complex assignments feasible**. For example, with database programs and graphing capacities available, extensive data collection and analysis projects become possible.
- **provides earlier entry points to some content areas**. First graders with word-processing programs, for example, can now become writers before they are fluent readers.
- **can extend and enhance what students produce**. For example, editing one's writing is easy on a word processor. And even sophisticated multimedia projects are now feasible, given the tools students have at their disposal.
- **lends authenticity to school tasks**. Students can now use the same tools as professionals, and their polished, professional-looking schoolwork seems "real" and important.
- **gives teachers the chance to become learners again**. From setting up new equipment to guiding students through technology-dependent projects, the teacher's new role is open-ended and never totally mastered.

In addition, technology facilitates the management of grades and paperwork.

- **Computer-based grading programs** help teachers keep current records of student grades, allowing them to print out a progress report (itemized by assignment or test) any time a student or parent requests it.
- Following the lead of many colleges, middle school and high school teachers are increasingly asking for **assignments submitted electronically**. (An added bonus here is the elimination of the all-too-frequent broken printer excuse!)
- **Class or school Web sites** make it easier for teachers to communicate homework assignments and other important information to parents and students.
- **E-mail** eliminates the need for many of the notes or phone calls to parents. (Ask for the e-mail addresses of parents who wish to communicate online, along with other home contact information.)

"The computer can be much more than a back-of-the-room diversion for students," claims Dockterman. "It can be a powerful instructional tool that you can weave into your daily agenda to help you meet your instructional objectives."

There are countless examples of educational software designed to help students acquire necessary content, practice and master skills, understand concepts, and develop the "other good stuff." Most are in CD-ROM format, and Dockterman offers descriptions and reviews of many good ones in his book *Easy Ways to Make Technology Work for You* (see the resources list at the end of this chapter).

Does It Work?

Recognizing the prevalence of commercially produced software aimed at teachers and schools, the federal government is undertaking a $10 million study of 16 computer-based reading and math products from 12 different companies. Researchers are looking for the conditions and practices under which technologies are most effective.

"Our goal is to measure the effectiveness of technology as it improves the bottom line—student achievement and learning," says Susan Patrick, acting director of the Office of Educational Technology.

But not everyone agrees that technology in schools is effective at all. A commentary in the London-based *Economist* suggests that educational software and computers in schools have done little to boost achievement, even hindering it in some cases. The commentary notes significant methodological flaws in studies claiming that technology significantly increases learning and achievement. Citing both an Israeli study and the research of Stanford University's Larry Cuban, who has extensively studied computers in education, the commentary claims that the billions spent on classroom computers represent money not spent on teachers or textbooks.

"One of the vaunted advantages of computer-based learning, that it allows children to proceed at their own pace, has so far turned out to be wrong: educational software is much more one-size-fits-all than a good teacher, skilled at tailoring the lesson to the varied abilities of a class," the commentary asserts. Instead, it suggests, schools would be better off investing money in two proven strategies: cutting class size and improving teacher training.

Some educators worry that money for computer technology will come at the expense of field trips, art and music programs, physical education classes, and other programs.

What's the average classroom teacher to do?

For obtaining information to supplement teaching or aid in professional development, a computer with online access can't be beat. Through the Internet, we can introduce students to vast amounts of information and a huge selection of resources. My advice is to get as many computers for your classroom as you can, and use them as suggested throughout this book—but not at the expense of field trips, manipulatives, books, and other hands-on resources. Give students opportunities to learn how the real world works—not just the virtual world.

Technology Changes Teachers' Roles

The experts claim that technology can (and should!) move classrooms away from traditional approaches, where teachers do most of the talking and students do most of the listening. Instead, with technology to help students complete authentic tasks, teachers become coaches and facilitators. They provide structure and support students' performances. They design tasks and orchestrate their completion, intervene at critical points, facilitate the use or availability of the technology, troubleshoot, and provide feedback.

"What technology will not do is make the teacher's life simple," say Barbara Means and Kerry Olson. They use the metaphor of the theater to explain.

"Technology plays an important role, but it is a supporting role. The students are the stars. The playwright and the director—and the power behind the scenes—is, as always, the teacher."

Many of us fear the new technology because we don't yet know enough about it. But we don't always need to be the "experts."

"One of the best things that teachers can do with respect to technology is to model what to do when one doesn't know what to do," claim Means and Olson. And Washington teacher Martine Wayman concurs.

"It had never occurred to me that it was 'OK' not to know all the answers. It was such a relief to be 'given permission' to step aside and problem-solve with my students! I became a 'guide on the side' instead of a 'sage on the stage.'"

The Internet

The new technology is not limited to educational software for computers. The most obvious—and important—feature of the new technology is the Internet. Most educators would agree that the Internet has the potential for the most significant impact on teaching and learning.

The Internet connects your home or school computers to millions of other computers worldwide. It's like a giant library where you can go for news, entertainment, and information on any subject. It's also an electronic mail system (e-mail) and a vehicle for direct conversations (instant messaging and chat rooms) or live video feeds (Web cameras).

Using the Internet to increase student learning and understanding is touted as one of the most effective uses of technology. Judi Harris, technology specialist from the College of William and Mary, identifies three main categories of classroom Internet use: interpersonal exchange, information gathering and analysis, and problem-solving activities.

Interpersonal exchanges, says Harris, include activities such as e-mail, chat rooms, and instant messaging. Keypals, the electronic version of pen pals, is one good example. Another involves contacting professionals who can inform students. Authors Jennifer Richard Jacobson (*Truly Winnie* and *Moon Sandwich Mom*) and Toni Buzzeo (*Dawdle Duckling* and *The Sea Chest*) suggest that teachers arrange for interpersonal exchanges with real-life authors or illustrators. There's nothing more inspirational or enlightening, say Jacobson and Buzzeo, and "many writers are more than happy to take a virtual leap to interact with their readers."

They describe three basic approaches to interacting with authors (or anyone who has expertise to offer students): **e-mail**, which is basically writing a student or class letter and awaiting a response; **virtual chat**, in which students and author converse in real time with instant messaging software (download AOL's version free at www.aim.com); and a **webcam visit**, in which the author and students actually see each other as they talk (you'll need a digital video camera and software, such as that available free at www.paltalk.com).

No matter which approach you take, you will first need to contact the author and ask whether he or she would be willing to talk to your students. Set a time, agree on a procedure, then have students do the necessary background work (read and discuss the story, learn a little about the author, devise a list of questions, and so on).

Information gathering and analysis is the Internet activity most familiar to teachers and students. Students gather and analyze information when they conduct research online. The Internet represents a seemingly infinite amount of information at our fingertips. Ironically, it is this sheer quantity that hinders our use of this incredible tool.

Many school districts have their own technology coordinators or facilitators who help teachers use the Internet effectively. One good example is Dawn Moore, learning technologies facilitator from Schamburg Community Schools in Illinois.

Moore has developed an excellent online tutorial that presents information literacy strategies for teachers using the Internet in their classrooms. The site, http://web54.sd54.k12.il. us/district54/lts/dmoore/infoliteracy, features a tutorial on search engines, graphic organizers and bookmarks, tips for using *PowerPoint* to take notes, a list of good reference sites for students, guidelines for citing Internet references, and many, many more strategies for taming the Internet "monster."

In addition, Moore reminds teachers to teach students how to evaluate the quality of Web sites. "The Internet exposes our students to massive amounts of information," writes Moore. Anyone can publish his or her version of truth on the Internet, "and they do. Unfortunately, many students believe if it's on the Internet, it must be true." She urges teachers to model the analysis of Web sites and make sure they understand the difference between fact and opinion. She also suggests that students use a

Subject-Specific Web Sites

▶ Language Arts

DiscoverySchool.com

school.discovery.com

Here is a collection of useful teacher tools. By typing in a list of vocabulary words, you can create a glossary list with definitions, a pronunciation key, and more, or make a quick vocabulary quiz. The puzzle makers are easy to use. Almost instantly you can generate a word-search puzzle or crossword. Also, check out their extensive clip art, daily brain boosters, and lesson plans.

The Scoop

www.friend.ly.net/scoop/

It's like having your own personal librarian in your classroom! The Scoop includes book reviews, audio excerpts, author/illustrator interviews, contests, interactive reading adventures, and advice on how to arrange an author visit to your school. The biography pages are thorough yet concise. Look under the activity link to discover a collection of exciting things to do from some of the most well-known children's activity books out there.

▶ Math

Educational Internet Resources

www.terc.edu

Inquiry-based math and science activities are this site's specialty. The site includes a long list of projects to share at home or in the classroom. Perusing the site's News and Hands-On! sections can update your knowledge of current trends in math and science education as well as set you up with some relevant resources and research done on teaching these subjects.

MathMagic

www.forum.swarthmore.edu/mathmagic

MathMagic's mathematic challenges are leveled by grade and set up in a way that invites students to work together to solve problems. Look under Math Library and Quick Reference for help in teaching certain mathematic skills. Parents and students will find Dr. Math's advice useful during homework time.

MathMastery

www.mathmastery.com

This fun site will surely motivate your students. Kids can register to partner up with a sports star or a pop music celebrity to learn about math, play games, and receive free posters in the process. Teachers can register a class of 25 or more and participate in on-line math courses designed for grades 3 through 8, and set up a Progress Page for each student to keep up-to-date on his or her progress. Looking for new and original math problems? Visit DailyBrains to find problems created by teachers for teachers. The CyberChallenge is a perfect place for students to practice their math skills in a fun, pressure-free atmosphere.

▶ Social Studies

ePALS.com Classroom Exchange

www.epals.com

If you'd like to find e-mail pen pals for your students, ePALS offers a free service that connects educators globally for collaborative projects. You can browse through the mail requests from teachers from Japan, New Zealand, and all over the world, or post your own profile. This site also offers communication tools such as automatic translation in six languages and a school e-mail service that is safe and easy to monitor.

National Atlas

www.nationalatlas.gov

Since 1997, the government has been busy at work updating the National Atlas of the United States and making it available online. This site provides many different kinds of multimedia maps that can give you a summary of geographic information, such as a map of America's potentially active volcanoes, or link you to another site for more detailed information.

National Geographic On-line

www.nationalgeographic.com

National Geographic's site offers many resources for teachers and students to explore field science, conservation, cultural studies, and more. The Maps and Geography link will connect you with any map to enhance your lessons—from "U.S. Hurricane Paths" to current event maps of the Middle East. The "kids" link directs you to kid-friendly news articles, geography activities, games, and science experiment ideas.

▶ Science

www.exploratorium.edu

www.exploratorium.edu

An extension of the museum based in California, the Exploratorium Web site for teachers and students explores human perception and how it works within the world around us. Watch live webcasts of eclipses and Real Videos of an aurora, or virtually explore Antarctica. Check out the Learning Studio for optical illusions and memory games, or learn how to build classroom versions of its exhibits. New and captivating content is added regularly.

Eye on the Weather

http://weathereye.kgan.com

Created by an Iowa news team and local educators, this site offers lesson plans for real-life weather situations. Its activities are divided into age-appropriate categories and include lesson objectives and hands-on experiments. Visiting the "Teachers' Lounge" will help you to find what weather system lesson you are looking for.

NASA's K–12 Internet Initiative

http://quest.arc.nasa.gov

Share the excitement of NASA's scientific and engineering endeavors like flying in the shuttle and the International Space Station, exploring distant planets with amazing spacecraft, and building the aircraft of the future. This site includes resources from profiles of NASA experts, collaborative activities in which kids can work with one another, and a place for teachers to meet one another.

Science Magazine

www.sciencemag.org

Featuring amazing pictures, information about careers in science, and links to scientific networks, this site is a great match for teachers looking to keep their students up-to-date on current scientific events and findings. Look under the daily news or search the online magazine's archives to find the science topics that capture students' interests and meet your instructional needs.

Subject-Specific Web Sites (continued)

▶ Other Professional Resources

The Amazing Picture Machine
www.ncrtec.org/picture.htm
Enter your search word and this search engine delivers photographs, drawings, and other graphical resources. You'll find pictures of frogs, telephones, cars, and rhinoceroses among many others! This site also offers Web activities correlated to the standards. Click on the lesson link to search by subject or grade level. Each lesson has helpful suggestions about the prior knowledge your students will need for the activity, as well as possible difficult concepts or misconceptions students might have. Lessons also provide graphic organizers and procedures to save you lots of time!

Blue Web'n
www.kn.pacbell.com/wired/bluewebn
What you see is what you get with this excellent site. The Content Table makes finding any piece of information, from Web-based tutorials to unit and lesson plans, quick and easy—without even typing a word! In addition to expected curriculum areas like social studies and science, searchable items include the arts, business, foreign language, and community interest. The site lists exactly how much information is contained within a particular area. Aside from browsing the Content Table, you can also search by subject area or grade level.

Daily Dose of the Web
www.internet4classrooms.com/daily_dose.htm
Start the day with quick critical-thinking activities using Daily Dose's great resources. Bookmark this site for daily brainteasers, challenging questions, and math problems geared to all grade levels, as well as daily birthdays, quotations, and vocabulary words. Check out the Daily Buzzword at Word Central for starters!

edHelper.com
www.edhelper.com
This site boasts a collection of 10,728 lesson plans, 1,193 WebQuests, 679 file downloads, 8,641 additional Web sites, 4,200 free worksheets, plus updated daily educational news. The materials are as high in quality as they are in number in this impressive collection.

Global Schoolhouse
www.gsh.org
Teachers can find coworkers from around the world to share best practices with. Global SchoolNet combines smart teaching ideas with Web publishing, videoconferencing, and other online tools that bridge geographic gaps, allowing young people around the world to learn together. The more than 900 collaborative projects within the site are organized by grade, topic, and project date.

HomeworkSpot
www.homeworkspot.com
This useful Web site brings all the best homework-related sites together to benefit K–12 teachers, students, and their families. Pages are organized by grade level (elementary, middle school, and high school) and include an entire teacher's category with topics such as grants, integrating technology, special education, and jobs. Students can check out new Web sites, take a virtual field trip, or read the latest headlines. In the Reference section, almanacs, dictionaries, and homework hotlines are available. From the first day of school to the last, you will want to access this site frequently.

The Learning Workshop
www.thelearningworkshop.com
Register at The Learning Workshop and you will have access to online grade books and grade tracking, a class message board, and a personal and class calendar, among many other tools. Classroom management has never been so easy! Students can register to receive testing tips, have online access to their grades, and communicate with their classmates on a classroom message board. Click on Tutors to search the database, organized by ZIP code, to find a tutor in your area. And keep visiting this great site, because it has promised to add even more useful links in the future.

McREL
www.mcrel.org
Bookmark this standards reference site and pull it up as you write your weekly plans! McREL is an authoritative easy-to-use guide to the education standards. Nonprofit educational research group McREL provides an online database of standards that is searchable, written in the simplest language possible, and includes links to classroom activities.

ThinkQuest
www.thinkquest.org
Looking for educational Web sites that are really aimed at kids? ThinkQuest has a large library of informational sites created by kids (and their teachers) for kids. Every year ThinkQuest requests submissions from teams of grade-school students for their Web site competition. Click on Library of Entries to visit their gold mine of educational sites organized by topic and grade level.

▶ Technology

Instructor
http://teacher.scholastic.com/products/instructor
This online version of *Instructor*, a monthly magazine for teachers, provides a comprehensive collection of lesson plan resources as well as information about current educational trends and timely advice that is updated regularly. Select "Web sitings" for a list of the best Web sites to help kids learn while navigating the net.

TeachNet
www.teachnet.org
Teachers Network supports educators in a range of teacher-related topics from learning how to grow professionally to what to do in tomorrow's classroom meeting. This site includes professional resources, grant opportunities, bulletin boards where you can talk with other teachers about specific topics, and more than 500 teacher-created projects. Visit the Daily Classroom Special for timely themes and methods to information about them for your classroom.

Teach-nology
www.teach-nology.com
This impressive Web site has something for every teacher's needs. A vast amount of information is organized so that everything can be found easily and quickly. Click on Web Tools for Educators and you will find tools to create anything from bus passes to student contracts. Teachers can even create their own free Web site. Check out Ideas That Worked to find projects, icebreakers, counseling strategies, and more! Teach-nology also provides excellent technology tutorials. Sign up for its newsletter and receive free weekly teaching tips.

Web Site Evaluation Checklist

Use this checklist to help you and your students identify trustworthy Web sites. The more checks the Web site has, the more reliable a source it is.

Criteria	Yes	No
A. Authorship/Sponsorship: Who Put up the Site?		
Is the name of the individual or group creating the site clearly stated?		
Is the source for information in the site cited where necessary?		
Is there a way for users to make comments or ask questions?		
Has the author been responsive to any questions regarding copyright, trademark, or ownership of all material on the site? Sites that knowingly violate copyright statutes or other laws should not be linked, listed, or recommended.		
B. Purpose: Every Site Has a Reason for Being There.		
Is the site's purpose clear and does content reflect its purpose, be it to entertain, persuade, educate, or sell?		
Is advertising minimal so it does not overshadow the content?		
Does the site enrich the user's experience and expand the imagination without promoting social biases (gender, racial, religious, or other types)?		
C. Design and Stability: A Great Site Has Personality and Strength of Character.		
Is the information on the site easy to find and easy to use?		
Is the site design appealing?		
Is the text easy to read, and not cluttered with distracting graphics, fonts, and backgrounds? Are pages consisting mainly of links well organized and useful for exploring the subject?		
Do the pages load in a reasonable amount of time and without problems?		
Do design elements and features on the site, such as searchable databases, animations, graphics, sound files, introductory and transitional pages, etc., enhance and not hinder the accessibility and enjoyment of the site?		
Are the interactive features explained clearly?		
D. Content: A Great Site Shares Meaningful and Useful Content That Educates, Informs, or Entertains.		
Is the title of a site appropriate to its purpose?		
Is the site's content easy to read and understand?		
Are spelling and grammar correct?		
Is there enough information to make visiting the site worthwhile?		
If there are large amounts of information on the site, is some kind of search function provided? There should be at least an outline of topics covered, allowing the users to find topics and move among them easily.		
Is the information current and accurate? If the topic of the site is one that changes, it should be updated regularly. A "last updated" date is a plus.		
Are links to more information on the topic provided?		
Are the skills required to use the site's features and structure appropriate or appropriately challenging?		

Web site checklist, such as the example on page 144, and that teachers remind them that they need a variety of sources to verify and support the information they find.

Using the Internet for **problem-solving activities** often involves science or math simulations, such as shuttle launches, space missions, ozone layer repair, and stock market investments; cyberhunts, in which students are provided with clues to a puzzle and they search the net for answers; sequential problem solving, in which a student completes one part of an activity before passing it on to the next student; or social action projects, in which students in different locations address the same real-life issue or problem. Harris describes a "save the beaches" project initiated online by middle school students in South Windsor, North Carolina, and involving students worldwide. Read about these and other problem-solving projects at http://lrs.ed.uiuc.edu/Mining/May95-TCT.html. Donald Leu, professor at the University of Connecticut, describes an Internet project for younger learners that involves sequential problem solving and interpersonal exchanges at a global level. The project, developed by Canadian teacher Dale Hubert, is based on book *Flat Stanley* (Jeff Brown's, HarperCollins, 1996). As Leu explains, Hubert and his third-grade students make a Flat Stanley on paper and write e-mail about experiences they create for him. They send both to a collaborating class. The second class writes new

Flat Stanley adventures and sends them and the protagonist himself back to the first class. The project can also include a chain of many participating classes, with each receiving regular adventure updates. To learn more, visit Hubert's Web site at http://flatstanley.enoreo.on.ca.

Ideas abound for facilitating learning with Internet activities. Explore the sites listed throughout this chapter. Contact a technologies facilitator or specialist for your school, even if that person is simply a colleague who knows more about Internet technology and application than you do. Read the monthly articles on instructional technology in *Instructor* magazine (available online at www.scholastic.com/instructor). Or do your own Internet interpersonal exchange, information collection, and problem-solving activities by exploring cyberspace.

A Few Words of Caution About the Internet

Like almost everything else, the Internet has its drawbacks.

The same reason that makes the Internet such a wonderful resource for schools is also why it has the potential to be dangerous for children: Anyone has access. Not only can you find virtual tours of museums and cities, simulations of science experiments, video feeds of events almost anywhere in the world (or space!), and countless documents and information sources, you can also find pornography, the rantings and ravings of hate groups, and people who prey on children.

To protect students and yourself, stay current with school policies and procedures for Internet use. Many schools have software programs that block access to inappropriate sites. At the very least, never leave students unattended as they "surf the net" or even use designated sites. Sometimes even the most harmless-sounding sites can expose children to highly inappropriate content. There was an incident in my area recently involving a link on a police Web site that led to a pornographic site, surprising both the police department and the young child who found it.

Another drawback that deserves mention is the tendency children (and even some adults) have to view everything found on the Internet as "gospel." One of the most important lessons we can teach students is to evaluate the reliability and accuracy of the information they receive. They must ask themselves, "Who is offering the information, and what vested interest do they have in that information?" That, of course, holds true for *any* information, not just that found online. A general rule that I give my seventh and eighth graders is that .org, .gov, and .edu sites will probably be more reliable for research than most .com sites, which usually have a commercial interest in the information they offer. Of course, my students also learn that some .com sites can be the source of wonderful material, and some .org sites represent the most biased of opinions. As Wisconsin teacher Alexis Ludewig notes, students and teachers must learn to read "with a critical eye" and select Web sites appropriate to the task at hand.

Ludewig also notes that "use of time" is an important consideration with Internet activities. As anyone who has ever done a Web search or surfed the Net just for fun knows, it's easy to get sucked into cyberspace and spend hours online without even realizing it.

A TEACHER TESTIMONIAL

"I cannot envision teaching without incorporating technology as a regular part of the daily classroom learning experience for kids," says sixth-grade teacher Martine Wayman. "In this information age, we no longer need to cram students' heads with bits of information because there is simply too much for anyone to know. Instead, we must teach children to use technology as a tool to access information quickly and efficiently."

Wayman's use of technology in the classroom began with her own discovery of how technology could transform her own life and guide her professional development. With a computer and online networks, she began communicating with teachers nationwide—sharing classroom strategies and philosophies. Soon she was leading online educator chats. From there it was a natural step to take telecommunications into the classroom, showing her students how they could communicate with other students and adults via the Internet.

Before long, Wayman's class was accessing current databases to use for their own research projects. They were discussing their topics with professionals in their fields and pursuing their investigations with people all over the country.

Motivation and enthusiasm spread quickly among her students.

"I saw non-readers read. I saw non-writers write."

Soon Wayman felt the need to change her teaching style and her "traditional" classroom to one that was less teacher-directed and more student-directed.

"Technology provided the impetus to radically change my teaching strategies in order to better meet the needs of children today," she explains. "My students became more self-directed. They took responsibility for their own learning and worked cooperatively with me and other students to plan projects and activities that not only met the district curricular requirements but were also true to life rather than simply classroom-oriented. When students saw real value in what they did, they worked harder and obviously enjoyed learning much more."

And it doesn't stop there. Wayman has collaborated with colleagues and scientists to develop a "real-life" science curriculum using the Internet and NASA data sets. As she and thousands of other technology-minded teachers are discovering, the new technology offers unlimited opportunities for improving schooling and for personal and professional growth.

But time is a precious commodity in classrooms. We must ensure that we use the Internet wisely and not as a time-filler or babysitter.

Making Technology Work in the One-Computer Classroom

In teacher Cassie Balzer's class, students collaborate on math assignments by "beaming" questions and answers to each other. Balzer's class is one of three fifth-grade classes in the Souderton, Pennsylvania, district equipped with hand-held computers for each student. The tiny computers allow students to write, calculate, do research, and interact with each other and the teacher. The new technology is woven into the fabric of this classroom. But even in classrooms with only one or several computers, teachers can still harness the power of these learning and teaching tools.

Each month, *Instructor* magazine features examples of using classroom computers effectively. In a recent issue, for example, authors AnJanette Brush and Joy Brewster show teachers how to take students on virtual tours of museums worldwide. With even just one computer (and ideally, a data projector to project the computer screen onto a larger screen), you can take students to St. Petersburg, Russia; Monticello; the Monterey Bay Aquarium; the Smithsonian; and many more of the world's "must-see" sites. Brush and Brewster identify some of the best—those that "offer purposeful and meaningful information, collections, and activities for the classroom":

✔ **United States Holocaust Museum** at www.ushmm.org. Holocaust survivors tell their stories, accompanied by photographs and much more.

✔ **State Hermitage Museum**, St. Petersburg, Russia, at www.hermitage.ru. Emphasizes European history, the Middle Ages, and art history.

✔ **Smithsonian Institution** at www.smithsonianeducation.org/students. The IdeaLabs section offers activities for every content area. And check out the Everything Art

section for a "treasure trove of visual information."

✔ **American Museum of Natural History** at www.amnh.org. One neat aspect is the Meet the OLogists section, where students learn all about scientists and their work.

✔ **Monticello**—Thomas Jefferson's Home in Charlottesville, Virginia, at www.monticello.org. Take a virtual tour, or spend "A Day in the Life" of the third president.

✔ **The Monterey Bay Aquarium** at www.montereybayaquarium.org. "No class with enough bandwidth will be able to resist the links to the live Web cameras placed throughout the aquarium," note Brush and Brewster.

✔ **Exploratorium**, San Francisco, at www.exploratorium.org. Features museum exhibits, science news, and experiments.

✔ **Indianapolis Art Museum** at www.ima-art.org. The Geometry & Art section helps boost middle schoolers' geometry skills as they learn how artists use geometry.

✔ **The Mint Museum of Art**, Charlotte, North Carolina, at www.mintmuseum.org. With an award-winning site on Mesoamerica, "students can watch a video reenactment of a high-stakes Aztec ballgame or explore an interactive timeline," report Brush and Brewster.

✔ **Dupage Children's Museum**, Illinois, at www.dupagechildrensmuseum.org. Allows kids to solve an engineering challenge, then communicate online with a real engineer.

In *Teaching in the Cyberage*, Kristen Nelson expands on the work of Judi Harris to include brain theory in Internet activities. This book features fully developed Internet lessons (grades 4–12) that help students develop their interpersonal exchange skills, information-gathering and analysis skills, and questioning and problem-solving skills. It also supplies Web site descriptions and rubrics for assessing students' understanding and use of multiple intelligences, Internet skills, and information literacy skills.

Technology for Special-Needs Learners

Technology-based resources can also help us meet the needs of students with physical, sensory, or cognitive disabilities. Two of the many good Web sites devoted to special-needs learners are:

✔ The Alliance for Technology Access, at www.ataccess.org

✔ The National Center to Improve Practice, at www2.edc.org/NCIP

In addition, computer software and hardware can be adapted for disabled students. Mac users can visit http://Apple.com/accessibility to learn how. PC users can visit www.microsoft.com/enable/default.htm and find links to accessibility aids.

John Sacco of Tom Snyder Productions reports that many software companies have developed tools to help disabled students and those with different learning styles. "Reading for Meaning" (Tom Snyder Productions) "uses audio recordings along with on-screen text to help boost students' reading comprehension skills." Sacco offers other good examples, including:

✔ Kidspiration, a visual thinking tool that uses outlines and diagrams to help kids organize and develop ideas. www.inspiration.com

✔ Intellikeys, a programmable alternative keyboard for students with physical, visual, or cognitive disabilities. www.intellitools.com

✔ TouchWindow, a tool that allows students to navigate through software using their fingers to move pictures, words, or objects on-screen. www.riverdeep.net

❖ Assigning Homework

As its name implies, homework includes those tasks and assignments students complete at home. Homework is a way to extend learning and practice time. It's a way to encourage student responsibility for learning. And it's a means of assessing how well students have learned what you have tried to teach.

It's important to avoid misusing homework. For example, using homework to make students teach themselves is a mistake many beginners make. Researcher Gaea Leinhardt of the University of Pittsburgh found that novices often used homework to finish an incomplete math lesson, or they jumped right from presenting new lessons to assigning independent practice. This made the homework more difficult to do (and thus more punishing), and it decreased the likelihood the students would complete it.

Instead, homework should be an opportunity to practice newly learned skills—skills you have taught and students have practiced in class under your guidance. Leinhardt found that expert teachers regularly assigned math homework, but only after at least two rehearsals in class where they guided and monitored student efforts.

This guided practice is very important. It means working and talking through examples of the homework you will assign. For example, if you want students to go home and make a list of ten nouns and ten adjectives they can find in their kitchen, first guide them together through a listing of nouns and adjectives they can identify in the classroom. This gives students the opportunity to see the assignment modeled, and it allows you to correct any misunderstandings they may have.

When assigning homework, check your school or district policy. Many districts now have

---

HOMEWORK SHOULD-NOTS

Many teachers with the right intentions assign homework for all the wrong reasons.

Homework should NOT be:

- a task just for students having difficulty
- a chance for students to finish work they couldn't finish in school
- busywork or punishment
- a way for students to teach themselves

Homework Ideas That Work!

These are homework ideas I use with my seventh- and eighth-grade students. They can be adapted to any age level or subject area, and they are a great way to differentiate assignments. Completed assignments can be shared with the class to give students public speaking experience. Use these ideas to generate homework ideas of your own. Add extra depth by having students expand the assignments with online research.

1 Draw a floor plan (to scale) of your bedroom or home. Or design your ideal bedroom. You can write a description or make an architectural design.

2 Collect family stories. Make a list, with a three- or four-sentence description, of those funny, scary, or poignant tales told at family reunions or gatherings. (This is good raw material for later writing assignments and a great way to involve families in schoolwork.)

3 Write an itinerary for the ideal one-week vacation. List several facts about the location you choose, including how far away it is and what type of weather you could expect.

4 Make something that you bring to show the class. Describe how you made it.

5 Invent a new game (board game, athletic game, etc.) and teach everyone how to play.

6 Visit a museum or attend a performance and make a list of at least five interesting things about the experience.

7 Interview your mother, father, family member, or neighbor about his or her job. (Visit the job site, if possible.) Write down at least five reasons why you would like this job and five reasons why you wouldn't like it.

8 Memorize a poem or write your own to recite to the class.

9 Using old magazines and other items, make a collage that shows who you are—your likes, interests, career goals, and so on.

10 Spend an hour watching an animal—the family dog or cat, a bird, squirrel, insect, worm, etc.—and write down as many details as you can. What does it do? Does it make noises? What do you notice about its appearance? Be very specific. (Older students might enjoy modeling their observations on Henry David Thoreau's detailed descriptions of animals in "Neighbors," a section of *Walden*.)

11 Develop a scrapbook (or *PowerPoint* presentation) about an exciting geographical location. Solicit materials from tourism departments or embassies, or find information online.

12 Read a biography or autobiography of a famous person. Make a hat or piece of clothing representing that person, and wear it while delivering a short speech or talk that person might have made.

13 Make a diorama about a scene from a novel or a historic event.

14 Conduct a class (or school) survey about the types of pets students have. Draw a graph to present your data by grade level, gender, or some other way.

Homework Hints for Parents

The following suggestions for helping children with homework are offered by the National Education Association in conjunction with the National PTA.

▶ Assume that your child will have studying to do every night.

▶ Ask your children if they understand their homework. If they don't, do a few examples together.

▶ Ask children to show you their homework after the teacher returns it to see where they are having problems and where they're doing well.

▶ Ask your children's teachers what you can do to support what they are studying.

▶ Remember that you and your children's teachers want the same thing—to help your children learn.

▶ Don't be afraid to contact teachers if you and your child don't understand an assignment, or if your child is having a lot of trouble. Many schools have a homework hot line or a school Website were assignments are posted.

▶ Don't do children's work for them. Help them learn how to do it themselves.

▶ If possible, set up a quiet, comfortable study area with good lighting and the necessary school supplies.

▶ Set a family "quiet time" when you and your children can work together on homework, reading, letter writing, and playing games.

▶ Allow your children to study in the way each learns best. For example, some children work best with background music while others must work in silence. It's best to leave the television off during homework time.

▶ Show your children that you think homework is important. If you are at work during homework time, ask to see their work when you get home.

▶ Encourage your children to do their best. Give praise for good effort as well as achievement.

▶ Maintain a portfolio of your child's "best pieces."

▶ Ask your child's school or teacher for tips about helping your child develop good study habits.

▶ Help older students organize their assignments by recording them on calendars or planners, along with due dates, dates turned in, etc.

From "Helping Your Student Get The Most Out of Homework." Copyright 2002–2004 NEA.org. www.nea.og/parents/homework.html hints.

HOMEWORK CAN WORK

Here's some advice to help you see that it does.

- Explain the purpose of every assignment and why it's important to complete it.
- Offer guided practice of new skills in the classroom before assigning homework on those new skills.
- Communicate your homework expectations to students and parents, including how much homework they can expect, what parents can do to help, and the consequences of unfinished or missed assignments.
- Acknowledge students' efforts in completing homework and encourage parents to do the same.
- Encourage parents to create an atmosphere conducive to homework. (The sofa in front of a blaring television is not a good place!)
- Don't grade homework. Remember, it's intended as practice or enrichment, not a test.
- Do collect, check, discuss, or in some way show that you value students' efforts and that it's worth their while to complete homework assignments.
- Assign homework that will enrich students' experiences and allow them to express individuality and creativity.
- Use assignment logs to help students remember to do their homework. Many schools now purchase commercially prepared assignment books to use with students as young as second or third grade. These weekly logs, or ones you prepare yourself, give students and parents a complete and accurate listing of all assignments. It's also a good idea to have parents sign the logs as assignments are completed. Many schools call these assignment logs "study buddies."
- Post homework on your class or school Web site. This acts as a backup for students and is a way for parents to monitor assignments.

Find more great homework tips for teachers from the Corporation for Educational Technology at www.buddyproject.org/jfy/teachers/articles/homework.asp.

guidelines concerning when and how much homework can be assigned. The National Education Association makes these suggestions:

✔ Homework should not exceed 10 to 20 minutes per day for students in grades K though 2.

✔ Students in grades 3 through 6 can handle 30 to 60 minutes daily.

Homework for junior high school students will vary by subject, and students may need help organizing and meeting deadlines for long-term projects or papers.

❖ In Summary

Motivation is the key to learning. As experienced teachers know and research confirms, personal desire or motivation must underlie any attempt to learn. Good teachers capitalize on students' interests and curiosity; with effective instructional strategies, teachers can motivate students and foster a natural desire to learn.

Teaching strategies that cut across curricular areas and help motivate students include organizing instruction into integrated, thematic units; using cooperative learning and group approaches; recognizing and teaching to multiple intelligences; accommodating individual learning styles; giving students choices about what they learn and how; stressing thinking skills; asking good questions; offering culturally responsive curricula; harnessing the power of technology in meaningful ways; praising and encouraging students effectively; holding imagination and creativity in high esteem; acknowledging the importance of active teaching, engaged time, and academic learning time.

Helping children become independent and enthusiastic lifelong learners—isn't that what good teaching is about?

❖ **Works Cited**

Bach, Richard. *Jonathan Livingston Seagull*. New York: Macmillan, 1970.

Bloom, Benjamin S. *Taxonomy of Educational Objectives: The Classification of Educational Goals.* (Handbook I, Cognitive Domain). New York: Longmans, Green, 1956. (For a user-friendly online description of the taxonomy developed by Kent School District in Washington, see www.Kent.wednet.edu/KSD/MA/resources/blooms/blooms.html.)

Brandt, Ron. "Why People Learn." *Educational Leadership* 53, no.1 (September 1995). Available: www.ascd.org.

Brophy, Jere. "On Praising Effectively." *Elementary School Journal* (1981): 269–278.

Brophy, Jere. "Toward a Model of the Value Aspects of Motivation in Education: Developing Appreciation for Particular Learning Domains and Activities." *Educational Psychologist* 34, no.2 (1999): 75–85.

Brush, AnJanette, and Joy Brewster. "Great Museums On-line." *Instructor,* January/February 2004, 30–35.

Buzzeo, Toni. *Dawdle Duckling*. New York: Dial Books, 2003.

Buzzeo, Toni. *The Sea Chest*. New York: Dial Books, 2002.

Caruthers, Loyce. "Classroom Interactions and Achievement." *What's Noteworthy on Learners, Learning, Schooling*. Aurora, CO: Mid-continent Regional Educational Laboratory, 1995. Available: www.mcrel.org/topics/noteworthy.asp.

Clark, Barbara. *Growing Up Gifted: Developing the Potential of Children at Home and at School*. 6th ed. Upper Saddle River, NJ: Merrill/Prentice-Hall, 2002.

Cohen, Elizabeth. *Designing Groupwork: Strategies for the Heterogeneous Classroom*. 2nd ed. New York: Teachers College Press, 1994.

Cohen, Elizabeth. *Working for Equity in Heterogeneous Classrooms*. New York: Teachers College Press, 1997.

Cohen, Elizabeth, and R. A. Latan "Equity in Heterogeneous Classrooms." In J. Banks and C. Banks, eds., *Handbook of Multicultural Education*. 2nd ed. New York: Teachers College Press, 2003.

Daniels, Harvey. *Literature Circles: Voice and Choice in Book Clubs and Reading Groups*. 2nd ed. Portland, ME: Stenhouse, 2002.

"Department to Study Technology's Role in Raising Student Achievement." Press release. U.S. Dept. of Education, February 13, 2004. Available: www.ed.gov/news/pressreleases/2004/02/02132004.html.

Dockterman, David A. *Easy Ways to Make Technology Work for You*. New York: Scholastic, 2002.

Evans, Timothy. "The Tools of Encouragement." *CYC-Online*. Child and Youth Care International, June 2004. Available: www.cyc-net.org/cyc-online/cycol-0604-evans.html.

Fanning, James. "Expanding the Definition of Technological Literacy in Schools." *What's Noteworthy on Learners, Learning, Schooling*. Aurora, CO: Mid-continent Regional Educational Laboratory, 1995: 33–37. Available: www.mcrel.org/topics/noteworthy.asp.

"Focus on Differentiated Instruction." *Curriculum•Technology Quarterly* 9, no. 3 (Spring 2000). Available: www.ascd.org/handbook/demo/ctq/8spr00.html.

George, Jean Craighead. *Julie of the Wolves*. New York: Harper, 1972.

Hait, Helen. "Effective Instruction for Creating a Classroom Community: A Brief Study of Contributing Factors in Group Work." *Educational Insights* 8, no. 3 (March 2004). Available: www.ccfi.educ.ubc.ca/publication/insights/v08n03/articles/hait.html.

"Helping Your Student Get the Most Out of Homework." National Education Association, 2004. Available: www.nea.org/parents/homework.html.

Jacobson, Jennifer Richard. *Moon Sandwich Mom.* Morton Grove, IL: Albert Whitman, 1999.

Jacobson, Jennifer Richard. *Truly Winnie.* Boston: Houghton Mifflin, 2003.

Jacobson, Jennifer Richard, and Toni Buzzeo, "Meet Favorite Kids' Authors On-line." *Instructor,* October 2003, 25–27.

Jensen, Eric. "Brain-based Learning: A Reality Check." *Educational Leadership* 57, no. 7 (2000): 76–79.

Jensen, Eric. "Brain-based Learning: Where's the Proof?" Available: www.jensenlearning.com/truth.html.

Katz, Lilian. "The Project Approach." ERIC Clearinghouse on Early Education and Parenting, 1994. Available: http://ceep.crc.uiuc.edu/eecearchive/digests/1994/lk-pro94.html.

Kiester, Edwin Jr. and Sally Valente. "How to Teach Your Child to Think." *Readers' Digest,* June 1991, 140–144.

Kohn, Alfie. "Choices for Children: Why and How to Let Students Decide." *Phi Delta Kappan* 75, no. 1 (September 1993): 8–20. Available: www.alfiekohn.org/teaching/cfc.htm.

Kohn, Alfie. *Punished by Rewards: The Trouble With Gold Stars, Incentive Plans, A's, Praise, and Other Bribes.* Boston: Houghton Mifflin, 1999.

Leinhardt, Gaea. "Expertise in Mathematics Teaching." *Educational Leadership* 43, no. 7 (April 1986): 28–33.

Leu, Donald Jr. "Flat Stanley Goes Cyber." *Instructor,* January/February 2003, 28–31.

McCombs, Barbara. "Learner-Centered Principles and Technology." *Teacherline,* January 2001. Available: http://2kbb2.pbs.org/teacherline/resources/articles/article_jan01.cfm.

McCombs, Barbara. "Understanding the Keys to Motivation to Learn." *What's Noteworthy on Learners, Learning, Schooling.* Aurora, Co: Mid-continent Regional Educational Laboratory Winter 1995: 5–12. Available: www.mcrel.org/topics/noteworthy.asp.

Means, Barbara, and Kerry, Olson. "The Link Between Technology and Authentic Learning." *Educational Leadership* 51, no. 7 (April 1994): 15–18.

Meier, Deborah. Interview. *Educational Leadership* 52, no. 1 (September 1994).

Merrow, John. "In Schools We Trust: An Interview with Deborah Meier." *The Merrow Report.* Original airdate January 1997. Available: www.pbs.org/merrow/tv/trust/interviews.html.

Moore, Dawn. "Information Literacy Strategies—Using the Internet." Schamburg Community Schools, 2004. Available: http://web54.sd54.k12.il.us/district54/lts/dmoore/infoliteracy.

Nelson, Kristen. *Developing Students' Multiple Intelligences.* New York: Scholastic, 1999.

Osborne, Alex. *Applied Imagination.* New York: Scribner, 1963.

Rocco, Michael. "Hand-held Program Doing Well in Souderton Schools." *Lansdale Reporter,* April 25, 2004.

Rogers, Michele. "Windows of Opportunity." *Sonoma Medicine* 54, no. 3 (Summer 2003). Available: www.sonic.net/~scma/magazine/scp/sm03/rogers.html

Ruenzel, David. "Ron Brandt's Address at Brain Connection's Conference Brain Research and Effective Teaching." *Brainconnection,* 2000. Available: www.brainconnection.com.

Sacco, John. "Electronic Learning: Special-Needs Solutions." *Instructor,* 2004. Available: http://teacher.Scholastic.com/products/instructor/specialneeds.htm.

"Screen It Out: Teaching With Computers." *The Economist* 365, no. 8296 (October 26 2002): 13.

Sousa, David. "Is the Fuss About Brain Research Justified? In a Word, Absolutely." Center for Development and Learning, 1998. Available: www.cdl.org/resources/reading_room/brains_research.html.

Stephens, Karen. "Praise: Like Sugar, It Should Be Sprinkled, Not Poured." *Child Care Exchange,* 2002. Available: www.childcareexchange.com.

Strube, Penny. *Theme Studies: A Practical Guide.* New York: Scholastic, 1993.

Sylwester, Robert. "What the Biology of the Brain Tells Us About Learning." *Educational Leadership* 51, no. 4 (December 1993/January 1994).

Tomlinson, Carol Ann. "Mapping a Route Toward Differentiated Instruction." *Educational Leadership* 57, no. 1 (September 1999): 12–17. Weiss, Ruth B. "Brain-Based Learning." *Training and Development* 54, no. 7 (July 2000).

❖ Resources

Brain-Based Instruction
Given, Barbara K. *Teaching to the Brain's Natural Learning Systems.* Alexandria, VA: Association for Supervision and Curriculum Development, 2002.

Greenwald, John. "Retraining Your Brain [Fast ForWord]." *Time Magazine* July 5, 1999.

Jensen, Eric. *Brain-Based Learning.* Del Mar, CA: Turning Point Publishing, 1995.

Nickelsen, LeAnn. *Memorizing Strategies & Other Brain-Based Activities That Help Kids Learn, Review, and Recall.* New York: Scholastic, 2003.

Nunley, K., and G. Van Tassell. *Practical Brain Applications of Current Brain Research,* 2001. Available: www.brains.org.

Sousa, David. *How the Brain Learns: A Classroom Teacher's Guide.* 2nd ed. Thousand Oaks, CA: Corwin Press, 2001.

Sylwester, Robert. *A Biological Brain in a Cultural Classroom: Enhancing Cognitive and Social Development Through Collaborative Management.* 2nd ed. Thousand Oaks, CA: Corwin Press, 2003.

Wolfe, Pat. *Brain Matters: Translating Research into Classroom Practices.* Alexandria, VA: Association for Supervision and Curriculum Development, 2001.

Cooperative Learning and Group Work
Cohen, Elizabeth G. "Making Cooperative Learning Equitable." *Education Leadership* 56, no. 1 (September 1998): 18–21.

Differentiated Instruction
Tomlinson, Carol A. *The Differentiated Classroom: Responding to the Needs of All Learners.* Alexandria, VA: Association for Supervision and Curriculum Development, 1999.

Yatvin, Joanne. *A Room With a Differentiated View: How to Serve All Children as Individual Learners.* Portsmouth, NH: Heinemann, 2004.

Encouragement and Praise
Brophy, Jere. *Motivating Students to Learn.* New York: McGraw-Hill, 1998.

Dinkmeyer, D., and L. Losoncy. *The Skills of Encouragement.* Delray, FL: St. Lucie Press, 1996.

Evans, Timothy. "The Encouraging Teacher." In G. M. Gazda et al., eds. *Human Relations Development.* Boston: Allyn & Bacon, 1995: 261–69.

Motivation and Student Achievement
Marzano, Robert, et al. *Classroom Instruction That Works: Research-Based Strategies for Increasing Student Achievement.* Alexandria, VA: Association for Supervision and Curriculum Development, 2001.

McCombs, Barbara. *The Learner-Centered Classroom and School: Strategies for Enhancing Student Motivation and Achievement.* San Francisco: Jossey-Bass, 1997.

McCombs, Barbara, and Nadine M. Lambert. *How Students Learn: Reforming Schools Through Learner-Centered Education.* Washington, DC: American Psychological Association, 1998.

McCombs, Barbara, and James Pope. *Motivating Hard-to-Reach Students.* Washington DC: American Psychological Association, 1994.

Meier, Deborah. *In Schools We Trust: Creating Communities of Learning in an Era of Testing and Standardization.* Boston: Beacon Press, 2003.

Multiple Intelligences
Armstrong, Thomas. *Multiple Intelligences in the Classroom.* Alexandria, VA: Association for Supervision and Curriculum Development, 1994.

Fogarty, Robin, and Judy Stoehr, eds. *Multiple Intelligences.* Palatine, IL: IRI/Skylight Publishing, 1995.

Gardner, Howard. *Creating Minds.* New York: Basic Books, 1993.

Gardner, Howard. *Multiple Intelligences: The Theory in Practice.* New York: Basic Books, 1993.

Gray, Lynell, et al. *Multiple Intelligences.* Washington, DC: NEA Professional Library, 1996.

Haggerty, Brian. *Nurturing Intelligences: A Guide to Multiple Intelligences Theory and Teaching.* Menlo Park, CA: Addison-Wesley, 1995.

Starko, A. J. *Creativity in the Classroom.* New York: Longman Publishers, 1995.

Project Approach
Chard, Sylvia. C. *The Project Approach: Making Curriculum Come Alive.* New York: Scholastic, 1998.

Chard, Sylvia. C. *The Project Approach: Managing Successful Projects.* New York: Scholastic, 1998. (Chard's Web site, project-approach.com, features examples of projects such as the two shown on pages 114–117. You can also view highlights of the Project Approach CD Chard has developed, which is available for purchase.)

Harmin, Merril. *Inspiring Active Learning: A Handbook for Teachers.* Alexandria, VA: Association for Supervision and Curriculum Development, 1994.

Katz, Lilian G., and Sylvia C. Chard. *Engaging Children's Minds: The Project Approach.* Norwood, NJ: Ablex, 2000.

Sharan, Yael and Shlomo. *Expanding Cooperative Learning Through Group Investigation.* New York: Teachers College Press, 1992.

Technology and Education

Ashdown, David. *Hyperstudio Made Very Easy!* New York: Scholastic, 2000.

Cuban, Larry. *Oversold and Underused: Computers in the Classroom.* Cambridge, MA: Harvard University Press, 2001.

Green, Timothy. *PowerPoint Made Very Easy!* New York: Scholastic, 2003.

Harris, Judi. *Virtual Architecture: Designing & Directing Curriculum-Based Telecomputing.* Eugene, OR: International Society for Technology in Education, 1998.

Kassem, Lou. *Middle School Blues.* Boston: Houghton Mifflin, 1986.

Means, Barbara, and G. D. Haertel, eds. *What Research Should Tell Us About Using Technology in Schools.* New York: Teachers College Press, 2005.

Nelson, Kristen. *Teaching in the Cyberage.* Arlington Heights, IL: Skylight Professional Development, 2000.

Thornberg, David. *The New Basics: Education and the Future of Work in the Telematic Age.* Alexandria, VA: Association for Supervision and Curriculum Development, 2002.

Theme Teaching

Gamberg, Ruth, et al. *Learning and Loving It: Theme Studies in the Classroom.* Portsmouth, NH: Heinemann, 1988.

Kotch, Laura, and Leslie Zachman. *The Author Studies Handbook: Helping Students Build Powerful Connections to Literature.* New York: Scholastic, 2001.

Chapter Four

Assessment and Evaluation

"Authentic achievement involves the challenge of producing, rather than reproducing, knowledge."

—Fred M. Newmann, professor, University of Wisconsin

Each year, you and your students will take a long trip together. Destination: increased learning and achievement. Where you start, the route you take, and when you get there will vary from class to class and student to student. But the map that guides you along your way—student assessment—remains the same.

Effective assessment means much more than just giving paper-and-pencil tests and assigning letter grades. The process occurs before, during, and after lessons, units, or marking periods. It is a way of charting students' progress. And it provides a vehicle for instructional planning. In fact, experts say good assessment drives instruction. You can't plan for effective instruction until you know where students are, where you want them to go, and how you want them to get there. Assessment also gives parents, students, and others a profile or report on student achievement. And with student input and ownership, assessment can even motivate students to perform and produce.

Assessment of student achievement has undergone a major overhaul in the last two decades. This overhaul has resulted in two major complementary assessment trends: **authentic assessment**—assessment derived from best practices in the classroom;

Authentic assessment, based on authentic learning, simply means that students work on real problems and real tasks or projects, and their academic growth is viewed in terms not only of the outcomes they produce but also the processes they undertake. With authentic assessment, the line between teaching and testing becomes blurred because students continue learning during the assessment. In fact, many of the assessments presented in this chapter are also good instructional strategies.

and **standards-based assessment**—assessment derived from general academic standards and objectives developed by each state and used to explain the concepts and skills students are expected to master at each grade level. Each informs teaching and helps us fine-tune our instruction to the specific needs of individual students. Good teaching incorporates multiple forms of assessment, and good teachers balance students' individual needs with grade-appropriate expectations as they plan instruction and assessment.

Balanced assessment includes both new strategies and traditional tools, such as objective tests and standardized achievement tests. Today's teachers are challenged to maintain this balance in light of national legislation, which has placed standardized tests in a more prominent role than ever. Standardized assessment of achievement has become the linchpin of the federal legislation now driving America's public schools.

❖ Assessment in the National Spotlight

On January 8, 2002, the No Child Left Behind (NCLB) Act was signed into law by President George Bush. NCLB, which had been in development for more than 10 years, reflects national concerns over low educational achievement and expectations for our students. According to the U.S. Department of Education, "Some schools operate without a clear set of expectations [for what] teachers and students should achieve in critically important subjects." As a result, the federal government now requires each state to establish its own **standards of learning** outlining what students should know and be able to do in the core content subjects—reading, math, and science. States are also responsible for designing tests to measure those standards.

Several important points for educators to understand about NCLB legislation include:

✔ Taxpayer dollars will go only to states that have established standards and expectations for improving schools or teaching a solid academic curriculum.

✔ States are required to administer their own annual tests aligned with state standards for grades three through eight to measure how successfully students are learning what is expected by the standards. According to the Department of Education, the tests serve as "accountability systems [that] gather specific, objective data through tests aligned with standards." Test data "is used to identify strengths and weaknesses in the system." States not establishing standards and measuring them with annual achievement tests are not eligible for federal funding.

✔ NCLB requires all schools to make **adequate yearly progress** (AYP), by showing yearly test score gains in reading/language arts and math, and improvements in either graduation rate (for high schools) or attendance rate (for elementary and middle/junior high schools). If a school fails to meet AYP goals after two consecutive years, the school must offer supplemental education services for students or school choice (parents may send their children to a better-performing school), and/or the school must take "corrective actions" such as personnel changes or curriculum and instruction reform. Costs are subtracted from federal funding received.

All Agree on High Standards

The U.S. Department of Education reports that 88 percent of Americans support holding schools to higher standards. Like the rest of the nation, educators believe in setting high standards for teaching and learning, which has become a primary focus for staff development and teacher trainings.

"School leaders have embraced the standards and accountability movement," claims the 2003 Wallace Foundation report *Rolling Up Their Sleeves: Superintendents and Principals Talk About What's Needed to Fix Public Schools*. "Many indicate they have been focusing on student achievement, teacher quality, and accountability for quite some time [prior to the NCLB initiative]." The report also notes that "superintendents in urban districts seem to be especially responsive to implementing standards."

At the classroom level, former sixth-grade teacher Clair Berube speaks for many teachers when she praises standards-based education: "I would have been unable to teach without the Virginia Standards of Learning," claims Berube, now an assistant professor. "They gave me a wonderful road map that I coordinated with my curriculum guide and the district's guidelines."

Indeed, almost everyone agrees with the idea of standards-based teaching and learning. But the translation of the law into practice has posed some serious challenges for many public school educators.

Challenges for NCLB

"The problem is not the standards but, rather, how the standards are assessed," writes Berube, who says that "something went terribly wrong" when states started measuring how schools achieved standards with multiple-choice, high-stakes tests and equating this achievement with school success. This is one of the strongest criticisms of the legislation—that all stakes hang on standardized test scores, which are only one measure of school success.

A key concern is that since schools vary greatly in average class size and access to qualified teachers, textbooks, and technology, it is unfair to require all schools in a state to meet the same standards in the same time frame. "Judging schools solely on the percentage of students who pass a single test each year does not accurately reflect a school's performance," claims the National Education Association and the Northwest Evaluation Association. James Popham, professor emeritus at the University of California, Los Angeles, points out that measuring school success "exclusively" by students' performance on standardized tests impacts every level of school evaluation. For example, he cites the government-sponsored Blue Ribbon Schools program, which has been revamped since the enactment of NCLB so that schools are recognized soley on the merit of their performance on the required state tests.

Another issue is lack of funding for new programs or program changes outlined in the legislation. Some 89 percent of the nation's superintendents and 88 percent of principals see NCLB as "an unfunded mandate," according to the 2003 Wallace Foundation report. For example, this lack of funding has resulted in hastily prepared standardized tests that often contain content errors and may be poorly matched to content standards. There are even cases in which states have simply recycled older standardized tests to cut costs, calling into question the reliability of the test.

Another point of concern is that high-stakes testing can unduly pressure—rather than challenge and support—administrators, teachers, and students. High-pressure situations occur when school districts link grade retention decisions or graduation requirements directly to students' standardized test scores. In many districts the test results are being used to measure teacher and administrator performance, according to a report prepared by Public Agenda for the Wallace Foundation report. Superintendents and principals interviewed for the report claim that test scores result in a much tougher scrutiny of teachers and principals. Standardized test scores at the classroom level may impact teacher evaluations and even tenure decisions; schoolwide scores may help determine principal evaluations and reassignments.

"The pressure on teachers and administrators to improve these [standardized test] scores is enormous," writes former professor Dave Posner. He notes that until recently, teachers in California were offered a cash bonus relative to improved test scores. Other states, such as Florida, have offered students cash bonuses for scoring well. What can happen in these high-stakes situations? Education writer and consultant Mark Goldberg has identified numerous examples of states cited for testing irregularities. "A high-pressure atmosphere in which jobs and bonuses—not to mention the school's reputation and even real estate values—are at stake can cause teachers and administrators to alter best practices and even to engage in unethical behavior," Goldberg writes. He notes that even graduation rates have been altered by classifying dropouts as students leaving the district.

Finally, many teachers and administrators approach the challenge of helping students prepare for the tests by narrowing the curriculum and "teaching to the test." Even before NCLB, my children's elementary school placed high priority on high test scores. Every year after Christmas, teachers were directed to stop teaching social studies so they could schedule a double math period. Yes, we usually had the highest test scores in the county. But our children missed out on instruction that could have better prepared them to understand our complex world.

We are witnessing what the National Center for Fair and Open Testing, in a 170-page report, has found after reviewing the first two years of NCLB: The heavy reliance on standardized tests, together with severe penalties for not meeting adequate yearly progress, is resulting in a narrowing of the curriculum and intensive teaching to the test.

What are the consequences of teaching and learning by standardized tests? David Posner argues that students who can only solve standardized test problems may lack the skills and learning necessary to tackle difficult real-life problems. "Individuals equipped only with the ability to solve routine problems would be those most vulnerable to displacement by automation," he claims.

Further, many question the assumption that improved test scores mean increased achievement. Do we judge musical or athletic performance with a multiple-choice test? Yet that's what we're trying to do with important skills and abilities in the areas of mathematics, science, and language.

"Achievement should not be measured by how well we train our students to take multiple choice tests," says Berube. "If we are not careful, we could become a nation of people who score high on standardized tests but who cannot understand, analyze, synthesize, and evaluate what we have truly learned."

What Can We Do?

Now, more than ever, we teachers have a duty and moral obligation to understand assessment and how we can use it to improve achievement.

"Assessment-related ignorance is the overriding obstacle," says Professor James Popham. He urges educators at every level to understand the assessments they use. Until they do, "they'll not be able to protest the misapplication of the wrong test in their own settings." As he notes, "traditional standardized tests are wonderful for certain purposes, but when you apply them for other purposes, purposes for which they were not intended, you get distorted results."

Popham suggests that we could vastly improve standardized tests by making them "measure a smaller number of super-important skills," with many different items targeting that small number of critical skills. These would give us the most accurate picture of a student's achievement. Yet, as they stand now, most tests attempt to measure too many skills with too few test items. Further, Popham posits, "accountability tests should look more like the writing-sample exams where we try to find out if a kid can write a decent persuasive essay by having the kid actually write a persuasive essay."

As advocates for children and quality instruction, we can become assessment savvy and urge our state- and district-level administrators to develop appropriate standardized measures. In the meantime, Popham suggests that teachers and schools "spend much more time doing instructionally informative classroom assessment and limit the amount of large-scale assessment time to an absolute minimum."

Many assessment procedures are specific to the content area. These content-specific procedures are discussed later in this chapter. Following are strategies and ideas that can generally apply to assessment in most subject areas.

MEASUREMENT MATTERS

Backward design works as a three-stage process (see page 162). Below is a very abbreviated example of a first-grade unit on linear measurement developed by West Virginia teacher Susan Naylor. You can find the entire unit, Measurement Matters, at http://reinvent.k12.wv.us/lt/homepage.nsf/PreviewHomePages/math.

Stage 1. Desired Results (Select the enduring understandings or big ideas you want students to know, based on actual standards and objectives.)
   a. Why does length matter?
   b. Why do we need a "standard" way to measure length?
      • Students will understand that one attribute of objects is length, and length can be used to compare and order objects. There are many ways to measure length and it is important to have a "standard" unit for measuring length.
      • Students will know key terms such as *standard, nonstandard, inch, centimeter, ruler, tape measure*.
      • Students will be able to measure length with nonstandard units, measure length with inch and centimeter rulers, and compare and order objects by length.

Stage 2. Assessment Evidence (What formal and informal assessments can measure student knowledge, based on specified performance descriptors?)
   a. Nonstandard measuring—students use dominoes, paper clips, and crayons to measure classroom objects.
   b. Inch-by-Inch—students use inchworm manipulatives, then inch rulers, to measure classroom objects.
   c. Scavenger Hunt—students use inch and centimeter rulers to measure, compare, and order classroom objects.
   d. Measure Me!—students use inch and centimeter sides of tape measure to measure and record different parts of their bodies.
   e. Other Evidence—teacher observation, class discussions, and learning log entries of measurement activities.

Stage 3. Learning Plan (These are the actual classroom activities and teacher instruction leading to student achievement and understanding.)
   a. Introduce unit with discussion about the kinds of things we measure length of, and why length matters.
   b. Demonstrate how to use dominoes to measure a blackboard eraser. Students then work independently or in pairs to measure other classroom objects using dominoes, recording their results.
   c. Students re-measure the classroom objects using other units of measurement, such as crayons or paper clips. Students discuss why the measurements are different, why it matters, and what they could do about it (all use the same unit of measure—a "standard").
   d. Read the story *Inch by Inch* by Leo Lionni. Use inchworm tiles to introduce measuring in inches, a "standard" measure.

❖ Starting With Standards

Assessment specialists Grant Wiggins and Jay McTighe have developed a process to help teachers use state standards to design assessment and guide instruction. The process, called Understanding by Design, is a framework for **backward design**. It's "backward" only because it runs counter to traditional practice.

As Wiggins and McTighe explain it, teachers start by specifying the desired results (the standards and objectives), asking themselves, "What is it I want students to understand and be able to do as a result of instruction?" Next, they design the assessments for measuring student achievement of these desired results. Only then do they actually plan the instruction.

The goal here, say Wiggins and McTighe, is teaching for understanding. Teachers play the critical role of "designers of student learning." As such, they can be most effective by basing instruction on the following key ideas:

✔ A primary goal of education should be the development and deepening of student understanding.

✔ Students reveal their understanding most effectively when they are provided with complex, authentic opportunities to **explain, interpret, apply, shift perspective, empathize,** and **self-assess**. When applied to complex tasks, these "six facets" provide a conceptual lens through which teachers can better assess student understanding.

✔ Effective curriculum development reflects a three-stage design process called "backward design" that delays the planning of classroom activities until goals have been clarified and assessments designed. This process helps to avoid the twin problems of "textbook coverage" and "activity-oriented" teaching, in which no clear priorities and purposes are apparent.

✔ Student and school performance gains are achieved through regular reviews of results (achievement data and student work) followed by targeted adjustments to curriculum and instruction. Teachers become most effective when they seek feedback from students and their peers and use that feedback to adjust approaches to design and teaching.

✔ Teachers, schools, and districts benefit by "working smarter" through the collaborative design, sharing, and peer review of units of study. (Toward this end, Wiggins and McTighe have developed a subscription-based Web site devoted to the development and peer review of curricular units. Check it out at www.ubdexchange.org.)

❖ Authentic Assessment

The scope and depth of our curriculum, combined with our students' varied skill levels, require us to measure student learning with more than paper-and-pencil tests. Authentic assessments include teacher observations, learning log entries, scavenger hunts, and other subject- or need-appropriate assessments like those listed in Naylor's Measurement Matters lesson on page 161.

Authentic assessment reflects a concern that traditional assessment tools (including standardized tests) do not accurately measure thinking and problem-solving skills, in-depth subject knowledge, or how well students can direct their own learning.

Further, traditional assessments ignore the learning styles of many students. They are presented in a visual or written mode and require children to retrieve information in a visual way. If a student's strengths and dominant learning style is auditory or kinesthetic, he or she is seriously handicapped on written tests. These are the students we know to be "bright, but just not good test-takers."

The intent of an "authentic" assessment is to assess fairly and accurately the real learning of *all* students. Authentic assessment should actively involve students, give them feedback from teachers and peers, allow them to make choices and demonstrate their strengths and successes, and encourage them to build on what they already know.

There are many different ways teachers can assess student knowledge and achievement authentically. Some of the best include portfolios, exhibitions, performances, journals, projects, presentations, and experiments. Effective teachers design these assessments to be part of the learning process itself. Many call it **performance-based teaching**.

Jay McTighe, director of the Maryland Assessment Consortium, speaks for many educators when he suggests that teachers **teach** for performance, not just **measure** it. He offers seven instructional principles that reflect a performance orientation:

✔ **Establish clear performance targets**. In a sense, this requires teachers to use their performance assessments as a goal for their teaching and learning. And doesn't it make sense that both our teaching and our assessment should reflect what we expect students to understand and be able to do as a result of their learning?

"A performance-based orientation," says McTighe, "requires that we think about curriculum not simply as content to be covered but in terms of desired *performances of understanding*."

✔ **Strive for authenticity in products and performances**. Do the activities you assign to students reflect the world outside the classroom? For example, have your future scientists conduct actual experiments or formulate hypotheses. Future builders or engineers could demonstrate knowledge of area by measuring the square footage of their classroom or homes.

✔ **Publicize criteria and performance standards**. Let students know ahead of time what you expect a good performance or product to look like. Knowing the standards actually improves

the performance, say McTighe and other assessment experts.

✔ **Provide models of excellence**. Publicizing the performance standards is not enough. "If we expect students to do excellent work, they need to know what excellent work looks like," says McTighe. Athletic coaches have their players review films of winning and losing performances to help them understand how to improve their own efforts. Classroom teachers need to do the same. What does a well-designed and -executed art project look like? What does a well-written paper look like? Students need to see and analyze these models to know how to improve their own.

✔ **Teach strategies explicitly**. "In every field of endeavor, effective performers use specific techniques and strategies to boost their performance," says McTighe, offering such examples as athletes who visualize great performances, writers who seek critical feedback, and law students who form study

DIFFERENTIATED LEARNING PRODUCTS

Not everyone has to demonstrate learning in the same way. Many educators have found that students need to be given choices about how they will demonstrate what they've learned. We call this "differentiating the product." Students know their strengths and interests, and having a choice motivates them and helps them succeed.

Author and educator Barbara Clark explains that performance assessments can be produced for visual, oral, or written presentation. She offers the following as examples of products that can verify that learning has occurred and also serve as part of the learning process:

1. **Verbal Products:** role-play, simulations, panel discussions, audiotapes, debates, lectures, and tutorials
2. **Visual Products:** charts, illustrations, filmstrips, graphs, collages, murals, maps, time lines, flowcharts, diagrams, posters, and advertisements
3. **Kinesthetic Products:** dioramas, puzzles, games, sculpture, and exhibits
4. **Written Products:** journals, diaries, logs, reports, abstracts, letters, essays, thought or position papers

For more on differentiated instruction, see Chapter Three.

groups. He urges teachers to present specific strategies to improve academic performance, such as graphic organizers to show connections, brainstorming techniques to help generate ideas, mnemonics to improve retention and recall.

✔ **Use ongoing assessments for feedback and adjustment**. Just as the reviewing, feedback, and revising phases help us improve our writing, regular assessments throughout the learning process help students improve their performance. Scrimmages and dress rehearsals help athletes and performers identify problems and fine-tune their performances. Practice tests, review processes, and peer response groups, says McTighe, could help students do the same. Assessment should enhance performance, not simply measure it.

✔ **Document and celebrate performance**. Experts insist that we can motivate students to keep trying harder by focusing on what they can do and how they have improved.

Following are additional teacher-tested tips for developing authentic assessment:

✔ **Use a variety of tasks and products** to match the learning styles and needs of different types of learners.

✔ **Plan assessments that require an audience**. A real audience, whether it be peers, parents, community members, or younger children, motivates children to produce quality performances and products. When my junior high students present their research projects, we always invite parents and grandparents, who appreciate the opportunity to participate.

✔ **Give students the chance to assess each other**. Using an evaluation guideline that I prepare, my seventh and eighth graders offer constructive comments to classmates presenting research projects. (Parent visitors also are asked to participate.) This task not only keeps them focused as audience members, it helps them think about improving their own presentations.

✔ **Teach students to assess themselves** by showing them how to identify their strengths and weaknesses. Help them use self-questioning strategies. Pose questions such as *What kind of writer am I? Where would I like to improve? What will help me improve?* Write down the questions and ask the students to respond in writing.

✔ **Involve parents in the assessment process**. For example, share student portfolios with parents by displaying them at conference time or sending them home. One goal of assessment is accountability, so show parents what their children have learned and can do.

Portfolio Assessment

One of the most popular forms of authentic assessment is the portfolio. A portfolio contains representative work samples selected in a variety of ways for various purposes.

Students can collect work samples over time to demonstrate how much they've learned and how far they have progressed. Since the intent is often to document progress, student portfolios might include not only polished pieces, but also the earlier, less-skilled work that a professional portfolio would not include.

Portfolios can contain more than just "flat" pieces of writing or artwork. They can include audiotaped or videotaped performances, computer disks, photographs of projects, and often, student, parent, and teacher evaluations of the contents.

Information and ideas abound on establishing and maintaining portfolio assessment, and you must pick and choose to create the system that works best for you and your students. Some good resources to get you started are listed at the end of this section.

There are different types of portfolios to serve different purposes.

✔ **Showcase portfolios** celebrate a student's best work.

✔ **Descriptive portfolios** demonstrate what a student can do without evaluating it.

✔ **Evaluative portfolios** assess and measure the quality of student work against some standard.

✔ **Progress portfolios** document work over time in a particular subject area.

What Should It Contain? A student portfolio can contain many different types of work, depending upon its purpose and the content area it represents. In many elementary schools and middle schools, one portfolio serves all integrated subjects.

In his book *Portfolio Assessment: Getting Started*, Allan DeFina identifies items that could be included in a language arts portfolio. Many of these could serve other content areas equally well.

✔ essays and reports
✔ letters
✔ poetry and other creative writing
✔ sequels/spin-offs to stories
✔ problem statements/solutions
✔ reader-response logs/reviews
✔ journal entries
✔ interviews
✔ posters/artistic media
✔ collaborative works
✔ workbook pages, quizzes, tests
✔ attitude surveys
✔ reading lists and reviews
✔ self-assessment checklists
✔ self-assessment statements
✔ teacher comments
✔ teacher checklists
✔ peer reviews
✔ parent observations and comments

Potential Problems Despite the widely acknowledged benefits of portfolios, a realistic appraisal of their merits must also include a mention of possible problems. For example, regularly reviewing and evaluating the portfolios of 30 or so students (many more if you're a middle- or high-school teacher) can be a time-management nightmare. DeFina suggests setting up a rotating schedule in which you review two or three portfolios every day. This way, you'll be able to see each student's portfolio at least once during the month.

Scoring Authentic Assessment

While observing student performances and reviewing portfolios, teachers must have some reliable way to score these alternative assessments. And they do, using predetermined criteria. In some content areas, such as science, there are commercially developed performance assessments. But most teachers using performance assessments develop their own scoring rubrics.

A rubric is simply a scoring or evaluation tool that lists important features that should be present in the performance or product. It also indicates levels of quality for each feature. For example, what makes a good student report good and a poor report poor? What does a great project presentation look like as compared to a poor one? What are the features of a successful science experiment?

While some rubrics focus on product content, others focus on organization, writing mechanics, presenting abilities, or other matters of form. Scoring rubrics communicate to students (and parents) that certain identifiable skills *are* valued and expected, such as synthesizing information from several sources, speaking clearly and making eye contact during oral presentations, developing a good introduction in an essay or research paper, or using transitions between paragraphs.

Consider, for example, one criterion of a rubric for assessing a student's written story: *Clearly creates and communicates setting.* The various quality levels of this criterion might be described like this:

Great: Puts in enough details to give the reader a clear sense of time and place.
Good: Includes some details about setting, but could use a few more to clarify.
Fair: Very little detail about setting; may have described place but not time, or vice versa.
Poor: No details about setting.

I've developed the rubric on reproducible page 167 for scoring middle schoolers' research papers. The individual criteria listed for each of the three skill areas can be fine-tuned for different types of papers and for different skill levels. For example, more experienced students may be required to use four to five reference sources. Each rubric should be adapted to the project criteria and students' abilities.

DESIGN YOUR OWN RUBRIC

Designing your own customized rubrics with the help of 4teachers.org is simple and convenient. This federally funded project, developed by the High Plains Regional Technology in Education Consortium, features rubric templates you can adapt for your own purposes. (See the example I developed for scoring my seventh and eighth graders' oral presentations on page 168.) This must-see Web site helps teachers integrate technology into the classroom and offers numerous online resources and tools. It's also free and easy to use. Find it online at http://rubistar.4teachers.org/index.php.

A ready-to-use rubric form is provided on page 170. See Creating a Rubric (page 169) for some good examples of language and descriptors to use in creating your own rubrics.

Creating Rubrics To create your own rubrics, researcher Heidi Goodrich suggests that you collaborate with students using these general steps applied to any specific situation:

1. Show students models of good and poor work and identify the key characteristics of each.
2. List the key criteria of good work.
3. Describe various levels of quality for each criterion.
4. Practice using the rubrics on sample work.
5. As students work on the actual assignment, ask them to assess themselves and peers occasionally using the rubric.
6. Give students time to revise their work based on the feedback from self- and peer evaluation.
7. Use the same rubric to assess student work yourself.

Some expert teachers suggest that for each separate assessment, you identify five or six qualities, ranked in order of importance, that a project must possess to be outstanding. These important qualities can be presented in the form of a checklist you refer to as you evaluate each performance or product.

But no matter which performance assessment you use—commercially prepared or teacher developed—be sure to assess the assessment tool. Does the assessment require students to demonstrate exactly the kind of knowledge or understanding you are attempting to measure? Does it reflect what you are teaching? Is it reliable? (That is, will the student's score be consistent no matter who is scoring?) We should always be able to justify the assessment we give of a student performance.

Focus only on the criteria in the rubric and avoid comparing students' papers. Finally, don't make students guess what it is they need to do or demonstrate. Experts agree that students should know the scoring rubrics ahead of time and even help develop individual assessment instruments.

❖ Traditional Assessment

Much of the time, authentic assessment gives us the best picture of what students know and can do. But there is still an important role to be played by more "traditional" assessments such as objective tests. For example, such tests can be an accurate measure of students' factual knowledge. They can tap other types of learning as well.

"I use a multiple-choice test to find out if my students know particular pieces of science knowledge, such as the boiling point of water at sea level," says Marilyn Bachman, a sixth-grade teacher in California. Bachman, who uses performance assessments extensively, explains that, "Teachers need to know that it's okay to combine traditional tests with performance assessments, as long as they are aware that what you test for is what you get."

Other experts agree that no single assessment form is sufficient. Each has its strengths and weaknesses, and each has its place.

Traditional methods such as objective tests or standardized achievement tests also allow us to compare students to standards or norms, and this is important, stresses assessment authority Grant Wiggins. Drawing upon a baseball-card analogy,

Research Paper Evaluation Rubric

	EXCELLENT	VERY GOOD	SATISFACTORY	NOT SATISFACTORY
RESEARCH SKILLS				
adequate number of reference sources				
appropriate types of sources— books, experts, magazines, Internet, video, encyclopedia				
synthesized information from many sources				
listed references in a bibliography				
Comments:				
WRITING SKILLS				
strong introduction and thesis statement				
writing reveals true understanding of topic				
paragraphs all relate to thesis or main topic				
paraphrased and quoted, did not plagiarize				
explicit tie-in with overall unit theme				
Comments:				
MECHANICS				
met required length				
carefully proofread final draft				
avoided grammatical and usage errors				
neatly typed/presented				
Comments:				

Oral Presentation Rubric: I-Search Projects

Teacher Name: _____

Student Name: _____

Category	4	3	2	1
Content	Shows a full understanding of the topic.	Shows a good understanding of the topic.	Shows a good understanding of parts of the topic.	Does not seem to understand the topic very well.
Preparedness	Is completely prepared and has obviously rehearsed.	Seems prepared but could have used a couple more rehearsals.	Somewhat prepared, but it is clear that rehearsal was lacking.	Does not seem at all prepared to present.
Speaks Clearly	Speaks clearly and distinctly all the time (100–95%), and mispronounces no words.	Speaks clearly and distinctly all the time (100–95%), but mispronounces one word.	Speaks clearly and distinctly most of the time (94–85%). Mispronounces no more than one word.	Often mumbles or cannot be understood OR mispronounces more than one word.
Posture and Eye Contact	Stands up straight, looks relaxed and confident. Establishes eye contact with everyone in the room during the presentation.	Stands up straight and establishes eye contact with everyone in the room during the presentation.	Sometimes stands up straight and establishes eye contact.	Slouches and/or does not look at people during the presentation.
Enthusiasm	Facial expressions and body language generate a strong interest and enthusiasm about the topic in others.	Facial expressions and body language sometimes generate a strong interest and enthusiasm about the topic in others.	Facial expressions and body language are used to try to generate enthusiasm, but seem somewhat faked.	Very little use of facial expressions or body language. Did not generate much interest in topic being presented.
Time Limit	Presentation is 10–15 minutes long.	Presentation is 8–9 minutes long.	Presentation is 6–7 minutes long.	Presentation is less than 6 minutes OR more than 15 minutes.
Volume	Volume is loud enough to be heard by all audience members throughout the presentation.	Volume is loud enough to be heard by all audience members at least 90% of the time.	Volume is loud enough to be heard by all audience members at least 80% of the time.	Volume often too soft to be heard by all audience members.

Creating a Rubric

When you are creating general rubrics, think about the changes that may occur over time and across a variety of student responses (e.g., student comments in discussion, questions asked, written work, exam answers, assignments).

Some of the following verbs are useful:

demonstrates	represents	generates	selects
writes	considers	contributes	participates
listens	responds	applies	
speaks	produces	collaborates	
shows	uses	reads	

Some of the following competence qualifiers are suitable:

- At the *highest level of competence:*

often	evident	predictably	level
many	thoughtful	well-developed	varied
strong	consistently	purposeful	independently
clear	most	complete	excellent
always	sophisticated	frequently	articulate
several	insightful	competent	

- At the *second level of competence:*

usually	at times	good	some
competent	often	on occasion	acceptable
satisfactory	suitable	adequate	

- At the *third level of competence:*

only with assistance	unclear	unsupported by	disorganized
basic	undeveloped	fair	generalized
incomplete	inaccurate	weak	
irrelevant	seldom	evidence or example	
with support	imprecise	inconsistent	

- At the *lowest level of competence:*

weak	off topic	incomplete
lacking in organization	shows little knowledge of	muddled
little evidence of	student is unable to	has limited skill with
even with assistance	undeveloped	
not evident	unsatisfactory	

From *75 Language Arts Assessment Tools* by Mary Sullivan (Scholastic, 2003). © by Mary Sullivan.

Rubric Form

Highest Level			Lowest Level

The student…

From *75 Language Arts Assessment Tools* by Mary Sullivan (Scholastic, 2003). © by Mary Sullivan.

Wiggins explains, "I don't know how to judge the value of a batting average of .280 unless I have some comparative information. It may turn out that hitting three out of ten, which sounds poor, would land a player in the majors."

Using both performance-based and traditional methods, many schools report individual student performance on a novice-expert continuum, Wiggins continues. He explains that teachers identify carefully delineated steps describing what a student should have mastered from the novice to the expert level. See pages 172 to 173 for an example of a developmental reading scale that describes the progress from novice to expert reader. In my own state of West Virginia, individual achievement results on the state's standardized test (the WesTest) rank students from novice to distinguished performance. Called "performance descriptors," these rankings show the extent to which students have mastered specific standards. They are like the rubrics we use to assess authentic learning. (See the following section on Standardized Tests for an example of these performance descriptors.)

Developing Your Own Test

Keep these time-honored tips in mind when developing traditional objective tests:

✔ A multiple-choice answer set should include the correct answer (expressed in specific terms), two choices that are clearly wrong, and one choice that could almost be correct. (This encourages careful thinking and discriminating.)

✔ The matching portion of an objective test should include more answer choices than the number of items. This prevents using the simple process of elimination and challenges students to really know the material in order to pass the test. Moreover, when you include additional answer choices directly related to the knowledge or content tested, you can cover more ground in a shorter test. (That is, in eliminating the

---

OTHER WAYS TO EVALUATE LEARNING

In her study, "A+ Teachers," teacher Ruth Tschudin found that effective teachers use formal written tests sparingly; more often, they rely on other evaluation techniques. You might try some of these techniques, but don't forget to document the results.

- **Use oral and open-book quizzes**. For example, have students consult reference materials on a particular topic, then demonstrate their knowledge through an oral quiz. Many teachers believe individual oral tests are more accurate and less threatening than paper-and-pencil tests.

- **Have students test each other** on math facts, spelling skills, state capitals, and other factual knowledge. The payoffs? Students who are more relaxed, and fewer papers to correct, say teachers.

- **Use frequent small tests instead of fewer large ones**. This minimizes test anxiety, encourages small successes, and reveals problems sooner.

- **Observe students in practical, problem-solving situations**. Students demonstrate many observable skills when they are passing out papers, collecting soup-can labels for educational supplies, finding information in the library or on a computer, tutoring a classmate, writing thank-you letters to class visitors, playing learning games, or taking care of the classroom plants and pets. You could develop a checklist of observable skills and periodically assess each student. Available at www.uwplatt.edu/education/WIselin/pdf/teachers.pdf.

---

extraneous choices, students must still think about the content.)

✔ On matching tasks, provide the definitions or descriptions in the left column, and the one- or two-word answers in the right column. That way, students don't get bogged down rereading lengthy items each time they search for a new match.

✔ On true-and-false items, avoid writing statements made false by just the most minor of details. You are testing for overall understanding, not trying to trick students.

In general, when I use objective tests, I encourage students to write notes on the items that seem confusing. I find that highly able students often read too much into an objective question. By explaining their thinking, students reveal their knowledge and understanding and are less intimidated by "the test." I reward them for correct thinking even when their answers aren't correct.

Model Developmental Reading Scale
Grades K–3

How do students develop as readers? This scale was adapted from one designed by teachers from the Upper Arlington, Ohio, school district. The scale charts major steps along the path to becoming a proficient reader. You can use this scale to assess each student's progress and tailor instruction accordingly. At the end of the school year, kindergartners should have reached Step 4; first graders should be in Step 7; second graders in Step 8; and third graders in Step 9.

Prereader

Step 1

- Engages briefly with books or pictures on a one-on-one basis
- Relies on others to read or share books

Step 2

- May participate in shared reading experiences
- Enjoys looking at books on his or her own or being read to
- May repeat words or phrases with familiar books
- May make up his or her own story with books

Step 3

- Responds to books during shared reading experiences
- Begins to choose books on his or her own
- Able to retell a story using pictures after repeated listening experiences (demonstrates the awareness that the meaning, sequence, and words in a book remain the same with repeated listening experiences)

- Knows how to progress from the beginning to the end of a book

Emergent Reader

Step 4

- Able to engage in reading reenactments
- Memorizes some texts
- May invent text
- Mimics reading behaviors
- Displays directionality (left to right, top to bottom, and return sweep) by running finger along entire lines of text
- After a pattern has been established, is able to read the pattern

Step 5

- Knows the difference between a letter and a word
- Is moving toward a one-to-one correspondence
- Rereads familiar stories or environmental print (e.g., signs, logos, cereal boxes)
- Reads own written messages

- Able to retell a familiar story without the book
- Uses primarily meaning (picture) and his or her own language as cues when reading text
- Able to predict story events, words, and endings
- May need encouragement to take risks

Step 6

- Uses one-to-one correspondence to monitor and then self-corrects
- Locates some known words and unknown words
- May predict and confirm a word by using beginning and ending letters/sounds
- Begins to integrate meaning, language, and visual print as cues
- Begins to develop fluency with familiar text
- May need support in selecting appropriate reading material
- Begins to use known, high-frequency words to monitor reading

Model Developmental Reading Scale (continued)

Progressing Developing Reader

Step 7

- Has good control of early reading strategies (directionality, one-to-one word matching, ability to locate known and unknown words)

- Begins to build a core of high-frequency words known automatically

- Demonstrates understanding through discussion, retelling, and/or extensions

- May compare or contrast his or her experiences with story

- May make connections with other literature

- Makes predictions using book language and story structure

- May read new text word by word but shows some evidence of phrasing

- Regularly searches the print, checks, and self-corrects most errors that interfere with meaning

- Comments upon patterns, characters, plot, and setting with prompts

- Chooses both new and familiar books

- Begins to analyze words and make connections

- Is moving toward independence

Transitional Reader

Step 8

- Reads most texts with fluency, phrasing, and expression

- Uses a variety of strategies when reading

- Recognizes which errors are important to self-correct; often corrects silently

- Demonstrates understanding of material read in a variety of ways: discussion, retellings, changes in expression, rate, inflection when reading aloud, and through book/story extensions

- Makes good predictions using prior knowledge

- Makes good use of reading time; often chooses to read

- Views self as a reader; often takes risks

- Usually selects appropriate reading materials; begins to read a greater variety of longer and more complex texts

- Makes some generalizations about patterns, characters, plot, setting, and genre

- Retellings include some of the following elements: setting, sequence of events, main idea, characters, and conclusion

Fluent Reader

Step 9

- Reads with phrasing, fluency, proper intonation, and expression

- Uses a wide variety of strategies automatically

- Rarely makes miscues; consistently monitors reading for understanding

- Demonstrates good comprehension

- Demonstrates involvement with nuances in books

- Makes informed predictions using prior knowledge

- Independently makes connections

- Spends quality time reading

- Reads a variety of genres for information and pleasure

- Welcomes challenges as a reader

- Independently makes generalizations about pattern, characters, plot, setting, genre, style, and purpose

- Produces retellings that are effective and complete

- Revisits the text to support ideas and understandings during literary discussions

❖ Standardized Tests

Just mention the words "standardized test" and watch those around you squirm. Standardized tests make people uncomfortable. Their use is associated with unfair tracking policies, discrimination, denied opportunities, real estate values, negative student labels, cultural bias, political diatribes, teacher evaluation, and other such misuses.

But for the foreseeable future, standardized tests will remain a fact of school life. States complying with the No Child Left Behind mandate are required to administer annual standardized tests to assess student achievement. (See the discussion of NCLB at the beginning of this chapter.) These tests provide a convenient, uniform way to track a school's progress. While many argue that standardized tests don't truly measure achievement, others believe that the tests are the most objective and scientific measures we have. Either way, you must familiarize yourself with the content and format covered and be aware of the testing dates for your state and/or district; your future, your students' futures, and your school's very existence may depend on the results of these tests.

Look closely and you'll discover that much of the standardized testing controversy stems from abuse—not proper use—of the tests. Using standardized test results exclusively to label students or place them in special programs, for example, is one such abuse. Test developers and program coordinators argue vehemently that a student's test scores should be just one of *many* different pieces of information contributing to placement decisions.

Standardized achievement tests are potentially powerful tools for instruction. And for certain purposes, such as measuring students against standards or norms, standardized tests perform well. Differences in standardized test scores often reveal differences in opportunities to learn.

A standardized test's usefulness depends on how much you know about it. Here are some important facts about standardized tests:

✔ **Most of the state standardized tests developed recently in response to NCLB are criterion-referenced tests**. That is, the test compares an individual student's performance on certain skill objectives with some performance standard. Student results are reported along some continuum of mastery.

✔ **Before NCLB, many if not most standardized tests were norm-referenced**. That is, they compared a student's performance on certain skill objectives with that of other children at his or her grade level. A score of 70 percent would indicate that the child had scored higher than 70 percent of test-takers at his or her grade level.

✔ **A standardized achievement test is designed to indicate strengths and weaknesses in specific skill areas**.

✔ **A standardized intelligence test measures a student's use of previously learned skills to solve new problems or situations**. In addition to cognitive abilities, it includes social perceptiveness, creativity, and other factors indicating intelligence.

✔ **A test is valid when it actually measures what it purports to measure and reliable when a student scores the same on different versions of the test**.

✔ **Test results should never replace teacher judgment**; they should supplement and support that judgment.

✔ **Test results are potentially most useful when they disagree with teacher judgments**. Like a red flag, they warn us to proceed cautiously. Are there learning problems you haven't perceived? Is that shy, unobtrusive child who never demands your attention gifted? Is a child achieving more than you thought? Was a student sick or distracted during the test?

✔ **Results are reported in various ways**, including composite scores (stanines, grade equivalents, percentile rankings), scores in major skill areas, individual item analysis (students' responses on each test question), and most recently, rankings along a continuum of mastery. (See the box on page 175). Each type of score serves a specific purpose and is more appropriate or helpful in some situations than others.

ONE EXAMPLE: A CONTINUUM OF MASTERY

Performances of students taking West Virginia's annual WesTest are reported as descriptions of how well certain content areas or standards have been mastered. The following example lists the performance descriptors for West Virginia's fourth-grade geography standard:

Distinguished
- The student demonstrates exceptional and exemplary performance with distinctive and sophisticated application of knowledge and skills that exceeds the standard in geography. The student analyzes the physical and human processes that shape the earth's surface and predicts future changes. The student constructs complex time zone maps and population pyramids to derive information about places in the world. The student uses maps to predict the future effects of geography on population density, distribution and movement. The student draws conclusions about the selected regions of the world with respect to migration patterns with regard to economics, religion and language.

Above Mastery
- The student demonstrates competent and proficient performance and shows a thorough and effective application of knowledge and skills that exceeds the standard in geography. The student explains and assesses the physical and human processes that shape the earth's surface. The student constructs selected maps and population pyramids to summarize information about their place in the world. The student uses maps to evaluate the effects of geography on population density, distribution and movement. The student compares and contrasts selected regions of the world with respect to migration patterns with regard to economics, religion, and language.

Mastery
- The student demonstrates fundamental course or grade-level knowledge and skills by showing consistent and accurate academic performance that meets the standard in geography. The student identifies and describes the physical and human processes that shape the earth's surfaces. The student uses maps, globes, and population pyramids to explain their place in the world and the effects of geography on population density, distribution, and movement. The student describes selected regions of the world with regard to economics, religion, and language.

Partial Mastery
- The student demonstrates basic but inconsistent performance of fundamental knowledge and skills characterized by errors and/or omissions in geography. Performance needs further development. The student identifies the physical and human processes that shape the earth's surface. The student uses grade-level geographic tools to recognize their place in the world. The student uses simple maps to describe the effects of geography on population. The student identifies the movement of economics, religion, and language between selected regions of the world.

Novice
- The student demonstrates substantial need for the development of fundamental knowledge and skills, characterized by fragmented and incomplete performance in geography. Performance needs considerable development. The student names the physical and human processes that shape the earth's surface. The student uses maps to recognize their place in the world. The student recognizes a few regional religions and languages.

From the "West Virginia Content Standards and Objectives" at West Virginia Department of Education Web site (http://wvde.state.wv.us/csos).

✔ **Test manuals are full of useful information** about interpreting and using test results. Try at least to skim the manual of any test you routinely give.

✔ **Test scores reveal important discrepancies.** Differences in average test scores among certain groups of students often reveal differences in opportunities to learn.

✔ **Not all standardized tests are created equally.** Some are more valid (measure what they claim to measure) and reliable (individual scores remain consistent over multiple tries) than others. The test manual should report these validity and reliability factors.

✔ **Comparisons among students are helpful.** Comparing one student's test performance to national or state norms allows us to see what that student has learned in given subject areas in relation to other students.

Item Analysis: A Closer Look

One aspect of standardized testing that holds particular promise for improving practice is the individual item analysis. The item analysis lists the skill-area objectives represented on the test and the actual test questions addressing those objectives. It shows the number of questions in each skill area answered correctly by each student.

In the area of English language usage and mechanics, for example, an item analysis might reveal that a particular student consistently misses items on sentence structure (run-ons or fragments). Further, more than half of the students in a class miss the same items. Clearly, this is a content area that subsequent instruction must target. That same student might also repeatedly miss items testing knowledge of end marks, but his or her classmates do much better in this area. Here, then, the teacher can plan for more individualized help on using periods, commas, question marks, and exclamation marks.

Of course, the usefulness of item analysis depends on two factors: the timeliness of the test results, and the accuracy, validity, or reliability of the test items themselves.

Learning How to Take the Test

Students need practice in marking answer sheets, pacing themselves, and making reasonable guesses on questions they don't know. They need to understand the purpose of standardized testing and practice with special strategies—for example, eliminating incorrect answers for multiple-choice questions.

Both experienced teachers and test makers agree that students need to learn how to take tests. That doesn't mean teaching to the test or focusing curriculum on test content; it means making students familiar with the testing format and general test-taking strategies.

Many teachers, for example, design their own classroom tests to fit standardized-test format. On a spelling test, they might ask their students to pick the correct spelling of a word from among four different choices. Or on a math test, they might list four possible answers and have students indicate the correct one after working the problem.

Be careful not to rely on certain test formats exclusively, however. One year I had a group of seventh graders who seemed to have an unusually difficult time with spelling. I discovered that in grade school, these students had been assessed with spelling tests requiring them to recognize correct spellings, rather than actually spell the words. That requires a different form of information processing and learning. When I explained to them the difference between visual recognition and actual spelling and showed them how to study the spellings, their performances improved dramatically.

In *Test Scores Count! A Handbook for Teaching Test-Taking Skills*, author Sharon Koenigs identifies four major skill areas for taking standardized tests. Short lessons and practice activities can easily be designed around each of these areas.

✔ **Understanding instructions and following directions**. Following oral and written instructions, understanding the vocabulary of test directions, using answer sheets, interpreting different formats.

✔ **Using time efficiently**. Budgeting time, saving unknown questions for last, using extra time to check answers.

✔ **Guessing wisely**. For example, eliminating answers in multiple-choice questions.

✔ **Applying special strategies to specific types of test questions**. For example, avoiding, in most cases, answers that include "all" or "none" in true/false items.

When giving tests, you can enlist help from parents, too. Keeping family members informed about testing procedures is not only essential for home-school communications but also enables parents to provide the support and atmosphere children need before a test. Many teachers send home a letter such as the one on reproducible page 177.

Dear Parent,

Throughout the school year, your child will take many different types of tests. I want
_____ to feel relaxed and confident in
testing situations, and I need your help. Please explain that tests, including standardized
achievement tests, are among the most important tools we have for helping children. A
good test can identify a child's strengths and weaknesses and show where he or she
needs extra help. At school, we talk about the purpose and importance of testing. And
we practice various test-taking skills such as following directions and using time wisely.
There are also some things you can do to help your child do better on tests.

Before a Test, Children Need:
- a full night's sleep
- a good breakfast on test day
- comfortable school clothing
- a little understanding if they're anxious or upset

How to Talk With Your Child About Tests:
- Mention that you value tests because they are designed to help children learn better.
- Encourage your child to take the test seriously and do as well as possible, but reassure
  him or her that he or she will not be in trouble for items missed.
- Never add pressure in the form of threats or rewards attached to test results. Do not
  make comparisons to siblings, either.
- Stress that every child is unique in terms of strengths and learning styles and deserves
  to be loved for that uniqueness.

Thank you for your help and support.

_____
Teacher

❖ Assessment by Subjects

Some assessment strategies are specific to a certain subject. When we consider individual subjects, we're not only concerned about *how* to assess learning but *what* to assess. Associations for specific subjects and professional organizations have developed sets of standards. These standards, created through the collaboration of thousands of teachers, researchers, professionals in the field, government agencies, and businesses, represent the closest thing we have to a national consensus about what constitutes effective teaching and learning in each of the subject areas.

Currently, under the No Child Left Behind Act, individual states are responsible for developing their own set of standards for subject areas. These state standards often reflect the standards developed by national associations, but they also account for textbooks and curriculum priorities adopted at the state level. To find your state standards, go to your state department of education's Web site, then find the standards or benchmarks. Linked to these standards by subject are standardized tests. New teachers need to be aware of their state's standardized testing schedule and other forms of assessment they'll be expected to use throughout the year. Many states, for example, administer a writing assessment at certain grade levels.

This section focuses on the subject-specific standards and assessment strategies suggested by the national professional organizations. These represent some of the best thinking on what teachers need to teach, what students need to know, and how we can tell when they've gained the targeted skills and knowledge. The Mid-continent Regional Educational Laboratory (McREL) has synthesized these suggested standards and compiled a list by subject area on its Web site: www.mcrel.org/compendium and also provides a helpful link to corresponding state standards, where applicable.

QUALITY VS. QUANTITY

Jay McTighe, Grant Wiggins, and other experts suggest that assessment should help students "uncover" knowledge rather than cover the entire text. Similarly, good subject-matter teaching is better served by quality than quantity. The following quote from the late Charles Kuralt seems to have a special message for teachers: *Cover fewer topics better.*

"The good memories are all of stopping and staying awhile. I realize I've always driven too fast through life, carrying in my baggage too much impatience and apprehension, missing too many chances, passing too many good people in the dust."

From *A Life on the Road.*

Reading and Language Arts

Many educators feel that reading is the single most important educational activity in a child's life.

In fact, the highest educational priority in this country today is helping all children learn to read. A special initiative known as Reading First has been developed through the NCLB Act, and federal funds are directed toward state and local reading programs that are based on "solid scientific research," meeting the requirements of the Department of Education. The overall goal is to increase the percentage of children who are reading at grade level or above, particularly in grades 1 through 3.

The Reading First initiative emphasizes "five skills identified by research as critical to early reading success":

✔ **phonemic awareness**—the ability to hear, identify, and play with individual sounds, or phonemes, in spoken words
✔ **phonics**—the relationship between the letters of written language and the sounds of spoken language
✔ **fluency**—the capacity to read text accurately and quickly
✔ **vocabulary**—the words students must know to communicate effectively
✔ **comprehension**—the ability to understand and gain meaning from what has been read

When we read, we try to understand the relationships of words and ideas within a passage and how the meaning of the passage relates to the world around us. Reading enables us to think, interpret others' thoughts, and ultimately express our own.

Reading and the other language arts are tools—tools that can be applied to all other curricular areas.

Six Skill Areas The two largest associations devoted to English language arts—the National Council of Teachers of English (NCTE) and the International Reading Association (IRA)—recognize six language arts skills:

✔ reading
✔ writing
✔ speaking
✔ listening
✔ viewing
✔ visually representing

Around this framework of skills, the two associations have collaboratively identified general standards for teaching and learning language arts. As the NCTE explains in its publications, the standards are offered as principles to build on, not prescribed spelling lists or "one-size-fits-all" lesson plans.

What's Important
Explaining the standards in various publications, the NCTE and IRA state that students need to know how to read to satisfy a wide range of purposes. They need to read fluently and thoughtfully and be able to interpret and evaluate a range of superb literature.

Further, students need to write for many purposes and audiences. They need to write with ease and clarity, organizing their ideas logically and presenting them to others in both written and spoken forms.

In terms of technology, the standards suggest that students should know how to use computers and other technology to find the information needed to solve real problems and to communicate clearly and correctly to real audiences. Technology will help students use language for authentic purposes; for example, they can practice literacy skills by sending e-mail messages.

The standards support bilingual education, while at the same time acknowledging that students need to know and be able to use standard English to enter mainstream society and to gain employment.

Recognizing the contemporary importance of the visual media, the standards call for students to be able to think critically about film, television, and other visual modes. They must learn to listen effectively and also communicate in the visual forms.

In general, students need to know how to use the power of the English language to find the information they need to solve real problems and to communicate clearly and correctly with real audiences.

A Balanced Approach In the 1990s, educators advocated a "whole-language" approach to language arts instruction. This meant exposing children to real literature in the form of trade books (as opposed to

---

LANGUAGE ARTS RESOURCES

Each of these resources offers abundant information to support language-arts teaching and learning.

- **Council for Teachers of English** (www.ncte.org) To order the standards document or various materials and lesson ideas in support of the standards, visit the Web site or call (800) 369-6283. Or contact the council at 1111 West Kenyon Rd., Urbana, IL 61801.

- **International Reading Association** (www.reading.org) Contact the association at 800 Barksdale Rd., P.O.B. 8139, Newark, DE 19714, or call (302) 731-1600.

- **National Writing Project** (www.writingproject.org) Contact the NWP at the University of California, 205 Bancroft Way #1042, Berkeley, CA 94720-1042, or call (510) 642-0963.

basal reader stories developed around certain basic skills lessons) and real writing before they had gained the requisite skills. The idea was to give students rich, authentic experiences to enhance motivation and learning. As they attempted to write a letter to the mayor in support of a new park, for example, first or second graders would have the opportunity to check and polish their spelling and punctuation so that the letter would be well received.

The whole-language movement positioned itself against direct instruction, a traditional, "top-down" method characterized by focused, teacher-directed lessons and worksheet drills on basic skills. In direct instruction classrooms, young students read canned "stories" of the "Dick and Jane" variety—passages developed by textbook writers to correspond to specific words or skills just learned. This approach often divorced skills from real-world contexts of literature and writing and frequently reduced comprehension and motivation. However, the approach was systematic and sequential, and students' acquisition of skills could be easily assessed.

Today, most experts prefer a balanced approach. Literacy expert Regie Routman explains that a balanced approach to teaching language arts includes not only many opportunities for students to read and respond to real literature, it also incorporates the explicit teaching of spelling, punctuation, phonics, and other "basics." In *Literacy at the Crossroads*, Routman offers numerous strategies for sharpening students' basic skills as they engage in real reading and writing tasks. (See Works Cited at the end of this chapter.)

One good example of a balanced approach to reading instruction is the **Four Blocks Literacy Framework.** This multimethod, multilevel framework, developed by Pat Cunningham and Dottie Hall of Wake Forest University, has allowed students in thousands of elementary classrooms to develop their reading, writing, listening, and speaking skills, while engaging in genuine literacy activities.

The Four Blocks—Guided Reading, Self-Selected Reading, Writing, and Working With Words—represent four different approaches to teaching children to read.

"Four Blocks is based on the premise that there is not just one way that educators can teach *all* children to read," says Cheryl Sigmon, former classroom teacher and language arts consultant for the South Carolina Department of Education. Sigmon, who now writes and consults about Four Blocks, explains that this approach provides a framework that allows teachers the opportunity to expose all kids to all four approaches each and every day—without ability grouping. Sigmon describes the four blocks as follows:

During the **Self-Selected Reading Block**, teachers give students class time to select and read from a wide variety of materials. This self-selection motivates students to read, and in reading frequently, they "will figure out a great deal about reading on their own," says Sigmon, pointing to the example of how the Harry Potter series has made reading pleasurable for many reluctant readers. At this stage, says Sigmon, students learn the joys and rewards of reading.

The **Guided Reading Block** is where students learn that "the ultimate objective of reading is to gather meaning from print," Sigmon notes. Here, teachers guide students in applying reading skills, such as decoding, in the context of "real" reading. Teachers teach a specific comprehension skill or reading strategy daily, then connect students to the guided text with "prereading" activities (establishing prior knowledge, teaching critical vocabulary, establishing purpose for reading, asking for predictions about text).

In the third block, **Working With Words**, students approach reading from the "word level." They learn the high-frequency words that comprise the greatest percentage of text. Tapping all learning styles and modalities (even clapping, snapping, and chanting letters and words!), teachers teach students 110 to 120 words per year. Students also explore words, letters, sounds, and patterns by manipulating letter tiles, discovering which rhyming words in a poem have the same spelling pattern, or applying decoding strategies to guess words in sentences that their teacher has covered.

The **Writing Block** helps students apply much of what they've learned in the other blocks, says Sigmon. She refers to research showing that some 60 percent of students can learn to read from their own writing. "Writing provides the greatest opportunity for children to apply their own phonetic understanding," says Sigmon, noting that students must **encode** or match letters to the sounds they wish to write—to get words on paper—and they must **decode** or match sounds and symbols—to take the words off the paper. Teachers provide daily mini-lessons on an element of grammar, mechanics, or the writing process that they want students to focus on. Students are given time to write each day and integrate that focus skill or concept in their writing. The daily writing is student-directed, usually focusing on a topic they want to tell their teacher and their classmates. Thus audience becomes an important part of the writing. Ultimately, students "publish" polished pieces and read them to other students.

"Multilevel, multi-approach, and *daily*—these are the magical ingredients of a framework that's changing America's schools!" Sigmon writes.

Originally created for first grade, 4 Blocks can by modified to enhance language arts instruction at many grade levels. To learn more, read Sigmon's monthly online column at www.teachers.net/4blocks/column.html, visit her Web site www.cherylsigmon.com, or read the books by Sigmon or Cunningham listed in the Works Cited section at the end of this chapter.

Assessing Language Arts. The IRA and NCTE Joint Task Force on Assessment has issued the following language arts assessment guidelines:
✔ The interests of the student are paramount in assessment.

✔ The primary purpose of assessment is to improve teaching and learning.
✔ Assessment must reflect and allow for critical inquiry into curriculum and instruction.
✔ Assessments must recognize and reflect the intellectually and socially complex nature of reading and writing and the important roles of school, home, and society in literacy development.
✔ Assessment must be fair and equitable.
✔ The consequences of an assessment procedure are the first, and most important, consideration in establishing the validity of the assessment.
✔ The teacher is the most important agent of assessment.
✔ The assessment process should involve multiple perspectives and sources of data.
✔ Assessment must be based in the community.
✔ All members of the educational community— students, parents, teachers, administrators, policy makers, and the public—must have a voice in the development, interpretation, and reporting of assessment.
✔ Parents must be involved as active, essential participants in the assessment process.

Sample Assessments. While portfolio assessment is probably the most widely used alternative in assessing language arts learning, there are many ways to use performance-based assessments.

My students and I develop a **scoring rubric** to assess their research and presentation skills (see sample rubrics, pages 167 and 168). Each year I ask my seventh and eighth graders to identify their own topic for research within a broad theme relating to our literature study. The categories are so broad (for example, technology or intelligence) that students can justify almost any topic. And justifying their topics is often a good exercise in divergent thinking.

The basic requirement of the project is to accumulate enough information from a variety of credible sources (print and nonprint) to put together a 10- to 15-minute presentation and to develop several "products" of their choosing such as posters, overhead transparencies, collages, drawings or charts, songs, models, video clips, and poems. Students spend several weeks researching and creating, then formally present their projects to the class and to parents and other invited adults. (Along the way they've earned points for developing a project bibliography and outline and meeting deadlines.)

Our scoring rubric, featured on page 168, focuses on the content of the project and key elements of an oral presentation, such as posture, enthusiasm, and volume. For each element, I list criteria for performance at four levels, ranging from 1 (below expectations) to 4 (above expectations). Students have this rubric ahead of time, so they know exactly what is expected. While students are presenting, I simply make notes under each category, and at the end of the presentation, I circle the score that reflects the level of performance achieved in each category. The rubric's scoring scale allows me to add the scores of the individual elements together to find a total out of 28 possible points, which I can choose to convert into a grade.

Also, I give each member of the audience a scoring sheet to evaluate the presentations themselves. I always collect and look at these others. In most cases, the other evaluations confirm my own. Where they don't, I stop and take a closer look. I ask evaluators to write comments, and these I share (anonymously, of course) with the presenters when I give them their final evaluation sheet.

Rubrics like these can be adapted for almost any kind of a project at any grade level. Usually it's beneficial to have students help determine the important features of a project. And always share the rubric with them ahead of time.

To assess my middle schoolers' understanding about Greek mythology and the epics of Homer, I ask them to draw "superhero" cartoons illustrating the qualities valued in ancient heroes, and the characteristics or values of society revealed in these stories.

There are many different ways to assess authentic language arts learning and at the same time give students important choices and ownership, integrate subject areas, and extend the learning. Original songs, poems, alternative endings, role-playing, collages, and drawings allow students to express their understanding of a literary work. Reader responses, where students react to a literary work, not summarize it, reveal thinking and comprehension, as does telling or writing a story from a different perspective. Instead of multiple-choice tests on homonyms, metaphors, haikus, adjectives, or vivid verbs, have students demonstrate understanding *by creating and using their own literary and language devices.*

Specific Reading Assessments. As mandated by NCLB and its Reading First initiative, states must regularly measure student progress in reading skills in grades 1 and 2. In addition, as part of the annual state standardized testing, all children in grades 3 through 8 are tested in reading.

Aside from mandated standardized tests, there are numerous assessments available on all aspects of reading. One good source is a searchable reading assessment database (K–3) developed by the Southwest Educational Development Laboratory (www.sedl.org/reading/rad). (See the list of domains for assessing primary-grade students from SEDL on page 183.) Another good source of assessments and assessment information is Kathleen and James Strickland's *Making Assessment Elementary* (listed in Works Cited at the end of this chapter). This book includes entire chapters on reading and writing assessment, and chapters on portfolios, tests, grades, and other assessment instruments. The authors describe such reading assessment strategies as surveys and interviews, a Concepts About Print test, miscue analysis, oral reading assessments, journals and logs, written response to literature, and many more.

Perhaps the most frequently used, informative, and easy-to-learn reading assessment is the **Running Record**, a tool used to assess oral reading skills and determine reading level. Developed by New Zealand educator Marie Clay and featured in Clay's Reading Recovery Program, the Running Record is a shorthand method in which a teacher records all of the

Here is a sampling of domains for teaching and assessing primary-grade students, created by the Southwest Educational Development Laboratory:

- reading comprehension
- language comprehension
- decoding
- linguistic knowledge
- background knowledge
- cipher knowledge
- lexical knowledge
- semantics
- syntax
- phonology
- phoneme awareness
- knowledge of alphabetic principle
- letter knowledge
- concepts about print
- phonological awareness

Available at www.sedl.org/reading/rad.

reading behaviors exhibited by a student as he or she reads a short passage.

The Running Record is "an essential tool," claim authors Mary Browning Schulman and Carleen daCruz Payne, that helps teachers "gain insight on the strategies the student uses effectively and those with which the student needs help." As such, it's an excellent example of the way assessment can inform instruction.

The record helps teachers easily document the following reading behaviors and miscues, say Schulman and Payne:

✔ accurate reading
✔ substitution (of words)
✔ omission
✔ insertion
✔ repetition or reread
✔ self-correction
✔ intervention (teacher assistance)
✔ intervention (teacher encouragement to try)
✔ student uses initial sound to problem-solve

For strategies, forms, and tips on taking and using Running Records, see Schulman and Payne's *Guided Reading: Making It Work*, listed in the Works Cited at the end of this chapter. Consult the Reading A–Z Web site (www.readinga-z.com/newfiles/levels/ runrecord/runrec.html) for helpful charts and guidelines for Running Record symbols and marking conventions, a sample of an actual Running Record for a student, and tips on how to analyze and score the record.

The error and accuracy rates provided by Running Records help teachers determine each student's reading level with a high degree of accuracy. Coupled with the use of developmental reading scales such as the one featured on pages 172 and 173, the Running Record can provide a well-rounded snapshot of a reader. Teachers can quickly identify and teach skills and strategies that the student lacks and chart progress by comparing Running Record tests over time.

Specific Spelling Assessments Student achievement in spelling must be viewed in the context of four distinct developmental levels of spelling, according to experts Mary Jo Fresch and Aileen Wheaton. These developmental levels, described on page 184, vary from student to student, and they cannot be neatly categorized by grade level, Fresch and Wheaton point out. However, there are some general grade-level benchmarks to help teachers determine what concepts and skills their students can be expected to know or learn.

Phase one, **Print and Symbol Awareness**, generally begins at home or in preschool. Most students reach the second phase, **Print and Sound Awareness**, in primary through early intermediate grades. Most students reach and may remain in the third phase, **Print and Sound Connections**, during the upper primary grades through middle school. And finally, students generally make the transition to Phase Four, **Self Reliance**, anywhere from early intermediate to middle school.

Like assessments in other subject areas, the goal of spelling assessments—formal or informal—is to inform and improve instruction. Fresch and Wheaton describe a variety of spelling assessments that can be used together to

Overview of Four Phases
of Development of Word Knowledge

PHASE	CHARACTERISTICS
Print and Symbol Awareness	• Scribbles • Imitates reading and writing • Is aware of print • Learns alphabet • Strings letters to create message
Print and Sound Awareness	• Attempts at spelling become more logical as relationships between letters and sounds begin to be used ("kak" for cake) • Develops sight vocabulary for reading and writing; uses obvious strategies to spell (such as using the letter c for "sea," u for "you") • Exchanges short vowel for closest long (a for short e; e for short i) • Common errors include affrications ("jriv" for drive, "chrip" for trip), nasal ("bop" for bump), exaggerated sounding ("palena" for plane)
Print and Sound Connections	• Develops larger reading and writing sight vocabulary • Correctly uses short vowels • Marks long vowels (sometimes incorrectly, may add the "e marker" when not needed or place two vowels side by side to mark first one as long) • Uses -d for past tense, adds -ing • Understands that words have two elements—beginning consonant pattern, and a vowel plus ending, such as in the word "black" (bl-a-ck) or in the word "fed" (f-e-d)
Self-Reliance	• Begins to internalize rules • May overgeneralize newly learned patterns and rules (adds "e marker" when not needed or doubles letters before adding any ending) • Begins to correctly double consonant before adding endings • Invents at the juncture or schwa position (spells "needle" as neddle, or "rabbit" as rabit) • Spellings show orthographic awareness available for word attack • Reads efficiently, fluently • Attends less to words as literacy processing quickens

From *Teaching and Assessing Spelling* by Mary Jo Fresch and Aileen Wheaton (Scholastic, 2002). © by Mary Jo Fresch and Aileen Wheaton.

provide a well-rounded assessment of a student's spelling growth and areas for development. Some of these tools include a Spelling Knowledge Inventory, which reveals the range of grade-level words students are able to spell; anecdotal notes, in which teachers might record, for example, that students' spellings are influenced by pronunciations ("gonna" for "going to"); analysis of written work, in which teachers watch for consistent, correct usage of word features; and interviews of students to determine their understandings of certain words or word features. (See Fresch and Wheaton's *Teaching and Assessing Spelling* listed in Works Cited for more teaching and assessment strategies and tools.)

Specific Writing Assessments Portfolios and rubrics, discussed earlier in this chapter, are two of the most helpful types of writing assessment. Another is the 6+1 Traits model of the teaching and assessment of writing. Based on more than 20 years of research and development at the Northwest Regional Educational Laboratory, the 6+1 Traits model identifies the major components of effective writing:

✔ **Ideas** (the content)
✔ **Organization** (internal structure or logical pattern of ideas)
✔ **Voice** (the writer's style, feelings, convictions)

6 + 1 TRAITS PERFORMANCE CONTINUUM

WOW!
Exceeds expectations

STRONG
Shows control and skill in this trait; many strengths present

EFFECTIVE
On balance, the strengths outweigh the weaknesses; a small amount of revision is needed

DEVELOPING
Strengths and need for revision are about equal; about halfway home

EMERGING
Need for revision outweighs strengths; isolated moments hint at what the writer has in mind

NOT YET
A bare beginning; writer not yet showing any control

From *6+1 Traits of Writing* by Ruth Culham (Scholastic, 2003). © by Ruth Culham.

✔ **Word Choice** (rich, colorful, precise language)
✔ **Sentence Fluency** (the flow and sound of word patterns)
✔ **Conventions** (precise grammar and mechanics)
✔ **Presentation** (form and layout)

Good writing in any genre and at any age displays these traits, say model developers.

The 6+1 Traits model gives teachers "a method of looking at the main characteristics of writing and assessing them independent from one another," notes former Montana English Teacher of the Year Ruth Culham, who pioneered research on the model. It's an assessment tool that "far exceeds the limited information a single grade or score provides," she adds.

The model implies a tightly woven interaction of standards, curriculum, and assessment. It fosters a conversation between writer and reader, says Culham. "If, as a result of the conversation, the writer improves a little with each draft, that's huge. If he or she can maintain that growth from paper to paper, that's gargantuan."

Culham cautions that the traits are not a curriculum but a shared vocabulary—a common standard of what good writing looks like at any age. Assessment of each trait follows a continuum from poor to superb performance (see the graphic on page 185). (Detailed lessons and activities for each trait, scoring guides, and sample student papers can be found in Culham's book, listed in Works Cited.)

Using state standards as a guide, teachers must know which forms of writing students are expected to know at a particular grade level. They need to collect and score formal writing samples from students throughout the year. Some schools require an example of various forms from each student by year's end, evaluated with scoring marks and indications of improvement.

Mathematics

Teaching mathematics is a tough job. It's an area fraught with problems (no pun intended) and challenges, and the greatest challenge is to teach students how to think well and how to apply their thinking and knowledge in solving complex problems encountered in real life. Problem solving is probably the most important skill students can take into the 21st century.

Our ideas about the teaching and learning of mathematics have changed dramatically in the past two decades. Those changes are reflected in and result from the mathematics standards developed by the National Council of Teachers of Mathematics (NCTM).

"The teaching envisioned in the Professional Standards for Teaching Mathematics is significantly different from what many teachers themselves have experienced as students,"

explains author Shirley Frye.

Frye, a math teacher of 40 years and former president of NCTM, describes the standards as a shift *away from*:
- ✔ the teacher as the sole authority for right answers.
- ✔ mere memorization of math facts and procedures.
- ✔ emphasis on finding the correct answer.
- ✔ the concept of mathematics as a body of isolated concepts.

Instead, the standards advocate a shift *toward*:
- ✔ using logic and mathematical evidence to verify student responses.
- ✔ mathematical reasoning.
- ✔ conjecturing, inventing, problem solving.
- ✔ the concept of connected mathematical ideas and applications.

The goal of mathematics teaching, says Frye, is to help students develop "mathematical power," and for educators to realize that *what* students learn depends on *how* they learn it.

Beyond Arithmetic Our own experiences as students and the back-to-basics movement cause many of us to confuse competency in arithmetic—applying the basic operations of adding, subtracting, multiplying, and dividing—with competency in mathematics. But just as reading is more than decoding, mathematics instruction and learning is much more than simple computation.

SEE MATH STANDARDS IN ACTION

In a new video, the NCTM offers a look at the math standards and principles in the classroom. *Principles and Standards for School Mathematics: Vision to Reality* ($19.95) explores the major math themes in each of four grade bands, with actual footage of teachers implementing the standards in their classrooms.

In an overview of its most recent version of the standards, NCTM notes that, "We live in a mathematical world. Whenever we decide on a purchase, choose an insurance or health plan, or use a spreadsheet, we rely on mathematical understanding. The World Wide Web, CD-ROMs, and other media disseminate vast quantities of quantitative information. The level of mathematical thinking and problem solving needed in the workplace has increased dramatically. In such a world, those who understand and can do mathematics will have opportunities that others do not."

Mathematics instruction must emphasize not only numbers and operations but also geometry and measurement, patterns and relationships, probability and statistics, and algebra.

In addition to these target content areas, NCTM outlines five critical **mathematical processes** that students need to learn and practice:

✔ problem solving (the ability to apply and adapt strategies to solve a variety of types of problems)
✔ reasoning and proof (the ability to develop arguments and support these with proofs)
✔ communication (the ability to clearly and effectively explain and evaluate mathematical thinking and use mathematical language with precision)
✔ connections (the ability to find common links among mathematical ideas and applications of mathematical concepts to other subject areas or fields of study)
✔ representation (the ability to make and use models to organize, record, and communicate mathematical ideas

Teaching Strategies To extend mathematics teaching approaches to match a broadened concept of mathematics, the NCTM standards call for in-class discussions and writing about mathematics, cooperative learning, in-depth questioning, and asking students to justify their thinking and communicate mathematically.

The key is "asking students to explain their thinking—at all times, not just when they make mistakes," claims math-teaching expert Marilyn Burns. "I constantly probe, 'Why do you think that? Explain why that makes sense. Tell me more about how you reasoned.'"

Burns continues that questioning students gives them important messages, such as that their ideas are valued; math is about reasoning, not just memorizing; and they should always look to make sense of mathematical problems.

MATH RESOURCES

The National Council of Teachers of Mathematics (NCTM) has developed a set of content standard expectations specific to each of four grade bands: pre-kindergarten through grade 2; grades 3 through 5; grades 6 through 8; and grades 9 through 12. For information on these expectations, free activities and lesson plans, interactive Web sites, and much more to support standards-based mathematics teaching, visit NCTM at www.nctm.org/standards. Or contact the NCTM at 1906 Association, Reston, VA 20191-1502, or call (703) 620-9840.

You can also tap into the seemingly limitless online resources for mathematics teaching from just about any of the major Web sites listed in this book. But a more direct route would be to access **Eisenhower National Clearinghouse for Mathematics and Science Education** (www.enc.org). Among the many offerings are journal articles, lesson ideas and plans, links to find instructional resources online, and a copy of the NCTM standards. The clearinghouse also publishes *Update*, a free newsletter, and has produced two free compact discs showcasing effective instruction and assessment. Contact the clearinghouse at the Ohio State University, 1929 Kenny Rd., Columbus, OH 43210, or call (800) 621-5785.

Ten Goals for Teaching Math. After reviewing the first math standards issued by NCTM in 1989, educational writers and consultants Leanna Landsmann and Mary Harbaugh identified 10 features of good mathematics teaching. Their ideas are as relevant and practical today as they were when they were first published:

✔ Build on prior knowledge.

✔ Look at how kids reach answers, because process is as important as product.

✔ Foster positive attitudes toward mathematics early on.

✔ Make math active and hands-on.

✔ Use manipulatives—plenty of them—and not just with the very young.

✔ Think of math as a language to reason and explore with. Make mathematical reasoning and problem solving a primary goal in all lessons. Include writing and discussion activities to help children clarify their thinking.

✔ Help children see math as a useful subject that can be applied to the real world.

✔ Think of math as more than arithmetic. Measurement, geometry, statistics, estimation, probability, and algebra are all important in the elementary grades.

✔ Use calculators to develop conceptual understanding or save valuable time while problem solving.

✔ Boost achievement with cooperative learning.

Alternative Assessments To assess true understanding and problem solving, the NCTM standards call for a variety of assessments, including written explanations of mathematical understanding, the solving of real-life problems with real-life materials, portfolios, teacher observations, checklists, and collaborative work in groups to solve problems or complete tasks. Further, they call for assessment and evaluation to become a regular and ongoing part of instruction, with an emphasis on how students think and how they arrive at answers to problems.

Scored Discussions Colorado math teacher Eilene Leach describes her use of an alternative assessment that she learned from colleagues teaching social studies—the scored discussion. This assessment, which can be adapted for most grade levels, offers these advantages, says Leach. Scored discussions:

✔ allow students to learn from each other.

✔ allow success for students with different learning styles.

✔ permit students greater ownership of their learning.

✔ are easily scored and graded.

In Leach's class, a scored discussion involves a group of three to six students who sit at the front of the class to discuss and solve a problem in a certain amount of time.

"When I first tried a scored discussion, I was afraid the students would hate it," Leach admits. But she was wrong. "Those students in front of the class were trying their best, since they were working in front of their peers. The students in the audience listened intently. I learned more about how the students reasoned than I had by watching them in cooperative

A Scored Discussion

LEFT SEAT 1 ___Lisa___   RIGHT SEAT 1 ___José___
LEFT SEAT 2 ___Hank___   RIGHT SEAT 2 ___Nicole___
LEFT SEAT 3 _____   RIGHT SEAT 3 _____

1. Determining a possible strategy to use (3)

L 1 ___✔___   R 1 ___✔___
L 2 _____   R 2 _____
L 3 _____   R 3 _____

2. Successfully communicating a strategy (3)

L 1 ___✔___   R 1 _____
L 2 _____   R 2 _____
L 3 _____   R 3 _____

3. Correctly applying a property (2)

L 1 _____   R 1 _____
L 2 ___✔___   R 2 _____
L 3 _____   R 3 _____

4. Recognizing misused properties or arithmetic errors (2)

L 1 _____   R 1 _____
L 2 _____   R 2 ___✔✔___
L 3 _____   R 3 _____

5. Drawing another person into the discussion (2)

L 1 ___✔___   R 1 _____
L 2 ___✔___   R 2 _____
L 3 _____   R 3 _____

6. Asking a clarifying question (3)

L 1 _____   R 1 _____
L 2 _____   R 2 ___✔___
L 3 _____   R 3 _____

7. Moving the discussion along (1)

L 1 _____   R 1 ___✔✔___
L 2 _____   R 2 _____
L 3 _____   R 3 _____

1. Not paying attention distracting others (-2)

L 1 _____   R 1 _____
L 2 _____   R 2 _____
L 3 _____   R 3 _____

2. Interrupting (-2)

L 1 _____   R 1 ___X___
L 2 _____   R 2 _____
L 3 _____   R 3 _____

3. Making an incorrect application or assumption (-1)

L 1 _____   R 1 _____
L 2 _____   R 2 _____
L 3 _____   R 3 _____

4. Monopolizing (-3)

L 1 _____   R 1 _____
L 2 _X_ (Hank corrected   R 2 _____
his own mistake.)
L 3 _____   R 3 _____

5. Making a personal attack (-3)

L 1 _____   R 1 _____
L 2 _____   R 2 _____
L 3 _____   R 3 _____

Discussion Scoring Rubric

Name _____ **Lisa** _____

Positive	Tally	Negative	Tally
1. Determining a possible strategy to use (3)	**3**	1. Not paying attention distracting others (-2)	___
2. Successfully communicating a strategy (3)	**3**	2. Interrupting (-2)	___
3. Correctly applying a property (2)	___	3. Making an incorrect application or assumption (-1)	
4. Recognizing misused properties or arithmetic errors (2)		4. Monopolizing (-3)	___
5. Drawing another person into the discussion (2)	**2**	5. Making a personal attack (-3)	
6. Asking a clarifying question (3)	___		
7. Moving the discussion along (1)	___	Total **8**	

groups. Best of all, the approach took no more time than preparing, administering, and grading a short quiz."

Using the scored discussions primarily to assess problem-solving skills, Leach has developed a scoring rubric to use as she evaluates student performance. The students score points on the basis of the strategies they apply, the errors they recognize, the questions they ask, and the communication skills they exhibit (for example, drawing others into the discussion or not monopolizing the discussion). They can lose points by not paying attention, distracting, interrupting, or personally attacking others, making an incorrect application or assumption, or monopolizing the discussion.

To adapt the scored discussion to your own grade level or a different content area, try negotiating with students the important features of a discussion. What type of learning or knowledge is it that the discussion should reveal? This negotiation is a good problem-solving exercise in its own right, and students will "own" the assessment if they've helped develop it. Further, it forces students to think about their learning and what it is they are trying to accomplish.

Also, share the scoring rubric or evaluation instrument with students ahead of time so they know exactly what is expected of them. The illustration shows a completed scored discussion tally. You'll find a blank scored discussion reproducible on page 190.

Building Models Researchers at the University of Wisconsin claim that fundamental ideas about mathematics and science become clearer to elementary students when they create and discuss models. In a recent classroom experiment, the Wisconsin researchers asked first- and second-grade students to construct working models of their elbows out of such materials as cardboard tubes, rubber bands, clay, craft sticks, and balloons. The students were also asked to explain the models they built.

Many of the students thought that a good model was one that looked like, rather than acted like, a real elbow. Their first attempts revealed this misunderstanding and enabled their teachers to explain that function is the important concept. Most went through several revisions of their models before producing ones that moved in the same way a human elbow moves. But by the end of the experiment, their understanding of elbows far surpassed that of a group of second, fourth, and fifth graders who had not made models.

Researchers Richard Lehrer and Leona Schauble explain that models, whether of atoms, the solar system, or elbows, help scientists and mathematicians solve problems and search for evidence.

"Students should be able to approach science through fundamental mathematical ideas such as spatial visualization, data, measure, and uncertainty," says Schauble. This approach, she adds, reflects the way real mathematicians and scientists work, and it helps students make sense of their world and connect learning to real life.

Used as an alternative assessment, a model allows for different learning styles, different approaches, hands-on learning, and a look at students' deeper understandings.

A Scored Discussion

LEFT SEAT 1 _____   **RIGHT SEAT 1** _____

LEFT SEAT 2 _____   **RIGHT SEAT 2** _____

LEFT SEAT 3 _____   **RIGHT SEAT 3** _____

---

1. Determining a possible strategy to use (3)

L 1 _____   R 1_____
L 2 _____   R 2_____
L 3 _____   R 3_____

2. Successfully communicating a strategy (3)

L 1 _____   R 1_____
L 2 _____   R 2_____
L 3 _____   R 3_____

3. Correctly applying a property (2)

L 1 _____   R 1_____
L 2 _____   R 2_____
L 3 _____   R 3_____

4. Recognizing misused properties or arithmetic errors (2)

L 1 _____   R 1_____
L 2 _____   R 2_____
L 3 _____   R 3_____

5. Drawing another person into the discussion (2)

L 1 _____   R 1_____
L 2 _____   R 2_____
L 3 _____   R 3_____

6. Asking a clarifying question (3)

L 1 _____   R 1_____
L 2 _____   R 2_____
L 3 _____   R 3_____

7. Moving the discussion along (1)

L 1 _____   R 1_____
L 2 _____   R 2_____
L 3 _____   R 3_____

1. Not paying attention, distracting others (-2)

L 1 _____   R 1_____
L 2 _____   R 2_____
L 3 _____   R 3_____

2. Interrupting (-2)

L 1 _____   R 1_____
L 2 _____   R 2_____
L 3 _____   R 3_____

3. Making an incorrect application or assumption (-1)

L 1 _____   R 1_____
L 2 _____   R 2_____
L 3 _____   R 3_____

4. Monopolizing (-3)

L 1 _____   R 1_____
L 2 _____   R 2_____
L 3 _____   R 3_____

5. Making a personal attack (-3)

L 1 _____   R 1_____
L 2 _____   R 2_____
L 3 _____   R 3_____

Other Alternatives Other authentic assessments of mathematical learning include individual interviews, teacher observations, student portfolios, group projects, written reflections, and self-assessment. Descriptions of these and other methods can be found in resources listed throughout this chapter.

Science

"Our young people must be exposed to science both because it is useful and because it is fun. Both of these qualities should be taken at a truly high value."—Edward Teller

Good science instruction enables children to become good thinkers. In learning scientific process and inquiry, they learn to look closely at the world around them—to observe, take notes, ask questions, solve problems, discover, experiment, guess, keep careful records, make inferences, and draw conclusions. The goal of science instruction, the experts agree, is scientific literacy.

What does it mean to be science literate? The experts suggest that students who are science literate:

✔ know basic science concepts
✔ understand the process of scientific inquiry
✔ understand how science affects their daily lives
✔ understand the relationship of science, technology, and society
✔ are aware of careers in science
✔ understand the socio-historical context of science

Ongoing Assessments In its *National Science Education Standards*, the National Research Council offers many ideas about science assessments. When engaging in ongoing assessment, teachers of science:

✔ use multiple methods and systematically gather data about student understanding and ability
✔ analyze assessment data to guide teaching.
✔ guide students in self-assessment
✔ use student data, observations of teaching, and interactions with colleagues to reflect on and improve teaching practice

✔ use student data, observations of teaching, and interactions with colleagues to report student achievement and opportunities to learn to students, teachers, parents, policymakers, and the general public

The document offers further explanations for each item under the standard. For example, under "Using multiple methods," you'll find some of the forms assessment can take, including student

---

WHAT IS THE SCIENTIFIC METHOD?

The scientific method is a practice used to find truths about our world. Using the steps of the scientific method, scientists move from observations to a proposition (hypothesis) that they test systematically and revise until the proposition can no longer be disproved. Then it becomes a theory, a building block of science. Students can use this simplified version of the scientific method to conduct their own research:

1. Make an observation and pose a question that will guide your research.
2. Develop a hypothesis, an educated guess about your question that is consistent with what you have observed.
3. Use your hypothesis to make predictions.
4. Test those predictions by experiments or further observations. Adjust your hypothesis in the light of your results.
5. Repeat steps 3 and 4 until your predictions match the experiment results and/or observations.

When consistency is obtained (step 5), a hypothesis becomes a theory and provides a set of guiding points that explain observable events. A theory is the framework within which observations are explained and predictions are made.

Students can find an excellent explanation of scientific method in an interactive format online. The site, developed by J. Stein Carter at the University of Cincinnati, Clermont College, illustrates the concepts with an activity that presents an observation and question, asks the student to pick a hypothesis from among six choices, allows the student to test one of 25 variables, and then asks for a prediction of change (six different choices). After clicking on "Do the experiment," the student learns the "results" and can go back to hypothesize, predict, and test again. The site is available at www.biology.clc.uc.edu/courses/bio104/sci_meth.htm. Check out other projects and activities on the university's biology home page, www.biology.clc.uc.edu.

interviews, formal performance tasks, investigative reports, written reports, pictorial work, models, inventions, portfolios and "other creative expressions of understanding." The document notes that teachers choose assessment tools according to learning goals and student experience.

Necessary Changes Our entire system of science education must change, the *Standards* authors stress. And with it, the way we assess science teaching and learning. The new standards advocate *less* emphasis on assessing:

✔ what is easily measured
✔ discrete knowledge
✔ scientific knowledge
✔ what students don't know
✔ only achievement

The standards call for *more* emphasis on assessing:

✔ what is most highly valued
✔ rich, well-structured knowledge
✔ scientific understanding and reasoning (how do you know your answer is correct?)
✔ what students do understand
✔ achievement *and* opportunity to learn

In addition, the standards advocate that students engage in ongoing assessment of their own work and that of others and that teachers help develop science assessments.

Performance Assessments In the last ten years, the emphasis in science class has gone from textbook learning *about* science to hands-on learning to *do* science. And it doesn't take a rocket scientist to figure out that the best way to assess students' understanding of science is by having them actually perform a science task. Performance assessment lets us measure what students know by watching what they do.

Performance assessment in science should include three basic features, according to Janet Brown of the University of California and Richard Shavelson, director of the Stanford

Education Assessment Laboratory. Brown and Shavelson have teamed with scientists and classroom teachers to develop performance assessments for hands-on science classrooms.

They say that science assessments should always:

✔ present students with a concrete, meaningful task
✔ include a response format with which students communicate their findings
✔ score not just the "right" answer but the reasonableness of the procedure used to determine the answer

Some Examples What does it look like in practice?

Brown and Shavelson offer the example of fifth-grade teacher Dianne Flood, who uses performance assessments to assess her students' thinking, not just their recall of facts.

In a 12-lesson chemistry unit called Mystery Powders, Flood teaches her students the concept of confirming and disconfirming evidence by having them test how certain powders (cornstarch, for example) react with certain indicators (iodine, for example). Throughout the unit, Flood assigns three different 15-minute performance assessments to check student understanding.

In one performance assessment, Flood asks students to identify two mystery mixtures, each consisting of two powders. She asks them to use what they have learned about the indicators and what they can observe to identify the mixtures. The assessment is just another learning activity, but students work independently to make their own discoveries. (Other assessments might require students to work in pairs or groups.)

Teacher observation is an important part of performance assessment, and Flood circulates around the room while the students are working. She gives them an assessment notebook to record their findings, which she later scores based on a scoring system developed by Brown, Shavelson, and colleagues.

"Performance assessment gives me clues to changes I need to make in my teaching," Flood explains. In one assessment, for example, she discovered that students understood the concept of decide how to approach it. In the first step, for example, students must decide how to wet the towels and whether it is necessary to get each towel completely wet. Students then measure their results—again, choosing from a variety of methods. Finally, they record their findings and the methods they used in special assessment notebooks, which the teacher scores based on a previously developed scoring instrument.

In each case, the performance assessments are viewed as another learning activity, the students work on a real problem using real materials, they record and describe their thinking and methodology, and there isn't simple recall of fact or one right answer.

Other assessments could include learning logs, where students record their thinking, or graphic organizers, where students graphically illustrate everything they've learned about a topic and how all of that learning is interrelated. (See the examples in Chapter Three.)

confirming evidence, but not disconfirming evidence (that is, ruling out a substance because of a nonreaction). She also found that many students accurately recorded their observations, but they didn't record the tests those observations were based on. It was obvious where she needed to adjust her instruction.

Brown and Shavelson also offer the example of students who demonstrate their knowledge of science and scientific procedure by using laboratory equipment and problem-solving skills to find out which of three brands of paper towels absorbs the most water. There's more than one way to solve the task, and each student must

Developing Performance Assessments Many good science assessments are available commercially or publicly through the print or electronic media. (See the integrated science units and assessments offered by the Regional Educational Laboratory at AEL mentioned in Chapter Three.) And some teachers like to develop their own. But Brown and Shavelson caution that, "Performance assessments in science need a great deal of fine-tuning. In fact, our research has shown us that assessment development needs to be a team effort—teachers, scientists, curriculum writers, and assessment specialists working together."

To view many different types of performance assessments developed by Brown and Shavelson, see their book, *A Teacher's Guide to Performance Assessment* (Sage Publications, 1996). The focus is on middle-grades science, and the authors give clear instructions on how to use and score each type of assessment.

In their work on science education in grades K though 12, Shavelson and colleagues have identified four types of science achievement:

✔ Declarative—"Knowing that"
✔ Procedural—"Knowing how"
✔ Schematic—"Knowing why"
✔ Strategic—"Knowing about knowing"

Their work focuses on different assessment methods that account for these different types of achievement, including multiple-choice items, constructed response, concept maps, performance assessment, and student science notebooks.

For more information on assessing student achievement in science, see the Stanford Education Assessment Laboratory's Web site at www.stanford.edu/dept/SUSE/SEAL. The site features papers, assessment instruments, and links to other sites.

Social Studies

"Social studies is the integrated study of the social sciences and humanities to promote civic competence." That should be the guiding principle behind social studies teaching and learning, according to *Expectations of Excellence: Curriculum Standards for the Social Studies* issued by the National Council for the Social Studies.

"The primary purpose of social studies is to help young people develop the ability to make informed and reasoned decisions for the public good as citizens of a culturally diverse, democratic society in an interdependent world," writes Lynn Page Whittaker in an executive summary of the standards document. To accomplish this, Whittaker points out, social studies must draw upon the interrelated disciplines of anthropology, archaeology, economics, geography, history, law, philosophy, political science, psychology, religion,

National elementary social studies teacher of the year Tarry Lindquist shares her ideas about standards and teaching strategies in three books:
• *Ways That Work: Putting Social Studies Standards Into Practice* (Heinemann, 1997)
• *Social Studies at the Center: Integrating Kids, Content, and Literacy,* with Douglas Selwyn (Heinemann, 2000)
• *Seeing the Whole Through Social Studies* (Heinemann, 2002)

and sociology, as well as appropriate content from the humanities, mathematics, and natural sciences.

Social studies, perhaps more than any other discipline, illustrates the concept that all knowledge is interrelated. (It is not, however, included in the No Child Left Behind annual standardized testing mandate, as are language arts, math, and science.)

"In essence," writes Whittaker, "social studies promotes knowledge of and involvement in civic affairs. And because civic issues—such as health care, crime, and foreign policy—are multidisciplinary in nature, understanding these issues and developing resolutions to them require multidisciplinary education."

What's Important The teachers, college professors, and other professionals who developed the standards suggest that social studies teaching and learning incorporate these thematic strands:

✔ culture and cultural diversity
✔ time, continuity, and change
✔ people, places, and environment
✔ individual development and identity
✔ power, authority, and governance
✔ production, distribution, and consumption
✔ science, technology, and society
✔ global connections
✔ civic ideals and practice

Each of the thematic strands draws on all the social science disciplines, and all are interrelated.

Social Studies Self-Assessment Quiz

Assess your social studies instruction and learn how you can improve it with this quiz developed by Tarry Lindquist. To create the quiz, Lindquist pulled a few specifics from each of the ten NCSS thematic strands. The quiz represents primary-intermediate and middle-school expectations all mixed together.

1. Culture: Can your students compare/contrast how groups, societies, and cultures meet human needs and concerns? Did they have opportunities to show how language, folktales, music, and art express culture and influence behavior?

Score: _____

2. Time, Continuity, and Change: Can your students demonstrate an understanding that different people may describe the same event in diverse ways? Give reasons for the differences? Use knowledge of facts and concepts drawn from history? Do historical research to reconstruct or reinterpret the past?

Score: _____

3. People, Places, and Environments: Can your students create, interpret, use, and distinguish various representations of the earth, such as maps, globes, and photographs? Locate and distinguish varying landforms and geographic features? Did your kids explore ways that the earth's physical features have changed over time? Talk about how these changes may be connected?

Score: _____

4. Individual Development and Identity: Did your students share the unique features of their nuclear and extended families? Identify and describe ways regional, ethnic, and national cultures influence daily life? Explore factors that contribute to their personal identity, such as interests and perceptions?

Score: _____

5. Individuals, Groups, and Institutions: Can your students identify the different roles they play in group situations, such as family member, peer, or club member? Explain influences such as religious beliefs, laws, and peer pressure on people, events, and culture?

Score: _____

6. Power, Authority, and Governance: Did your students examine the rights and responsibilities of individuals in relation to their social groups? Can they explain the purpose of government? Distinguish among local, state, and national government and identify representative leaders?

Score: _____

7. Production, Distributions, and Consumption: Did your students learn how scarcity and choice govern our economic decisions? Can they distinguish between needs and wants? Identify examples of private and public goods and services? Comprehend the relationship of price to supply and demand?

Score: _____

8. Science, Technology, and Society: Can your students identify and give examples of how science and technology have changed lives? Describe how science and technology, such as building dams and farming rain forests, have changed the environment? Can they suggest ways to monitor technology to protect the environment, individual rights, and the common good?

Score: _____

9. Global Connections: Can your students describe how language, art, music, and belief systems facilitate global understanding or cause misunderstanding? Analyze examples of international conflict, cooperation, and interdependence? Demonstrate understanding of issues related to universal human rights?

Score: _____

10. Civic Ideals and Practices: Can your students identify and give examples of key ideals of the United States, such as human dignity, liberty, justice, equality, and law? Did they practice civic discussions? Learn civility? Make reasoned arguments and compromise? Share opinions? Respect other points of view?

Score: _____

How to Score:
If your students didn't do anything like this, but you're thinking about it for next year, give yourself one star (★).

If you've tried something like this but don't feel comfortable—or need to gather more resources, give yourself two stars (★★).

If your students had these or similar experiences, give yourself three stars (★★★).

0 to 14 Stars: **Budding**
15 to 24 Stars: **Blossoming**
25 to 30 Stars: **Bouquet**

Specific suggestions for student performance are offered for each strand.

"In my opinion, the NCSS standards represent good thinking by credible people," says Washington teacher Tarry Lindquist, a noted author. The standards "give us a solid means to assess your own programs, and provide us with suggestions for those areas in which we find our instruction lacking."

To help you assess your own social studies instruction and give you some ideas about how to improve, Lindquist offers a Self-Assessment Quiz (see page 195).

And Don't Forget In addition to the thematic strands, expert teachers include two other important aspects of social studies teaching.

The first is "presenting multiple histories, stories, and perspectives," suggests Tamara Glupczynski of Columbia Teachers College. The idea is that history, like any story, differs depending upon who's telling it. Dr. Martin Luther King Jr.'s account of the civil rights movement, for example, would certainly differ from Alabama governor George Wallace's account. By considering multiple perspectives, students get a broader picture of the world.

The second aspect, related to the first, is the idea of teaching with **primary sources:** diaries, letters, speeches, photos, and other documents or artifacts created or used during or immediately following the event they describe, by people who had firsthand knowledge of the event. **Secondary sources**, such as textbooks, interpret primary sources to present an overview of historical people, places, or events. Teaching with primary sources allows students to interpret history for themselves, based on evidence contemporary to the event or person. Analyzing primary sources encourages higher-order thinking skills and provides a necessary complement to a linear reading and factual recall approach commonly used with textbooks. One good example of a primary source commonly used with a unit on World War II or the Holocaust is *Anne Frank: The Diary of a Young Girl.*

Alternative Assessments Traditional assessments alone cannot do an adequate job in social studies, because the teaching and learning of social studies can no longer be "traditional."

"For social studies to perform its mission of promoting civic competence, students must learn not only a body of knowledge but how to think and be flexible in using many resources to resolve civic issues," writes Lynn Page Whittaker. When students organize and conduct a letter-writing campaign to protest a community ordinance, or initiate a recycling drive to reduce landfill volume, or write to pen pals in Asia, or collect clothes and toys to send to North Dakota flood victims, they are "doing" social studies. The tie-ins to other subjects and skills are not only easy, they're unavoidable.

GEOGRAPHY STANDARDS

Articles abound deploring Americans' lack of geographical knowledge. What should we learn and be able to accomplish with geography? *Geography for Life: National Geography Standards* identifies 18 standards organized around six essential elements of geography. Joseph Stoltman, a geography professor from Western Michigan University, explains that, according to the standards, the geographically informed person knows and understands:

The World in Spatial Terms

1. How to use maps and other geographic representations, tools, and technologies to acquire, process, and report information from a spatial perspective
2. How to use mental maps to organize information about people, places, and environments in a spatial context
3. How to analyze the spatial organization of people, places, and environments on Earth's surface

Places and Regions

4. The physical and human characteristics of places
5. That people create regions to interpret Earth's complexity
6. How culture and experience influence people's perceptions of places and regions

Physical Systems

7. The physical processes that shape the patterns of Earth's surface
8. The characteristics and spatial distribution of ecosystems on Earth's surface

Human Systems

9. The characteristics, distribution, and migration of human populations
10. The characteristics, distribution, and complexity of Earth's cultural mosaics
11. The patterns and networks of economic interdependence on Earth
12. The processes, patterns, and functions of human settlement
13. How the forces of cooperation and conflict among people influence the division and control of Earth's surface

Environment and Society

14. How human actions modify the physical environment
15. How physical systems affect human systems
16. The changes that occur in the meaning, use, distribution, and importance of resources

The Uses of Geography

17. How to apply geography to interpret the past
18. How to apply geography to interpret the present and plan for the future

Order the standards from the National Geographic Society at P.O.B. 1640, Washington, DC 20013-1640, or call (800) 368-2728. You can view the 18 standards online at www.nationalgeographic.com/education/xpeditions/standards. Also available on this Web site are activities, links, and lesson plans sorted by standard and grade level.

"Assessment should no longer be viewed as separate from instruction," insists Pat Nickell from Kentucky, who helped write the standards. "Just as the worker is evaluated on an ongoing basis on the products or services generated, student evaluation is most authentic and equitable when it is based upon the ideas, processes, products, and behaviors exhibited during regular instruction."

Assessment and teaching must be tied to real problems and issues.

Former *Instructor* editor-in-chief Mickey Revenaugh tells the story of how fourth graders in a class in which she volunteers learned a "real" history lesson after their principal announced one day that all students would be required to buy a special 25-cent stamp to put on each homework assignment they turned in.

The students were really upset, Revenaugh reports. "Within minutes, the students were making protest signs, drafting letters, and planning a rally outside the principal's office. That's when their teacher broke the news: The whole thing was a ruse to help them understand American history. For one brief, red-hot moment, these fourth graders had stepped into the shoes of the Colonists facing the Stamp Act."

Examples of Alternative Assessments

Following are some of the many ideas gleaned from colleagues who have successfully used performance-based alternatives to traditional teaching and assessment.

✔ **Invention Convention.** Tarry Lindquist integrates social studies and science and asks her fifth graders to demonstrate knowledge and thinking skills by asking them to "become" scientists and inventors who have changed the world. First, the students each select a significant invention (from any era) and research the "who, what, where, why and how." Next, they draw diagram posters of their inventions and label them so they are visible anywhere in the classroom. Posing as newspaper reporters, they then write stories (with quotes from the inventors) about their invention. They also create ads to sell the inventions. Next, as the inventors, they write letters to a friend describing what they did and how they felt on the day their invention finally worked. And the culminating activity is a mock science convention where students present their research and inventions, try to convince the audience how important the invention is, and answer questions. After the convention, the posters are hung around the room in chronological order to create a time line of inventions.

✔ **Dramatizations.** As scholar Barbara Clark argues convincingly, "Combining theater and history can lead to a memorable meeting of the minds." Many teachers have discovered the effectiveness of having students "act out" important events, role-play important characters, or write and perform their own plays on important concepts. Such activity requires deep understanding of the underlying principles and draws on the strengths of different learning styles.

✔ **Reader Response Logs.** Many teachers have discovered the benefits of teaching social studies through literature. For example, they might have students read fiction about a culture or time period studied. Since literature is not written in a vacuum but reflects the people, places, and prevailing thoughts of certain time periods, the possibilities are endless. To assess student learning, you might ask them to write about the characters' experiences according to what they know about the time period. I've learned that Mark Twain's *The Adventures of Huckleberry Finn* helps middle schoolers learn more about the American experience than any other single piece of literature. Not to mention the chance to explore the issue of censorship.

SOCIAL STUDIES ONLINE

A site to bookmark for frequent visits, the National Council for the Social Studies (NCSS) Web site at www.ncss.org offers access to the social studies standards and much more. This site is also a great source for lesson plans and teaching resources such as current events information and maps on Iraq.

The Arts

Researchers and teachers cite indisputable evidence that the arts stimulate higher-order thinking skills and improve the quality of our lives. But in our nation's quest for high standardized-test scores and more "basics," we've cut or eliminated arts programs everywhere. My own local elementary school shares a traveling art teacher with ten other elementary schools in our district. For individual students, that translates to one 30-minute art period every six weeks.

"When we dilute or delete arts programs, we unravel the infrastructure that assures the cultural future of the nation," warns scholar and writer Charles Fowler. "But far worse, the absence or meagerness of the arts in schooling denies children access to the vast treasury of American and world culture. The result? Their education is incomplete, their minds less enlightened, their lives less enlivened."

Fowler writes, "We do not need more and better arts education to develop more and better artists. We need more and better arts education to produce better educated human beings, citizens who will value and evolve a worthy civilization."

The arts—music, visual arts, dance, drama—*are* "basic." Artistic expression is the essence of our humanity, argues Fowler.

"The arts, like the sciences, are symbolic systems that convey meaning about the world," he says. "The great thinkers of any age do not express themselves solely by the written word." (Does the name Leonardo da Vinci come to mind?)

"By denying children the arts, we starve our civilization," Fowler continues. "We produce children who are more fitted for an age of barbarism than the advanced civilization of the information age."

In the last decade, Harvard professor Howard Gardner and other educational psychologists have even argued convincingly that music and the arts represent distinct forms of intelligence, equally important as verbal or mathematical intelligence.

Achievement in the arts has always been assessed by performance or portfolio. In fact, the arts provide models for alternative and authentic assessments in other subjects. Further, the arts are vehicles themselves for assessing what students know, understand, and can do in other content areas. When a student acts out a poem, or paints a picture depicting the forces of gravity, or composes a song about families broken by the Civil War, he or she is demonstrating knowledge and understanding.

❖ In Summary

Good assessment of learning is authentic. It attempts to measure thinking skills and deeper understanding, not just factual knowledge or rote memorization. It accounts for the unique learning styles of individual students to accurately reflect their *real* learning.

Authentic assessment actively involves students, gives them feedback from teachers and peers, allows them to make choices and demonstrate their strengths and successes, and encourages them to build on what they already know. It is part of the learning process itself. When students develop portfolios, plan exhibitions, design performances, write in journals, undertake experiments, create projects, or offer presentations, they are *still learning*, not just demonstrating what they already know. They're demonstrating what they *can do* with what they know.

Good assessment also includes a wide array

VOLUNTEER ART PROGRAM

When budget cuts severely curtailed regular art education at Cameron Elementary School in West Virginia, parents stepped in and organized a volunteer art program. Working in teams at each grade level, they collected materials, planned and presented activities, and cleaned up afterward for art classes held twice per month. This is just one example of how volunteers can enrich the experiences of children beyond what is available in school.

If you want to organize a volunteer art education program in your school, or find yourself in the position of designing your own program, see page 200 for some helpful hints.

Fostering Creativity in Children's Art

When you come up with new ideas, imagine things that don't exist, or think of new ways to use everyday items, you are exercising creativity. Creativity, says Sandra Duncan, publisher of *Early Childhood Today*, is the ability to make something original or do the same task in many different ways. We can help children develop creativity through art if we recognize that the process of art is more important than the final product.

Duncan offers four ways you can foster creativity in children's art and create an environment that encourages children to explore and investigate.

Provide open-ended art activities.

Creativity is about the process of creating—not the product. By giving children product-oriented activities you limit their ability to exercise creativity. Ditto sheets, coloring-book pages, connect-the-dots, and activity sheets all limit creativity because they force children's artwork to look alike. Rather than display a model of the art project for children to replicate, encourage children to use their imagination. Instead of passing out coloring-book pages, all with the same line drawings, turn on some music and have the children draw what they hear!

Provide significant blocks of free time for children to work in a relaxed and encouraging atmosphere.

Create a classroom that invigorates the five senses. Don't simply draw or paint—feel the texture of the paper, smell the crayons, listen to the sound of a crayon being sharpened, and watch the colors change as paints are mixed!

Encourage spontaneous exploration.

Place puppets, musical instruments, and other objects around the classroom. Provide a constant, easily accessible supply of basic materials such as chalk, markers, paste, construction paper, brushes, and paints. Allow children to discover the properties of these items and how to use them. Can the children use their fingers as a paintbrush? Draw a picture in the dirt using a stick? Make their bodies the same shape as a tree? Describe what the color purple feels like? March around the room in a happy, sad, or funny way?

Respect children's creativity.

Share children's work with others. Display artwork in the classroom, the lobby, or in local libraries and pediatricians' offices. Don't criticize children's work. Ask open-ended questions about a child's creation. Rather than asking, "What is your picture of?" ask the child to tell you about his or her work.

Excerpted from "Fostering Creativity in Children's Art" by Sandra Duncan, *Early Childhood News*, May/June 1996. Reprinted by permission of the publisher.

of measures. There is a time and a place for standardized tests, traditional teacher-made tests, informal assessments, self-assessments, and other measures. But any one measure has limitations and should be used as a piece of a larger repertoire.

Finally, good assessment matches some type of standard. What is it that we want students to know and be able to do? And for the first time in the history of American education, we have some consensus on that question: standards for teaching, learning, and assessment in each of the major content areas.

❖ Works Cited

Aborn, Allyson. *Everything I Do You Blame on Me!* King of Prussia, PA: Center For Applied Psychology, 1994.

Berube, Clair T. "Are Standards Preventing Good Teaching?" *The Clearinghouse* 77, no. 6 (July/August 2004).

Brown, Janet, and Richard Shavelson. "Does Your Testing Match Your Teaching Style?" *Instructor,* September 1994, 86–89.

Brown, Janet, and Richard Shavelson. "New Ways to Measure What Students Know and Can Do." *Instructor,* March 1994, 58–61.

Burns, Marilyn. "How I Boost My Students' Number Sense." *Instructor,* April 1997, 49–54.

Clark, Barbara. *Growing Up Gifted: Developing the Potential of Children at Home and at School.* 6th ed. Upper Saddle River, NJ: Merrill/PrenticeHall, 2002.

Culham, Ruth. *6+1 Traits of Writing: The Complete Guide, Grades 3 and Up.* New York: Scholastic, 2003.

Cunningham, P. M., D. P. Hall, and C. M. Sigmon. *The Teacher's Guide to the Four Blocks.* Greensboro, NC: Carson-Dellosa, 1999.

"The Facts About . . . State Standards." Available: www.ed.gov/print/nclb/accountability/state/standards.html.

Farkas, Steve, et al. "Rolling Up Their Sleeves: Superintendents and Principals Talk About What's Needed to Fix Public Schools." *A Report from Public Agenda for the Wallace Foundation.* New York, 2003.

Farrace, Bob. "The Nature of the Test: W. James Popham on Assessment." Interview. *Principal Leadership* 4, no. 1 (September 2003).

Fowler, Charles. "The Arts are Essential to Education." *Educational Leadership* (November 1989): 60–63.

Fresch, Mary Jo, and Aileen Wheaton. *Teaching and Assessing Spelling.* New York: Scholastic, 2002.

Frye, Shirley M. "Communicating the Next Message of Reform through the Professional Standards for Teaching Mathematics." ERIC Digest No. ED335238, 1991. Available: www.ericfacility.net/ericdigests/ed335238.html.

Gehret, Jeanne. *Eagle Eyes.* Fairport, NY: Verbal Images Press, 1991.

Goldberg, Mark F. "The High-Stakes Test Mess." *The Education Digest* (April 2004).

Goodrich, Heidi. "Understanding Rubrics." *Educational Leadership* 54, no. 4 (December 1996/January 1997): 14-17.

"Grant Wiggins on Assessment." *Instructor,* October 1995, 16.

Koenigs, Sharon. *Test Scores Count! A Handbook for Teaching Test-Taking Skills.* Aurora, CO: Mid-continent Regional Educational Laboratory, 1987.

Kuralt Charles. *Life on the Road.* New York: Putnam, 1990.

Language Arts Standards. 4th ed. Mid-continent Regional Educational Laboratory. Available: www.mcrel.org/compendium/SubjectTopics.asp?subjectID=7.

Leach, Eilene. "An Alternative Form of Evaluation that Complies with NCTM's Standards." *Mathematics Teacher* 85, no. 8 (November 1992): 628–632.

Lehrer, Richard, and Leona Schauble. "Building Models Enhances Understanding." *WCER [Wisconsin Center for Education Research] Highlights* 9, no. 1 (Spring 1997). Available: www.wcer.wisc.edu/publications.

Lindquist, Tarry. "Social Studies Now: How Does Your Teaching Rate?" *Instructor,* May/June 1996, 36–37.

McTighe, Jay. "What Happens Between Assessments?" *Educational Leadership* 54, no. 4 (December 1996/January 1997): 6–12.

National Center for Fair and Open Testing (FairTest). "Failing Our Children: How No Child Left Behind Undermines Quality and Equity in Education, and an Accountability Model that Supports School Improvement." Available: www.fairtest.org.

National Council of Teachers of English. *Standards for the English Language Arts.* Urbana, IL: NCTE, 1996.

National Council of Teachers of Mathematics. *Principles and Standards for School Mathematics.* Reston, VA: National Council of Teachers of Mathematics, 2000.

Posner, Dave. "What's Wrong With Teaching to the Test?" *Phi Delta Kappan* 85, no. 10 (June 2004).

"Questions and Answers on *No Child Left Behind*—Reading." U.S. Department of Education. Available: www.ed.gov/nclb/methods/reading/reading.html.

Routman, Regie. *Literacy at the Crossroads: Crucial Talk About Reading, Writing, and Other Teaching Dilemmas.* Portsmouth, NH: Heinemann, 1996.

Schulman, Mary Browning, and Carleen Payne daCruz. *Guided Reading: Making It Work.* New York: Scholastic, 2000.

Sigmon, Cheryl. *Modifying Four-Blocks at the Upper Grades.* Greensboro, NC: Carson-Dellosa, 2001.

Stoltman, Joseph. "The National Geography Content Standards." *ERIC Digest,* March 1995. Available: www.ericfacility.net/ericdigests/ed381480.html.

Strickland, Kathleen and James. *Making Assessment Elementary.* Portsmouth, NH: Heinemann, 2000.

Wiggins, Grant, and associates. "Authentic Education." 2004. Available: http://authenticeducation.org.

Wiggins, Grant, and Jay McTighe. *Understanding by Design.* Upper Saddle River, NJ: Merrill/Prentice Hall, 2001.

Viorst, Judith. *The Tenth Good Thing About Barney.* New York: Aladdin Books, 1987.

❖ Resources

<u>General Assessment</u>

Fiderer, Adele. *40 Rubrics & Checklists to Assess Reading and Writing.* New York: Scholastic, 1999.

Olson, Lynn. "Federal Education Law Failing, Report Argues." *Education Week,* June 9, 2004. Citing a report from the National Center for Fair and Open Testing, Olson reports that NCLB's heavy reliance on standardized tests coupled with strict penalties for failing to meet annual yearly progress results in a "narrowing of the curriculum and intensive teaching to the test."

Strickland, Kathleen and James. *Making Assessment Elementary*. Portsmouth: NH: Heinemann, 2000. (Interactive CD included.)

Sullivan, Mary. *75 Language Arts Assessment Tools*. New York: Scholastic, 2003.

Wiggins, Grant, and Jay McTighe. "Understanding by Design Exchange." Available: www.ubdexchange.org. Subscription rates: $45 per individual; $499 per school. An ASCD cooperative Web site devoted to the development and peer review of curriculum units.

Portfolios
Clemmons, J., et al. *Portfolios in the Classroom: A Teacher's Sourcebook*. New York: Scholastic, 1993.

DeFina, Allan. *Portfolio Assessment: Getting Started (Grades K–8)*. New York: Scholastic, 1999.

Grace, Cathy, and Elizabeth Shores. *The Portfolio Book: A Step-by-Step Guide for Teachers*. Beltsville, MD: Gryphon House, 1998.

MacDonald, Sharon. *The Portfolio and Its Use: A Road Map for Assessment*. Beltsville, MD: Gryphon House, 1997.

Rubrics
Arter, Judith A., and Jay McTighe. *Scoring Rubrics in the Classroom: Using Performance Criteria for Assessing and Improving Student Performance*. Thousand Oaks, CA: Corwin Press, 2001.

Running Records
Clay, Marie. *Concepts About Print: What Have Children Learned About the Way We Print Language?* Portsmouth, NH: Heinemann, 2000.

Clay, Marie. *Running Records for Classroom Teachers*. Portsmouth, NH: Heinemann, 2000.

Shea, Mary. *Taking Running Records*. New York: Scholastic, 2002.

Chapter Five

Teaching Kids to Care

"As a teacher I feel I have a moral obligation to help the children in my classroom grow toward becoming full human beings and to feel successful. Teaching cognitive skills is not enough."

—*Jean Medick,*
Michigan teacher and author

If teaching academic subjects was all we had to do as teachers, our jobs would be much simpler than they are now. But anyone who's been in a classroom more than a few days or weeks knows that academic instruction is just one aspect of a much larger task. As teachers, we play a role in nurturing and facilitating social and emotional development as well as intellectual growth. Children's affective needs and abilities are closely tied to their cognitive needs, and we are challenged with addressing the whole child—heart and mind.

In short, we need to teach children to care—about themselves, each other, their schools and communities, and the world at large. Think about it. Would caring children bully each other? Intentionally disrupt classroom activities? Vandalize schools and communities? Engage in self-destructive behavior? Hate each other for their racial or ethnic differences?

This chapter addresses those affective concerns—behavior problems; discipline; self-esteem; prejudices based on cultural, racial, gender, or socioeconomic stereotypes; peer conflicts; and social climate—that have such a significant impact on teaching and learning. These are the concerns foremost on the minds of most novice teachers and even many veterans.

❖ Caring Teachers

Of course, teaching kids to care presupposes that we teachers do. Student behavior is closely linked to our own. Our actions, attitudes, and expectations greatly influence how students act.

There are important personal qualities that can help us influence behavior and performance in positive ways. Teachers who are warm, patient, tolerant, interested in students, and willing to use humor achieve the best results. You can smile and be cheerful and still maintain a businesslike, work-oriented approach.

"Hold sacred the opportunity to be a role model for your students," suggests Pennsylvania teacher Laurie Borger. "Honesty, respect, compassion, and understanding are two-way streets. You must show the way for our youth to follow. Apologize when you make a mistake, and they will do the same."

"Be honest with kids!" stresses Martine Wayman, a veteran from Washington. "Tell them what you need from them and let them know that it's okay to disagree with you as long as they do it with respect. Give them regular opportunities to reflect on how they feel their school year is going and what they would like changed."

"Be yourself!" suggests California veteran Pamela Shannon. "Share things about yourself with your class. Smile. Give 'warm fuzzies.' Be kind but firm. Let the students know where they stand." (See page 206 for tips on how to show students you care.)

Prevention Is the Best Policy

There are many things teachers can do to increase the odds that students will be on their best behavior. Classroom research shows that effective teachers spend very little time dealing with student misconduct. It's not that they ignore behavior problems; they have established strategies for preventing many problems in the first place.

You can significantly reduce student misconduct with good classroom management—routines, consistent enforcement of negotiated rules, careful lesson planning, and smooth transitions between lessons (see Chapter One).

You can also significantly reduce student misconduct with effective instructional strategies—giving students choices, offering projects and themes, addressing different intelligences and learning styles, and keeping them actively engaged (see Chapter Three). Motivated, engaged students are not likely to cause many problems.

Good teachers also address students' emotional needs by nurturing their self-images, teaching them to be responsible and fair, showing them how to resolve conflicts, emphasizing cooperation, and teaching them to value individual differences and talents.

Teacher Behaviors

Observing expert teachers in a landmark study more than 25 years ago, researcher Jacob Kounin discovered that they shared three important behavioral qualities—qualities that enabled them to nip most problems in the bud:

✔ **Expert teachers are "with it."** They let their students know that they are aware of what is happening at all times. They regularly monitor and scan the classroom and position themselves where they can see all students.

✔ **Good classroom managers can also overlap activities**. That is, they can do more than one thing at a time without disrupting the class as a whole. They can work with individuals or a small group and still, almost unnoticed, deal with other students who have questions. (Give students routines for seeking your help and teach them to discern which questions warrant your immediate attention. See Chapter One.)

✔ **The experts also maintain the momentum in teaching a lesson**. They keep attention focused on instruction and not on misbehaving students by avoiding extended reprimands or overreactions. They ignore minor inattention. And they promptly attend to more serious misbehavior in nondisruptive ways—eye contact, a brief comment, a question directed to the offender. But lesson momentum is possible only if a teacher is well prepared. False starts, backtracking, and confusion can destroy a lesson—and student attention.

How to Show Students You Care

If you love children and love learning (and what good teacher doesn't?), communicate your feelings to students with these tips offered by Linda Brown Anderson, special-education teacher from Prescott, Arizona. Most of what Anderson suggests is just good teaching.

Listen. Most of us have been taught to teach, keep order, and attend to the endless details that make up each school day. Often we don't take the time to listen. How can we sharpen our listening skills? One way is by making eye contact with students while they are speaking. After students finish speaking, invite questions and comments from their classmates. This tells students that their statements are important.

Share something about yourself. Sharing something personal—but not intimate—with children is a nice way to demonstrate that you respect them as fellow human beings.

Value humor. Humor doesn't have to be disruptive. Appropriate humor is healthy and can bring teachers and students together. Laugh and enjoy.

Admit you don't know everything and acknowledge mistakes. It's amazing how difficult it is for most adults, especially teachers, to say, "I don't know." Some teachers fear that admitting errors damages their credibility. I've found that when I'm honest, I become more credible. For instance, my class recently read a short story about a boy who died because of an enlarged heart. A student asked me why that condition could cause death. I said I didn't know. Hearing me say that made it easier for students to ask questions and to admit they didn't always know the answer.

Be tough. My students sometimes think I'm too strict. From the moment class begins until the bell signals its end, they are at work. Invariably during the week before a major holiday, they come into class, look at the assignment posted on the board, and say plaintively, "Mr. Brown is showing movies in his class all week. Can we have movies or free time in here?" When I say no, they plod dolefully to their seats—but then get to work. I'm demanding for a good reason. We have such a limited time allotted each day for formal learning. When teachers are always prepared and ready, students get the message: Learning is important, and so are they.

Be curious. People who love learning are in a perpetual state of curiosity. Curiosity is contagious; so, too, is the joy and excitement of being alive in an endlessly fascinating world. Gently prod your students: Why is this? Why is that? What do you think? How can we find out? Lead by example. Join children as they pursue subjects that really interest them and you.

Reward effort. Every child needs to know that education is a journey, not a destination. To keep children engaged in the process, consistently reward academic exertion as well as achievement.

Spend time with children who need to be drawn in. These are the children whose behavior is occasionally problematic, children who have minimal interactions with you and their classmates, children who seem to lack motivation. Has the child mastered even a small academic skill? Show approval. Focus on the positives. Such children need consistent attention but don't always get it. Sometimes it seems as if the children who are well-behaved receive more of our attention. Is this because they reinforce our success as teachers? Maybe. But I really feel that I am not a successful teacher unless every student in my class feels successful. (On some days that's easier said than done.)

Value yourself. This is a tough one. Our society defines people's value in monetary terms, and most teachers are woefully underpaid. As educators, we need to remember this: We touch children's lives. Valuing children and valuing education are among the characteristics of a great nation.

Important Qualities

Other teacher qualities associated with good student behavior and discipline were identified by Jere Brophy and Joyce Putnam in their extensive review of classroom research. They include:

✔ **Ego strength and self-confidence.** These qualities enable a teacher to hear student complaints without becoming authoritarian or defensive.

✔ **Positive attitude.** Students respond well to teachers who like and respect them. Veterans strongly recommend getting to know students, communicating a sincere interest in their lives, and establishing good rapport.

✔ **High expectations.** When teachers help students perceive themselves as able and responsible, students tend to act that way. (See the section on expectations in Chapter Three.)

✔ **Authoritative leadership.** Effective teachers seek feedback and consensus on decisions and make sure that students understand their decisions. This is more effective than either authoritarian rule (where decisions are absolute) or nondirected laissez-faire leadership.

> *Teacher-educator Tamara Glupczynski notes another important quality: being yourself. She advises, "If your personality is quiet and soft-spoken, establish a classroom culture where you are still in charge, but kids know you. Routines should support your needs. Don't try to be someone you're not—kids can tell."*

HOW TEACHERS DEAL WITH STUDENTS WHO ARE DIFFICULT TO LIKE

Keep these tips in mind when a student has your blood pressure rising.

- "I pretend that someone in my classroom is watching me teach. This keeps me on my toes and helps me deal with all my students fairly."—Rhonda Houchins, Pittsfield, IL

- "Each day I spend five minutes talking to the child about anything but school issues. After a few weeks, I have learned something about the child and can relate to him."—Amy Lynn, Lumberton, NJ

- "In my mind, I separate the child from the irritating behavior. Once I have put my finger on what it is that annoys me, I don't have as much difficulty with the child."—Anne Fitzpatrick, Seattle, WA

- "I put my feelings aside and focus on the fact that I am a professional."—Andrea Green, Alief, TX

- "I try to keep in mind that I may be the only person who likes this child, so I look for positive things and try to keep my sense of humor."— Lee Smith, Columbus, OH

- "I make at least one positive statement about that child each day. Even on the child's worst day, I tell myself one positive thing about the child, sometimes just liking the color of the child's shirt."—Lisa M. Schultz, Columbus, OH

- "Keep in mind that the most unlikeable child is the one who most needs to be liked."—Beth Raker, Granger, IN

- "I have lunch with the student and talk about the child's interests. This gives me something positive to focus my attention on."—Sherry Milner, Foxworth, MS

"How Teachers Deal With Students Who Are Difficult to Like" by Shelley Krapes, *Creative Classroom*, August 1997, p. 30. © 1997 Children's Television Workshop. Used by permission of Children's Television Workshop.

When Personalities Clash

Sometimes, despite our best intentions, we find ourselves actively disliking one of the children in our charge. The child may be rude, disrespectful, disruptive, obnoxious, or otherwise annoying. It's just human nature; some personalities clash. But instead of feeling guilty about our feelings, we can take positive steps to improve them, says school psychologist and teacher Shelley Krapes, a columnist for *Creative Classroom*. Here are Krapes's suggestions:

✔ First, try to understand where the behavior is coming from. Is the child distressed by a death, divorce, new baby, learning disability, or some other overwhelming experience? Speaking to the child's parents may shed light on underlying causes and help you develop sympathy through understanding.

✔ Help yourself manage negative feelings by reflecting on a past situation where a similar conflict occurred. Discuss the situation with a friend or by writing your thoughts in a journal. Making and understanding these connections can help you let go of some of your current hostility and resentment.

✔ Use positive strategies when dealing with the child, such as addressing specific behaviors with precise language that describes what needs to be done ("I see the milk has spilled. We need to get a sponge," rather than, "You're such a mess. I can't take my eyes off of you for a second."). Seat the child near to you or a helpful student, praise the child liberally but sincerely, give the child choices to promote self-worth and feelings of control, be firm and consistent about your rules, and express displeasure with the child's behavior without criticizing the child.

✔ Set a goal. If the situation between you and the child has not improved after two or three months of your best effort, it may be time to recommend professional psychological/educational testing. Some problems are very complex and may be beyond your control.

See below for ideas on how other teachers handle students who exhibit irritating and unlikable behaviors.

❖ What Is Discipline?

"To me the worst thing seems to be for a school principally to work with the methods of fear, force, and artificial authority. Such treatment destroys sound sentiments, the sincerity and the self-confidence of the pupil. It produces the submissive subject."—Albert Einstein

"The first idea that the child must acquire in order to be actively disciplined is that of the difference between good and evil; and the task of the educator lies in seeing the child does not confound good with immobility, and evil with activity . . . our aim is to discipline for activity, for work, for good, not for immobility, not for passivity, not for obedience."
—Maria Montessori

Gone are the days (thank goodness!) when children were to be seen and not heard. When classrooms were quiet places where compliant students sat all day in rows of desks, listening to their teachers speak. When curious, active boys were "just being boys," but curious, active girls were "unruly tomboys." Our concept of, and goals for, good discipline have changed dramatically.

Good discipline is *not* the same thing as punishment. *Discipline*, related etymologically to the word *disciple*, means to teach or instruct. The term is used here as a broad concept encompassing the steps taken to ensure appropriate behavior or to correct misbehavior. The goal, of course, is *self*-discipline. For teachers, discipline means:

✔ **Instruction**—teaching *students* responsibility for their behavior, strategies for governing their own actions, and the value of following reasonable rules

✔ **Management**—collaborating with students to create and enforce classroom rules and routines

✔ **Positive reinforcement**—recognizing good behavior as well as establishing negative consequences for misbehavior

It's impossible to talk about discipline in school without talking about classroom management and instructional strategies; the three are closely related. For example, students who repeatedly fail at school tasks become frustrated. They may stop trying, or they may act out feelings of anger and hostility. Others misbehave when they are confused or bored. Still others misbehave because they feel alienated or disliked by classmates. Teachers can prevent many of these problems by nurturing a strong group identity and class community; by carefully planning and pacing lessons; by capitalizing on students' interests, abilities, learning styles, and choices; by keeping kids actively involved and challenged; and by ensuring that all students have opportunities to succeed.

The key concept here is prevention. Good discipline strategies are those that prevent problems. This means attending to the students' physical needs, so they are not uncomfortable; attending to their intellectual needs, so they are not bored, confused, or frustrated; and attending to social and emotional needs, so they feel secure, valued, and part of the group.

❖ Behavior Problems

When does a student's behavior cause a discipline problem? When it interferes with your teaching and the students' learning. We're not talking here about noisy, happy students hard at work. Behavior problems are those that interfere with classroom life; for example, an angry, hostile student who constantly picks fights.

There are many other less extreme examples of problem behaviors: students who can't seem to control annoying habits such as pencil tapping, whistling, or talking out at inappropriate times; students who continuously whine, complain, or tattle; those who always "forget" their homework or claim their assignments are too difficult; or those who withdraw and want only to be left alone. Each of these problem behaviors interferes with your teaching and with student learning.

But besides these specific problem types, there are more pervasive problems affecting a much larger portion of school-age children. Generally, these involve a total disregard for the feelings and rights of others. They just "don't care."

"So many children feel perfectly free to cut others down," writes Michigan Teacher Jean Medick of her fourth- and fifth-grade students. "When I ask them why they said a hurtful thing to someone for no apparent reason, they answer, 'I don't know.' It's like a sport—something to do."

Poor Self-Image

Students with behavior problems share one characteristic: a very poor self-image. And a

> ## "I-MESSAGES"
>
> Many experienced teachers use a technique known as the "I-message" when they discuss problem behaviors with students. The "I-message" lets you tell a student how his or her behavior makes you feel. For example, "Could you please move your feet? When they're in the aisle, I'm afraid I might trip over them and get hurt." This statement includes the three necessary components of effective "I-messages":
>
> 1. Describe the behavior.
>
> 2. State the effects of the behavior.
>
> 3. State how it makes you feel.

poor self-image or low self-esteem manifests itself in the following pervasive problems, which Medick and other veterans find particularly disturbing:

1. negative feelings about themselves and low self-worth
2. much physical and verbal fighting
3. insensitivity
4. lack of self-discipline
5. inattentiveness, poor listening skills, inability to stick to a task or concentrate
6. disregard for their property, that of others, or the school's
7. stealing, and the attitude that if they take something and can get away with it, it's okay
8. failure to put things away or clean up after themselves
9. doing only what they want to do and nothing more
10. constant socializing
11. apathy, boredom, depression, and withdrawal
12. constant demand for their rights, with little regard for the rights of others

WHEN YOU CAN'T DO IT ALONE . . .

Even in learner-centered classrooms that meet students' social, emotional, intellectual, and physical needs, there may be situations where the best strategies and intentions fail. At some point during most teachers' careers, there comes a child whose problems are too great to be handled in class.

"We need to support teachers in the notion that they will need help with some students," says Dr. Adele Brodkin, clinical associate professor of child and adolescent psychiatry at New Jersey Medical School. "There are some behaviors and situations teachers shouldn't be expected to deal with. After they've exhausted all of the instructional and behavioral strategies they know, they need to seriously think about referrals."

Brodkin, an expert on kids in crisis, suggests that some children may need professional counseling. Abuse, neglect, domestic violence, drugs and alcohol, and bitter custody battles are among the serious problems overwhelming many young students and making it difficult or impossible for them to function well in school.

"Trust your gut feelings," Brodkin suggests. "If you notice a child repeatedly doing something negative that he never did before, chances are, something is wrong in his life."

She gives the example of a child who suddenly refused to go to school. The parents immediately assumed that something had happened at school; the teachers assumed something had happened at home. Actually, there was a bully on the bus. In another case, a child decided she didn't want to go to school because she felt she had to stay home and "protect" a sick parent.

Brodkin cautions that we need to look beneath the surface to the underlying causes of the behavior. "They're not always as obvious as you think." And that's where we teachers need outside help and support.

Too often, says Brodkin, schools take the easy way out and label children ADD (attention deficit disorder), ADHD (attention deficit hyperactivity disorder), or BD (behaviorally disordered). These conditions are vastly overdiagnosed these days by people who don't take the time to find out what's really wrong, Brodkin claims. "You can't observe a child running around during class and immediately conclude ADHD. Troubled or misbehaving children need complete diagnostic workups."

Advice From the Experts

Sarcasm, ridicule, and other verbal abuse used as discipline techniques are ineffective at best and hurtful at worst. They damage students' self-esteem and only reinforce the already low opinions many kids have of themselves.

Effective teachers discipline with encouragement and kind words more often than with rebukes or reprimands. They help students feel good about themselves. Their discipline techniques focus on improving a student's self-image and sense of responsibility.

Handling misbehavior isn't easy. But when you must, try to keep the following advice from veterans in mind. These tips represent the collected wisdom of many different teachers from around the nation:

✔ Take a deep breath and try to remain calm. It's natural to be overcome with frustration, resentment, and anger. But when you are, you become less rational, and your agitation becomes contagious.

✔ Try to set a positive tone and model an appropriate response, even if it means you must take a few moments to compose yourself. Acknowledge that you need time to think, time to respond. "This is upsetting me, too, but I need a few minutes to think before we talk about it."

✔ Make sure students understand that it's their misbehavior you dislike, not them. "I like you, Jason. Right now, your behavior is unacceptable."

✔ Give the misbehaving student a chance to respond positively by explaining not only what he or she is doing wrong, but also what he or she can do to correct it.

✔ Never resort to blame or ridicule.

- ✔ Avoid win-lose conflicts and emphasize problem solving instead of punishment.

- ✔ Insist that students accept responsibility for their behavior.

- ✔ Try to remain courteous in the face of hostility or anger. Showing students that you care about them and their problems will help you earn their respect and establish rapport.

- ✔ Treat *all* students respectfully and politely, and be consistent in what you let them say and do. Be careful not to favor certain students.

- ✔ Be an attentive listener. Encourage students to talk out feelings and concerns and help them clarify their comments by restating them. (See the section in this chapter on Active Listening.)

- ✔ Model the behavior you expect from your students. Are you as considerate of your students' feelings as you want them to be of others? Are you as organized and on-task as you tell them to be?

- ✔ Specifically describe misbehavior and help students understand the consequences of misbehavior. Very young children may even need your explanations modeled or acted out.

- ✔ Be aware of cultural differences. For example, a student who stares at the floor while you speak to him or her would be viewed as defiant in some cultures and respectful in others. (For more on cultural differences, see Chapter Two.)

- ✔ Discourage cliques and other antisocial behavior. Offer cooperative activities to encourage group identity.

- ✔ Teach students personal and social skills— communicating, listening, helping, and sharing, for example.

- ✔ Teach students academic survival skills, such as paying attention, following directions, asking for help when they really need it, and volunteering to answer.

- ✔ Avoid labeling students as "good" or "bad." Instead, describe their behavior as "positive," "acceptable," "disruptive," or "unacceptable."

- ✔ Focus on recognizing and rewarding acceptable behavior more than punishing misbehavior.

- ✔ Ignore or minimize minor problems instead of disrupting the class. A glance, a directed question, or your proximity may be enough to stop misbehavior.

- ✔ Where reprimands are necessary, state them quickly and without disrupting the class.

- ✔ When it's necessary to speak to a student about his or her behavior, try to speak in private; this is especially true of adolescents who must "perform" for their peers, and public reprimands or lectures often trigger exaggerated, face-saving performances.

Five Persistent Problems

The majority of "difficult" student behaviors fall into five distinct categories, according to expert Bill Rogers. In his extensive work on behavior management in Australia and worldwide, Rogers has identified five "tricky personalities" and the strategies teachers can use to handle them. (These tips and more can be found in Rogers's book, *Behavior Management: A Whole-School Approach*.)

1. **The Chatterbox.** What can you do about the student who distracts others with nonstop talking?

- ✔ Give a positive direction or reminder, followed by "thanks." For example, "Emma, Lisa, facing this way and quiet, thanks!" The key, says Rogers, is to focus on the desired behavior rather than the misbehavior. And using "thanks" rather than "please," even when correcting, communicates your expectation that the students will comply, he adds.

- ✔ Try a strategic pause. A pause communicates the expectation that students look toward you, listen, and subsequently respond. Even if you call a misbehaving student's name, says Rogers, try a pause before giving a positive direction or reminder so the student has time to focus.

- ✔ Keep the focus on the primary issue by knowing how to redirect. Frequently, students who are singled out will argue or sulk, which is secondary to the primary issue of their disruptive talking. Don't get drawn into these secondary issues, Rogers cautions. You can briefly acknowledge the student's feelings, then quickly shift focus back to the primary issue. For example, "But we were only talking about the work," argues the student. "Maybe you were, but I want you to face the front and listen, thanks. You'll need to know this stuff," responds the teacher, redirecting the focus and continuing the lesson.

2. **The Clinger**. This dependent student rarely does anything without demanding the teacher's immediate help and attention. To wean him or her of this dependency:

✔ Start with tactical ignoring. Keep the focus on the lesson, or on acknowledging and reinforcing students who follow the rules and ask for help at appropriate times. For example, while you are conferring with one student, ignore the student pulling on your arm and wanting you to look at his story. When he sits down and waits quietly (maybe after a reminder), go to him enthusiastically, reinforcing his improved behavior.

✔ Combine simple directions and reminders with hand signals. "Hands up without calling out, thanks" or "Please wait your turn." Well-established hand signals are effective, too, such as a blocking hand to signal that a student should wait.

✔ Give students alternatives. An established routine such as, "Ask three before you ask me," works in many situations, Rogers suggests. In other words, students should ask three peers before seeking your help. Encourage students to help each other, turning to you for help only as a last resort, he adds.

3. **The Boycotter**. Sometimes students simply refuse to do their work, pulling teachers into a power struggle. If this happens:

✔ Give students a choice—with consequences attached. For example, "If you choose not to do the work now, you will need to do it during free time." Rogers explains that using

the word "choose" or "choice" is important, because students need to understand that they have control over how they behave. Their behavior is their responsibility.

✔ Provide take-up time. This refers to the time students have to respond to corrective discipline. If you turn briefly to respond to another student or survey the room, this gives the student a chance to save face while complying, and it eliminates a prolonged confrontation.

✔ Reestablish the relationship. After a student has complied, a simple smile or positive comment reassures the student that you aren't holding a grudge and his or her relationship with you is still secure.

4. **The Debater**. This student challenges everything a teacher says or does. With him or her, every small primary issue escalates into several major secondary ones.

✔ Distinguish between primary and secondary behavior. A student's words, tone of voice, body language, and "attitude" often distract us from the original, often minor infraction. For example, "Bradley, I notice that you haven't started. Any problems?" the teacher asks politely. "Yeah, well, I haven't got a pen, have I?" Bradley snarls in reply. Try to ignore this secondary behavior in the heat of the moment.

✔ Avoid unnecessary power struggles. It's tough not to overreact and get defensive when a student's attitude and body language are hostile. But overreaction only extends the conflict, warns Rogers. Instead, remain assertive, but civil, and redirect the student to the primary issue.

✔ Plan a follow-up. While it usually works better to ignore secondary behavior in the heat of the moment, plan an after-class discussion with students who habitually exhibit such behavior. Explain what their secondary behavior sounds and looks like, and how it affects your working relationship.

5. **The Sulker**. Like the debater, the sulker's secondary behavior is usually worse than the primary problem.

✔ Schedule an after-class chat. A private discussion helps the student to understand that the habitual secondary behavior is unacceptable. Such chats, says Rogers, are most effective early in the year to "nip in the bud" the problem and send the message that you will always follow up on such behavior.

✔ Time your invitation effectively. Inform the student of an after-class chat just before the recess bell, or just before class ends. That avoids any prolonged discussion of, "What have I done?"

✔ Keep your presentation positive. Teachers must correct and guide students in a positive and friendly manner. Avoid threatening body language or tone of voice, Rogers advises. A pleasant demeanor will help repair strained relationships.

✔ Offer to mirror the problem behavior. Many students don't see their behavior as teachers do. Their poor social skills, bad habits, and gambits for attention come across as rudeness, even if they don't necessarily mean to be rude. In a friendly, nonthreatening manner, demonstrate the postures, gestures, and tone of voice the student uses, then explain. "I don't speak like that to you. When you speak like that, it shows disrespect because of the tone and the way you say it." Explain how such behavior affects working relationships.

❖ Consequences

Etymologically, the word *punishment* is related to the word *pain*. In the days of rulers rapping knuckles, *punishment* was an appropriate term. What we mean today when we talk about punishment is "consequences"—what happens as a result of misbehaving.

Beware that some responses to misbehavior can reinforce the very behavior you are trying to correct. If misbehaving is the only way a student has of getting attention, then disciplinary action can reinforce an already low self-image. Misbehavior elicits the attention he or she wants, and the student usually continues to misbehave.

Tips From the Experts

The experts—experienced teachers, psychologists, and researchers—claim that disciplinary actions work best in settings where positive behavior is acknowledged and reinforced. Furthermore, discipline should always match a student's actions, because we are teaching students "about the basic relationship between cause and effect that rules all our lives, children and adults alike," writes Douglas Barasch. Here are some recommendations:

✔ Never discipline in the heat of the moment.

✔ Make sure the student knows what the infraction is.

✔ If necessary, delay discipline until an appropriate time.

✔ Discipline mildly, briefly, and infrequently.

✔ Never use schoolwork or homework as disciplinary measures.

✔ Don't discipline the class for one student's misbehavior.

✔ Never humiliate a student—physically or verbally.

Appropriate Responses to Misbehavior

Whenever possible, respond to misbehavior with logical consequences, such as taking recess time to have a student finish an incomplete assignment. This way, discipline becomes a direct result of the misbehavior, not just a random punishment. Some examples of mild, appropriate consequences, linked to common misbehaviors include:

✔ being last in the lunch line (pushing or cutting in line)

✔ a reassigned seat (constant talking)

✔ staying after school just long enough to miss walking home with friends (using project time to play with friends)

- removal of a privilege such as recess or free time (poor use of work time)

- arranging with parents for a student to lose a home privilege such as watching television (homework not turned in or done carelessly)

- time-out—removing a student from peers to sit alone and cool down or think before rejoining the group (loosing temper in a peer-group setting)

Time Out

Physically removing the disruptive student is a commonly used discipline technique referred to as "time-out." The intent is to give the student a chance to cool down and think while allowing the rest of the class to continue undisturbed. Used properly, the time-out can be an effective part of a positive discipline program.

Most experts believe that time-out can be a positive learning experience if used appropriately. To make it work well, keep these tips in mind:

- Use it for disruptive behaviors, not such transgressions as failure to do homework.

- Make the time-out area simple and unstimulating but never dark or scary.

- Never leave a student unsupervised in time-out. Many teachers place a time-out chair where they can see it, but the other students can't. Others use an area supervised by an aide.

- Limit the time spent in time-out. Psychologist Ron Drabman suggests no more than 10 minutes for 5- to 10-year-olds and 15 minutes for 10- to 14-year-olds.

- Include follow-up activities after the time-out, such as those described here. The time-out stops the disturbance, but the follow-up addresses the root of the problem.

Carl Calliari of Rowan University, New Jersey, offers a specific strategy for making time-out a time for learning.

First, says Calliari, explain to the class that the purpose of time-out is to help them become better behaved, to have time to think, and to learn how to make better decisions. Emphasize that when students are sent to the time-out chair, they need to go there immediately, without argument. And explain that it's not an automatic conviction; they get a chance to tell their side.

After sending a student to the time-out chair (positioned so you can see it, but students can't), ask him or her to answer, in writing, these questions on a "Time to Think" sheet:

1. Why do I think I was sent here?
2. What is my side of the story?
3. What do I think should happen to me?

Kindergartners or first graders may be too young to write their answers, but they are certainly not too young to think about and answer the questions. Calliari suggests they could record their answers on a tape player or tell you in person. Use pictures or visual prompts to help them remember or "read" the questions.

As soon as possible, confer with the student about his or her misbehavior. Students at one Virginia middle school must discuss a written plan with their teachers before they can return to class. The plan, which the students write, describes their disruptive behavior and explains how they will work to change it.

Asking students to think about and identify their misbehaviors and suggest strategies for improving are critically important components of the time-out process, stress the experts. Kids sometimes behave disruptively without realizing it; they hum, snap their fingers, talk out loud, and so on. Or they do so many things, they aren't sure what got them into trouble. Asking them to identify the problem makes resolving it much easier and forces them to "own up" to it.

Giving students a chance to explain their side of the story demonstrates your fairness and shows you are interested. And asking students what they think should happen as a result of the misbehavior helps them accept responsibility. It also gives them some control. They'll soon learn that their suggestions must be appropriate and fair to be acceptable.

Developmental Considerations

Tailoring our expectations and reactions to students' developmental levels is essential to teaching good discipline, writes Douglas Barasch.

Between the ages of 6 and 9, Barasch notes, children are developing a conscience—"a behavioral compass that guides them in distinguishing right from wrong." However, they are still limited in their ability to do everything that they know is "right." Children at this age can also understand the logic and reasoning behind rules of behavior. Discussions about what's right and wrong and why are possible and productive. In fact, if children don't learn to reason at this stage, it will be more difficult later to understand and regulate their own behavior.

Further, children between 6 and 9 sometimes become defiant as they test the boundaries of their independence and power. Lying, stealing, and obscene language are ways to test these boundaries. "They want to have an experience of power and they don't want to take into account the rules of the world," explains psychologist Sara Weber, whom Barasch cites. Parents and teachers must help children begin to reconcile their needs with "the rest of the world's needs," Weber continues.

In preadolescence, from ages 10 to 12, children test the limits of their independence even further. Our primary goal here, as teachers and as parents, is to teach children to make good decisions, says Barasch. "Punishments, when they're necessary, should be coupled with asking the child to do a lot of thinking about what she has done," he says.

❖ Positive Discipline

Halfway through her second year of teaching, Nina Shandler decided she was tired of nagging and punishing and yelling at her third and fourth graders. She disliked their misbehavior, but she disliked her own even more. She vowed that she would never speak another negative word to her students. And that's how she started her positive discipline approach.

"Positive discipline—using positive reinforcements to teach children responsible behaviors—takes tremendous *teacher* discipline," Shandler writes. "Faced with demanding, defiant behavior, we can find it difficult to look for and reward positive behavior. The glare of misbehavior obscures our vision, preventing us from seeing small acts of cooperation, bits of appropriate behavior, grains of responsibility."

Rewarding Behavior

Basically, positive discipline is acknowledging and rewarding appropriate behavior, and "disarming" misbehavior by refusing to give it "status." (When students engage in attention-seeking actions, for example, the teacher ignores or redirects attention elsewhere.)

Shandler, who is now a licensed psychologist and family therapist, describes a strategy she used in one difficult class. Carrying a clipboard for a week, she silently recorded negative behavior but never publicly acknowledged the students misbehaving. Instead, she commented only on positive behavior. At the end of the week, she posted the names of the well-behaved students on the bulletin board, pulled out some board games, and told them they had a free play period.

But before the other students could grumble and complain, she quickly asked everyone to help plan the next week's special activity. They agreed to make a spaghetti dinner in the classroom, deciding that every student who had gotten fewer checks for misbehavior the next week could participate. (This would reward students who were really trying to improve, her students reasoned.) The students who weren't playing the games were immediately motivated to control their grumbling and work hard to earn the right to participate in the next special event.

"By the end of three weeks, I felt rejuvenated," Shandler reports. "I recovered my enthusiasm for teaching. I enjoyed my students. And I liked myself again."

The key to positive discipline, says Shandler, is one "magic" question: "What did you do right?" By focusing on the positive, we affirm students' basic needs to be accepted and valued. We send the

Educator's Checklist on Human Relations

In the Classroom ✓

- ❑ Do I accept each student as he or she is?
- ❑ Do I help all students feel they belong?
- ❑ Do I show confidence in my students?
- ❑ Do I let them know I like them?
- ❑ Do I make each student feel he or she has something to contribute?
- ❑ Do my pupils bring their problems to me?
- ❑ Do I help them accept one another?
- ❑ Do I live up to agreements with students?
- ❑ Do I succeed in getting everyone to assume some responsibility?
- ❑ Do I help the group form a behavior code?

Outside of Class ✓

- ❑ Do I try to develop faculty cooperation?
- ❑ Do I do my share in determining and carrying out school policies?
- ❑ Do I aid associates with constructive ideas?
- ❑ Do I accept ideas from others?
- ❑ Do I refrain from interfering with the classroom affairs of associates?
- ❑ Do I refrain from shifting my responsibility to other teachers?
- ❑ Do I hold inviolate confidential information about my students?
- ❑ Do I transact school business through the proper channels?
- ❑ Do I avoid petty conversation about my associates?
- ❑ Do I hold inviolate confidential information about my associates?

With Parents and Community ✓

- ❑ Do I maintain friendly, cooperative relationships with parents?
- ❑ Do I hold all information confidential?
- ❑ Do parents feel sure that I deal justly and impartially with every child?
- ❑ Do I give all parents their fair share of time?
- ❑ Do I present a complete, fair, and meaningful evaluation to parents?
- ❑ Do I listen to and give fair thought to parents' opinions?
- ❑ Do I take an active part in community life?

Ethical Standards ✓

- ❑ Do I treat each child without prejudice or partiality?
- ❑ Do I respect the confidence of a student? Of a group of students?
- ❑ Do I refuse to use my position to promote partisan policies and sectarian views?
- ❑ Do I listen to and weigh parents' viewpoints carefully?
- ❑ Do I avoid making remarks that might discredit parents?
- ❑ Do I exercise my right to participate in the processes that determine school policy?
- ❑ Do I support school policy once it has been determined?
- ❑ Am I kind, tolerant, and loyal in my dealings with professional associates?
- ❑ Do I take pride in the achievements of my associates?
- ❑ Do I criticize with discretion?
- ❑ Am I proud of my profession?

message loud and clear that positive behavior pays. Positive behavior earns social recognition and status.

Five Basic Steps

A positive discipline approach incorporates five basic steps, says Shandler:

1. **Define a goal.** What is it you want students to know and value? Self-respect? Empathy? Responsibility? Cooperation? Tolerance? Keep your goal in mind.
2. **Recognize positive steps.** Practice recognizing the attitudes, actions, and skills that move students toward the goal. Can they now accept compliments and corrections? Do they concentrate on their work? Can they appreciate another viewpoint?
3. **Reinforce positives.** Help students notice their accomplishments, and reinforce or recognize even the smallest steps forward.
4. **Disarm negatives.** Undermine the power of negative attitudes and behaviors by ignoring them, changing the focus, or offering positive alternatives. Don't give negative behavior status by arguing with students, writing names on the chalkboard, or reprimanding publicly.
5. **Appreciate progress.** Remain optimistic by measuring progress often, remembering where you began.

Show Them You Care

"Whatever words we use or technique we employ, positive discipline nourishes children on a daily dose of caring," says Shandler. It isn't a quick fix, she warns, adding that our long-term efforts can guarantee no sure outcomes. But take heart, she advises, and believe that our students will take with them the message our positive approach sends: "You are a good person, worthy of self-respect and capable of self-discipline."

A Matter of Language

We can set a positive tone in our classrooms by changing many of our "don'ts" to "dos," says

behavior-management expert Bill Rogers.

"It is necessary to plan the language of discipline as carefully as we plan teaching and learning," says Rogers. "Positive correction comes from a conviction that corrective, assertive management is not inconsistent with the emphasis on positive teacher-student communications. Basically, it is substituting positive language, where possible, for negative language, while keeping the corrective focus." For example:

✔ "Walk quietly, thanks," rather than, "Don't run!"

✔ "Share the pencils on this table," rather than, "Don't argue and fight over the pencils."

✔ "Hands up without calling out, thanks," rather than "Don't call out."

✔ "If you hold the pen like this [teacher models], it will be easier," rather than, "Don't hold it like that! Here give it to me! I'll show you! No wonder you can't write neatly if you hold the pen like that."

✔ "Look this way and listen, thanks," rather than, "Don't talk when I'm teaching."

Our nonverbal language counts, too. Rogers points out that tone of voice, eye contact, body language, and proximity to students all affect how our words are perceived (positive or negative) by students.

"When considering our language in correction and management, we also need to consider the following principles if positive discipline is to operate," Rogers notes:

✔ Focus on the behavior rather than attacking the person.

✔ Be angry about issues that really count rather than a host of minor issues.

✔ Be brief when addressing behavior, even when using commands.

✔ Calm yourself before trying to calm the student.

✔ Balance correction with encouragement and the re-establishment of working relationships.

✔ Provide take-up time (sufficient time for students to comply) whenever possible.

✔ Concentrate and focus on primary behaviors (what the student did wrong) rather than on secondary behaviors (for example, the backtalk or "attitude" a student gives when corrected).

Assertive Discipline

A focus on positive behaviors is also the key aspect of a widely used strategy known as assertive discipline.

"The key to assertive discipline is catching students being good: recognizing and supporting them when they behave appropriately and letting them know you like it, day in and day out," explains Lee Canter, developer of the strategy.

In recent years, assertive discipline has been criticized as focusing only on the negative—a strategy of putting misbehaving students' names on the board or otherwise drawing attention to bad behavior. But that's misusing the system, Canter stresses. "As a general rule, a teacher shouldn't administer a disciplinary consequence to a student until the teacher has reinforced at least two students for the appropriate behavior. Effective teachers are always positive first."

Canter, who no longer advocates putting names on the board, recommends a three-step cycle in his positive discipline approach:

✔ Teach the specific behaviors you want; don't assume students already know. This means describing, discussing, modeling, and practicing.

✔ Use positive repetition to reinforce students who follow directions and rules. "Jason went back to his seat and got right to work."

✔ If the first two steps fail to prevent misbehavior, use the negative consequence you have established (and the students know) for such misbehavior. Always make this the last resort.

RESOURCES ON POSITIVE DISCIPLINE

Following are the resources Shandler recommends for a positive approach to discipline:

• *Reaching Out to Troubled Kids: 15 Helpful Ways to Bridge the Gap Between Parents, Teachers, and Kids,* by Kathleen McConnell (Sopris West, 1996)

• *Rethinking Student Discipline: Alternatives That Work,* by Paula M. Short et al. (Corwin Press, 1994)

• *Positive Discipline in the Classroom: Developing Mutual Respect, Cooperation, and Responsibility in Your Classroom,* by Jane Nelson, et al. (Prima Publishing, 2000)

• *Succeeding With Difficult Students,* by Jeffrey A. Kottler (Corwin Press, 1997)

• *Special Educator's Discipline Handbook,* by Richard E. Maurer (Center for Applied Research in Education, 1988)

For more resources on discipline, see the resources section at the end of the chapter.

"An effective behavior management program must be built on choice," Canter stresses. Students must know beforehand what is expected of them in the classroom, what will happen if they choose to behave, and what will happen if they choose not to behave. Students learn self-discipline and responsible behavior by being given clear, consistent choices. They learn that their actions have an impact and that they themselves control the consequences."

Remember, too, that discipline is a broad, preventive approach to managing the classroom, motivating students, and giving students many opportunities to learn responsibility and problem-solving skills. Assertive discipline is only one strategy among many that a teacher can use.

❖ A Caring Climate

What is the climate and social atmosphere like in your classroom? Are your students cooperative, responsible, caring, sharing, self-controlled, trusting, and accepting of themselves and others? Classrooms are social places where teachers must create the conditions conducive to teaching and learning. In the right atmosphere and environment, students (and teachers) grow and flourish; problems and misbehavior do not.

In positive classroom environments, students:

✔ dare to take risks.

✔ share their talents and encourage each other.

✔ know they are important.

✔ respect themselves, each other, and their communities.

✔ care for and trust each other.

Group Identity

Humans are social creatures who function best as members of a group. The feeling of belonging is a basic human need. You can foster group identity in your class by soliciting ideas, suggestions, and comments from all students, acknowledging and valuing everyone's opinion and contribution, teaching students to recognize the special talents and strengths everyone possesses, and accounting for differing learning styles.

To feel a part of a group, students must tolerate and respect other group members and feel tolerated and respected in turn. Jean Medick created an atmosphere of tolerance and respect with one very important classroom rule:

"A rule which I propose each year is that no name-calling, put-downs, sarcasm, or ridicule be permitted in our classroom," she writes. "This rule fosters an environment where individuals are free to be themselves, where students tolerate and come to accept others, and where all are free to learn. This is perhaps the most important rule in my classroom, and I enforce it. After a while, the children help enforce it."

"Without a clear feeling of community, a caring classroom is an illusion," says William Kreidler, conflict resolution expert. To achieve this sense of community and group identity, Kreidler suggests "whole-class team-building games that give students a chance to strive together toward a common goal. For example:

✔ **Name That Kid**. Start this game by having the class—including yourself—stand in a circle. Toss a ball or beanbag to a student across the circle. That student says three names—first the name of the person to the right, then the name of the person to the left, then his or her own name. He or she then passes the ball to the right and the next student says the three names. The object is to see how quickly the ball can go around the circle. For older students, have players toss the ball to someone across the circle instead of passing right or left.

✔ **We're All Connected**. Start the game by stating something such as, "Last summer I took a car trip to visit my sister in Montana." Ask if there is any student who can "connect" with you by making a statement that builds on your statement. (You may need to prompt students at first by asking, "Did anyone take a trip this summer? Visit a relative? Go to Montana? Ride in a car?") Have a volunteer take your hand and state a connecting thought such as, "We visited my aunt on Lake Cayuga." Ask if there is anyone who can build on that student's statement. The next volunteer, who might say, "I have an uncle who lives on a lake in Florida," takes the free hand of the previous volunteer. Continue as long as you can make connections. Three to five is a good start for younger students; with older students, try to connect the entire class.

Following are activities to further boost students' sense of belonging:

✔ Ask each student to share with the rest of the class something he or she likes to do—play a musical instrument, play a sport, pursue a hobby, develop a skill. Children who share experiences and learn about each other develop a closeness with one another.

✔ Create "proud-of" bulletin boards. Students can post individual and group work, drawings, and photographs they're proud of. (Be sure to display work of your own.)

✔ Discuss what a positive statement is and help students come up with several. Then ask them to write a descriptive positive statement on fancy paper cutouts to include on bulletin boards featuring the "Student of the Week" or "Student of the Month."

✔ Have the students conduct a group survey. Ask each student to complete a questionnaire that requests such information as birthplace, states visited or lived in, height, number of siblings, favorite hobbies, favorite subjects, and so on. In compiling the results, students should detect an interesting phenomenon: A group is composed of individuals with many different traits and experiences. Older students can use their math skills to create a composite student by averaging the questionnaire responses. For example: The composite student is a girl and standing 4 ft. 5 in. tall. She has one sibling, has visited three states, attended two different schools, and likes math best. Point out how all of the students contribute to this composite. (It would be fun to make this composite student the class mascot and develop stories or activities around him or her.) Think of other interesting ways to handle the questionnaire data. For example, create a verbal class portrait: "Our class consists of 12 boys and 11 girls. There are no only children. We range in height from . . ."

✔ Include yourself as part of the group and model your own sense of belonging. For example, describe activities as things "we" will do. Reminisce about events and activities as things "we" did together.

Cooperation

How can teachers get kids to like and respect their peers? One way is to assign them cooperative tasks and activities. Discussion and awareness activities expose our biases and social prejudice. But cooperative activities help overcome them.

The research evidence is consistent: racial and gender relations and relations in general improve markedly in classrooms where students interact cooperatively to meet specific goals. Just plain common sense tells us that getting to know people as individuals helps dispel generalized social stereotypes.

Whether your students paint a classroom mural, put on a play, or engage in some other cooperative activity, always stress these three concepts of cooperation:

✔ Everyone gets to participate.

✔ Everyone wins or loses.

✔ The better students work together, the more enjoyable and successful the activity will be for all who participate.

Teachers who stress cooperation and social responsibility in their classrooms offer students peer tutoring, small-group cooperative activities, and other chances to work together. Cooperative activities enhance group identity and significantly decrease classroom conflicts, says William Kreidler, a veteran teacher who now works for Educators for Social Responsibility. Kreidler suggests these noncompetitive games and activities for setting a cooperative tone:

✔ **Tug-of-Peace**. Tie the ends of a large rope securely together and place it in a circle on the floor. Ask students (any age will work) to sit outside the circle and grab hold of the rope. The object is for the students to raise themselves to a standing position by pulling hard on the rope. Obviously, they must all pull together. When they succeed, the group wins.

✔ **The Line Forms Here**. This quick and quiet cooperative activity can be used when your class is making a transition from one activity to another. Explain that without talking, students must form a line according to height, from the shortest to the tallest person. Once they've mastered this, have them form a line according to birthdays, alphabetical order of their names, or some other criteria. They will figure out a way to communicate silently and complete the task.

Kreidler also suggests small-group games to help students prepare for cooperative-learning tasks. One good example he calls Human Machines. Here, students develop cooperation skills as they pantomime a working machine, with each student representing a different cog, wheel, or part. The first few times you play this game, it's helpful to assign each group a machine to pantomime, such as a washing machine, blender, stapler, steamroller, or electric eggbeater. When each group has developed its pantomime, have students present their working machines to the class while classmates guess what kind of machine they're portraying.

Cooperation is also the focal point of an instructional strategy known as cooperative learning. **Cooperative learning** involves students working in small groups to help each other learn academic content in tandem with social skills. Proponents have claimed that cooperative learning improves race relations, allows the successful inclusion of students with disabilities, increases self-esteem, prepares students to collaborate in the workforce, and even increases achievement.

While much of the evidence is anecdotal or based on nonstandardized measures of achievement, many teachers incorporate some form of cooperative learning in classwork. (Various grouping strategies are discussed in Chapters One and Three.)

"I like groups," admits Washington teacher Martine Wayman. "Kids learn better that way. But make sure you allow time at the beginning of the year to teach how to work in groups. Many teachers assume kids already know how to do that and they don't!"

There are many different forms of cooperative learning. In his synthesis of the research on cooperative learning, Robert Slavin of Johns Hopkins University reports that, "For enhancing student achievement, the most successful approaches have incorporated two key elements: group goals and individual accountability. That is, groups are rewarded based on the individual learning of all group members."

A word of caution: Use cooperative learning selectively, especially for gifted learners. While heterogeneously organized cooperative groups may improve social skills and relations, when they are used as the major means of organizing instruction, "gifted students are in danger of serving as tutors to less able learners far too much of the time and miss the challenge of their

intellectual peers," says author and scholar Barbara Clark. Other experts concur. Roger Johnson, a strong supporter and promoter of cooperative-learning groups, told Clark that such groups "were never meant to be their whole learning experience. They were not designed to challenge them academically."

"Care" Projects

Teaching children to become more involved in their communities helps them learn to become more caring and concerned. From formal service programs to informal classroom projects, students nationwide are pitching in and helping out their communities. Imagine the boost to self-esteem when students realize how their efforts are needed and appreciated.

Martine Wayman describes the "Kids Care" projects she and her sixth graders undertake.

"One project we worked on was with a nursing home," Wayman reports. "We partnered with people there, visited them, wrote to them, and sang to them. I was awed by how touched and caring my sixth graders were!

"However, the Kids Care project that most touched our community was instigated by my online communication with another teacher in the Oklahoma City area," Wayman continues. "My students and I met and chatted with Dolores Choat, a third-grade teacher. We expressed our concern and desire to do something for or with them in light of the horrible disaster they had experienced." To honor the children who died in the bombing of the Federal Building, Wayman's students decided to plant a tree, purchase a commemorative plaque, and send teddy bears to Choat's class.

"The students raised over $500 for the project by selling cookies they baked at home," says Wayman. "With the money, we purchased a Western Rosebud tree (the Oklahoma state tree), bought teddy bears for each child in Dolores's class, made buttons for each bear, and purchased 45 pansies to plant around the base of the tree.

"With the help of our staff and music teacher," she continues, "we prepared a song to dedicate along with the tree. On the dedication day, the whole school met outside. We planted the tree, sang the song, and my students explained the meaning behind everything we did. We were able to videotape the entire ceremony and send the tape to the class in Oklahoma along with the bears. I can't begin to tell you the joy we experienced helping someone in need! My students will never forget this activity, and neither will their families."

Here are several more examples of how teachers have involved students in their communities:

✔ Martha Schuur's fifth graders help set up, serve, and clean up a lunch program for the homeless that her church-affiliated school in Los Angeles sponsors once a week.

✔ Tennessee teacher Margaret Schmitz suggests having students tape-record themselves reading a book. They can then donate the tape and book (placed in a resealable plastic bag) to a local day-care center or the pediatric floor of a local hospital.

✔ Vita Monastero of New York suggests having students produce a play or sing songs for a local senior-citizen center. Families and students can bake and make favors for the seniors, too.

✔ Patti Wingerd's fifth graders place flags by the graves of Civil War soldiers at a local Maryland cemetery. Her students also volunteer to plant trees as a restoration and beautification project at the battlefield nearby.

Character Education

What values should students be taught in the caring classroom?

Eleanor Childs, founder of the Heartwood Institute, a nonprofit ethics program, claims that of the many human qualities and attributes valued around the world, seven are universal: courage, loyalty, justice, respect, hope, honesty, and love.

Childs and several elementary teachers developed a program for teaching these values through multicultural literature.

"Children have big hearts if developed with care, and they must be helped to understand that the mind must work along with the heart—that they need to think before acting," explains the former defense attorney. "School is the perfect place—as a support to the home—for this kind of education to happen. Children need to learn these basic concepts as early as possible. These are basic universal ideas that teachers already deal with every day."

Pilot-tested in Pittsburgh schools, the Heartwood Ethics Curriculum is now used nationwide. Students learn a vocabulary for naming specific attributes they see in a character in a story, and they learn which behaviors express these attributes. By using literature, students can discuss problems and choices without the threat of getting too personal.

Teachers incorporating character education into the curriculum can choose their own literature or use lists developed by the Heartwood Institute and other organizations. When choosing your own books and stories, look for those that:

✔ feature children making difficult choices.

✔ enrich children's experience with other cultures.

✔ explore problems children can grasp.

✔ are not written around a particular message or an obvious choice.

For more information on the Heartwood Institute, or to receive a partial book list and activity cards, write to the institute at 425 North Craig St., Suite 302, Pittsburgh, PA 15213, or call (800) HEART-10 or (412) 688-8570. You can also e-mail the institute at hrtwood@aol.com or visit the Web site at www.heartwoodethics.org.

❖ Taking Responsibility

Individual and social responsibility are important goals in classrooms. Students must be responsible for their own learning and behavior, and for acting in the best interests of the group.

"A theme we discuss and explore all year is that freedom and responsibility go together," writes Jean Medick. "The children are free to sit where

QUALITIES AND ATTRIBUTES VALUED AROUND THE WORLD

Courage

Loyalty

Justice

Respect

Hope

Honesty

Love

librarian, file clerk, and pet/plant caretaker are all jobs students can easily and willingly handle. (Teachers with older students can add computer troubleshooter to the list.) Student jobs can also incorporate important learning objectives, such as sequencing and categorizing skills employed by the librarians who help keep the resources in the classroom library in order.

To make a job program work, keep these tips in mind:

✔ Post descriptions and requirements of each job.

✔ "Hire" students for an extended period—at least a week or two.

✔ Ask students to "apply" for a job on a sign-up sheet that you have devised, dated, and posted.

✔ Limit the number of times a student can request a job. For example, maybe aim for each student to have one or two jobs during a marking period.

✔ Compensate student workers by allowing them to earn credit toward some type of reward. This way, there are also consequences (no credits) if they fail to do the job.

✔ Early in the year, have students formally apply for the job program by listing their qualifications on an application form, describing prior work experiences at home and school, and stating why they want the job and think they can do good work. (It will boost their self-esteem to see how qualified they are!)

✔ Enrich students' vocabularies by using professional job titles such as administrative assistant, secretary, plant manager (erases boards, helps with recycling, and so on), botanist, and paramedic.

Making the Rules

Students who help make the rules are much more likely to obey them. That's what both research and experienced practice show.

Alfie Kohn, who writes about education and human behavior, bemoans "the absurd spectacle of adults insisting that children need to become self-disciplined or lamenting that 'kids just don't take responsibility for their own behavior'—while spending their days ordering children around."

and with whom they wish, as long as they behave responsibly and do their work. Seating arrangements change frequently. The freedom to move desks fosters social growth and provides me with important dynamics within the room. It also involves the children in relevant, and sometimes difficult, decision making."

Further, writes Medick, "A large number of classroom management responsibilities are handled by the children, including room cleanup. I do nothing for the children that they can do for themselves."

Many veterans agree that assigning students to routine classroom tasks is a proven method of helping them become more responsible. And with increased responsibility comes increased self-esteem and self-confidence, and a decrease in problems.

Student Employees

Many teachers institute a "job responsibility" program to help students learn the self-discipline to complete tasks they attempt and to become productive, cooperative members of the group. Messenger, chalkboard caretaker, classroom

Kohn insists that, "If we want children to take responsibility for their own behavior, we must first give them responsibility, and plenty of it."

Like so much else in teaching and learning, it boils down to issues of choice and control. Numerous studies show that people (including young students) who feel some control over their lives are happier and better adjusted than those who experience no self-determination.

"By contrast," writes Kohn, "few things lead more reliably to depression and other forms of psychological distress than a feeling of helplessness."

Kohn and others point out that it's a question of democracy—of living and practicing our democratic ideals and not just talking about them. The best way to prepare children to live in a democracy, says Kohn, is to help them "acquire both the skills of decision making and the inclination to use them," and the best way to accomplish that is if we "maximize their experiences with choice and negotiation."

One of the first tasks for any new school year must be to discuss and negotiate the classroom rules. Both teachers and students have a voice in this collaborative process. And don't forget to determine the consequences for breaking those rules. Also, make sure students discuss and understand *why* rules are necessary in the first place. (See Chapter 1 for some suggestions for involving students in establishing classroom rules.)

Problem Solving

To become socially responsible individuals, children need opportunities to solve their own problems in school. "This produces positive feelings, confidence, and a sense of being in control of one's behavior and life," notes Jean Medick.

Medick describes how she learned to let her fourth and fifth graders solve the problem of fighting.

"When children fought, I used to resort to scolding, lecturing, taking away recess, isolating, or sending children to the office," she recalls. "These procedures did not help [them] learn anything about how to prevent fighting or better ways to solve disagreements. But children can learn a great deal about the feelings people experience in fights, the causes of fights, and better ways to deal with situations that cause fights through group discussions using the problem-solving process."

Medick explains that even if only a few students are doing the fighting, the whole class can help to think of better alternatives. "They learn much about the way their classmates think and feel during these discussions. This promotes understanding and empathy that simply was not possible when I used the old

---

ACCEPTING RESPONSIBILITY

Accepting responsibility is an important aspect of learning to solve your own problems. Allowing students to take responsibility for their problems and responsibility for solving them gives them needed practice. Michigan teacher Jean Medick shares this real-life example:

John one day refused to do his schoolwork. His teacher explained to him that teaching was her responsibility, but learning was his. After signing a statement (at his teacher's suggestion) that he refused to do his work, he elected to go home. His mother picked him up (according to prearranged plans) and took him to work with her, where he spent the day alone. After that, he never refused to do his work again. Nor did he show resentment toward his teacher or his mother, because the choice had been his.

Obviously, this scenario would not be appropriate in every case, but this teacher knew the student and parent well enough to make an effective judgment call.

When you provide students with a choice, you place responsibility with them. And this is where it belongs, stress the experts. Make sure they understand the consequences of their choices; then let them decide. But also be sure to follow through. If a student elects to "suffer the consequences" rather than comply with the rules, those consequences had better be forthcoming. Make sure you involve families and the principal in something as unusual as the case of John.

---

methods," she discovered. "I, too, learn many things about the children from listening."

Medick also insists that her students be honest in problem-solving situations and never resort to the "I don't know" response. This frequent response "gets a kid off the hook" by allowing him or her to avoid responsibility in unpleasant or threatening situations.

"Sometimes I think the response, 'I don't know' really means, 'You figure it out, teacher—read my mind.' Early in the year, I tell all the children that responding with 'I don't know' on matters of behavior or interpersonal problems will be unacceptable because they are intelligent human beings capable of thinking," says Medick. "I also tell them that all other responses except put-downs are permitted in problem-solving situations—even 'I don't like you' or 'I think you are a mean or unfair teacher.' Once we know how people are honestly feeling, we can proceed to work things out."

Many of the discipline strategies advocated by teachers and child psychologists offer similar approaches to problem solving. The problem-solving process, which should involve the collaboration of your students, requires that you:

✔ Identify the problem.

✔ Determine the circumstances and behaviors that led up to the problem.

✔ Identify the feelings experienced by those involved.

✔ Ask yourself, "Have I ever experienced something like this before? What did I do? Did it work?"

✔ List and think through many different alternatives for handling the problem.

✔ Select one alternative and develop a plan.

✔ Put the plan into action.

✔ Evaluate the plan. Is it working? If not, choose another alternative.

THE RESPONSIBLE CLASSROOM

Marcia Leverte, Arden Smith, and JoAnn Cooper offer the following description of a responsible, caring classroom. Such a classroom features:

• mutual respect, not fear of ridicule.
• encouragement, not criticism or unconcern.
• shared responsibility, not sole responsibility or undependability.
• consequences for behavior, not punishment or inconsistency.
• shared decision making, not judgment or indecision.
• influence, not power or weakness.
• cooperation, not competition or control.
• teacher facilitation and leadership, not command or desertion.
• desire to learn from within, not imposed learning or indifference to learning.
• freedom and order, not dictatorship or chaos.

Remember to articulate each step of the process. You are not only solving problems, you are teaching students the problem-solving process so they can use it on their own.

❖ Active Listening

How many times do you tell your students to "listen and learn"? Listening is a critically important skill—for teachers as well as students. Indeed, listening is something we need to do a lot in behavior-management situations.

"Teachers are busy talking and many times forget to be quiet and hear what is said and left unsaid," notes Pennsylvania teacher Laurie Borger. "Listen," she urges. "Every day work on honest, open communication. [Without being judgmental,] allow young children to share with you what they need to. Be a role model of honest and understanding communication."

"Talk, listen, but be the adult, not the peer," adds Texas teacher Jane Kelling. "Kids will respect you for that."

Get the Whole Picture

If you listen to what students say and think, you'll discover that your perceptions of what goes on in the classroom are not necessarily the same as students' perceptions. Only by listening can you get the whole picture. Only by listening can you discover students' motives, thoughts, and feelings while at the same time communicating the message that you have confidence in their abilities to solve the problem.

When you actively listen, you attempt to understand what is really being said. You clarify and restate what students are saying. Active listening does not mean offering advice, opinions, judgments, analyses, or solutions—only restating what you hear the person saying. Think of yourself as a sounding board.

Active listening, like any skill, takes practice to perfect. But the payoffs can be tremendous. We learn what students are really thinking and feeling, and they learn to confide in a caring adult who allows them to explore their thoughts and feelings in reaching a solution to their problems.

Here's How It Works

Following is an example of active listening that occurred in Jean Medick's classroom.

Student: Jane doesn't like me anymore. She won't play with me at recess, and she won't eat lunch with me today.

Teacher: You're upset because Jane didn't play with you at recess and won't eat lunch with you today.

Student: Yes! She's my best friend, and she's being mean.

Teacher: Having Jane as a best friend is important to you, and it hurts you when she is mean to you.

Student: Yes, Jane's the best friend I ever had, and I don't want to lose her.

Teacher: You're worried about losing Jane as your best friend.

Student: She likes Patsy. Yesterday she said she'd play with me after school, but she didn't. She played with Patsy and they're going to eat lunch together today. I don't like Patsy! It's not fair!

Teacher: Your feelings are really hurt and you feel left out. And you don't like Patsy?

Student: Yes, I'm scared I won't have anyone to play with, and I don't like to eat lunch alone. Actually, I like Patsy okay. She's nice, but I guess I'm jealous.

Teacher: You feel scared and jealous at the same time.

Student: Yeah, but it's partly my fault. I haven't been very nice to Jane since I found out she played with Patsy.

Teacher: You think that you contributed to the problem by not being as nice as you usually are to Jane. What alternatives do you think you have?

Student: I guess I'll tell Jane I'm sorry for being mean, but I'm going to tell her she hurt my feelings, too.

By hearing her teacher repeat and clarify what she was saying, this student was able to evaluate her own thoughts and reach a decision about how she might handle her problem. Her teacher's active listening enabled her to grow as a problem solver. Imagine the boost to her self confidence and esteem when she realized that she could handle this problem on her own!

We expect our students to develop good listening skills in class, and we need to practice them, too. Students need adults who will really listen to what they say.

Kids Need Practice, Too

Veteran teacher and conflict resolution expert William J. Kreidler reports that most conflicts between elementary-age students are rooted in some form of miscommunication. Kids simply don't hear or understand what other kids are saying. To help them practice their listening, observing, and speaking skills, he suggests the following activities:

✔ **Get With the Beat.** Sit in a circle with students. Using a pencil or your hands, tap out a simple rhythm, then sigh (but not too deeply) and say, "Now I've got the beat." Repeat the same sequence again, including the sigh and the phrase, then ask for a volunteer to repeat the sequence. If the volunteer doesn't repeat the entire pattern, including the sigh and the words, say, "That's not quite right," and repeat the sequence. Then ask for a new volunteer to try to replicate it. Keep repeating the sequence until someone gets it right. Play the game again with a new beat, including some subtle movements, such as tapping your toe, that the students might miss at first. Because this is a listening game, your subtle movements should make some sound. Once students get the knack, they can be the ones to initiate the beat.

✔ **Pete and Repeat**. Paraphrasing what has been said is a useful listening skill to ensure that you've heard accurately. Begin this activity by explaining that paraphrasing is repeating what you heard someone else say using your own words. Give the whole group practice by having students paraphrase simple sentences such as:

✔ The book I'm reading is interesting.

✔ I saw some boring shows on television last night.

✔ I'm excited about the field trip we're taking.

When you think students have grasped the concept of paraphrasing, have them pair up. One partner will be Pete and the other Repeat. Explain that whenever Pete says something, he or she will stop for a moment and Repeat will paraphrase it. Pete should nod or say yes if it is an accurate paraphrase. Have all the Petes address this topic: things grown-ups do that make me mad. After a few minutes, have partners switch roles and continue the activity.

✔ **Body Sculpture**. In this activity, students try to re-create a pose by describing it to a blindfolded person. Divide the class into groups of three. Each student will play a role: the artist, the sculpture, or the clay. (Extra children in a group can play the clay.) Explain that the goal of the artist is to re-create the sculpture using the clay. The clay is blindfolded and stands behind the artist. The sculpture stands in front of the artist and strikes a pose. Students should choose a position they'll be able to hold for several minutes. The artist then describes the sculpture to the clay, and the clay tries to duplicate the pose. The clay may ask questions, but the artist cannot look at the clay until they both agree that they are finished. (Model the activity first, playing the role of

artist.) Repeat the activity so everyone gets a chance to be the artist. Then discuss what was a help or hindrance in communicating.

❖ Shoring Up Self-Esteem

Self-esteem is the driving force behind many of our actions and behaviors. It's the foundation of self-confidence. Without it, students can't succeed. And unsuccessful, unhappy students not only fail academically, they fail to behave properly in the classroom. They make life miserable—for you, the other students, and themselves.

Treating the Cause

Raising students' perceptions of themselves is treating the cause of poor behavior, rather than the symptoms. It's probably the most important discipline strategy you can employ. Giving students choices and some control over their learning goes a long way to boosting self-esteem. Teaching to students' individual strengths and learning styles and accounting for multiple intelligences ensures success for all—and success breeds self-confidence and self-esteem. Performance-based teaching and assessment make learning and schoolwork meaningful and relevant for students—another boost in how they feel about themselves.

Tending to students' emotional and social needs nurtures self-esteem, too. Children need to feel that they are valued members of a caring community. They need to know that people (including their teachers) listen to what they say and respect their opinions. As teachers, we can help children improve their self-esteem by establishing a climate of trust, acceptance, and caring.

Self-Esteem Strategies

"To develop a positive view of ourselves, we must be given opportunities to experience ourselves as positive, loving persons who are cared about and thought well of by others," explains Barbara Clark. "[Children] need to realize what others appreciate about them in order to feel self-worth," adds psychologist

Patricia Berne. Berne offers the following tips and activities for shoring up self-esteem:

✔ **Build in success for each child**, especially success that is continuous. Authentic assessment and student choice are two effective strategies.

✔ **State the positive**. Nurture self-esteem by acknowledging the positive in a non evaluating but validating way. For example, point out all the details in a child's picture or comment on his or her use of color, instead of simply saying, "That's a good picture."

✔ **Capitalize on successes**. If you build on a child's interests to enable him or her to succeed, go a step further and use those successes to broaden interests. One child Berne worked with loved toys, so she encouraged him to write the descriptions and prices of toys in a notebook. Later, his interests expanded to collecting and classifying plants.

✔ **Watch for growth sparks**. Children with low self-esteem believe they can't learn or relate well to others. Help ignite a spark of interest they never knew they had. When a learning-disabled student showed Berne a magic trick he learned from a cereal box, she detected his delight in the trick and noticed how his self-esteem was heightened by her enjoyment. She nurtured this newborn interest and built on it to provide success and positive experiences to share with his classmates.

✔ **Value and acknowledge**. Visible, tangible evidence of success greatly increases a child's self-esteem. Collect students' artwork and writings to show them the improvements they're making over time. (Portfolios help here.) Encourage families to display children's work, especially work that shows accomplishment.

✔ **Listen to suggestions** from students concerning different approaches to tasks and lessons. "Self-esteem grows when children feel involved and in control of their lives," notes Berne.

INCLUDING SHY STUDENTS

Some students are just shy and tend not to participate much in class discussions. Often these students do know the answers or have opinions to contribute but are reluctant to raise their hands. When called upon, they are startled or embarrassed, which only adds to their discomfort. Here's a strategy that really works:

Call the student's name *before* you ask a question. Then pause and slowly pose the question. This way you alert the student beforehand that a question is coming, and you give him or her enough time to focus on the question and an answer.

✔ **Empathize with students**. For example, acknowledge when a task is boring or frustrating. Your empathy often makes them less resistant to certain tasks, says Berne. When their feelings are recognized, children feel valued.

Don't forget to work with families in helping students build self-esteem. The National Parent Teacher Association has published a list of ways parents can help at home. (See page 229.)

❖ Bibliotherapy

One of the best techniques for helping students deal with their problems and emotions involves a resource that most classrooms and schools have plenty of: books! Bibliotherapy is the use of literature to address children's problems.

Many parents—myself included—have relied on books to get their children through emotional difficulties such as that first visit to the dentist or

Self-Esteem
12 Ways to Help Children Like Themselves

1 Reward children. Give praise, recognition, a special privilege, or increased responsibility for a job well done. Emphasize the positive things they do, not the negative.

2 Take their ideas, emotions, and feelings seriously. Don't belittle them by saying, "You'll grow out of it" or "It's not as bad as you think."

3 Define limits and rules clearly, and enforce them. But allow latitude for children within these limits.

4 Be a good role model. Let children know that you feel good about yourself. Also let them see that you, too, can make mistakes and can learn from them.

5 Have reasonable expectations for children. Help them to set reachable goals so they can achieve success.

6 Help children develop tolerance toward those with different values, backgrounds, and norms. Point out other people's strengths.

7 Give children responsibility. They will feel useful and valued.

8 Be available. Give support when children need it.

9 Show students that what they do is important to you. Talk with them about their activities and interests.

10 Discuss problems without placing blame or commenting on a child's character. If children know there is a problem but don't feel attacked, they are more likely to help look for a solution.

11 Use phrases that build self-esteem, such as "Thank you for helping," or "That was an excellent idea!" Avoid phrases that hurt self-esteem: "Why are you so stupid?" or "How many times have I told you?"

12 Show that you care.

"12 Ways to Help Children Like Themselves" reprinted by permission of the National PTA.

CELEBRATING INDIVIDUALITY

- New York teacher Pat Dickinson lets her sixth graders get to know each other by having them create **self-portrait collages**. As she explains it, "Students pair up and pencil sketch each other's heads and necks. Each child draws his or her face and hair. Next, to represent chest and stomach, each child makes a collage of magazine pictures of favorite foods. Then each student picks his or her very favorite thing in the world and draws that one object using tempera, ink, or charcoal. For the lower body, they design the wildest pair of shorts imaginable. Again with their classmates' help, students trace their arms and legs on construction paper and cut them out. Kids then take off their shoes, put them on their desks, and draw them with pencils. We connect all the parts together and wrap the arms of each figure around the drawing of their favorite things."

- Texas teacher Sandy Owens has her third graders, and later their parents, make a **"We're Unique" display**. "On the first day of school," says Owens, "I ask each of my third graders to make a flower out of assorted materials I place in the center of each group of four desks. When everyone finishes the flowers, I ask kids to sign one of the petals, then we staple the flowers to a bed of grass on a bulletin board titled WE ARE ALL DIFFERENT AND WONDERFULLY UNIQUE. Then I write the word *unique* on the chalkboard and we discuss its meaning, exploring how every flower is special in a unique way. We then discuss how students have different styles of reading, writing, and studying, and how some students may be better in math, spelling, and reading than others. We agree that we all have strengths and weaknesses and need to help one another. On parents' night, I ask parents to make flowers from the same assorted materials, and display each parent's flower next to his or her child's on the bulletin board. The students are delighted to see that their parents are unique, too."

- I ask my middle schoolers to create **personalized writing folders** with collages that illustrate who they are, what they like, and what they want to do and be. After cutting pictures and words from magazines, adding individualized artwork and graphics, and pasting on personal mementos such as concert tickets or photographs, the students take turns presenting their "pictorial autobiographies" to classmates. Besides celebrating their uniqueness and creativity, the decorated folders give them ideas for stories and essays during the year.

- Self-esteem through self-awareness is the goal of the **Me Museums** activity developed by Susie Edmond. She asks each student to bring in one empty shoe box. Then she has the student print his or her name on the box and decorate it with magazine photographs or illustrations to depict hobbies, interests, favorite foods, toys, or television programs. Edmond places the finished museums in a row on the windowsill and asks the students to bring in one small but special item each day for the next two weeks—items such as family photographs, souvenirs, small collectibles, and greeting cards. The items are exhibited in the museums, and students view each other's exhibits during free time.

They giggled and nodded in appreciation—there were other people who had problems with annoying siblings. And even as each was identifying with one of the characters, they could laugh at and understand how both children in the story had legitimate gripes as well as distorted perceptions. It may have been their first good lesson in the concept that "reality" depends upon our perception of it—that there are always two (or more) sides to every story.

You're Not Alone
Stories show children that they are not alone—that there are others experiencing the same problems they have. They offer a safe way to investigate important issues, feelings, and emotions.

Veteran teacher Betty Forney describes how she uses a well-loved children's story, Bernard Waber's *Ira Sleeps Over* (Houghton Mifflin, 1972), to begin each new school year. In the story, six-year-old Ira is invited to spend the night at his friend Reggie's house, but he's not sure his teddy bear is invited, too. He's afraid to leave the bear behind, but he doesn't want to look like a baby. Bravely, he decides to go alone. When it's time to go to bed at Reggie's house, Ira discovers Reggie has a teddy bear, too.

"Kids often fear the unfamiliar turf they face at the beginning of a school year," says Forney,

hospital, the first day of school, moving to a new town, or dealing with bullies. When my daughters were in elementary school, they loved Judy Blume's *The Pain and the Great One* (Bradbury Press, 1985), about sibling rivalry.

who's found that the story works well at all grade levels. "I always tell [students] to 'take along a teddy bear.'" Her fifth graders understand the symbolic meaning of the story and enjoy discussing what kinds of "teddy bears" are suitable at their age. Forney explains, "From lucky hats to big smiles to old friends, they suggest things they can take along to help themselves feel comfortable in strange settings."

Bibliotherapy is also helpful in situations where the problems—and stakes—are much greater. Writing about the emotional and behavioral problems of a third grader involved in a bitter custody battle, Dr. Melba Coleman suggested that the child's teacher give her access to such books as Sharon Dennis Wyeth's *Always My Dad* (Knopf, 1995) and Paula Danzinger's *The Divorce Express* (Dell, 1982). "Books like these can help both children and teachers deal with 'freaky Fridays and moody Mondays'—days in which children typically go to and return from stays with absent parents," Coleman explains.

Widespread Use

Bibliotherapy has been used by counselors since the 1950s and first became popular in classrooms in the 1970s, writes Mary Rizza of the University of Connecticut. Long advocated as a strategy for meeting the needs of gifted children, the technique is also used successfully with all types of children in all types of situations. And the publishing industry has responded. There are stories dealing with all kinds of issues and problems: facing bullies, getting along with friends, living with disabilities, coping with divorce, death, abuse, hunger, homelessness . . . the list goes on and on.

Author Barbara Clark points out that bibliotherapy is used in three distinct ways:
1. to help children develop a more positive self-concept.
2. to change attitudes and values.
3. to promote mental and emotional health.

As teachers, we have many opportunities to help shape students' attitudes in the books we select for literature units. For example, I use such books as Mildred Taylor's *Roll of Thunder, Hear My Cry* and Harper Lee's *To Kill a Mockingbird* to help counter the racial prejudices and fears in my culturally and ethnically homogeneous community.

Important Considerations

Teachers using bibliotherapy should keep these ideas in mind, advises Rizza.

First, it's not enough simply to have students read a story. They need to talk about what they've read.

"Always remember, bibliotherapy is a conversation starter, not ender," she writes. "It should be used to open up communication. Handing a book to a child in the hopes that he or she will understand your intention is not helpful. Connections need to be facilitated and open expression should be encouraged."

Story selection is a critical factor, too. And there are a lot of books to choose from.

"The quality of available literature is outstanding," says Rizza, citing a greater awareness and portrayal of real-life issues and multicultural sensitivity among today's publishers.

To find appropriate stories, Rizza suggests consulting with knowledgeable librarians or using readily available resources such as *Bookfinder 5: When Kids Need Books* by Sharon Spredemann-Dreyer (American Guidance Service, 1992), which lists books by subject, author, and title. A title that includes books helpful for students in grades K through 6 who are facing challenging issues such as a new sibling or the death of a pet is Laura Ann Campbell's *Storybooks for Tough Times* (Fulcrum, 1999). The book includes discussion questions as well.

It's also very important to fit the book to the student, Rizza stresses. "The story line and characters do not have to match your situation exactly, but be sure there is some commonality," she suggests. "There are many good stories available, so don't compromise. Choosing a story that a child cannot relate to will negate your good intentions."

A POIGNANT EXAMPLE

Former teacher Nina Shandler, who is now a family therapist, relates the story of how bibliotherapy helped a troubled third grader named Jerry. Jerry, who was diagnosed with attention deficit disorder, obsessive-compulsive behavior, and a mild form of Tourette's syndrome, had completely alienated his classmates with his odd behavior. Feeling excluded and ostracized, he cried himself to sleep every night, wishing he were dead.

After conferring with Shandler and Jerry's parents, his teacher read Jeanne Gehret's *Eagle Eyes* (Verbal Images Press, 1996) to the class. At the end of this story about a boy with behavioral difficulties, Jerry blurted out, "That kid's like me!" Shandler reports.

Over the next two days, the teacher read *Everything I Do You Blame on Me* (Center for Applied Psychology, 1994), about a child who struggles to gain self-control. Again Jerry blurted out comments like, "That's me!" and "Me, too!"

"Following the readings," writes Shandler, "the teacher explained to the class that there are complicated medical reasons for some children's behavior. She explained that some children have disabilities that make it very hard for them to pay attention and sit still, or to control their emotions and actions. She explained that these smart, well-meaning, creative children need patience and acceptance. A friend of Jerry's volunteered: 'Jerry really is like that.' His classmates nodded in agreement."

Later, after a positive discipline program and medication began helping Jerry in class, his classmates accepted him once more. "The sting of rejection faded," says Shandler.

writing could be original works based on the models they've read, or they could be a modification of, or alternate ending to, a published story. Either way, writing is a good way to get children talking and thinking about the problems and issues they face.

Rizza gives the example of a little girl whose pet dog was killed. A wise neighbor gave the grieving child Judith Viorst's *The Tenth Good Thing About Barney* (Aladdin, 1987), a story about a little boy whose cat died. Like the protagonist, the little girl wrote a list of good things she wanted to remember about her pet, and she drew pictures about each one. Rereading this "book" she had created helped the girl deal with her pet's death and the slow process of healing.

Rizza and other experts caution that we can't expect immediate results from bibliotherapy.

"Time is the critical factor," she points out. "For some children it will take time for them to incorporate the ideas or even want to deal with the issue. Talking about emotions may be difficult and the child may be resistant, but with the help from a caring adult, she or he can learn to deal with issues and not ignore them."

And make sure you actually read the story ahead of time, says Rizza. It should be closely related to the student's problem, offer suggestions for coping with the problem, and include a main character to whom he or she can relate.

Also, look for these three criteria when selecting a book, Rizza suggests. The book should:

✔ promote the exchange of information between teacher and student.

✔ enable the student to make the connection to her or his life.

✔ validate the student's feelings and responses to the crisis or issue at hand.

Writing Helps, Too

In addition to discussing and analyzing the stories they read, children will "heal" faster when they write their own stories, suggest the experts. Their

❖ Valuing Diversity

Biologists have realized for years the importance of diversity. Many different plants and animals contribute to the successful functioning of any ecosystem. Our adaptability and "staying power" on this planet depend upon preserving diverse life-forms.

The same can be said for cultural diversity. The differences among groups of people in lifestyles, thinking processes and philosophies, customs, land-use patterns, religions, and so on sustain and nourish our adaptability as a species. Cultures have been borrowing good ideas from other cultures for as long as there have been organized societies.

Our schools are the perfect forum for learning about and celebrating human diversity. After all, who should be more tolerant and accepting of differences than Americans, whose very nation owes its existence to multiple cultural, racial, and ethnic groups?

Culturally Responsive Curriculum

What is a culturally responsive curriculum? It's a curriculum that "capitalizes on students' cultural backgrounds rather than attempting to override or negate them," explains author Ismat Abdal-Haqq. Abdal-Haqq lists important characteristics. Culturally Responsive Curriculum, he says, is:

✔ integrated and interdisciplinary, not simply relying on one-time activities or "add-on" units.

✔ authentic, child-centered, and connected to the students' real lives. Principles and concepts are illustrated with examples from a student's culture and history.

✔ focused on developing critical-thinking skills.

✔ based on cooperative learning and whole-language instruction.

✔ self-esteem building and recognizes multiple intelligences and diverse learning styles.

✔ supported by appropriate staff development and preservice preparation.

✔ part of a coordinated, schoolwide strategy.

African Americans, Native Americans, Asian Americans, and Hispanic Americans are often treated inappropriately in textbooks and curriculum materials. Abdal-Haqq warns teachers to be aware of three such inappropriate treatments, including:

1. **The "sidebar approach."** Here, different ethnic experiences are relegated to a few isolated events set off from the rest of the text in boxes or sidebars.

2. **The "superhero" syndrome.** This is when ethnic groups are misrepresented by acknowledging only the "superheroes of history" from a race or culture. Booker T. Washington and Martin Luther King, Jr. were important African Americans, but so were the hundreds of thousands of black soldiers who have fought in every American conflict since the Revolutionary War.

3. **The "one-size-fits-all" view.** This view implies that there is a single Hispanic, African, Asian, or Native American culture and doesn't recognize that considerable diversity exists even within cultural subgroups. For example, there are more than 300 American Indian tribes, each with its own distinct language, value system, government, and social organization.

Just the Facts . . .

Common myths about various ethnic groups contribute to bias in teaching and materials. We teachers often unwittingly perpetuate those myths through the curriculum materials we rely upon. Textbooks, television, and movies often treat different ethnic groups in stereotypical and distorted ways.

One common myth is that all Native Americans live on reservations. In fact, only about 12.5 percent of the population live on reservations or trust lands, and about 66 percent live in metropolitan areas (U.S. Census Bureau data, 2003). Further, many people believe that American Indians receive financial support from the government simply because of their cultural identity. But funds, education, health services, and other benefits are payments for native lands, negotiated by treaties.

These and other myths about Native Americans and different ethnic groups only fuel our conflicts and misunderstandings of each other. As teachers, we must insist on fair and accurate sources of information about cultural diversity. (For related materials, see the cultural diversity resources listed in Chapter Two.)

English as a Second Language

Children from diverse ethnic and cultural backgrounds also have different language backgrounds. Sometimes, if English is not the child's primary language, he or she may have problems adapting to school. Many schools have special programs for English language learners Students who qualify for language instruction in English may be classified as English as a Second Language (ESL) students, English Language Learners (ELL), or students with Limited English Proficiency (LEP). If yours does not, try these strategies developed by the late Dr. Eleanor W. Thonis:

✔ **Provide a climate of warmth and caring** that nurtures a sense of comfort and ease for students who are coping with the demands of a new language.

✔ **Seat the student close to the front of the room**, where directions and instructions can be given with fewer distractions.

✔ **Speak naturally, but slowly**, to allow for comprehension to develop.

✔ **Use clear, simple language** (that is, shorter sentences, simpler concepts, and fewer multisyllabic words).

✔ **Support content-area instruction with visual materials** such as pictures, diagrams, and drawings.

✔ **Provide manipulative materials** whenever possible to make mathematics and science lessons meaningful.

✔ **Offer film and filmstrips with the sound track turned off**, and tell the story or explain the lesson in simpler language and less complex terms.

✔ **Do not call on the ELL student for a lengthy response**. Elicit one-word or gestural answers when appropriate.

✔ **Avoid correcting pronunciation, structural, or vocabulary errors** when the student speaks. Accept the student's response or restate the response correctly without comment.

✔ **Do not expect mastery** of the language or the accuracy of a native English speaker. Enjoy the flavor of the nonnative speech, especially when it does not interfere with comprehension.

OTHER STRATEGIES FOR TEACHING ENGLISH LANGUAGE LEARNERS

Interviewing several effective ELL teachers, writer and former teacher Jane Schall identified these important strategies for meeting the needs of students whose primary language is not English:

- Recruit volunteers who speak the same language as the ELL students.
- Get to know the students' backgrounds and cultures.
- Build understanding through role reversals. Ask someone to teach a lesson in a language unfamiliar to your students. Don't tell them what you are doing at first so they can experience the extreme frustration and confusion that occurs when we can't understand the language.
- Enlist the aid of peer tutors who speak the ELL student's language.
- Pair the ELL students with peers who will look out for them and help them deal with the physical environment and the classroom rules and procedures.
- Make these students feel included and give them extra language practice by frequently asking them to help you find items or accomplish classroom tasks.
- Use gestures and encourage other students to be expressive when describing things for the ELL students. Pantomime and modeling through body language are excellent communication techniques.
- Label objects and use lots of visuals.
- Read aloud, especially poetry or stories that have patterns and repetitions.

✔ **Assign a dependable classmate to assist** whenever additional directions are needed to follow through on assignments. (Try to limit your dependence on a single peer assistant and limit the amount of time the assistant is assigned to help the ELL student. Remember that the assistant needs to attend to his or her own learning first and foremost and that the ELL student may be receiving incomplete or confusing directions from the well-meaning peer assistant.)

Perhaps most important, don't isolate your English language learners or somehow set them aside as "different." Make them an integral part of your learning community. Students with a primary language other than English are wonderful resources for demonstrating to others the beauty and complexity of language. Don't let these valuable human resources remain untapped!

❖ **In Summary**

We know that teaching involves much more than instruction in the academic subject areas; part of our responsibility is nurturing and facilitating social and emotional development along with intellectual growth. Thus, by keeping in mind that students' affective needs and abilities are closely tied to their cognitive needs, we can incorporate techniques to address the whole student—heart and mind.

Behavior problems, poor self-esteem, prejudices and biases, peer conflicts, negative social climate, self-destructive behavior—these and other negative factors have a significant impact on how teachers teach and students learn.

To be well adjusted, students need to care—about themselves, their classmates, their families and communities, their personal integrity, the quality of their work, and their world at large. Many students are taught to care at home. Others need our guidance and help. Simply put, we need to teach kids to care by modeling that care ourselves—by providing a caring classroom climate, by listening to students' concerns and bolstering their self-esteem, by offering books and curriculum to help students develop character and values, by giving students opportunities to learn to respect other cultures and people, by giving students responsibilities and the chance to exercise them, and by teaching that actions and behaviors have consequences.

❖ Works Cited

Abdal-Haqq, Ismat. *Culturally Responsive Curriculum.* ERIC Digest. Available: www.ericfacility.net/databases/ERIC_Digests/ed370936.html.

Barasch, Douglas. "Discipline: How a Child Develops Through the Years." *Family Life,* August 18, 1997, 54–61.

Berne, Patricia H., and Louis M. Savary *Building Self-Esteem in Children.* New York: Continuum Publishers, 1981.

Brophy, Jere and Joyce Putnam. "Classroom Management in the Elementary Grades." in D. Duke, ed., *Classroom Management.* The 78th Yearbook of the National Society for the Study of Education, Part III. Chicago: University of Chicago Press, 1979.

Canter, Lee. "Assertive Discipline—More Than Names on the Board and Marbles in a Jar." *Phi Delta Kappan* 71, no. 1 (September 1989): 57–61.

Clark, Barbara. *Growing Up Gifted: Developing the Potential of Children at Home and School.* 6th ed. Upper Saddle River, NJ: Merrill/Prentice Hall, 2002.

Cooper, Joann, Marcia Leverte, and Arden Smith-Martenz. *Helping Children Deal with Disruptive Behaviors.* Warminster, PA: Mar. Co. Products, 1992.

Kohn, Alfie. "Choices for Children: Why and How to Let Students Decide." *Phi Delta Kappan* 75, no. 1 (September 1993): 8–20.

Kounin, Jacob. *Discipline and Group Management in Classrooms.* New York: Holt, 1970.

Kreidler, William. *Creative Conflict Resolution: More Than 200 Activities for Keeping Peace in the Classroom.* Glenview, IL: Scott, Foresman, 1984.

Lang, Laura. "Too Much Timeout." *Teacher Magazine* (May/June 1997): 6–7.

Medick, Jean M. *Classroom Misbehavior: Turning It Around.* East Lansing, MI: Fanning Press, 1981.

Rizza, Mary. "Using Bibliotherapy at Home." *Newsletter of the National Research Center on the Gifted and Talented,* Winter 1997, 6–7.

Shandler, Nina. "Just Rewards." *Teaching Tolerance* (Spring 1996): 37–41.

Slavin, Robert. "Synthesis of Research on Cooperative Learning." *Educational Leadership* (February 1991): 71–77.

❖ Resources

Cooperative Learning

Bennett, B., C. Rolheiser and L. Stevahn. *Cooperative Learning: Where Heart Meets Mind: An Interactive Resource Book.* Professional Development Associates, 1991.

Cohen, Elizabeth G. *Designing Groupwork: Strategies for the Heterogeneous Classroom.* 2nd ed. New York: Teachers College Press, 1994.

Cohen, Elizabeth G., Celeste M. Brody, and Mara Sapon-Shevin. *Teaching Cooperative Learning: The Challenge for Teacher Education.* Albany: State University of New York Press, 2004.

Johnson, David W. and Roger T. *Positive Interdependence: The Heart of Cooperative Learning.* Edina, MN: Interaction Book Company, 1992.

Conflict Resolution

Kreidler, William J. *Conflict Resolution in the Middle School.* Cambridge, MA: Educators for Social Responsibility, 1994.

Kreidler, William J. *Teaching Conflict Resolution Through Children's Literature.* New York: Scholastic, 1994.

Discipline

Albert, Linda. *A Teacher's Guide to Cooperative Discipline: How to Manage Your Classroom and Promote Self-Esteem.* Circle Press, MN: American Guidance Service, 1989.

Brodkin, Adele. *Fresh Approaches to Working With Problematic Behavior.* New York: Scholastic, 2001.

Canter, Lee and Marlene. *Lee Canter's Succeeding With Difficult Students: New Strategies for Reaching Your Most Challenging Students.* Workbook edition. Canter & Associates, 1993.

Maurer, Richard E. *Special Educator's Discipline Handbook.* West Nyack, NY: Center for Applied Research in Education, 1988.

McConnell, Kathleen *Reaching Out to Troubled Kids: 15 Helpful Ways to Bridge the Gap Between Parents, Teachers, and Kids.* Longmont, CO: Sopris West, 1997.

Mendler, Allen N. *What Do I Do When . . . ? How to Achieve Discipline With Dignity in the Classroom.* Bloomington, IN: National Educational Service, 1992.

Nelson, Jane, et al. *Positive Discipline: A Teacher's A–Z Guide: Hundreds of Solutions for Every Possible Classroom Behavior Problem.* Roseville, CA: Prima Publishing, 2001.

Short, Paula Myric, Rick Jay Short, and Charlie Blanton. *Rethinking Student Discipline: Alternatives That Work.* Bloomington, IN: Corwin Press, 1993.

"Tolerance.org"
www.tolerance.org
A Web project of the Southern Poverty Law Center. Search the site for ideas about conflict resolution and other means to promote harmony and tolerance.

English Language Learners

Asher, James J. *Learning Another Language Through Actions.* 6th ed. Los Gatos, CA: Sky Oaks Productions, 2000.

The Institute for Research in English Acquisition and Development (READ)
www.ceousa.org/READ

"Instructing Language Minority Children." *Research and the Classroom*, 5 (1994). National Center for Effective Schools, Wisconsin Center for Education Research, University of Wisconsin, 1025 W. Johnson St., Ste. 570, Madison, WI 53706; (608) 263-4730.

Spangenberg-Urbschat, Karen, and Robert Pritchard, eds. *Kids Come in All Languages: Reading Instruction for ESL Students.* Newark, DE: International Reading Association, 1994. To order, call (800) 336-READ, ext. 266, or log on to www.reading.org.

Walker, Michael, and Teresa Walter. *Amazing English! How-To Handbook: Instructional Strategies for the Classroom Teacher for Cultural Diversity, Language Acquisition, Literacy, Academic Content, Assessment.* Reading, MA: Addison Wesley, 1996.

Chapter Six

Home-School-Community Connections

"*The role of parents in the education of their*

children cannot be overestimated."

—*Mexican American Legal Defense
and Educational Fund*

Few ideas and issues in education enjoy as much support as the notion that family and community involvement are necessary for successful schooling and learning to occur. Indeed, many would argue that such involvement is the single most important feature of effective schools.

"Nothing is more important to success in schools than the quality of relationships between and among students, teachers, and parents," says Dr. James P. Comer, whose parent-involvement programs in New Haven, Connecticut, are widely replicated. Without this "personal touch," Comer maintains, "educational efforts in this country will fail."

The research clearly supports Comer's claims: Where parents volunteer their time and attention, students achieve more and like school better. Studies of effective programs for at-risk children consistently identify parent involvement as a key component.

Just think of it! Each year you could have well-qualified adult helpers to assist you all year long. In a class of 25 students, you have at least 25 parents, foster parents, or guardians with a vested interest in what you are trying to accomplish.

At home, adults can encourage and help motivate children, foster a good attitude toward school and work, provide practice and supplemental learning activities, and make sure children get the rest, food, and exercise they need to perform well.

In school, parents can volunteer to tutor individual students, read to groups or classes, share special skills or knowledge, help photocopy materials, organize field trips, and give you more time to teach.

In the community, parents can spearhead fund-raisers for schools and classes, lobby for better education budgets, promote positive public relations, sponsor school activities, serve on site-based management teams, and more.

And that's just parents! Add to that the growing numbers of community members and businesspeople willing to get involved, and your potential pool of human resources is almost limitless. This chapter explores the different ways that teachers, parents or other caregivers, and the community can unite their efforts for the good of children.

❖ Communication and Interpersonal Skills

Cooperation between teachers and parents doesn't just happen. It requires special skills on your part—skills such as good listening, tact, kindness, consideration, empathy, enthusiasm, and an understanding of parent-child relationships. No matter how you interact with parents and the community at large—through conferences, telephone conversations, e-mail, written notes or reports, lobbying or fund-raising efforts, working together in the classroom—good communication and interpersonal skills will enhance your efforts.

Veteran teachers stress the importance of effective communication skills.

"When working with parents, be honest," advises Pennsylvania teacher Laurie Borger. "And be sensitive! Remember that you are talking about their most valuable family resource—their family's future."

Adds Frank Garcia of California: "Always be tactful with parents. Think and plan what you are going to say to them, and how. Never be confrontational. Always speak in a pleasant voice, yet with firmness and authority when needed. Keep in mind that parents really love their children."

The Right Attitude

Garcia is right. Parents really *do* love their children. That's just one of several important ideas to keep in mind when establishing partnerships with parents. Writing about at-risk families and schools, L. B. Liontos lists other "beliefs" that teachers must adopt to work effectively with families:

✔ All families have strengths.

✔ Parents can learn new techniques.

✔ Parents have important perspectives about their children.

✔ Most parents really care about their children.

✔ Cultural differences are both valid and valuable.

✔ Many family forms exist and are legitimate.

Further, former teacher Oralie McAfee offers the following guidelines for working with families:

✔ Recognize that schools and homes have shared goals. Both are committed to the nurturing, development, and education of children. "Teachers must believe that parents have a crucial role in their children's education, and parents and teachers must trust each other," McAfee stresses.

✔ Respect caregivers and communicate that respect. Tone of voice, word choice, facial expressions, body language, expectations, how long we make people wait—all these communicate respect or lack of it. Many parents have personal, family, work, health, or other problems that we know nothing about. Avoid being judgmental, and give parents the benefit of the doubt.

✔ Acknowledge the changes in the American family. In most families, both parents work outside the home. Further, millions of American schoolchildren come from single-parent homes. Still others live with relatives or in foster homes.

To the preceding lists, add one more important item concerning attitude:

✔ Be positive! "Parents enjoy positive communication," says West Virginia teacher Jane Baird. "Most teachers only make contact when something goes wrong." Other veterans heartily agree. "Make sure if you give negatives that you also give positives—positive phone calls, letters, and so on," suggests principal Jane Kelling of Houston. West Virginian Marilyn Perkins communicates positive messages by mentioning every child in her class in every newsletter.

Plain Talk

Stanines, percentiles, standards, cognitive style, constructivist approach—using educational jargon is a good way to throw up a smoke screen. But if honest communication is your goal, take time to speak plainly. Translate your professional shorthand into meaningful words and explanations. Jargon reduces rather than improves your credibility with parents.

The late Erma Bombeck, a parent and columnist, illustrated this point beautifully:

"When my son, Bruce, entered the first grade, his report card said, 'He verbalizes during class and periodically engages in excursions up and down the aisles.'

"In the sixth grade, his teacher said, 'What can we do with a child who does not relate to social interaction?' (I ran home and got out my dictionary.)

"At the start of his senior year, Bruce's adviser said, 'This year will hopefully open up options for your son so he can realize his potential and aim for tangible goals.'

"On my way out, I asked the secretary, 'Do you speak English?' She nodded. 'What was she telling me?'

"'Bruce is goofing off,' the secretary said flatly.

"I don't know if education is helping Bruce or not, but it's certainly improving my vocabulary."

Stop, Look, and Listen

When people speak to you, what do you hear? Chances are it's only one-quarter of what they say. Researchers estimate that our listening efficiency is about 25 percent. Maybe that's proof of the adage, "You hear what you want to hear."

But listening is one of the most frequently used aspects of communication—and probably the most important. Good listening skills are essential in building partnerships with parents. They are the difference between talking *to* parents and talking *with* them.

If you genuinely want to hear what someone says, you can improve your listening skills, say the experts. Here's how:

✔ Maintain eye contact.
✔ Face the speaker and lean forward slightly.
✔ Ignore distractions.
✔ Nod or give other noninterrupting acknowledgments.
✔ When the speaker pauses, allow him or her to continue without interrupting.
✔ Wait to add your comments until the speaker is finished.
✔ Ask for clarification when necessary.
✔ Check your understanding by summarizing the essential aspects of what the speaker tried to say or the feelings he or she tried to convey.

DETERRENTS TO COMMUNICATION

Many factors can inhibit our ability to listen:

• distractions, such as 25 children about to let loose while you speak with a parent who has dropped by unexpectedly
• tension, when you may be defensive and trying to think of what to say next, instead of paying attention
• an environment that is too noisy, too crowded, or too uncomfortable
• impatience, when you think that what's being said is unimportant
• time, if you are in a hurry
• preoccupation with other matters
• impressions of the way a speaker looks, acts, or sounds

The Parent Interview

Practice your listening skills and acquire useful information in the process by interviewing your students' parents or caregivers. The interview is especially helpful if conducted during the first half of the school year. It makes a good "get-acquainted" exercise. It demonstrates that you are genuinely interested in families and their insights. And it gives you important information about students and parents.

You can conduct the interview in person or over the telephone (but send a note home first to say you'll be calling and why). Following are some possible questions for your parent interview:

1. Please tell me about your child—his/her likes and dislikes, strengths and weaknesses, and whatever else you think is important.
2. Please tell me about your child's interests, habits, chores, and responsibilities.
3. What are your hopes and dreams for your child?
4. What are your expectations from me and the school?
5. How do you think you can help your child learn?
6. Are there any unique situations or problems you want to share to help me understand your child better?
7. What kinds of communication do you like to receive from teachers—notes, newsletters, phone calls? How often would you prefer them?
8. What is a good time to call you?
9. What are some special hobbies or skills you could share with students?
10. What are your expectations about homework?

LEARN TO LISTEN

Keep these teacher tips in mind as you learn to listen to parents:

- Be alert for visual cues, body language, and other nonverbal signs. Pay attention to offhand comments that may give insight to personalities and family situations.
- Find out what parents know about what goes on in school and in your classroom. If their academic or social expectations are too high or too low, explain what you think are realistic expectations. **But first try paraphrasing what they have said to make sure you understand.** Your paraphrasing gives parents an opportunity to correct any misunderstanding on your part or to further explain their concerns.

After reviewing many different parent involvement studies, Dan Jesse reports that parents prefer informal relationships with teachers and informal, regular contacts through notes and phone calls. "They appreciate teachers who take the time to find out about their perspectives," Jesse writes, noting that many cite a "personal touch" as the factor that most enhances their relations with school.

The Open-Door Policy

Seeing is believing. If you really want parents to know what a great place your classroom is, how well their children are learning, or how much you want and need their involvement, invite them to school. Be sure to give working parents plenty of advance notice so they can make arrangements to take time off. Once there, parents can casually observe, participate in activities, or help you run the show. The changes in attitude that can occur from such visits are amazing. When parents feel welcomed and comfortable at school, they feel freer to communicate with teachers and become involved in the schooling process. Parents who visit and are involved in schools become teachers' strongest allies.

An open-door policy sets a good tone for school-home relations. But unless you issue a specific invitation, few parents will actually visit.

Here are teacher-tested strategies for encouraging classroom visits:

✔ Send letters inviting parents and caregivers to a Visitation Day. Tell them this day will be a window on their child's world at school. Send home an activities schedule so parents can plan to visit all or only part of the day. After the visit, encourage parents to write or call with comments or questions.

✔ Make lunch or breakfast dates with parents. Even those who work will often be able to spend a lunch hour at school or slip in before class starts. They won't see much of classroom activities, but just the chance to be greeted by you and to sit and talk with their children should give them a warm feeling of belonging.

✔ Invite parents to school for special classroom events. Are your students performing a play based on a history unit they've just completed? Will they be presenting the science reports they spent two weeks preparing? Ask families to share the moment. This gives them a chance to witness children's accomplishments and gives students an audience for their performances.

✔ Schoolwide events are another time to invite parents and caregivers. You could ask them to meet your class at the room, then accompany you as you go to the auditorium for a special assembly or program.

There are many different ways and occasions to bring parents to school. The important thing is to get them there. The more they feel that their presence is valued, the more likely they are to support your efforts and become involved in their children's learning.

Encourage all your students' parents or caregivers to visit your classroom. But you'll want to establish some guidelines, especially concerning unannounced visits. Some teachers

---

INVITE PARENTS TO SCHOOL

"The parents in our largely Hispanic area come to register their children at the beginning of each school year," says Mary Helen Ratje of Las Cruces, New Mexico. "I know some Spanish, but I always ask a fluent Spanish speaker to be with me as an interpreter. This way, I can ask parents to volunteer, describe how I need their help, and find out when they can come to school. These parents are often reluctant at first, but if you make them feel comfortable, they'll come back."

For more perspectives and ideas on bridging the home-school divide with families of students from diverse socioeconomic and cultural backgrounds, see page 274.

---

welcome unannounced visits, but many feel they are too disruptive. One strategy is to explain in a newsletter or group conference that valuable teaching time is lost when unannounced visits break students' concentration and your tight schedule. Instead, suggest that family members call first or come during a specially designated time.

Group visits might make some parents feel more at ease. Also, you will be more comfortable—and so will visitors—if you provide written guidelines on what you expect. Do you want visitors to wander around the room and interact with students? Or would you prefer them to be as unobtrusive as possible? Can you give them information that will make their observations more meaningful? What about providing copies of textbooks or materials so they can follow along with your lesson?

Invite your visitors to get into the swing of things. They can read stories to the class, dictate words for a spelling test, assist on an art project, or referee games on the playground. But whatever you do, make them feel at home.

❖ Parent and Community Involvement

The reason to hone communication skills and bring parents into school, of course, is to involve them to the fullest possible extent in their children's education. National opinion polls and surveys reveal that teachers consistently rank parent involvement as a top priority for the nation's schools.

"Involvement" is a term we use loosely to describe many different ways teachers and parents can team up to help students. In his comprehensive review of research on parent involvement, Dan Jesse concludes that parent involvement occurs in four ways: parents as teachers, parents as partners, parents as decision makers, and parents as advocates. These four categories serve well to delineate the roles you can encourage your students' parents to play.

Parents as Their Children's Teachers

Parents are their children's first teachers. No one would dispute the truth of this old adage. But recent research on learning and the human brain adds a new twist to the old adage: Parents are their children's most important teachers.

Research has shown clearly that intelligence is heavily influenced by the experiences a child has in the first years of life. Most scientists agree that intelligence is not a quotient fixed at birth, and they claim that much of our learning ability is developed during the first three or four years. Thus, our caretakers during this time—usually parents—have the greatest influence on how "smart" we'll be. Parents hold the key to "turning on" the receptors in children's brains.

Teachers can encourage parents to continue playing a critical role as "teachers" by reading to children, traveling together, discussing ideas and issues, providing creative outlets, modeling self-discipline and task commitment, and so on.

Parents as Partners With Teachers

This is the role most teachers think of when they think of parent involvement. As partners in education, parents can share special knowledge and expertise with children in school, volunteer in classrooms, encourage children to complete homework, and much more.

Tapping All That Talent Parents have a wealth of information, ideas, special skills, and hobbies to share. Tap some of that talent in mini-courses and enrichment classes taught by them.

The first step is to find out what special interests and occupations parents have. Use information from your parent interviews. You may want to create a language-skills unit based on students interviewing and writing feature stories about their parents. Or send a survey home explaining your purpose and asking for ideas. Cameron Elementary School in West Virginia conducts a schoolwide survey, developing a "speaker's pool" to which all of the school's teachers have access.

You'll probably discover a parent who can teach your class about tropical fish and setting up an aquarium. Or someone who can help children learn knot tying or the techniques of wildlife photography. Ask parents to describe their occupations—what it's like to be an engineer, police officer, auto mechanic, veterinarian, or

---

FREE RESOURCE ON PARENT INVOLVEMENT

A free publication from the U.S. Department of Education lists ideas you can share with parents on how they can become more involved. This publication emerged from a vigorous parent involvement effort that the department launched in 1995 called "America Goes Back to School: A Place for Families and the Community." Print out a free copy of the resource guide "America Goes Back to School" at www.ed.gov. (Enter the document title in the site's search field to access a printer-friendly file.)

CONTROLLING UNANNOUNCED VISITS

One teacher writes this note:

"We have set aside Wednesday morning as a special time for parents to visit. We will have some adult-sized chairs for you at the back of the room. Feel free to come in. A rough weekly schedule and some observation guidelines will be placed next to the chairs. If you have any specific questions, please make an appointment with me because I will continue working with the students throughout the morning. We look forward to sharing our school day with you. Hope to see you at school."

rancher. Are there parents who could help students understand different cultures and customs? Don't let these valuable resources go untapped; use every opportunity to enrich your students' education and involve parents in the process.

Parent instructors not only supplement the curriculum; they also serve as important role models for students—as career role models and as parenting role models for when students themselves are in a position to become parent instructors.

Some teachers set aside one day a month as mini-course day, organizing the day around various parent instructors who come to share their hobbies, talents, and skills. Other teachers find that occasional Friday afternoons are a good time to offer these enrichment activities.

One interesting variation on the parents-as-instructors idea is an enrichment program that exposes children to community experts in many different fields. Such programs are spreading like wildfire across the country. In Moundsville, West Virginia, the program is called Kids' Kollege; it's YMCA University in Agoura Hills, California; Kids College in La Crescent, Minnesota; and

Kampus Kids in Cameron, West Virginia. But no matter what it's called, the program basically features students selecting enrichment courses from a wide variety taught by parents, teachers, and other community members.

Among the 26 classes featured recently in Cameron were Fun with Chemistry, Knights in Armor, Native American Culture, Driving an 18 Wheeler, Dog Grooming, and Learning Russian. The more than 100 volunteers included parents, local high school students, community members, and teachers. It's an annual event that solidifies an entire community. And parents play the most significant role in planning and organizing the event.

In La Crescent, Minnesota, classes from Cow Milking 101 to Introduction to Careers in Television News give students "a chance to make the connection between the skills they learn in school and the skills they'll need for real-world careers," says teacher Scott Critzer.

"Our program gives students unique learning opportunities, provides teachers with alternative teaching topics, and increases parent involvement," explains YMCA University creator Cynthia Davidson.

"AIDE-ING" IN EDUCATION: PARENTS ENRICH CURRICULUM

Looking for "a new kind of parent involvement," the late Madeline Hunter realized that students' parents had much to offer and could enrich the curriculum beyond what even the most competent and committed professional staff could do. So, as principal of the UCLA laboratory school, she developed a program to enrich and extend the curriculum through volunteers who shared career expertise, hobbies and crafts, and cultural knowledge.

Hunter's "Par-aide in Education" program featured two important components: careful soliciting of parent information and presenters, and training of the parent presenters. First, Hunter and her teachers sent a letter to all parents inviting them to participate (see the sample on page 245). Then, they invited the parents who responded to a two-hour training and information session. Here,

teachers modeled sample lessons for the parents and gave them basic information on how to plan a lesson or activity (see the sample on page 246).

Further, a par-aide coordinator (teacher with some release time) helped parents plan their lessons and observed the actual presentations. Afterward, the coordinator gave parents feedback on what went well and tips for improving.

Hunter reported that everyone involved, including the students, was enthusiastic about the program. In fact, several parents decided to earn their teaching certificate as a result of their work as a par-aide.

"These 'riches' can be made available to students in any school," she wrote, "regardless of budget, school organization, methods, material or pupil-teacher ratio."

Sample Letter to Parents

Dear Parent,

We are anxious to take advantage of your very considerable talents, abilities, and interests in order to increase the richness of your child's program. As a result, we are initiating "Par-aide (Parent Aide) in Education" and, with parents joining us to augment the power of our instructional resources, are creating another "first" for education. You are busy people, but many of you already have indicated your eagerness to contribute your time and talents to the success of your child's education. We would like to poll your interest and availability for participation in one of three areas. In no way is this an obligation of a parent, just an opportunity.

Your contribution would be to list your name as a possible source of assistance at the time of need. If you wish to increase your involvement and make your child's school richer through your participation, please return the tear-off below. After we receive your reply, we will schedule a meeting to give you additional information. Indication of interest in no way commits you to the program.

Sincerely yours,

I am interested in learning more about the areas checked. I understand that this response does not commit me to participation in the program.

☐ **I. Knowing and valuing cultural differences**

My special cultural interest is _____. I could contribute to:

_____customs, _____folklore and literature, _____art, _____cooking, _____history, _____geography, _____special events and festivals, _____beliefs and religions, _____music, _____other: _____

☐ **II. Arts, crafts, and hobbies**

I could share my interests in

_____

_____

☐ **III. The world of work**

I could tell about

_____

_____

☐ **IV. An extra hand at school** (e.g., clerical work, preparation of games, materials, puzzles, charts, chaperoning field trips, etc.) I would be willing to

_____

Child's name: _____

Parent's or Guardian's name: _____ _____
                                            (Printed Name)   (Signature)

Excerpts from "Join the 'Par-aide' in Education" by M. Hunter. *Educational Leadership* 47, no. 2 (1959): 39. Used by permission of the Association for Supervision and Curriculum Development. Copyright © 1989 ASCD. All rights reserved.

Sample Format for a Parent Presentation

Your plan:	You might do or say:
1. Developing anticipatory set The teacher will get students ready and introduce you. Watch to see how the teacher: gains attention of the group, prepares students for your presentation, sets behavioral and content expectations.	Use some of those same signals and techniques when you work with the group.
2. Stating objective The students will know what they are going to do. After your presentation, students will: answer questions, ask questions, prepare/make/taste product demonstrated.	"Listen (watch) carefully, I'm going to tell you about _____. When I finish, I will ask questions so you will know how much you have learned." "You will be able to prepare some _____." "You will have a chance to make _____." "You will all play the game of _____." "I will answer your questions about what I have told you/demonstrated."
3. Purpose/meaning Why is your presentation important? Information and/or demonstration: • will help students value cultural differences and similarities • enables students to create/make a product, play a game, sing a song • Encourages students to increase their knowledge of occupation presented	"The information I give you (the things I tell you about) will help you see how we have benefited from this culture and the ways it's different from/similar to our own culture." "After we do this together, you will be able to do it at home for your family." "When I finish, you may want to read further about _____. I can give you some references."
4. Input Give information through: lecture, pictures, film, demonstration, display, charts, diagrams, response to questions.	Explain, describe, show. Include references, such as books, museums, trips, and programs, that students can use for added information. Provide or have students write down a list of supplies or ingredients for product demonstrated.
5. Modeling You show by doing or by showing examples of: craft, music, costumes, games, art, dance, things used in occupation.	"These are the special tools/ingredients/costumes used by the people of _____ when they _____." "Watch carefully while I show you how to _____."
6. Checking for understanding • Ask questions to check for understanding. • Help students identify similarities/differences between another culture and ours. • Determine if students can tell steps in procedure demonstrated. • Respond to students' questions.	"You have listened well. Now raise your hand if you know the answer to this question." Give the students knowledge of how well they did: "You really remembered. That's just right." If the answer is incorrect, maintain the student's dignity: "I can see how that may have been confusing. Let me make it more clear." "Let's list some ways we're the same/different." "Let's review now. What will you do first?" "That's a good question. I didn't cover it." or "You're really thinking about it. As I said _____."
7. Ending the lesson Finish with good feeling tone and help students move to next assignment by: • acknowledging good attending • reinforcing good questions asked • expressing your pleasure in talking to/with them • turning class back to the teacher	"I've enjoyed talking with you and answering your questions." "You've learned very quickly." "You've listened well and asked many good questions. It has been a pleasure to be with you." "Now it's time for your teacher to give you directions for your next activity."

Excerpts from "Join the 'Par-aide' in Education" by M. Hunter. *Educational Leadership* 47, no. 2 (1989): 40, Used by permission of the Association for Supervision and Curriculum Development. Copyright © 1989 ASCD. All rights reserved.

PARENTS CONTRIBUTE EXPERTISE

When my daughter Nora's teachers learned that her biologist dad had recently returned from a trip to the Galápagos Islands, they wasted no time in scheduling a special slide show and program. Like most parents, Nora's dad simply had to be asked, and he was more than willing to share his expertise.

When her daughter was in elementary school, professional writer and editor Janet Brydon spent at least one day per week in school as a writer's workshop volunteer.

"The first time I went into school I was really surprised at what's involved in working with children," says Brydon. "Teachers spend an incredible amount of time doing things for students, much of it on their own time. Teachers can't do it all, although many try. That's where volunteers come in."

Parent Volunteers As many teachers have already discovered, parent volunteers represent a valuable classroom resource. Extra hands, hearts, and ideas can only benefit students and make the tough job of teaching a little bit easier. In addition to the actual practices and volunteer programs highlighted in this section, here are some ideas for how you might involve parents in your classroom. (Please check privacy laws and distinct regulations regarding volunteers before offering these assignments.)

✔ **Tutors**: With individuals or small groups, parents can listen to children read, give spelling words, play math games, read aloud, or help out at learning centers.

✔ **Aides**: Parents can supervise individual reading time, project time, or other independent work periods.

✔ **Field trip assistants**: Let parents organize some of your field trips as well as going along to help.

✔ **Room mothers and fathers**: Have parents help with special parties and school activities.

✔ **Lunchtime and playtime supervisors**.

✔ **Clerical helpers**: They can photocopy materials, make teaching aids, help type or edit class newsletters, correct papers, and help with record keeping. (Parents shouldn't have access to confidential information about other children, however.)

✔ **Room coordinators**: With an active volunteer program, you'll need someone to juggle schedules, make assignments, and find last-minute replacements when necessary.

✔ **Presenters**: Let parents share their special expertise and knowledge with students in classroom demonstrations, workshops, and programs.

And don't forget that volunteering can occur after school hours, too. Parents who work full time can become involved by helping out at home: cutting out bulletin-board displays, counting soup can labels to exchange for school computers, calling other parents to invite them to school activities, and so on. They can volunteer in the evenings or on weekends as field trip chaperones, organizers of school activities, members of planning teams, and more. The contributions of these after-school volunteers are just as valuable as any others.

The first step is to solicit volunteers. Research shows that parents are more likely to volunteer if they know the teacher, have been to school and inside the classroom already, and receive regular communication from their child's teacher. And don't just limit yourself to parents.

Here are several good ways to seek volunteers:

✔ Ask for parent volunteers during parent conferences.

✔ Send home a letter requesting volunteers.

✔ Call and personally invite several parents to do a specific task.

✔ Ask parents already volunteering to convince other parents to get involved

✔ Recruit at local senior centers.

✔ Tie volunteering to community service projects at nearby high schools (cross-age tutoring, for example).

There are many roles volunteers can play at school. But no matter how you involve them, don't forget that they will need training and guidance. You'll want to brief them on your teaching goals and strategies, the type of classroom climate you are trying to create, and your expectations for them. Volunteers who work directly with children will need training in such areas as how to model difficult tasks, how to verbally encourage children, and how to avoid unintentional put-downs.

Also, show volunteers the ropes. Is there a special place to park? Can they use the teachers' lounge? Do they check in at the office? Should they call if they'll be late? Adapt your own guidelines for volunteers from the list on page 250.

It's also important to give your volunteers choices about what they'd like to do. Some parents are nervous about tutoring children and would rather make photocopies, while others hate machines and want to be with children. Like anyone else, volunteers do best at what they like best.

Tap your volunteers' preferences with a form like the one on page 251.

Keep in mind that problems may occasionally arise. Personalities may clash, volunteers may forget to follow the guidelines, feelings may get hurt. But based on our experience in Marshall County and the experiences of teachers nationwide, the benefits far outweigh the problems. Keep problems to a bare minimum by remembering that *you*:

1. make decisions concerning classwork.
2. assign and present all classwork and homework.
3. grade and/or evaluate all student work.
4. diagnose student needs.
5. discipline students.

Beyond that, just try to keep the lines of communication open. Urge volunteers and colleagues to talk about small problems before they fester into larger ones.

WINNING OVER PARENTS

Asking parents to volunteer also gives you the chance to establish better relationships with "difficult" parents. Just ask Sandy Spaulding of Sacramento, California.

"After blistering phone calls and confrontations with the father of one fifth grader, my partner and I decided this father needed to feel that he had something to contribute, that he was needed and accepted. That's when the idea of volunteering occurred to us."

Capitalizing on the parent's occupation as a computer repairman, Spaulding asked him to help the students learn to use some recently donated used computers. Immediately, she reports, he responded with a big grin, obviously pleased at having been asked.

"The help with the computers never materialized," she continues, "but this parent became a fully supportive ally of the teachers at our school. He even volunteered to donate all the food and cooking equipment (through his employer) for a fund-raiser pancake breakfast that enabled our fifth graders to take an overnight trip."

Finally, we must acknowledge our volunteers' contributions. Thank-you letters from teachers and students, volunteer pins and small gifts, certificates and plaques, banners displayed at school, and luncheons or banquets in their honor are among the ways that schools recognize their volunteers.

Do's and Don'ts Relationships with parent volunteers can sometimes be tricky. But the benefits are worth the time it takes to establish good working relationships. Here, Laurie Borger, Susie Davis, Mary Helen Ratje, Kathy Wesley, and Jackie Huff offer tips for getting (and keeping) parent volunteers and advice for avoiding pitfalls:

✔ **Do** show appreciation that someone is there to help you. Remember that busy parents are giving up their time to improve their children's education and facilitate your teaching. A kind word or simple "thanks" goes a long way.
✔ **Do** capitalize on the eagerness of primary students' parents. These parents are especially receptive to invitations to help, and once they develop the volunteering habit, they keep coming back year after year.

✔ **Do** make a special effort to communicate with parents who speak little English. Making sure that key communications are understood by parents is critical. You might enlist the help of a bilingual parent as a communication coordinator for notices such as field trips, early dismissals, and scheduling parent conferences. School personnel may also be able to assist with translating important communications into students' home languages.

✔ **Do** help parents feel less intimidated by asking them to call you by your first name. This shows parents that you consider them an equal partner in their child's education. Many parents, especially in economically disadvantaged areas, feel intimidated by schools. The simple gesture of using first names helps them feel more at ease.

✔ **Do** plan ahead so there is always something for volunteers to do. If they come in and there's nothing to do, you're going to lose them.

✔ **Do** encourage volunteers to call when they can't make it, and you call them if you don't need them that day. Both parties need to be reliable partners.

✔ **Do** remember that parents have special knowledge to share. One student's mother and grandmother came to school to make tortillas for the class. Another mother came to do a presentation on her native India.

✔ **Do** keep commitment high by sending home reminders about volunteering, at least until firm habits are established. I remind my volunteers every Friday in a folder I send home with each child. And I personalize the reminder by tying it to specific children. I might write something like, "Pete and Becky are looking forward to working with you on Tuesday." Parents hate to disappoint children.

✔ **Do** give volunteers options. We all get tired of doing the same thing. Our volunteers can choose to tutor students, create bulletin boards, photocopy materials, make games and activities, read to kids, or take them to the cafeteria at lunchtime.

✔ **Do** take time to get to know your volunteers. Talk to them, ask about their families. This is especially important if you are working with minority parents or those who speak English as a second language. Parents are more committed to someone they view as a friend.

✔ **Don't** sit back and wait for volunteers to come to you. Most parents will do what they can if you make them feel needed and welcome.

✔ **Don't** permit volunteers to bring preschoolers with them unless your school has special arrangements. Babies and toddlers can be distracting to everyone.

A VOLUNTEER PROGRAM IN ACTION

In my home district of Marshall County, West Virginia, an advisory team of parents, teachers, community members, and administrators has developed a school-volunteer program used in each of the county's 11 elementary schools. The individual schools adapt the program to their own needs.

At Cameron Elementary, for example, teachers indicate early in the year the types of volunteer help they'd like. Volunteers are solicited through letters sent home and contacts made by teachers. The volunteers indicate their work preferences on a special form (see page 251), then a program coordinator matches volunteers with teachers. (These arrangements are flexible and easily changed.)

Volunteers are invited to an orientation meeting, where they meet the principal and the coordinator of volunteers for that school (a "volunteer" position itself, which is filled by parents at some schools and teachers at others). They hear tips and advice from experienced volunteers, and they receive and discuss a list of guidelines for volunteers.

Once "on the job," the volunteers sign in when they come to school, then go directly to their assigned areas. Teachers or staff members assign tasks and duties and work out weekly schedules with their volunteers.

Cameron Elementary values its volunteers and expresses appreciation in many ways. The PTA pays for cafeteria lunches for those volunteers who work a full day. Teachers give their volunteers small Christmas gifts and host a catered luncheon at the end of the school year.

Several loyal parent volunteers have followed their children to Cameron Junior/Senior High School, where they help teachers photocopy and produce classroom materials.

Guidelines for Volunteers

**Thank you for sharing your time and talents with us here at _____.
We have developed some guidelines that will help you help students and teachers. Please feel
free to talk to the teachers you are working with, or contact _____
if you have any questions or concerns.**

1. Confidentiality: All information concerning students is strictly confidential and should not be shared with others.

2. Please call the school, and leave a message with the secretary if you are coming late or will be absent.

3. Please leave preschoolers at home. Try alternating babysitting with other volunteers.

4. Attire should be neat, clean, and comfortable—appropriate for an elementary school setting.

5. Please park at _____
_____
_____

6. Feel free to use the staff restrooms and the lounge facilities.

7. Volunteers need to be in the vicinity of a teacher when working with students. (This is a law in many states.)

8. Please avoid interrupting teachers while they are teaching. Questions and concerns can be addressed following instructional time.

9. Teachers will deal with discipline issues. Please bring any behavior problems to the attention of the teacher. It is inappropriate for volunteers to discipline students verbally or any other way.

10. Don't repeat the stories and personal information that students share with you. Do notify the teacher if a student tells you information that could affect his or her health or well-being.

11. Ask other volunteers or teachers for help when you need it.

12. You can get your assignments from _____
_____
_____

13. No political or religious preferences may be advocated.

14. The use of drugs, alcohol, and tobacco is prohibited.

Volunteer Preference and Availability

1. **Name:** _____

2. **Phone (day):**_____ **(evening):**_____

3. **Child's name and grade, if attending school:** _____

4. **Day or days available:** _____

5. **Time available:** _____

6. **Area preference. (Please rank from 1 to 3. We will do our best to place you where requested.)**

_____ **Kindergarten**	_____ **Office**	_____ **Special Education**
_____ **First Grade**	_____ **Gym**	_____ **Floater (wherever most needed)**
_____ **Second Grade**	_____ **Music**	
_____ **Third Grade**	_____ **Speech**	
_____ **Fourth Grade**	_____ **Guidance Counselor**	
_____ **Fifth Grade**	_____ **Reading Specialist**	
_____ **Sixth Grade**	_____ **Library**	

Other (please specify) _____

7. **Work preference. (Please rank from 1 to 3. We will do our best to place you where requested.)**

    Assist with:

_____ **Materials and Lessons**	_____ **Bulletin-board Construction**
_____ **Seatwork Monitoring**	_____ **Tutoring**
_____ **Videotaping**	_____ **Yearbook Layout**
_____ **Storytime Reading**	_____ **Word Processing**
_____ **Copying/Machine Operating**	_____ **Anything Needed**

✔ **Don't** expect volunteers to come to school during odd times of the day. While some parents who work close to the school may be able to help on a lunch hour, it's often more convenient for parents to come at the beginning or end of the day. For example, a mother who picks up her daughter after school once a week for gymnastics lessons may be able to come an hour early each week to help her child's teacher with special projects.

✔ **Don't** ask volunteers to tutor their own children, either individually or in groups. Most children do best working with volunteers other than their parents. Occasionally, some children are too distracted to have a parent even working in the same room. Most learn to adapt, but if they don't, assign the volunteer elsewhere.

✔ **Don't** have volunteers working directly with children if you don't feel absolutely comfortable about it. In one first-grade classroom, a teacher overheard a volunteer tutor telling a little boy, "You really can't read, can you?" The teacher quickly reassigned the well-meaning volunteer to other jobs where her unintentional remarks couldn't hurt.

✔ **Don't** put volunteers on the defensive. If a problem develops—if, for example, parents are preferential to their own children or overstep their bounds with you or the school staff—sit down and talk about it in a tactful, delicate way.

Parents Helping With Homework

Homework is often the most visible proof parents have of their child's learning and your teaching. It is the most common link between home and school life. In fact, it's probably the best way to involve parents, according to Johns Hopkins researcher Joyce Epstein, who directs the National Network of Partnership Schools and the Center on School, Family, and Community Partnerships.

"I'd like to see more attention to the type of involvement parents want most: how to work with their own child at home in ways that help the student succeed and that keep the parents as partners in their children's education across the grades," Epstein writes.

Epstein's definition of homework goes far beyond the traditional worksheets or assignments that students complete alone. She extends the definition to include "interactive activities shared with others at home or in the community, linking schoolwork to real life." Further, she defines "help at home" as "encouraging, listening, reacting, praising, guiding, monitoring, and discussing—not 'teaching' school subjects."

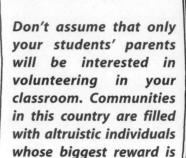

Don't assume that only your students' parents will be interested in volunteering in your classroom. Communities in this country are filled with altruistic individuals whose biggest reward is personal satisfaction.

ONE TEACHER'S EXPERIENCE

"My parent volunteers do all kinds of enriching activities with the children—more than I could do with 25 kindergartners and no aide," says Kathy Wesley of Port Angeles, Washington. "Working one-on-one or in groups of six, they play alphabet bingo, matching games, and other activities that reinforce what I'm trying to teach.

"I have volunteers for one hour every day of the week. Some parents even take off work to help out, and in our lower-middle-class area that means a lot. Parents also help

out twice a week in our computer lab, helping the children work programs that reinforce beginning sounds, number identification, and simple counting.

"I always urge my parents to ask questions if they don't understand something, and I tell them not to worry about things going wrong. I don't give them anything so critical that the class would fall apart if things went wrong.

"I can't imagine doing without parents in the classroom. They love volunteering, and the kids love them being there."

Heeding the abundant evidence that parents want to know how to help their children at home, Epstein and her colleagues at the Center on School, Family, and Community Partnerships developed an interactive homework process called Teachers Involve Parents in Schoolwork (TIPS). Epstein explains that TIPS homework assignments "require students to talk to someone at home about something interesting that they are learning in class."

For example, consider the TIPS language arts activity on pages 256 and 257. Here, students interview their parents about hairstyles of the past. They then write a paragraph based on the information they gather, and they share this paragraph with parents. Later, they develop another topic for a parent interview, asking questions and recording answers.

A TIPS math activity (pages 258 to 259) requires students to explain and demonstrate

---

TIPS FOR USING TIPS

- Introduce the TIPS process to students (through class discussions) and to parents (at an open house, parent conferences, or with a letter), making sure each understands that the intent of the process is not only to improve students' skills and abilities but also to involve children and their parents in an ongoing dialogue about learning.
- Adapt the activity prototypes to your curriculum and your students' skills and grade level.
- Allow children to complete the TIPS assignments with a grandparent, older sibling, or other caretaker if a parent is unavailable.
- Use a particular color of paper for TIPS activities, so they are immediately recognizable.
- Print assignments on two sides of a page so there's only one piece of paper to keep track of.
- Assign TIPS on Fridays, so families have more time to complete the activities.
- Realize that not every homework assignment has to be a TIPS activity, but schedule TIPS activities regularly enough to keep parents and children talking about schoolwork and to keep parents apprised of their children's work and progress.

OBTAINING TIPS MATERIALS

Currently, the TIPS program for elementary grades (K–5) includes a teacher's manual and prototype activities for math and science. There is a separate middle-grades manual and prototype activities in science, math, health, and language arts for grades 6 through 8. For more information, or to obtain these modestly priced materials, contact the Publications Department, Center on School, Family, and Community Partnerships, Johns Hopkins University, 3003 North Charles St., Ste. 200, Baltimore, MD 21218; (410) 516-8808. www.csos.jhu.edu/p2000.

---

graphs and graphing techniques. It also asks students to solicit and record a family member's opinion about the importance of graphs.

Primary students can practice grouping and classification with family members by using the TIPS Activity on pages 260 and 261.

These three examples illustrate the important features of any TIPS activity:
✔ clearly stated topic, skills, and objectives, stated in brief note signed by student
✔ list of materials needed (always common and inexpensive)
✔ clearly stated procedures
✔ discussion component that encourages children to talk about what they're learning and apply and analyze their skills
✔ invitation (and space) for parents to share observations, comments, and questions
✔ request for parent signature

In a true partnership between home and school, Epstein explains, educators say, "I cannot do my job without the help of my students' families and the support of this community," and parents say, "I really need to

PARENTS RUN A WRITING CLUB

"Parent volunteers figured prominently in the after-school writing club we established for our second graders," reports Wenda Clement of Indiana. "We sent a letter home inviting all second graders and their parents to participate. Forty-five children and 25 adults responded.

"First we made a videotape of one of our second-grade teachers demonstrating the writing process she teaches to children. Then we used the video to train our volunteers prior to their first session with the students.

"For seven weeks the young writers and their volunteer mentors spread out on the cafeteria tables with paper, markers, scissors, and glue. When a writer said, 'I'm done,' the adult helper read the text out loud so the writer could hear his or her own words. The volunteers then asked questions to help stimulate the children's thinking, then allowed more free writing time.

"After some initial editing done by the writers, the adult helpers became editors. The volunteers helped students make the necessary corrections and encouraged them to use a dictionary and other editing tools. After the students corrected everything they could, the volunteers completed the corrections and discussed them with the writers. Adults also typed stories on the computer for those students who wanted printed stories.

"During an author-sharing session presented to the entire second grade, several of the adult helpers came to bask in the success and joy of the young writers. Our volunteers were just as enthusiastic about our Quill Club as the students, and many asked to sign up for next year. Even our school's PTO got involved, providing hamburgers and chips for the kids."

know what is happening in school in order to help my child."

In a true partnership, she continues, teachers and administrators create family-like schools, and parents create "school-like families." School-like families "reinforce the importance of school, homework, and activities that build student skills and feelings of success. Family-like schools "recognize each child's individuality and make each child feel special and included."

The goal, and one to which we all must aspire, Epstein concludes, is "a caring educational environment that requires educational excellence, good communications, and productive interactions involving school, family, and community."

Parents as Decision Makers

In this role, parents are actually involved in running schools. Most often, this involvement occurs on site-based school improvement councils or decision-making teams. Such teams are mandated in some states and practiced voluntarily in others.

Unless you serve on such a committee, you may not have direct contact with these parents. But you can encourage your parent volunteers to become involved in such decision-making bodies. Your own volunteers, learning firsthand about schools and schooling, are in a perfect position to serve effectively as decision makers. And you are training them!

Site management teams help determine curriculum, plan school activities, set academic goals, organize parent and community outreach programs, and even hire administrators.

One prominent example of parents as decision makers is the school planning and management team approach advocated by James Comer, associate dean of the Yale Medical School and director of Yale's School Development Program. Comer and colleagues at Yale's Child Study Center developed a program that brings teachers and parents together as natural allies.

Years ago, Comer explains, schools didn't have to work at such partnerships. "Teachers lived in the communities where they taught. They interacted daily with parents and other community members, and there was a 'natural transfer of authority' from home to school." Today, he adds, with greater geographical, economic, and social separation, parents and teachers don't always have the same sense of shared purpose or common values.

The Comer School Development Program was first implemented in 1968 in two New Haven, Connecticut, schools. Today, it is the model guiding many schools nationwide. It calls for parents, teachers, administrators, and other school staff to form management teams that develop comprehensive plans for school improvement. Parents have a direct influence on school activities, goals, and even staff development.

Magruder Primary School in Newport News, Virginia, is one of many schools to adopt the Comer Model. Magruder's School Planning and Management Team worked to improve communication among teachers, parents, and the community, identified staff-development needs, and reviewed and rewrote academic goals.

Former principal Michael Williams-Hickman describes the team's efforts this way: "We raised our expectations for everyone—students, parents, and teachers. Then we told one another exactly what we expected the outcomes to be. We wrote our goals and shared them. We praised every success, no matter how small. Our students know that we value them."

To learn more about Dr. Comer's work on parent and community involvement, see the listing of articles and resources developed by the George Lucas Educational Foundation available at http://glef.org/php/people.php?id=c502819.

Parents as Advocates

Parents as advocates work directly for local, state, and national policies and legislation to improve education and support students. Advocacy efforts range from voicing support at school-board meetings and voting for school bonds and levies to lobbying state and national legislators for programs that support students and learning.

Strong advocacy often grows out of direct involvement in classrooms and schools.

"I count on parent support for ideas in the classroom, but I also count on their financial support," says Kathy Wesley. "Our district votes on a levy every two years, so if parents understand and experience first-hand the needs of schools, they're more supportive at the polls."

PARENTS SPEAK OUT

Sherrie Rogers of Port Angeles, Washington, represents a growing trend among parents. She doesn't sit back and wait to be asked. She volunteers her help each year to both of her sons' teachers.

"My whole focus is to make my kids realize that school is very important," Rogers explains. "This makes all the difference in the world in their education."

Dawn Beck of Pipersville, Pennsylvania, has no regular volunteering schedule, but she's always available when her son's teacher calls for help on special projects.

"The bottom line is, I love to see my son thriving and doing well. By being involved at school, I can help determine what goes on and what experiences he has. And I know my child is proud when I'm volunteering, even if he's too old to admit it." Beck adds, "The more I volunteer, the more my admiration grows for teachers and the more I appreciate their hard work."

I have covered four different ways that parents can be involved in their children's education and learning—as their children's teachers, as partners with teachers, as decision makers in schools, and as advocates for education policy. To this list, Johns Hopkins researcher Joyce Epstein would add two more types of parent involvement.

The first she calls "basic parenting obligations," and it includes the child-rearing skills and positive home conditions that enhance school learning. (For example, making sure that the child has enough sleep or making sure the child is supervised appropriately.) Epstein, who has studied parent involvement extensively and developed programs to involve parents, notes that most schools have workshops on parenting skills and basic parenting obligations. The problem, she continues, is that the workshops frequently don't accommodate parents' busy schedules, so many parents don't come. Epstein suggests audio recordings, videotapes, newsletters, computerized phone messages, and cable TV shows as ways to reach more parents.

Another type of involvement Epstein discusses is the "basic obligations of schools," which she describes as the "communications from school to home about school programs and children's progress." These communications include such things as newsletters, parent conferences, letters to parents, radio and television promotions about school events, and so on. They are the focus of the next few sections.

"Hairy" Tales/Family Interview

Dear Family:

In language arts I am working on using information we gather from others to write explanations. For this assignment, I am comparing today's hairstyles with those of the past. I hope that you enjoy completing this activity with me. This assignment is due _____.

Sincerely, _____ (student's signature)

Family Interview

Find a family member to interview.

Who is it? ....

_____

Ask:

1. In what decade were you born? (1950s, 1960s, etc.)

_____

2. What types of hairstyles were popular when you were my age?

For boys: _____

For girls: _____

3. What hairstyle did you have when you were my age? _____

4. Did your family agree with your choice of hairstyle? _____

5. What is your favorite current hairstyle and Why? _____

6. What is your least favorite current hairstyle and why? _____

Ask your family member to show you a picture of a hairstyle from the past. Draw a picture of the hairstyle here.

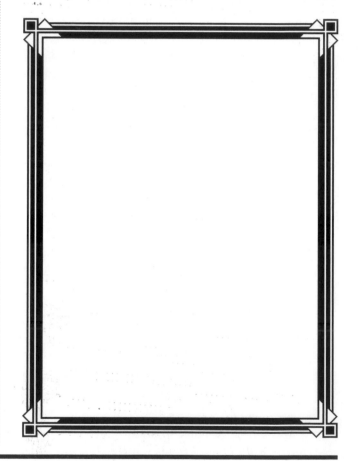

First Draft

Use the information from your interview to write a paragraph about hairstyles. Remember to:

- Give your paragraph a title.
- Be sure all of your sentences relate to your topic.
- Use descriptive words to help explain the ideas.
- If you compare hairstyles, tell how they are alike and how they are different.

Write your paragraph here.

Title: _____

_____

_____

_____

_____

_____

_____

• Read your paragraph aloud to your family member. Revise or add sentences if you need to.

Extension Activity

Select another topic for comparison—for example, clothing styles, ways to have fun, or rules at home and school. What topic did you choose? _____

Next to each Q line, write a question about this topic. Use your questions to interview your family member. Write the family member's answer next to each A line.

1. Q: _____

   A: _____

2. Q: _____

   A: _____

3. Q: _____

   A: _____

Home-to-School Connection

Dear Parent/Guardian:

Your comments about your child's work in this activity are important. Please write yes or no for each statement:

_____ My child understood the homework and was able to discuss it.

_____ My child and I enjoyed this activity.

_____ This assignment helps me understand what my child is learning in language arts.

Other comments: _____

_____

Parent signature: _____

"Hairy Tales" by J. L. Epstein, K. C. Salinas, and Vivian Jackson. *Teachers Involve Parents in Schoolwork (TIPS): Interactive Homework for the Middle Grades.* Baltimore, MD: Johns Hopkins University, Center on School, Family, and Community Partnerships, 1995. (Adapted from middle grades TIPS assignment for use in elementary grades.)

Math Graphs

Dear Family:

My class is learning how to read, understand, and create graphs. This activity will let me show you what I know about graphs. We can talk about why graphs are important. This assignment is due

_____.

Sincerely, _____ (student's signature)

Look This Over
Study the graph. Explain the answers to a parent.

How many circles? (3)

How many squares? (1)

How many rectangles? (4)

How many triangles? (2)

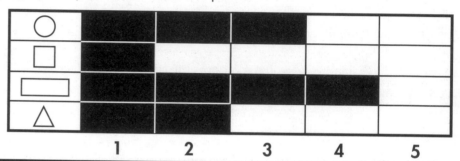

Now Try This
Color the graph to show how many examples there are of each object. Show a parent how you do this.

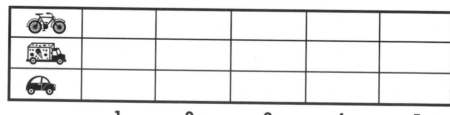

If you need some help, ask a parent to go over the examples with you. When you understand, explain to your parent what you did.

Practice Section
Study the graph and answer the questions.

1. How many sunny days? ___
2. How many rainy days? ___
3. How many cloudy days? ___
4. How many snowy days? ___
5. Snowy + cloudy = ___

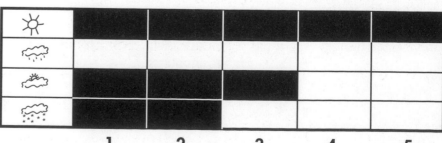

More Practice   Fill in the graph and answer the questions.

	1	2	3	4	5	6	7	8
🐖								
🐱								
🐰								

1. How many cats? ____   **3.** How many pigs? ____

2. How many rabbits? ____   **4.** How many more pigs than cats? ____

Answer to Now Try This

	1	2	3	4	5
🚲	■	■	■	■	
🚚	■	■	■		
🚗	■	■			

Let's Find Out

DISCUSS: Why do you think graphs are important?

MY IDEA: _____

_____

MY FAMILY MEMBER'S IDEA: _____

_____

Home-to-School Connection: Parent Observation

Dear Parent/Guardian:

How well do you think your child understands this skill?

___ **1.** My child seems to understand this skill.

___ **2.** Please check work. My child needs some help on this, but seems to understand.

___ **3.** Please help. My child still needs instruction on this skill.

___ **4.** Please note (add your comments here): _____

_____

Parent signature: _____

"Math Graphs" by J. L. Epstein and K. C. Salinas. *Teachers Involve Parents in Schoolwork (TIPS): Interactive Homework for the Elementary Grades.* Baltimore, MD: Johns Hopkins University, Center on School, Family, and Community Partnerships, 1992.

Grouping ABC's and Animals

Dear Family:

In science we are learning about systems of classification. This activity asks me to develop a classification system. I hope that you enjoy completing this activity with me. This assignment is due:

_____.

Sincerely, _____ (student's signature)

Procedure

1. Print the entire alphabet in capital letters here:

_____

2. Make up a rule for separating all the letters of the alphabet into three groups. Write your rule here:

_____

3. Below, give each group a title, then list the letters in each group under the title.

Group 1:	Group 2:	Group 3:

Family Interview

Who are you interviewing? _____

Explain your system of alphabet classification to a family member, then ask: Can you think of a different rule to make three groups out of all the letters of the alphabet? Write your family member's rule, group titles, and letters:

Group 1:	Group 2:	Group 3:

Try This!

You are a scientist who has been asked to classify a dog, a cat, a fish, a butterfly, a moth, and a turtle. Would you put them all in the same group or in different groups?

1. Explain your classification system for these animals.

I would group these animals into _____ (how many?) groups called: _____

My reasons are:

2. Use the following chart to show which group each animal belongs to and explain why the animal is in that group.

	Group	Reason
dog		
cat		
fish		
butterfly		
moth		
turtle		

Family Interview

Who are you interviewing? _____

Ask your family member to name six other animals. Will these animals fit the classification system you used above or do you need new categories? Fill in the chart to show your answer.

Animal	Group	Reason

Home-to-School Connection

Dear Parent/Guardian:

Your comments about your child's work in this activity are important. Please write yes or no for each statement:

_____ **1.** My child understood the homework and was able to discuss it.

_____ **2.** My child and I enjoyed this activity.

_____ **3.** This assignment helps me understand what my child is learning in science.

Other comments: _____

_____

Parent signature: _____

"Grouping ABC's and Animals" by J. L. Epstein, K. C. Salinas, and Vivian Jackson. *Teachers Involve Parents in Schoolwork (TIPS): Interactive Homework for the Middle Grades.* Baltimore, MD: Johns Hopkins University, Center on School, Family, and Community Partnerships, 1995. (Adapted from middle grades TIPS assignment for use in elementary grades.)

❖ Parent Conference

The parent-teacher conference is recommended by expert elementary teachers as a critically important way to communicate with parents. Parents of grade-school children report that they want regular conferences with their children's teachers.

However, these face-to-face encounters have the potential for becoming emotionally charged. Often the participants are nervous; in many cases teachers and parents are sizing each other up. At best, it is difficult to skillfully direct a parent conference, especially for new teachers. It's somewhat analogous to the accountant's task of sitting down with tax clients. Sometimes they are happy with their returns; sometimes they're not.

Part accountant, part diplomat, part psychologist, part friend—but totally a professional. These are the roles you play when you meet with your students' parents. Your challenge is to make parents feel comfortable, show them how to get involved with their child's learning, and establish a working partnership.

The basic purpose of a conference is to inform parents of their children's progress and school performance. They get to ask questions, and you gain valuable insights into students' home lives. The conference also provides a great opportunity to solicit classroom volunteers.

No two teachers conduct conferences the same way. Like teaching, conducting a conference includes elements of personal style. This section offers tips, ideas, and activities from a large sampling of professionals.

Planning the Conference

As with teaching, planning is critical to an effective conference. Here are some important steps to include:

✔ Decide whether the student will be part of the conference. (For tips on student-led conferences, see page 264.)

✔ Prepare a send-home that invites parents to meet with you, states the purpose of the conference, and lists potential times, including both afternoon and evening slots. Have parents call or send a note to reserve a time slot. Note: When divorced parents share custody, don't forget to invite both.

✔ Decide upon the goals for the conference (one or two will do).

✔ Prepare an agenda that you share with parents before the conference. Include such topics as your general impression of the child, his or her progress in each academic area, standardized test scores, your goals for the child in each content area, and strategies you will use to meet goals.

✔ Plan (and write down) questions to ask, points to make, and suggestions to offer.

✔ Take a moment to note some positives such as the child's strengths and recent accomplishments. Beginning the conference on a positive note immediately takes parents off the defensive and helps them listen to your concerns.

✔ Ask parents to bring to the conference a list of their child's strengths and weaknesses as they perceive them. (Include these parent observations on the reproducible parent-teacher conference form on page 265.)

✔ Prior to the conference, fill out the Teacher Observations section of the conference form on page 265 or simply take notes on the child's areas of strength and challenge. Develop reasonable actions to be taken and be ready to elicit parent input so that these actions can be informed and supported by the family.

✔ Collect samples of student work to display.

✔ Prepare to explain your goals and teaching strategies.

✔ Schedule enough time for questions and discussion.

✔ Pull together necessary materials such as a daily schedule of classroom activities, a checklist of skill areas and notes on student progress, sample work, test scores, and reports from other teachers where appropriate.

Arranging the Setting

Try making the conference area as comfortable as possible. Experienced teachers report that such amenities as adult-sized chairs; soft, relaxing music; and refreshments put parents as ease. Also, try to greet parents at the door and sit with them at a table or in chairs facing each other. (Never put the teacher's desk between yourself and parents.) If you provide paper and pens, parents can take notes to follow up on at home. And make sure you have a few activities for the younger siblings who invariably tag along.

Many teachers find it helpful to hang a "Conference in Progress" sign on the door to prevent interruptions. Further, many suggest setting a table of materials that parents can take home—for example, information on homework and grading policies, newsletters, suggestions for how to help children at home and at school, and invitations to school activities or parent-group meetings.

Conducting the Conference

First off, briefly review the agenda you prepared in advance. Then, communicate the specific information you have gathered about the child. Listen carefully to parents' responses, answer their questions, explain each point, and ask them if they can confirm your impressions. Set goals together for the child's future progress.

When you are delivering news about an academic or behavioral problem, author Susan Swap and others suggest certain strategies:

✔ Focus your comments and efforts only on things that can be changed.
✔ Limit the number of suggestions for improvement so that parents are not overwhelmed.
✔ Speak plainly and avoid jargon and euphemistic language.
✔ Be tactful, but not so tactful that you don't adequately communicate the problem.
✔ Ask for and listen to parents' reactions.
✔ Schedule a follow-up conference.

Conclude each conference by recommending specific steps parents or caregivers can take to help improve their child's education. You might also hand out a list of general suggestions such as the ones on pages 267 and 268. Thank parents for their interest and invite them to call, send a note or e-mail, or stop by after school if they wish to talk to you. Assure them that you want to keep the communication channels open all year.

Following Up

After each conference, take a few minutes to jot down the gist of what was said. Taking notes during the conference generally is not a good idea, because it can make parents uncomfortable and take your focus off active communication. However, limited time and other factors may make note taking during the conference both a benefit and a necessity.

Wisconsin teacher Alexis Ludewig makes a case for taking notes during the conference. She points out, "I've found that note taking indicates to the parent that you are taking what they say seriously. [Note taking is] another form of active listening and gives me the specific points to conclude the conference with a full summary where the parent can accept, add to, or refute. Also, in my school, conferences are often set up back-to-back so there isn't time to make notes between conferences. It is important to not forget key points and decisions so note-taking is really a must for me during the conference."

Remember to write down specific questions that parents want answered. List any commitments made by either you or the parents. Make follow-up calls or send notes, where necessary.

While the vast majority of encounters with parents are pleasant and productive, an exceptional few can lead to problems. We hate to acknowledge it, but we live in an age of litigation. For your own protection, keep a record of all personal contact you have with parents. This doesn't have to be anything more formal than a separate sheet of paper for each student that notes the date, nature, and outcome of any personal conference, letter, or telephone call. Better yet, keep a listing on your computer, where it's easily stored and retrieved. Not only does this record keeping help to protect you legally, it jogs your memory for any necessary actions or follow-ups.

Finally, evaluate your own performance. Were you well prepared? Was the atmosphere informal and friendly? Did you use time well? Did you begin on a positive note? Did you encourage parents to talk and offer suggestions? How could the conference have been improved? When it's all over, ask yourself what you have learned that will help you teach the child.

Learning From Experience

Most teachers have stories to tell about one or two particularly memorable parent conferences. Veteran Judy Smith shares an incident that taught her some valuable lessons. Here's what happened:

Smith had decided that one of her students should be retained, so she scheduled a conference with his parents. The only time they could meet her was before school. They arrived late, leaving Smith only 10 minutes to explain why she thought the child should be retained.

"So I hit them with the facts right away," she recalls. "They became angry and left angry. The bell had already rung, and the kids were waiting to get into the classroom. I was upset from the conference, but I had to control myself and have a nice day.

"I blew it," Smith continues. "It was my worst conference and my worst day of teaching ever!"

From the experience, Smith learned some valuable lessons that she passes on to others:

1. Never schedule a conference that important under time pressure.

2. Build up to telling parents you think their child should be retained—don't blurt it out all at once. "Now, we come to the conclusion together," says Smith, explaining how she first shows parents the evidence and talks about how difficult the next year will be for the child.

Inviting Students

Decide ahead of time whether you want to invite students to come with their parents. Opinions among veterans differ sharply in this respect, but many argue convincingly that having students present clears up a lot of misunderstandings and prevents situations where children tell parents one thing and teachers tell them something quite different.

At Central Park East School in New York City, teachers invite not only parents but as many family members as can come.

"The conference clears the tangle of misunderstandings between the school and the family," explains Deborah Meier, founder and former co-principal of this famous and successful "alternative" public school. Meier suggests that when there are disagreements, it's better to talk about them in the child's presence and let the child observe adults working out their differences.

Also, "[h]aving the child present makes it much harder for the adults to discuss the child in psychological terms," Meier states in an

ESTABLISHING FRIENDLY PARTNERSHIPS

To conduct successful conferences or work with parents in other capacities, establishing good rapport is critical. To be a friendly partner:

• Meet parents in a nonauthoritarian way.

• Sympathize and empathize.

• Try to see the child from the parents' view.

• Help parents feel good about themselves and their child.

• Be positive and enthusiastic.

• Let parents know that you are interested in their child as an individual— one who has strengths, weaknesses, and his or her own way of learning.

• Don't compare one child with another.

• Avoid getting too personal. If problems at home affect the child's behavior at school, report the behavior and ask parents if they have any ideas about the cause. But don't press.

• Respond to parents as individuals, realizing each has a unique personality and set of concerns.

• Try not to interrogate. People are more open if you don't put them on the defensive.

• Discuss, but never argue. And don't criticize.

• If parents need help with a problem, suggest ways they might solve it.

Sample Parent-Teacher Conference Form

Name of Child _____

Parent/Guardian _____

Date _____ **Grade** _____

Student Strengths	Parent/Guardian Observations	Teacher Observations
Areas for Improvement		

	Home	School
Action Plan		

interview. "As a parent, I cannot do anything about someone's psychological theories about my child. What I can do something about is homework, making sure my child comes to school on time, clarifying to the teacher what the child is confused about."

Dr. Dorothy Rich, founder and president of the Home and School Institute, also advocates inviting students. "I strongly suggest that, whenever possible, children be present at the conferences and included in on a team approach to making their school year successful," she says.

In some schools, teachers not only invite students, they ask them to direct the conference. "We believed that kids might be able to do a better job of reporting their progress than we could," explains second-grade teacher Nancy Litton. Litton and her colleagues at Wildwood Elementary School in Piedmont, California, offer these suggestions, based on their experiences with student-led conferences:

✔ Encourage students to select work samples to share at the conference. For example, you might list the major curricular areas and ask students to select something they've done in each area. Lianne Morrison's students generate lists of projects they've completed in several different subjects. Then individually, they choose which projects they'd like to share.

✔ Personalize your conference format. Although students direct the conferences,

the Wildwood teachers plan the specific activities. For example, fourth-grade teacher Bev Schmidt has parents observe unrehearsed group literature discussions, then she asks the students individually to share their portfolios with their parents. Nancy Litton, on the other hand, has her first graders read to their visitors for five minutes, play a math game, and compare several stories they've written.

✔ Model the process and allow students to practice directing their conferences. First-grade teacher Suzanne Latham does this by pretending to be a student and asking the children to play the role of the parents as she directs a practice conference.

✔ During the actual conferences, take the backseat. Let students do the talking and demonstrating.

✔ You can facilitate the conferences if you prepare visitors ahead of time. The Wildwood teachers write letters describing the process and benefits of student-directed conferences and suggesting ways the parents might respond. "I just remind them that if they sit back, are observant, and let the child take charge, they'll learn a lot," says Lianne Morrison.

What if parents want to discuss concerns and problems privately with teachers? The Wildwood teachers schedule "traditional" conferences in the fall and again whenever a parent or teacher desires one. The student-directed conferences are planned for spring, when students have developed a large body of work to select from and share.

What about the inevitable situation where a parent simply can't or won't attend the conference? Here, the Wildwood teachers allow students to invite another adult, or they ask another staff member to substitute for the parent. But to accommodate as many parents as possible, some of the teachers even allow for early morning (before school) conferences.

Helping Your Child at Home

Here are some suggestions for how you can help your child become a better learner and show that you care.

- Encourage your child and express your pride in his or her efforts and accomplishments.

- Make sure your child gets eight or nine hours of sleep each night.

- Keep your child healthy by providing:
  1. regular medical checkups, vision screenings, and booster shots
  2. a balanced diet
  3. regular exercise
  4. clean hair and fresh clothes

- Please notify me of any medical problems.

- Make sure your child has a good attendance record and arrives to school on time. Missing school means children fall behind in their work. They become anxious and frustrated when they can't keep up.

- Establish a time and place for studying. Give your child a quiet corner to read and do homework.

- Discuss homework assignments and discreetly monitor your child's progress. Offer praise or help when appropriate.

- Your child will regularly bring home completed papers and assignments for you to review. Ask to see these graded papers.

- Read to your child, and encourage him or her to read to you. Let your child see you reading. Remember: The best way to communicate the importance and value of reading is to read. Be a reading role model.

- Be an effective reading tutor by asking your child to find specific details in a passage, paraphrase a paragraph, or describe a character.

- Please stay in touch with me. I am happy to discuss any problems your child is having. Let's talk, and together we can try to find solutions.

I suggest the following enriching books and activities:

_____

_____

_____

_____

_____

_____

(teacher signature)

Thank you for your interest and concern. I appreciate your support!

Send-Home Sheet

Dear Parent:

Television has become another member of your family and mine; we eat meals near it, learn from it, and spend more time with it than with any single individual. Unfortunately, television is central in our children's lives—as tutor, baby-sitter, teacher, entertainer, and salesperson all rolled into one.

Has television grown so powerful we can no longer control it? No. But it very well might unless we act now to harness its influence and channel its awesome power. Television, like a potent drug, can either enhance or cripple a person's life. What can a parent do? Follow these guidelines—they will make a difference!

WHAT CAN YOU DO AT HOME?

Start now. Many children are already habitual TV viewers by the age of 2. Harmful viewing habits can be changed only by substituting new habits. Do a little at a time—some each day.

Put the TV in a little-used room. With the TV in an area away from the living room and other places where heavy family activity occurs, children will watch less and plan more what they watch.

Plan to have one night a week with the TV off. Meet as a family and pick a no-TV night. Decide whether you want to do things together or have time alone.

Avoid using the TV as a baby-sitter. You would not leave your child alone in the care of a stranger. A television cannot respond to a cry for help, nor can it tell when a child is frightened.

Plan ahead what to watch. With a TV viewing guide, decide what you and your kids will watch each night. Don't just turn on the set to see what's on.

Seek out programs made for kids. Help your children plan to watch programs designed for their ages, interests, and maturity.

Watch TV with your children. View their programs with them and help them evaluate what they're watching in light of your family's values and traditions.

Help kids distinguish between make-believe and real life on TV. Explain that terror and violence on TV shows is only acting and is not like real-life violence.

Discuss TV commercials selling junk food. Help young children see that ads are trying to persuade them to spend money by developing buying habits that could be unhealthy. Let your children help select nutritious family foods and snacks.

Use TV to start family activities. Make a list of TV-advertised products and see how many you have in the house. Watch different news programs the same night and see if all use the same lead stories. Play along with your favorite game show as a family, or play your own version with the TV set off. Do a TV-commercial product test and compare your results with theirs.

Find leisure activities besides TV. Watching TV is relaxing, but so is a good crossword puzzle or game of cards. If you break the TV habit, your child will have a better chance of avoiding an addiction. Buy a puzzle book to work on together or a model rocket to build together.

Read to your child. Start at an early age to help your child discover the magic in reading. Children of all ages enjoy being read to by their parents.

No need to try all these ideas at once. Start small by picking one you want to try and doing it. Post this list on your refrigerator and choose as a group one idea to try each week.

WHAT YOU AND SCHOOL CAN DO

Work with teachers and administrators. Support the use of quality educational television programs in school.

Acknowledge that appropriate TV viewing is a skill that can be learned. Bring in speakers from the PTA and local TV stations.

Let your feelings be known. Write newspapers, TV stations, networks, the FCC, and advertisers; tell them what you like and don't like.

_____
(teacher signature)

These ideas come from the Illinois State Board of Education and appeared in *Instructor*, March 1978.

Arranging Group Conferences

Many teachers have discovered the efficiency and effectiveness of group conferences. Bringing parents together in one large group accomplishes several purposes.

First, it saves time. Only once do you have to describe the direction and scope of your class activities, talk about individual learning styles, explain your strategies and goals for the year, describe curriculum materials, or explain grading policy.

Second, group conferences can help the more reluctant parents feel at home in school. An esprit de corps can develop among parents of classmates.

Group conferences are also a great place to describe how parents can help in school and to solicit volunteers. When parents see others volunteering, they'll be more willing to go along.

Group conferences can take many different forms.

Retired first-grade teacher Susie Davis scheduled a group conference before the first PTA

PARENT CONFERENCES:
SPECIAL CAUTIONS AND CONSIDERATIONS

Given the wide range of personalities and situations you'll deal with, occasional problems are inevitable. Parent-teacher conferences are fraught with potential pitfalls. To avoid them, heed this advice from experts Laurie Borger, Susie Davis, Dorothy Rich, Charles Edwards, Frank Garcia, and Jane Kelling:

- **Realize that your evaluations and impressions of their children affect many parents' own sense of self-worth**. Be sensitive! Remember, you are talking about their most valuable family resource—their family's future.

- **Know your school's policy regarding parent conferences**. If there isn't one, ask the front office staff to inform parents that they need to make an appointment for conferences. Make sure they understand that it is not appropriate to send a parent to your classroom unannounced during the school day.

- **Defuse explosive situations** by asking parents to be seated and by remaining calm and unemotional. (Your mood is contagious.) Let parents talk first so you can find out exactly what they are upset about. Then give your side of the story. If you are wrong, admit it. Let parents know that even if you disagree with them, you are interested in doing what is best for the child, just as they are.

- **Include the principal** if you expect problems beyond your expertise or jurisdiction.

- **Be sympathetic** in the face of mistrust or open hostility. Understand the fundamental fear most people have about placing their children in a "stranger's" hands for extended periods of time.

- **Communicate clearly** your position on an issue, and make sure listeners understand what you are and are not willing to do.

- **Don't wait until you meet with parents to alert them to a big problem**. Conferences are not the time for surprises. Use the telephone, send informal letters, and send classwork home regularly to let parents know how their children are progressing.

- When parents want to linger and chat, **politely end the conference** by summing up what's been said, then standing and moving toward the door. Make sure parents know how much time is allotted, especially when you schedule back-to-back conferences. Display a clock where everyone can see it, then occasionally note how much time is left.

- **Proceed cautiously in presenting information** collected by psychologists, social workers, nurses, and others. Always report who actually gathered the information.

- **Help caregivers understand achievement test results**. Explain that a child's scores make sense only when compared with his or her daily performance in school or at home. Achievement tests are only one measure of performance. Their purpose is to guide instruction, not evaluate students or teachers.

- When questioned about your grading policies, **explain how district or school policies influence how you assign grades**. What does a grade in a certain subject mean? Does an A mean that the child is working above grade level? Or does it mean that the child is completing all work perfectly, even if that work is below grade level?

meeting of each new school year. She called it an information meeting.

"This helped me to get to know parents right away," says Davis. "I explained my expectations and procedures, and I answered parents' questions." During the information meeting she also encouraged parents to volunteer as classroom helpers.

Eva Schmidler of Los Angeles designed a two-hour group conference incorporated into a regular school day. First, parents observe a language lesson and examine textbooks and supplementary materials. Then, while students attend physical education class, she talks to parents about children's special needs, overall academic goals, and how she hopes to instill in all children feelings of belonging and individual importance while they learn to function as a class unit. After students return to the classroom and have a snack with parents, an aide leads math, social studies, and reading activities for parents and children while Schmidler begins brief individual conferences. During the mini-conferences, parents see examples of their children's work, and they have the chance to ask questions in private.

Schmidler has found that after being in the classroom for group conferences, parents are more relaxed and have fewer anxieties when it is time for individual meetings.

Illinois teacher Jim Bellanca developed a two-hour "Parents Together Night," where parents get to know each other and the teacher. He discusses teacher and parent roles, expectations for academic performance, student responsibility, and social skills. Afterward, parents ask questions, sign up for an individual conference, sign up to volunteer, review texts and materials, look at learning centers, and chat.

Successful group conferences can be elaborately orchestrated activity sessions, or simple chat sessions centering on issues and concerns important to all. Either way, parents appreciate when we make a sincere effort to communicate and establish partnerships. And they respond in kind.

❖ Other Ways to Reach Parents

For those times when face-to-face conferences are not possible or necessary, you can communicate effectively in other ways. Telephones, e-mail, fax machines, class Web sites, newsletters, and handwritten notes are all good ways to maintain communication with parents.

Phone Home!

Telephone calls are the next best thing to being there. They are an effective tool for maintaining good school-to-home communication. And in this age of the answering machine, it's easier than ever to reach parents by phone.

Experienced teachers offer these telephoning tips:

✔ Make a practice of calling at least one parent a week to relay good news. Keep track of these "sunshine" calls and make sure each family receives at least two during the school year.

✔ Telephone etiquette demands that we address the person we are calling by name. Many students have different last names from their parents. Make sure you know the name before you call.

✔ Keep track of all calls made—good news or bad. Note the date, nature of the call, parents' responses, and outcomes. (A paper trail is very important for teachers today.)

✔ Make your first call to any home a positive one. One good idea is to make welcoming calls just before the new school year begins. Many kindergarten and first-grade teachers find that welcoming calls not only help establish good rapport with parents, they ease young students' anxieties about going to school.

✔ Call or e-mail those parents who don't respond to a written invitation for group or individual conferences. A call lets them know you're interested, and it could encourage those who are hesitant.

Recently, technology has enhanced the telephone's effectiveness as a bridge between home and school. In some schools, each teacher has an answering machine or voice mail. They record a brief daily message about learning activities, homework, and what parents can do to extend or support the learning. Then parents can call anytime from anywhere to receive the information.

In other schools, teachers can store a message in a computer, then direct the computer to call all or just some parents to deliver the recorded message. Often, the computer will keep track of calls completed so teachers know exactly who received the message.

The Written Word (Electronic or Otherwise)

E-mail, or electronic mail, is the technological development that truly gives meaning to the concept of a "global village." In seconds, we can communicate with people all over the world. Our world will never be the same. And neither will education. Through e-mail, students are corresponding with other students, soliciting information, and establishing mentorships with adults and professionals— worldwide. My own children and students think nothing of exchanging notes and information with students in South Africa. The ease of the exchange still leaves me awestruck.

For school-to-home communication, e-mail has vast potential. As more and more homes obtain computers and Internet access, e-mail is fast becoming an important link between teachers and parents. If you have e-mail access at school, take advantage of this incredible tool.

Other forms of writing are effective, too. Newsletters, monthly calendars, informal letters or notes, and interim reports are all ways teachers write to parents. In fact, writing is the most frequent form of communication between home and school.

Basically, there are two types of written messages sent home: messages for the whole class and messages about individual children. Most common among whole-class messages are the newsletter and the open letter to parents. Most common among the individual messages

are the personal note to parents and weekly or monthly progress reports.

Newsletters Surveys of parents consistently prove that they read school newsletters and consider them a useful source of information. Parents indicate that classroom newsletters are even more helpful.

You are limited only by your imagination in what a class newsletter can include. Here are some ideas to get you started:
- ✔ announcement of upcoming events
- ✔ invitations to class activities or open house
- ✔ reminders
- ✔ lists of items parents could collect or save for class projects
- ✔ thank-you notes to families who help out
- ✔ descriptions of study units and suggestions of ways parents can supplement units at home
- ✔ library schedule
- ✔ reprints of articles you think are important
- ✔ explanations of grading policies, standardized testing, and other means for assessing and evaluating performance
- ✔ explanations of behavior standards and consequences for misbehavior
- ✔ highlights of community resources such as a museum exhibit, play, concert, or television show
- ✔ children's writing and artwork
- ✔ news about classroom pets, trips, celebrations

The format can be as simple as a typed letter to parents or as complicated as a professional-looking document with headlines and columns. (Most word-processing software has the capabilities for producing multicolumn documents and other professional-looking features.) But no matter which format you use, use the same one each time so the newsletter becomes instantly recognizable. Keep the format clean and uncluttered. Headings help parents locate different topics, and simple graphics, such as boldface, help to summarize main points and capture attention.

Also consider:

✔ **Length:** Keep newsletters brief and to the point. One or two pages (back-to-back, so it's one piece of paper) are plenty for a weekly newsletter. More than that, and it becomes too expensive and time-consuming.

✔ **Tone:** Tone, in the literary sense, is the author's attitude. Newsletters project an image of you and your class. What attitude do you want to convey? Dignified and serious? Whimsical and playful? Humorous? Proud and full of school spirit? Child-oriented? Solid as a rock? Caring and responsive? These and other images are created by the words you use and the way your newsletter looks in content, format, and neatness. Avoid jargon, and always proofread any newsletter (or any written product) you send out.

✔ **Frequency:** How often you send home a newsletter depends upon your purpose. If you are suggesting supplemental activities, a weekly newsletter is probably your best bet. If you are trying to showcase student work and highlight achievements or contributions, a less frequent newsletter will suffice. A weekly update can be more informal, less cumbersome, and more timely. Also, many teachers report that parents find it easier to get in the habit of reading a weekly newsletter. However frequently you send a newsletter, try to send it on the same day each week or month so parents will learn to expect it and look for it. And don't forget to date it.

Open Letter to Parents Teachers who don't regularly produce newsletters—and even many who do—find that a general letter to all parents can be useful. For example, try starting the school year with an open letter to parents. This letter can cover nitty-gritty details you wouldn't want to include in a personal welcoming call to each family (information about homework policies and student supplies, for example). Send other letters throughout the year to make special announcements, explain a new policy, ask for volunteers, and so on.

Personal Notes A recurring theme in this chapter is that first contacts with parents should be positive ones. This way, you can gain parents' trust and confidence before you have to enlist their help if a problem should develop.

Share good news about individual children with their parents. These warm touches on paper go a long way in cultivating good relationships with both parents and students. Has a child accomplished an academic goal? Helped you or someone else? Finished her or his homework on time? Tutored a younger child? Led a group? Let parents in on the good news. Good-news notes allow you to recognize and reward the efforts of individual children. For example:

Dear Mr. and Mrs. Jones:

I thought you would be pleased to know how well Amanda is doing in reading. Her work improves every day, and her cheerful attitude brightens the whole classroom.

Sincerely,
Mrs. Howard

Two words of caution: Keep track of the good-news notes you send out so every student occasionally receives one. (Some teachers routinely write several a week.) And never distribute the notes en masse. They are not special if everyone gets one.

Unfortunately, not all your personal notes will be good news. Perhaps you've noticed that a child seems sick or constantly tired. Another is having difficulty in math and risks a failing grade. A shy child seems to be withdrawing more every day. You need to tell parents. But if you have already contacted them on a positive note, chances are they'll be more responsive now to problems. Always let them know you share the problem.

No matter what the nature of your personal note, always invite a response. Urge parents to call you, schedule an appointment, or write back. If they don't, call them. Show them that you care.

❖ Building Multicultural Home-School Partnerships

Sometimes, racial, cultural, socioeconomic, and language barriers inhibit partnerships and interactions between home and school. That's when it's important to make a special effort to involve and forge connections with families you may find difficult to reach. Some parents feel awkward or intimidated about approaching school staff, especially if they are nonnative speakers of English or have had negative schooling experiences themselves. What teachers may interpret as standoffish or uncooperative behavior from these parents may just be confusion, nervousness, cultural misunderstandings, or uncertainty.

The first step is to learn more about our students' cultures and backgrounds. In doing so, we bring into perspective similarities and differences that can enhance our relationships with students and their families.

Case Studies: Asian-American Families

Findings from case studies on home-school relationships can help us examine behaviors that we may assume have a "professional" connotation, but which may read quite differently to parents of different cultural backgrounds. Researchers report that some Asian parents, for example, feel that it is disrespectful to talk to teachers. They feel that to approach a teacher may be misconstrued as "checking up" on that teacher. Because they see teachers as professionals with authority over their children's education, they sometimes regard teachers who seek parent involvement as incompetent.

"Sometimes, the contrast of belief systems is profound," explains Gary Huang in a report on communicating with Asian-American children and their families. He refers to the 1989 shooting of five Cambodian schoolchildren in Stockton, California. "After the tragedy," Huang reports, "the greatest fear of the Cambodian community was not of the recurrence of killing, as school personnel supposed and painstakingly tried to assuage, but the haunting spirits of the dead." Not until school officials performed a folk religious ceremony on the advice of a Cambodian consultant did parents send their children back to school.

Huang also describes several "hidden" aspects of cultural differences that can seriously affect school-home relations.

✔ **Time:** Whereas mainstream Americans have a linear concept of time, Asians perceive time as a simultaneous process, where many things can happen at once. Thus, they may come late to a parent conference (with no apology or explanation) or appear to be inattentive when teachers address them.

✔ **Communication:** Whereas Anglo-Americans communicate primarily through clear, explicit verbal articulation, Asians rely more on nonverbal cues (such as body language), the context of the interaction, and presumptions of commonly held beliefs.

Add to these differences a language barrier, and it is easy to see how large a gulf separates many teachers from the families they serve. How can we bridge that gulf? In the case of Asian-American families, Huang offers these suggestions:

✔ Explain that parent involvement is a tradition in American education.

✔ Communicate with Asian parents individually rather than in group meetings, and orally rather than with written notes.

✔ Be attentive to nonverbal cues.

✔ Pay attention to periods of silence; they may indicate hesitancy and disagreement with what's being said, or they may be a chance for the parent to reflect on what's being said.

✔ Offer family-literacy and English-language-proficiency programs to bring parents into the school and help them understand how American teaching and learning occur.

To better improve home-school relationships with parents you may find hard to reach, consider contacting local cultural community leaders in your area to learn about home-school attitudes and how to open lines of communication.

Bridging the Home-School Divide

The following is a brief list of ways that teachers can build bridges between home and school when working with students from diverse socioeconomic and linguistic backgrounds.

- **Make teaching culturally relevant.** Gloria Ladson-Billings (1994) recommends teaching a "culturally relevant" curriculum in which students and their families feel represented in the curriculum. Some ways teachers can do this is by teaching multiple perspectives of history, bringing the cultural values of the children into classroom discussions, and choosing literature that reflects the experiences of the students that you teach. Make efforts to find literature in the native language of your students. Send these books home with your students so that parents who cannot read in English can still engage in literacy experiences with their child. Parents are more likely to build partnerships when they feel their children are respected and their communities and heritages are valued.

- **Create an environment in which students can see authentic uses of their home language** and non-English-speaking families can better connect with the school's mission and purpose. When possible, environmental print that is posted in the school and is geared to the community, including school letters home, should be translated into the languages available in the learning community (Schwarzer, Haywood, and Lorenzen, 2003). Schools can also make a language connection through placement of signs written in representative languages (e.g., "Office/Oficina," welcome banners, and the schools' mission statement or creed if it is posted).

- **Make sure you understand the needs and concerns of students' families**. In your back-to-school letter (which should be translated for families of non-English-speaking families), have parents fill out a portion where they tell you about themselves and their special relationship with their child. (Again, you may need help with translation as the writing comes back to you.) Ask parents frankly about their schedules and future availability in case they need to be contacted.

- **Plan flexibly for conferences**. When planning for conferences, keep in mind that some parents might not be available during school hours. If you would like to have a parent meet with you or attend an event, be sensitive to parents' varied schedules and announce meetings and other events several weeks in advance so that families may arrange for time off work or childcare. In some cases, going the extra mile is the only way to ensure you will make personal contact with families. For example, during his year as a teacher in an Alaskan Eskimo school, Jim Henry made home visits when parents couldn't show up for conferences. Henry reports that he was always well received. "In fact, these visits frequently revolved around food and parents presenting me with things to eat."

- **Open lines of communication with difficult-to-reach parents by keeping two-way journals** that students can carry back and forth once a week (or more or less frequently, as needed) from home to school. Teachers can use it to communicate on a variety of issues, including the child's behavior, skills the child has mastered or may need work on, interesting discussions that occurred in class and might continue at home, and goals for specific learning issues.

Essentially, it offers parents an additional way to remain involved and informed about their child.

- **Link a parent-involvement outreach program with a student performance** to encourage parent involvement. Salt Lake City, Utah, teacher Tim Bailey advises, "One of the best ways to communicate with parents and get them to show up to school is to have the children performing before the event that you want the parents there for. If you're having a PTA involvement drive, then have students perform before giving the parents the PTA spiel."

- **Organize a community-wellness or informational event at the school** to create other incentives for parents to come to the school. One successful model is a community health fair held in a school's cafeteria, in which school staff can volunteer alongside local health/safety professionals whom children's families may not otherwise have the opportunity to meet. Free services such as blood pressure and vision screenings, home-safety information sessions, and nutritious door prizes can be offered. A health fair provides an excellent opportunity to bring families into the school where they can receive some health benefits and identify local health resources, meet their children's teachers, and help them view the school as a community resource. Such community-based events help families build trust in the school and become more invested in the school community.

By Tamara Glupczynski, 2004

Connecting With Migrant Families

Migrant families pose a special challenge. Having their children attend school when they could be working in the fields or babysitting younger siblings is often a hardship for these families; expecting these parents to volunteer time at school is unrealistic. Many times, these families do not stay at one school long enough to develop effective partnerships with teachers.

But the involvement of migrant families in their children's education is as important as the involvement of any parents—even if that involvement is simply communicating to their children positive attitudes about education. One study of high-achieving and low-achieving migrant children conducted by the Center for Educational Planning showed that the parents of the high achievers held positive attitudes about school and could talk about the ways school was helping their children. Conversely, the parents of the low achievers had negative attitudes toward school and couldn't acknowledge anything beneficial about their children's schooling. Neither group helped their children with homework, so attitude appeared to be the important difference.

How do teachers and schools help migrant parents and others develop positive attitudes toward schooling? Through effective communication. Whether that communication takes the form of newsletters, phone calls, parent conferences, invitations to visit school, or even home visits, make the effort to communicate in the parents' primary language. Make *all* parents feel welcome and valued, and respect all families for the strengths each has.

Breaking Down Other Barriers

Economic differences that cut across racial and cultural lines are another barrier to effective school-home partnerships. Strategies for breaking down these barriers include:

ERIC DATABASE AIDS UNDERSTANDING

An excellent source of information and resources on culturally diverse students and their families is the ERIC database at www.eric.ed.gov. Search among more than 107,000 full-text articles published after 1993. A broad search for "parent involvement" yields more than 1,300 hits!

✔ regular meetings to discuss homework, behavior, and curriculum
✔ special parenting skills seminars
✔ offering adult-education classes to get parents into the school
✔ teaching parents how to help children at home
✔ activities for parents and children to learn together

Yale educator James P. Comer recalls that as a young minority student himself, he was supported and motivated by his own mother's intense involvement in his education, and by his teachers' personal attention and caring. Comer's School Development Program (mentioned earlier in this chapter) emphasizes helping teachers learn how to earn the trust and respect of the inner-city families they serve.

This chapter reviews many different ways to involve parents. But it's important to realize that there is no one "best" way for parents to participate in their children's education. Teachers and schools must adapt the strategies most suited to their situations. To get a good idea of how you and your school are currently involving parents and the community, try completing the checklist and questionnaire on pages 276 and 277. These offer a good indication of the direction you'll want to take.

No matter what your plan for involving parents, there is support and help readily available. The federal government funds a number of state resource centers for parent involvement. (See the list on page 278.) And in addition to the ideas suggested in this chapter, there are many more field-tested approaches offered through the resources listed here.

Checklist for Improving Parental Involvement

		YES	NO
1.	There is a place in the building for parents to gather informally.	❑	❑
2.	The office has a friendly, informal atmosphere.	❑	❑
3.	Parents are viewed by school staff as teaching resources.	❑	❑
4.	School staff members are aware of cultural and language barriers.	❑	❑
5.	Efforts are made to involve culturally and linguistically diverse parents.	❑	❑
6.	Communication between teachers and parents is effective.	❑	❑
7.	The atmosphere in the school is not bureaucratic.	❑	❑
8.	There are clearly defined policies regarding parental involvement in this school.	❑	❑
9.	There is a schoolwide homework policy in place.	❑	❑
10.	There is an in-service program for staff that addresses parental involvement.	❑	❑
11.	There is an in-service program for the Board of Education that addresses parental involvement.	❑	❑
12.	Training programs for parents are available.	❑	❑
13.	Parents are truly empowered to make decisions in this school.	❑	❑
14.	Families are a priority in this school.	❑	❑
15.	The businesses in the community are involved in the school.	❑	❑
16.	Community involvement is evident in this school.	❑	❑
17.	Parents are asked about their children's thinking and behavior.	❑	❑
18.	Parents routinely work in classrooms with children on learning activities.	❑	❑
19.	Parents in this community advocate for children's rights.	❑	❑
20.	Parents are promptly notified about problems with their children.	❑	❑

Adapted from "What's Noteworthy on Learners" in Learning, Schooling, Winter 1995. Published by Mid-continent Regional Educational Laboratory, 2550 S. Parker Rd., Ste. 500, Aurora, CO 80014.

Assess Your School's PPPQ
(Parent Perspectives and Participation Quotient)

This questionnaire is an informal way to assess what you are currently doing to learn about parents' perspectives. Your responses may also help you discover other ways to involve parents in school life.

Directions: Circle at least one response for each item. If more than one response describes your school, circle all that apply.

1. Most of our written communications (for example, informational letters, newsletters) could best be described as:
   a. jargon-free.
   b. jargon-lite.
   c. jargon-infested.

2. When we consider starting a new program or changing a practice, we usually:
   a. include parents and community members in the planning discussions from the start.
   b. inform everyone before the change actually occurs.
   c. hold informational meetings and/or issue news releases when the change is under way or near completion.

3. We get information on parents' perspectives about effective classroom practice primarily from:
   a. surveys of parents, followed by in-depth interviews and/or focus groups that represent all groups in our community.
   b. those parents who speak at open meetings.
   c. parents who have conferences with teachers or who contact the school when they have a question or concern.

4. At meetings to acquaint parents with new practices, we most often:
   a. provide opportunities for parents to understand and experience new practices for themselves.
   b. describe planned changes and encourage discussion in small groups.
   c. explain changes/answer questions.

5. Most of our parents:
   a. have visited classes and/or served as volunteers, guest speakers, or substitute teachers.
   b. come to school only for conferences, open houses, or athletic and other school activities.
   c. rarely come to the school (except perhaps when there is a problem).

6. Most of our parents get much of their information about classroom activities and assignments:
   a. by participating in assignments and regularly reviewing samples of their children's work.
   b. from letters and newsletters from teachers.
   c. from informal conversations with their children.

7. Teachers in our school would probably say that:
   a. parents as well as students should understand why teachers have chosen a particular curriculum and teaching method.
   b. students can probably benefit from knowing why their curriculum is important and why teachers have asked them to do assignments in a certain way, but this knowledge isn't essential.
   c. parents and students should trust teachers to make the decisions; they probably don't want to know the reasons as long as the students seem to be doing okay.

8. When a parent is critical of a program or practice, our usual approach is:
   a. to understand the nature of the concerns, to look for ways to solve the immediate problem, and to consider what general actions may be needed.
   b. to resolve the immediate problem.
   c. to minimize the conflict as quickly as possible by finding some way to appease the critical parent.

9. A fair estimate of the number of parents who have had a positive, personal contact with a teacher or administrator during this school year would be:
   a. more than half of all parents, including those from all ethnic/socioeconomic/political groups.
   b. about half of all parents, most of whom are mainstream and middle class.
   c. fewer than half of all parents, and few or none from some segments of society.

10. Our school regularly provides the following opportunities for parents to share their ideas and concerns with the school:

_____

SCORING
a = 3 points; b = 2 points; c = 1 point. For question 10, score 1 point for each item listed. Then add the points to get your total score.

30+	You are probably building parents' support for change.
16–29	The embers of dissent may be smoldering. They could flare up at any time, especially if you have not involved all groups.
15 or less	Keeping parents so distanced from school is likely to create problems if you aren't facing an outright conflict right now.

Parent Resource Centers

Families in a number of states from Maine to California have the opportunity to seek support from parent information and resource centers, many of which opened after receiving grants as part of the Goals 2000: Educate America Act. These parent centers respond to local conditions with their own priorities and activities, but they share a common objective to help families get involved in their children's learning.

Each center serves the entire state in which it is located or a region of that state and includes both urban and rural areas. While information and assistance may be provided to any parent, the centers are required to target areas with high concentrations of low-income, minority, and limited-English-proficient parents.

A list of the centers is provided below. Call to find out the specific services offered, including parent-to-parent training activities, hot lines, mobile training teams, resource and lending libraries, support groups, and referral networks. For additional parent resources in other states, visit the National Coalition for Parent Involvement in Education at www.ncpie.org (click on State Parent Information).

Appalachia Educational Laboratory (WV)
P.O.B. 1348
Charleston, WV 25325
(304) 347-0400
www.ael.org

Black Hills Parent Resource Network (SD)
P.O.B. 218
Sturgis, SD 57785
(800) 219-6247
www.bhssc.org/sdprn

Center for Early Adolescence (NC)
University of North Carolina at Chapel Hill
211 N. Columbia St.
Chapel Hill, NC 27514
(919) 968-8850

Center on Families, Communities, Schools, and Children's Learning (MD)
Johns Hopkins University
3505 N. Charles St.
Baltimore, MD 21218
(401) 516-8800

Children's Home Society of Washington (WA)
3300 NE 65th St.
Seattle, WA 98115
(206) 695-3200
www.chs-wa.org

Council of the Great City Schools (DC)
1301 Pennsylvania Ave. NW
Ste. 702
Washington, DC 20004
(202) 393-2427
www.cgsc.org

Family Resource Project (ME)
P.O.B. 2067
Augusta, ME 04338-2067
(207) 582-2504

Family Strengths (NH)
85 N. State St. 2
Concord, NH 03301
(603) 228-5429

Greater Washington Urban League (DC)
3501 14th St., NW
Washington, DC 20010
(202) 265-8200

Home and School Institute/Mega Skills Education Center (DC)
1500 Massachusetts Ave. NW
Washington, DC 20005
(202) 466-3633
www.megaskillsHSI.org

Iowa Parent Resource Center (IA)
1025 Penkridge Dr.
Iowa City, IA 52246
(319) 354-5606

Institute for Responsive Education (MA)
Northeastern University
21 Lake Hall
Boston, MA 02215
(617) 373-2595
www.responsiveeducation.org

National Coalition for Parent Involvement in Education (VA)
3929 Old Lee Highway
Ste. 91-A
Fairfax, VA 22030
(703) 359-8973
www.ncpie.org

National PTA (DC)
1090 Vermont Ave. NW, Ste. 1200
Washington, DC 20005
(202) 289-6790

National School Boards Association (VA)
1680 Duke St.
Alexandria, VA 22314
(703) 838-6722
www.nsba.org

Ohio Parent Information Center (OH)
5812 Madison Rd.
Cincinnati, OH 45227
(513) 272-0273

Parents and Children Together (HI)
1485 Linapuni Street, Ste. 105
Honolulu, HI 96819
(808) 847-3285
www.pacthawaii.org

Parents First Resoucre Center (TN)
3703 Park Ave.
Nashville, TN 37209
(615) 460-9810

Parents as Partners in Education (OK)
4801 Classen Blvd., Ste. 212
Oklahoma City, OK 73118
(405) 478-4078
www.parentsaspartners.org

Parents Plus (WI)
402 N. Commercial St.
Neenah, WI 54956
(920) 720-9890

Prevent Child Abuse (NJ)
103 Church St.
New Brunswick, NJ 07102-3031
(732) 246-8060
www.preventchildabusenj.org

Southwest Educational Development Laboratory (TX)
211 E. Seventh St.
Austin, TX 78701
(800) 496-6861
www.sedl.org

Vermont Family Resource Project (VT)
P.O.B. 646
Middlebury, VT 05753
(802) 388-3171
www.vermontfamilyresource.org

❖ In Summary

There are many different ways to involve parents and the community in children's schooling. But there's really only one reason for it: to provide the best possible education for children. In this respect, you and your students' parents share a common goal.

❖ Works Cited

Bombeck, Erma. *At Wit's End.* Garden City, New York: Doubleday, 1967.

Brandt, Ron. "On Parents and Schools: A Conversation with Joyce Epstein." *Educational Leadership* 47, no. 2 (October 1989): 24–27.

Center for the Study of Parent Involvement. *Proceedings: Families and Schools: A Global Perspective for a Multicultural Society.* Available from the center at 370 Camino Pablo, Orinda, CA 94563; (510) 254-0110.

Comer, James P. "Educating Poor Minority Children." *Scientific American* 259, no. 5 (November 1988): 42–48.

Comer, James P. *School Power.* New York: Free Press, 1995.

Gough, Pauline B. "Tapping Parent Power." *Phi Delta Kappan* 72, no. 5 (January 1991): 339

Huang, Gary. "Beyond Culture: Communicating with Asian American Children and Families." *ERIC Digest,* ED 366673, 1993. Available: www.eric.ed.gov (Search by title).

Hunter, Madeline. "Join the 'Par-aide' in Education." *Educational Leadership* 47, no. 2 (October 1989): 36–41.

Jesse, Dan. "Increasing Parental Involvement: A Key to Student Achievement." *What's NOTEWORTHY on Learners, Learning, Schooling.* Aurora, CO: Mid-continent Regional Educational Laboratory, 1995. Available: www.mcrel.org/topics/noteworthy.asp.

Ladson-Billings, Gloria. *The Dreamkeepers: Successful Teachers of African-American Children.* San Francisco: Jossey-Bass, 1997.

Liontos, Lynne Balster. *At-Risk Families and Schools: Becoming Partners.* Eugene, OR: ERIC Digest, ED 342055, 1992.

McAfee, Oralie. *A Resource Notebook for Improving School-Home Communication.* Charleston, WV: Appalachia Educational Laboratory, 1984.

The Parent Institute. *What's Working in Parent Involvement.* Monthly newsletter. P.O.B. 7474, Fairfax Station, VA 22039-7474; (800) 756-5525.

Ramirez-Smith, Christina. "Stopping the Cycle of Failure: The Comer Model." *Educational Leadership* 52, no. 5 (February 1995): 14–19.

Schwarzer, D., A. Haywood, and C. Lorenzen. "Fostering Multiliteracy in a Linguistically Diverse Classroom." *Language Arts* 80, no. 6 (2003): 453–460.

Swap, Susan McAllister. *Enhancing Parent Involvement in Schools.* New York: Teachers College Press, 1987.

❖ Resources

Comer School Development Program, Yale Child Study Center
http://info.med.yale.edu/comer

Comer, James P. "Schools That Develop Children." *The American Prospect* 12, no. 7 (April, 2001). Available: www.prospect.org/print/V12/7/comer-j.html.

Mariconda, Barbara. *Easy and Effective Ways to Communicate With Parents.* New York: Scholastic, 2003.

Multicultural E-Rolodex at Multicultural Pavilion
www.edchange.org/multicultural/resources/organizations.html
An online listing of organizations dedicated to progressive education and the creation of communications between home and school.

Novelli, Joan. *Instant Send-Home Letters.* New York: Scholastic, 2002.

The Parent Institute
www.parent-institute.com
Resources (some free) for both parents and educators.

Chapter Seven

Teachers Helping Teachers

"Being collegial means being willing to move beyond the social façade of communication, to discuss conflicting ideas and issues with candor, sensitivity, and respect."

—*Carl D. Glickman*,
Renewing America's Schools

No matter how much you love teaching, sometimes you can't help feeling overwhelmed. Many of us still teach in self-contained classrooms with little time or administrative support for teaming or team planning. For much of the day, there's not another adult in sight. Those you do see in the teachers' lounge (when you don't have lunch or playground duty) have their own concerns. You can't ask them for help. You can't go to them with a problem or concern. They're busy, and besides, they might think you're incompetent!

Or will they?

Actually, your colleagues are your best bet for surviving anything from the first year of teaching to a particularly difficult student to a midcareer change in teaching assignment. Teachers are each other's allies.

Think of the collective wisdom and practical knowledge of your school's veterans. The faculty in a single elementary school with 15 or more teachers represents hundreds of years of classroom experience with thousands of students. That's a great source for a lot of helpful information.

Teachers—all teachers—need formal and informal networks for tapping and sharing this information. When teachers help teachers and learn from each other, everyone benefits, especially the students. As researchers Judith Warren Little and Tom Bird have observed in *Resources and Practice*,

"[Teachers] accumulate such skills and wisdom as they can by themselves and then take their inventions with them when they leave. Superb teachers leave their marks on all of us, but they leave no marks on teaching."

This chapter describes some of the ways teachers can leave their mark on teaching and on each other. Teachers can work together to improve teaching—from the first years on. Whatever name they go by—mentors, lead teachers, helping teachers, team teachers, coaches, advisers, friends—your experienced colleagues have a lot to offer. And whether your relationship is formal or informal, relish this chance to work together.

❖ Mentor Teachers

Whom do we go to most often for help and advice? A friend. A trusted colleague. A mentor. Someone whose opinions we value. It's only natural for teachers to seek the companionship of like-minded colleagues.

In many districts today, teachers are assigned mentors, advisers, or helping teachers in addition to those they choose informally. These mentors are not *tor*mentors sent to spy upon or evaluate their colleagues. Rather, they are experienced teachers recognized for their effective teaching and their willingness to help others—experienced professionals supervising and overseeing the efforts of their less-experienced or sometimes burned-out colleagues.

Doctors do it. Lawyers do it. So do other professionals. They'd never leave novices to learn by trial and error. But in teaching, the internship portion of professional training has traditionally been absent. Teacher-mentor programs are one way to address this need. They are one good example of the "teacher-helping-teacher" model at work in many of our best schools.

Many Roles for Mentors

Companionship, support, technical feedback, opportunities to observe different models of teaching or reflect and analyze practice—such are the rewards of a good mentor-mentee relationship.

Researchers Judith Shulman and Joel Colbert identify five important ways mentors can assist:

✔ Inform new teachers about school policies and procedures, or help them find out about them.
✔ Share knowledge about new materials, unit planning, curriculum development, and teaching methods.
✔ Assist with classroom management and discipline.
✔ Provide opportunities to observe other teachers using different teaching models.
✔ Encourage new teachers to reflect on their teaching practices and help them adapt new strategies for their classrooms.

"The first four types [of mentor assistance] help teachers survive," say Shulman and Colbert, "but the last one represents the key to continuous learning."

Another important role played by teacher mentors is helping new teachers learn about their state's content standards and benchmarks. In addition, mentors can make sure their mentees

---

MENTORS' THOUGHTS ON MENTORING

"Just as I learned how to teach over time, I am still learning to be an advisor," says Susan Audap. "The hardest thing about advising for me is empowering without overwhelming."

Another teacher admits that "sometimes I resent being a mentor because almost everyone expects you to be perfect. I feel like I'm being watched all the time, and when I fail or make a mistake, everyone hears about it."

In Kathleen Devaney's *Building a Teachers' Center*, author C. San Jose sums it up this way: "It's fairly easy to walk in and tell someone what to do. It's not too difficult to listen to a problem and say what you would do. But to listen to people and then help them think through what is the next best step for them is an extraordinarily demanding way to work."

know state and district testing schedules and the ways they are expected to prepare their students for those tests.

A mentor can also individually consult with the new teacher, observe and coach in the mentee's classroom, or model teaching strategies in his or her own classroom.

And there's the emotional side to mentoring, too. Even the best of teachers needs someone to lean on now and then. One California mentor recalls, "When the kids were noisy and the day had fallen flat, then I would listen, comfort, console, and bolster. Such emotional support brought a special closeness, and we became personal friends during this time. This greatly enhanced our work professionally."

Confidentiality Is Critical

The mentoring process succeeds through close contact and continuing support. And confidentiality is critical. Mentors and mentees must develop a bond of trust. Mentors do *not* evaluate the teachers they are mentoring; they help and support them.

"One of my early successes was with a teacher who had absolutely no idea how to plan lessons around a particular unit," recalls one Los Angeles mentor quoted in *The Mentor Teacher Casebook*. "Although her lessons were extremely creative, they were just a hodgepodge of activities. We sat down with several textbooks and the instructional guide, and I showed her how to plan a unit around a list of objectives. I'll never forget the look on her face when we had finished. It was as if I had shown her the most marvelous thing in the world. You can imagine how good I felt when this teacher put together the next unit, completely on her own."

Fostering Good Relationships

Productive encounters between mentors and mentees, between veterans and beginners, don't just occur spontaneously. Both parties must work hard to make good things happen.

Most important is to keep an open mind. "Be willing to look at more than one way of doing things," advises veteran Cathey Graham. "A

mentor can give you a different perspective. If you start your career by always looking for new ideas, you will continue to do this and not become stale or stagnant."

Whether you have been assigned a mentor (this term is used to mean any helping teacher) or just choose to work with a willing colleague, remember several important steps in setting the stage for a healthy relationship:

✔ **Overcome your initial reluctance**. Sure you feel vulnerable. It's only natural. To have someone watching, discussing, analyzing your teaching can be unnerving. But try to push your self-doubt aside and concentrate on how much you stand to gain.

✔ **Try to get along**. Ideally, your most suitable mentor would be one teaching the same grade, subject, or type of students in the same building—with a personality complementing your own. But reality is something different. In formal programs, where mentors are assigned, you probably won't have a choice. If you do, try for a close match. Either way, remember that even if your mentor seems very different from you, your working relationship can still be a good one. Acknowledge and explore your differences, and try to understand different points of view.

✔ **Ask for help when you need it**. Professionals admit they have a problem and know when to ask for help. Your experienced colleagues are ready and waiting to help, but they don't want to intrude. You may have to take the first step. "If I knew then what I know now, I wouldn't have been afraid to ask for help or materials," says California veteran Sandra Tatum of her first year. Tatum speaks for most veterans when she urges new teachers to seek necessary help from their colleagues.

✔ **Communicate effectively**. Perhaps you don't understand how a mentor can be useful. Ask questions. Voice your concerns. If something about the mentoring process bothers you, speak up. And try not to become defensive. Mentors want to help, so let them know how they can.

✔ **Consider the mentor's perspective.** It's difficult being a beginner or a teacher in a new setting. But helping newcomers is no easy task, either—especially if the help is unasked for or even unwanted, as sometimes happens in formal mentor programs. If mentors are too assertive or forthright, they may come across as pushy. But if they aren't assertive enough, they may be doing you a disservice. If you understand these difficult demands, perhaps you'll be more inclined to focus on good intentions and overlook minor faults.

Susan Audap, principal of William L. Cobb Elementary School in Los Angeles, recalls her own shaky start as a teacher: "What got me through my first year was an advisor who came to my classroom once a week for an hour or two. On a scale of one to ten, my classroom control was a two, and this was not a rough school. When my advisor worked with my kids they were wonderful. With me they were a mess. What I learned from her was that the kids were not the problem. I was."

That first year was tough for Audap. But it was also a time for growing, sharing, and learning. "Sometimes I needed soothing, sometimes I wanted to share triumphs, sometimes I needed to be invigorated. I met these needs by talking and working with other teachers, advisors, parents of my students. I cannot overstate the importance of these relationships. We shared a vision of how wonderful classrooms could be, and we shared the work of making them that way. It didn't happen overnight."

Much later, Audap herself became a mentor for new teachers. And based on her earlier experiences, she knew what they needed.

"What I can do is treat my new colleagues as I was treated," Audap explains. "They are tender shoots who need sustenance when they begin to wilt, support as they grow, and someone to rejoice when they flourish and bloom."

A TWO-WAY STREET

Experienced teachers really *do* want to help their less-experienced colleagues, because they benefit as well. Helping others is a wonderful learning process. And it's emotionally and professionally satisfying, too.

For many veterans, including Ruth Donnelly, mentoring new colleagues is payback for the help they received as new teachers. "One [colleague] made all the difference in what happened for me. She told me, 'Honey, you are going to be a great teacher. I can see that. Be careful how you part your lips. Do a lot of observing, active listening, and careful thinking about what you are about. You come with new ideas and enthusiasm and you also need to learn the wisdom and experience of others. And come to me whenever you want or feel the need. I will be there for you.' She was correct, and I share her words with all new staff at my site."

Another mentor describes the relationship between herself and her mentees this way: "Feedback is a two-way street, and my mentees have been very responsive with me. They have helped me with how I am doing and whether or not I am meeting their needs. Most of the input has been positive. When it has been negative, I have tried to be a good listener and adjust to their suggestions, whenever possible and appropriate. . . . Mentees have conveyed fears, frustrations, tears, successes, and lots of laughter to me. It has allowed me to get to know these special individuals personally as well as professionally."

Often, mentors and their mentees become firm friends and partners. As one veteran describes the relationship that developed between him and the beginner he mentored, "We began to exchange lesson plans and reading materials. Now we observe each other whenever we use a new approach or special activity. We also meet regularly, during lunch or conference periods. Jeff and I have become professional buddies. We share ideas, jokes, learning theories, rooms, books, teaching strategies, and our real concern about effective teaching. I started out helping Jeff, but I ended up becoming his teammate."

❖ Partnerships

Generally speaking, any two teachers working together either formally or informally have formed a partnership. While mentor-mentee relationships can certainly be viewed as partnerships, the concept will be used here to mean relationships between colleagues of equal status or experience. Natural partnerships develop between team teachers, peer coaches, and the colleagues who teach nearby. But there are also some notable exceptions, such as the partnerships you can develop with colleagues online, or special situations like the one experienced by Ann Wildberger and the late Doris Dillon.

One Real-Life Experience

Every partnership and every situation is unique, but the experiences of others provide valuable insights. Consider, for example, the international partnership forged by Doris Dillon and Ann Wildberger. In 1992 Wildberger took a leave from her teaching position in Toronto, Ontario, and moved to San Jose to research children's literature, study the California educational system, and grow professionally. Volunteering her services as a media specialist, Wildberger teamed up with language-resource teacher and media specialist Doris Dillon.

Wildberger describes her experiences in the Winter 1995 issue of *The California Reader*: "Together we have developed a learning environment that goes beyond the traditional shadowing experiences. [Doris] provides me with opportunities beyond the

school site. I assist her with media techniques and procedures. We view each other as equals who have a genuine interest in the well-being and learning of the other.

"We share Canadian and American trends, books, authors, and experiences," Wildberger continues. "We have identified our weaknesses and work cooperatively at helping each other become better teachers and leaders. There is no competition or extra workload, just a simple agreement to help each other."

While in San Jose, Wildberger also assisted in classrooms, helped team teach, planned and implemented parent-training workshops, and participated in administrative processes. She acknowledges that it was a time of great professional growth.

And her partner, Doris Dillon, benefited, too. "We immediately began to connect and share," noted Dillon. "It quickly became clear that this unique liaison was going to be a once-in-a-lifetime experience for both of us."

Dillon stressed that "she was important to my professional growth, and I was an important link to her professional growth."

And that's exactly what partnerships are all about—teachers helping each other to grow and learn. Team teaching, travel, common hobbies and interests, book groups, and special interest groups are some of the many ways teachers can work and learn with other teachers. Maybe the best thing about forming partnerships is that

---

SUCCESSFUL RELATIONSHIPS

In a study of how teachers can help each other, Judith Warren Little a professor of education at U.C. Berkeley, identified six major features of successful relationships between mentors and the teachers they advise:

1. **A common language** to describe, understand, and refine teaching. (Make sure you are both talking about the same thing when you use a term such as *constructivism,* for example.)

2. **A focus on just one or two key issues** at a time.

3. **Emphasis on the hard evidence** revealed by classroom observations and records. (For example, a mentor's recorded observations that transitions between lessons average eight minutes is more valuable than a subjective statement such as, "Transition times are too long.")

4. **Skillful interaction** during conferences together.

5. **Predictability** based on trust in each other's intentions.

6. **Reciprocity** of skills and knowledge—giving each other's efforts a full measure of energy, thought, and attention.

---

they're not regulated by district policy. Partners are free to create and foster their own meaningful connections.

Tips on Establishing Partnerships

Wildberger and Dillon offer some advice on creating a successful collegial partnership:

✔ Partners' needs do not need to be parallel.

✔ Differences in age and experience can be positive factors.

✔ You must feel comfortable, not competitive, with each other.

✔ Partners must be learners first and teachers second.

✔ Be honest with yourself and each other.

✔ Partners must communicate and recognize each other's needs.

✔ Identify both your strengths and your weaknesses.

✔ Be flexible.

✔ Identify a network of resources from which to draw and share.

Often, partnerships are created among teachers who are trying to meet a common need or goal. In my own teaching setting, for example, two colleagues and I became partners to write a grant for a new computer lab. Each of us was frustrated with the lack of computer opportunities for our students, and we realized that we could pool our time and talents to secure a computer lab that would meet our needs. Collaborating in the writing and development of the grant application, we ultimately received state grant monies for a 10-station mini-lab. Our partnership continued as we worked together to set up the lab, equip it with software, teach students to use the hardware and software, and introduce our colleagues to the lab and its many potential uses.

Online Partnerships

Every time you exchange ideas with a colleague you have created a "partnership." And now, thanks to technology, our opportunities for developing informal partnerships are almost infinite. Every teacher who has access to a computer and the Internet can find like-minded colleagues all over the country or even the world to share ideas with or talk to. Many of these informal partnerships become long-term friendships. (See network resources on page 294 for professional groups that can help you connect with other teachers.)

Team Teaching

Linda Farr of San Jose and two of her colleagues had a great idea. They would each plan and develop a super science unit and teach it to one another's students. They wouldn't simply rotate classes, but they would divide all three classes into three groups composed of kids from each class.

The idea worked, and the payoffs were tremendous. The students completed two very good science units. And in mixed groups, they got to know and work with students from the other classes. The teachers used their time and energy more efficiently by each concentrating on one unit and doing it very well.

The nature and frequency of teaming largely depend on the individuals involved. There are countless combinations. Teachers in many schools are free to initiate team teaching, usually with administrators' blessings.

How do you choose a teammate? Farr advises teaming with colleagues who have the same philosophical leanings and similar classroom-management strategies. On the other hand, you might profit by joining forces with someone quite different. Exposure to different teaching styles and strategies stimulates both beginning and experienced teachers. In whatever shape or form, team teaching has a lot to offer:

✔ opportunities to brainstorm and share ideas

✔ more efficient use of time and lesson preparations

✔ capitalizing on teachers' strengths and expertise

✔ peer coaching opportunities and chances to observe other teachers in action

✔ students benefiting from different personalities and teaching styles and the chance to work with other kids

✔ shared resources

"Teaming is just a better use of personnel," Farr concludes.

And the resulting companionship is fun, too. Team teachers report higher job satisfaction than those who don't team teach. We work with children day in and day out, and sometimes it's just nice to speak and work with an adult.

❖ Peer Coaching

Peer coaching involves a special kind of partnership. As peer coaches, two teachers agree to observe and critique each other's teaching. It's a reciprocal relationship in which colleagues help each other implement new teaching strategies. They analyze evidence from their observations and plan ways to change. Peer coaching is a way to make significant improvements in your teaching—with a little help from a friend.

Learning new teaching strategies is difficult and demanding. It's easy to make mistakes and get discouraged. Coaching helps by providing much-needed support. In fact, research shows that without sustained feedback and support of the type offered by peer coaching, teachers have a difficult time learning to use all those new strategies they hear about in workshops and in-services.

1. **Pick Your Own Partner.**
   Coaching should be a comfortable, nonthreatening experience involving someone with whom you share a mutual trust and commitment to help. Perhaps you've already established a rapport with a colleague who once served as your mentor. Or perhaps you just respect the opinions and advice of the teacher who teaches across the hall. Successful coaching starts with trust and often leads to friendships.

2. **Seek Training.**
   Seek training, if it's available. Coaching is a skill that must be learned, like any other. Many districts now offer coaching partners training in factual data gathering, constructive feedback, and observation and analysis of teaching. (For more information on peer coaching, see the resources listed at the end of this chapter.)

3. **Focus on Something Specific.**

"Peer coaching needs to be centered around something people are trying to master, no matter what that is," emphasizes staff developer Beverly Showers, who along with colleagues at the University of Oregon developed peer coaching as an alternative to traditional one-shot in-services. Focus on a specific problem or strategy. Sit down with your coaching partner during lunch, after school, or any time the students are absent to discuss what types of observations to record. Identify your concerns and map out strategies for working together. Educational consultant Charlotte Danielson offers some specific guidelines. Drawing on empirical research, Danielson has identified 22 components of teaching that promote improved student learning. She organizes these components into four categories or "domains": planning and preparation, the classroom environment, instruction, and professional responsibilities. Danielson calls this framework "a foundation for professional conversations." Peer coaches can focus on one or several components as they collaborate to improve teaching skills. (See the whole framework on page 288).

4. **Conduct Systematic Observations.**

Coaching is most effective when partners conduct systematic observations and keep thorough and appropriate records. The Checklist for Observing Teaching reproducible on page 289 is an observation instrument you can adapt to your own needs. Or develop your own observation instruments with your partner's help. Instruments might help you record what each student is doing during a lesson (on-task behavior), or how teacher and students are interacting, for example. Or you and your partner could just agree on a systematic process of note taking. Data-gathering procedures could also include audio- or videotaping, anecdotal record keeping, seating charts indicating student interaction and on-task behavior—whatever lends itself to the specific focus of the coaching.

Classroom Observations

The classroom observation probably produces the most anxiety—yet has the potential to be the most beneficial aspect of teachers helping each other. It's stressful because it exposes your classroom behavior to careful scrutiny; beneficial because it is a window on teaching— a way to analyze real teaching of real students. Whether you are a new teacher, an experienced teacher in a new role, or a seasoned veteran, observations offer a means for reflecting on practice. And reflection helps us grow.

It works like this: Two teachers sit down together and agree to focus on a specific problem or concern. With that concern in mind, one teacher then observes a lesson, recording specific behaviors, comments, interactions, and other classroom happenings. Afterward, the observer presents his or her observations to the teacher observed. Together, they reflect on what happened and try to develop strategies for improvement.

Suppose, for example, you wanted help with classroom discipline. There are no severe behavior problems in your class, but the noise level and general rowdiness sometimes get out of hand. You ask a colleague to watch you teach a science lesson to help you figure out what's going wrong.

After the observation, you sit down together and go over his detailed notes. He has recorded how many minutes were spent on each of the three experiments the students did, and how much time elapsed between the end of one experiment and the beginning of another.

You learn that these transition times were much longer than you realized. And you can see from the observation notes that here was where most of the misbehavior occurred. When you paused to reprimand those misbehaving, you delayed the experiments even further, inviting more misbehavior.

The solution here is obvious. Keep students busily engaged and on-task by reducing dangerous transition times and stepping up the pace. Your colleague shares some of his strategies. And he also suggests that some minor misbehavior is better ignored so as not to disrupt the lesson.

Framework for Teaching

This framework, developed by Charlotte Danielson, identifies 22 components of teaching that promote improved student learning. It can serve as a foundation for teachers to discuss education.

Domain 1: Planning and Preparation

Component 1a: Demonstrating Knowledge of Content and Pedagogy
- Knowledge of content
- Knowledge of prerequisite relationships
- Knowledge of content-related pedagogy

Component 1b: Demonstrating Knowledge of Students
- Knowledge of characteristics of age group
- Knowledge of students' varied approaches to learning
- Knowledge of students' skills and knowledge
- Knowledge of students' interests and cultural heritage

Component 1c: Selecting Instructional Goals
- Value
- Clarity
- Suitability for diverse students
- Balance

Component 1d: Demonstrating Knowledge of Resources
- Resources for teaching
- Resources for students

Component 1e: Designing Coherent Instruction
- Learning activities
- Instructional materials and resources
- Instructional groups
- Lesson and unit structure

Component 1f: Assessing Student Learning
- Congruence with instructional goals
- Criteria and standards
- Use for planning

Domain 2: The Classroom Environment

Component 2a: Creating an Environment of Respect and Rapport
- Teacher interaction with students
- Student interaction

Component 2b: Establishing a Culture for Learning
- Importance of the content
- Student pride in work
- Expectations for learning and achievement

Component 2c: Managing Classroom Procedures
- Management of instructional groups
- Management of transitions
- Management of materials and supplies
- Performance of noninstructional duties
- Supervision of volunteers and paraprofessionals

Component 2d: Managing Student Behavior
- Expectations
- Monitoring of student behavior
- Response to student misbehavior

Component 2e: Organizing Physical Space
- Safety and arrangement of furniture
- Accessibility to learning and use of physical resources

Domain 3: Instruction

Component 3a: Communicating Clearly and Accurately
- Directions and procedures
- Oral and written language

Component 3b: Using Questioning and Discussion Techniques
- Quality of questions
- Discussion techniques
- Student participation

Component 3c: Engaging Students in Learning
- Representation of content
- Activities and assignments
- Grouping of students
- Instructional materials and resources
- Structure and pacing

Component 3d: Providing Feedback to Students
- Quality: accurate, substantive, constructive, and specific
- Timeliness

Component 3e: Demonstrating Flexibility and Responsiveness
- Lesson adjustment
- Response to students
- Persistence

Domain 4: Professional Responsibilities

Component 4a: Reflecting on Teaching
- Accuracy
- Use in future teaching

Component 4b: Maintaining Accurate Records
- Student completion of assignments
- Student progress in learning
- Noninstructional records

Component 4c: Communicating With Families
- Information about the instructional program
- Information about individual students
- Engagement of families in the instructional program

Component 4d: Contributing to the School and District
- Relationships with colleagues
- Service to the school
- Participation in school and district projects

Component 4e: Growing and Developing Professionally
- Enhancement of content knowledge and pedagogical skill
- Service to the profession

Component 4f: Showing Professionalism
- Service to students
- Advocacy
- Decision making

Adapted from *Enhancing Professional Practice: A Framework for Teaching* by Charlotte Danielson. Association for Supervision and Curriculum Development, 1996. (You can preview the first chapter from Danielson's book at www.ascd.org/readingroom/books/danielson96book.)

Checklist for Observing Teaching

Here are some things to look for when observing a colleague in action. Agree beforehand which of these areas you will focus on each time you make observations and comments.

Classroom Management	Active Teaching and Instructional Techniques	Teacher-Student Interaction
❏ Has efficient classroom routines in place	❏ Explains a lesson's relevance and purpose	❏ Encourages responsibility and independence
❏ Manages time effectively (allocated time, instructional time, engaged time)	❏ Explicit instructions	❏ Uses motivational techniques
❏ Creates a physical environment conducive to teaching and learning	❏ Maintains task focus	❏ Uses questioning techniques
❏ Arranges seating and organizes groups to minimize cliques and enhance cooperation	❏ Lesson presentation	❏ Makes direct eye contact
❏ Conducts well-organized lessons	❏ Paces lesson appropriately	❏ Boosts students' self-esteem
❏ Leads smooth transitions between activities	❏ Periodically checks for understanding	❏ Models positive behavior
❏ Provides learning centers, independent activities	❏ Provides examples, asks questions	❏ Offers specific, appropriate praise
❏ Handles paperwork, checks assignments	❏ Incorporates guided practice	❏ Allows all students opportunities to respond in class
❏ Delegates routine tasks	❏ Supports independent practice	❏ Solicits ideas from students
❏ Uses peer and cross-age tutors	❏ Includes review time	❏ Communicates high expectations
❏ Organizes cooperative activities	❏ Integrates subject matter	
❏ Firmly and fairly enforces classroom rules	❏ Assigns materials that reflect an appropriate level of difficulty	
❏ Has an effective repertoire of discipline strategies	❏ Groups students effectively (tailoring instruction and curriculum to needs and abilities of students)	
❏ Assesses how much students already know on a topic	❏ Provides opportunities for hands-on learning	
❏ Enforces rules and discipline equally	❏ Capitalizes on "teachable" moments	
	❏ Treats students with courtesy and respect	
	❏ Provides leadership	

You resolve to make these changes. And you ask your colleague to observe once more, just to help you assess the new strategies.

This is a simple example. But it illustrates the concrete results and immediate usefulness of a technique custom-tailored to each teacher.

And don't forget that the observation process works two ways. An observation can also involve one teacher trying to demonstrate a strategy or technique that another is trying to learn. Most of your colleagues will be happy to demonstrate certain techniques or connect you with someone who can.

Successful Observations In The *Mentor Teacher Casebook*, Acosta, Shulman, and Colbert state that successful classroom observations depend on several conditions:

✔ conferring beforehand to agree on the purpose for the observation

✔ analysis based on credible and concrete evidence (a written record or a teacher-student interaction chart, for example)

✔ discussion and problem solving in pre- and post-observation conferences

✔ an atmosphere of mutual respect and trust

✔ an assurance of confidentiality

Observing Videotapes Technology continues to play an increasingly larger role in classroom observations as more and more teachers observe themselves and each other on videotape. The advantages of videotaped lessons are obvious. First, you don't have the problem of trying to arrange an observation that fits your observer's schedule. Second, no one has to cover for an observer to come to your classroom. Also, both you and your colleague can observe and discuss the videotape at your convenience. And perhaps most important, you can observe the videotape together, replaying sections that seem especially relevant or important. You can see (and hear) firsthand the behaviors and interactions in question. (Before you use videotape in the classroom, check to see if your district has a policy regarding the taping of students and classrooms.)

Always Debrief Follow up each observation with a conference for offering technical feedback. Technical feedback is specific information on how a teacher uses certain skills or strategies, not an evaluation of general teaching ability. Coaching conferences are collaborative problem-solving sessions; they often result in the partners jointly planning a lesson with which to experiment. The teacher experiments with a new lesson while the coach observes, and the process continues with a new cycle of analysis, problem solving, and experimenting.

Repeat the Cycle Try to implement the changes suggested by your coach, then schedule another (or several) follow-up observations to document your success. There's always room for improvement. With peer coaching, professional teachers engage in the continual study of teaching.

An Alternate Approach

Perhaps the best testimonials for peer coaching come from teachers who participated in studies conducted by Beverly Showers and Bruce Joyce. The researchers report that the teachers became so skillful in collaboration and enjoyed the coaching experience so much that they wanted to continue their collegial partnerships even after they had improved their practices and met their initial goals. This reaction led the researchers to rethink their approach of using peer coaching as a vehicle for implementing specific training. Now they advocate organizing entire faculties into peer-coaching teams for the continual study of teaching.

Further, Showers and Joyce have changed their peer-coaching model in two other important ways.

First, they suggest omitting the verbal feedback part of the coaching process. Even though this feedback and debriefing is a key component to most coaching models, including their own earlier model, Showers and Joyce now argue that such feedback often sounds like evaluation and tends to sabotage collaboration, despite teachers' best intentions.

"The collaborative work of peer coaching teams is much broader than observations and conferences," they write. Rather, teachers learn best from one another "while planning instruction, developing support materials, watching one another work with students, and thinking together about the impact of their behavior on their students' learning."

This rethinking and redesigning of the peer coaching model has led to a second change; Showers and Joyce have redefined the meaning of "coach." When two teachers observe each other, they explain, "the one teaching is the 'coach' and the one observing is the 'coached.'"

You decide: coaches as demonstrators of strategies or observers of their colleagues' teaching skills and methods. Either way, collaboration with colleagues can improve teaching performance.

❖ Professional Development Teams

Many school districts are creating formal opportunities for teachers to interact and help each other as members of professional development teams. The team concept comes from solid evidence on what helps professionals to grow and develop. It's actually a new approach to teacher evaluation.

"We know that adults respond primarily to positive reinforcement, that they want to be involved, that they prefer to operate in a collegial and collaborative environment," explains professional development expert Tom McGreal of the University of Illinois at Champaign-Urbana. McGreal notes that teachers who were already organized into grade-level teams or interdisciplinary teams or curriculum teams realized that the team approach could be effective for staff development and evaluation, too.

With the team approach, "Everybody is involved in a professional development plan all the time," says McGreal. He gives the example of several primary teachers who want to develop an ungraded classroom. As a team, these teachers might engage in action research, do peer coaching, develop curriculum, and attend or conduct workshops.

"Our school dedicates every other Monday to ongoing professional development instead of a faculty meeting," notes Utah teacher Tim Bailey. "In addition, we have 90 minutes a week to meet as a grade-level team to discuss our curriculum and strategies."

"I'm seeing more collaboration, more collegial conversation than ever before in the 25 years I've been working in schools," McGreal claims. And due to this increased collaboration, "Schools are getting better—a lot better."

Read more about the team approach to professional development (described under Action Research) in Chapter Eight.

❖ Teachers' Support Groups

Another way that professionals interact is through various support and study groups. Support groups consist of teachers in close geographic proximity who meet regularly. These groups can be either formally organized around certain topics or teaching strategies, or informally organized as moral support groups.

Sometimes It Helps Just to Talk

Informal support groups, such as those where teachers meet once a month at their favorite restaurant, usually involve teachers talking about teaching. They express their joys and concerns, share stories, and just generally give each other a sympathetic ear and moral support. Talking about teaching with other teachers helps us reflect on our own practice.

What's the result of all this talk? Improved practice, increased collegiality, professional growth, and decreased isolation, frustration, and burnout.

New Teachers Need Support

As a new teacher, Susan Audap remembers being so obsessed with teaching that she used to "eat, drink, and sleep teaching." She'd seek out other beginners to talk about lessons and kids and instructional strategies and anything else pertaining to classroom life. Later, as an adviser to new teachers, she saw the same needs in her advisees.

But camaraderie, as important as it is, is not the only payoff of support groups. Barbara Diamond, a veteran teacher and teacher educator from Michigan, says that exchanging ideas with colleagues is one way teachers gain the self-confidence to make decisions about what is best for their students.

"Beginning teachers must include time for fueling the knowledge base from which instructional decisions should flow," says Diamond. "Initially, this could be informal meetings with other teachers in the building or in the district. Gradually, these meetings could become more focused and formalized." Diamond adds that participating in support groups can mean the "difference between teachers who enjoy their jobs and feel that they're effective and contributing, and those who become frustrated and burned out."

Veterans Need Support, Too

Support groups aren't just for beginners. Experienced teachers, who are just as isolated in their classrooms, also benefit from meeting and talking with their peers. Frequently, veterans form support groups organized around a particular curriculum area, teaching strategy, or professional interest. A group typically focuses on a particular topic that interests its members, such as cooperative learning, teaching to multiple intelligences, or designing a balanced literacy program.

After identifying a focus, support group members might review and discuss the research on a topic, watch videos or analyze commercially available programs, or try to model and demonstrate relevant teaching techniques. As they implement and practice the strategies they're studying, group members support each other with feedback and coaching (see the section on Peer Coaching).

Activities for Support Groups

Researchers Bruce Joyce and Beverly Showers, who have written about study and support groups, suggest these activities for group members:

✔ Ask a group member to read about a topic and share what he or she learns at the next meeting.

✔ If your group is interested in a certain teaching technique, send one teacher to a seminar for training, so he or she can then be the on-site trainer at the next group meeting.

✔ Plan a group "field trip," visiting a school that has a program your group would like to implement.

✔ Invite speakers and experts on certain techniques to give classroom demonstrations in your area.

✔ Observe each other's classes and offer feedback.

If there is no support group in your area, you may have to start one. It's a daunting task, but you don't have to tackle it alone. Team up with like-minded colleagues to discuss the idea, identify the group's focus, establish procedures and meeting schedules, and build a plan for action.

Some Examples In the middle/high school where I teach, teachers are sharply divided on the strategy of block scheduling. Those of us who want to implement the strategy decided informally to pool our efforts to educate and assuage the fears of our colleagues who oppose the idea. We have visited schools with block scheduling, gathered journal articles and personal testimonials, and even worked out several different versions of a block schedule for our small, rural setting.

Another district hosts periodic curriculum parties, where each teacher brings 100 copies of an idea to share with colleagues. Teachers can initiate curriculum-sharing parties on any level or scale.

Support groups put teachers in touch with others who share their interests and concerns. And it's not just talk. Talking stimulates thinking and reflecting on what it is we do in the classroom. And above all, teachers must be thinkers—not technicians applying a prescribed curriculum or strategy, but professionals whose expertise, judgments, and decisions guide the classroom.

❖ Networks

Closely related to teacher support groups are the various teacher networks emerging everywhere. Networks allow teachers to seek professional development among peers with similar interests. In the past 20 years, hundreds of teacher networks have been created in this country. Some are small and locally based, others are large and comprise thousands of members nationwide. Some are state-supported, while private organizations or universities fund others. Most focus on a particular subject matter, teaching strategy, or reform issue. And all have a tremendous impact on the way teachers teach and learn.

A Kentucky Example

One such network is the Kentucky Education Association's T^2—Teachers to the Power of Two. With 400 expert teachers acting as resources for their colleagues around the state, the network operates on the principle that teachers learn best from other teachers.

Basically, KEA members who want help with some aspect of their teaching simply contact T^2 and are then given a list of colleagues with expertise in that area. Funded by the Business Partnership for Kentucky Schools, the network pays for travel, expenses, and substitute teachers while a teacher seeks the necessary help and professional development.

Consider the experience of veteran teacher James Elmore, who contacted the network seeking help with developing hands-on science materials for his fifth-grade classroom. With support from T^2, Elmore observed science teacher Ray Ferguson (from across the state) and learned from Ferguson how to make and use the materials he needed.

Thousands of teachers have used the network since its inception in 1992. And the network is now available online, further expanding its impact. For more information on T^2, call KEA at (800) 231-4532 or visit the Web site at www.kea.org/professionaldevelopment/t2. You can also access information from the Web site at www.kea.org.

Authentic Professional Development

Members describe their networks as "a professional family" or "a support group of teachers, professors, and other professionals." Networks give teachers the chance to hear about the successes and failures of other teachers. And they meet a consistent demand for authentic professional development—development stemming from teachers' own interests and needs. With like-minded colleagues, network

---

ANATOMY OF AN ONLINE DISCOVERY

Talk about discovery learning! Looking for information on teacher centers one day, I logged onto the Internet and did a Web search using Yahoo!. I came up with 81 matches, including Getty ArtsEdNet at www.getty.edu/artsednet. The site description read "online service arts education from the Getty Center for Education in the Arts" and offered "lesson plans and resources for teachers." Intrigued, I clicked on the site and received a menu of choices from ArtsEdNet, including:

- Image Galleries and Exhibitions
- ArtsEdNet Talk
- Lesson Plans and Curriculum Ideas
- Highlights (exhibitions at the Getty Museum)

ArtsEdNet Talk caught my eye, and I clicked on to find out what it was all about. I discovered an online international network of teachers and learners who converse, via e-mail, on various topics suggested by participants. The network even features special guests who answer questions submitted by network participants. One of the many network tools is a "continuously updated archive of the ArtsEdNet Talk discussions," which "can be sorted by author, date, subject, or thread."

What possibilities for communication and interaction among colleagues! What unlimited avenues for sharing ideas, activities, strategies, and concerns! And networks such as this one exist in virtually all subject areas and for all special interest groups.

members can pool their knowledge and expertise and develop new ideas about how to improve their practice.

"Many educators trace the rise of networks to teachers' near-universal distaste for the ubiquitous, one-shot in-service seminars offered by districts, state agencies, and consultants," writes professional development expert Joanna Richardson. "Teachers' attitude about such training seems to be: If you aren't going to give us practical learning experiences, we'll do it ourselves."

NETWORKS: A FEW GOOD EXAMPLES

Here are just a few of the multitude of online networks serving educators. As you explore these respected, long-lived networks, you will meet people who can inform you of other, more local opportunities and experiences.

- **Bread Loaf Rural Teacher Network**
  Middlebury College
  Middlebury, VT 05753
  (802) 388-3711
  www.strom.clemson.edu/teams/literacy/RTN.html
  This network brings together rural teachers who want to improve students' experiences with literature and writing. It is sponsored by Middlebury College's Bread Loaf School of English and funded by the DeWitt Wallace Reader's Digest Fund.

- **California Subject-Matter Projects**
  http://csmp.ucop.edu
  This network focuses on improving teaching at all grade levels and in all subject areas with standards-based materials, professional development opportunities, and teacher forums.

- **International Education Consortium**
  8225 Florissant
  St. Louis, MO 63121
  (314) 872-8282
  http://csd.org/staffdev/iecweb/iec.html
  A network of humanities teachers that shares and generates resources to help teachers "prepare students to approach and appreciate the complex situations they are certain to encounter in our international and multicultural society."

- **National Geographic EdNet**
  National Geographic Society
  www.ngsednet.org
  Social studies teachers and others interested in integrating geography into the curriculum can build a web of contacts and resources through this nationwide network. Members can participate in the following online communities: Geography Action!, Geography & Literacy, Forces of Nature, International Studies in the Schools, and more.

- **IMPACT II**
  285 W. Broadway, Ste. 540
  New York, NY 10013
  (212) 966-5582
  www.teachnet.org
  This network documents and disseminates school-change projects and produces publications and videos created by teachers. More than 30,000 teachers have received IMPACT II grants. The site also features "Talk to Teachers," a bulletin board that invites teachers to discuss, share, and imagine.

- **Teachers Helping Teachers**
  www.pacificnet.net/~mandel
  This site bills itself as "By Teachers, For Teachers." Its stated purpose is to provide basic teaching tips to new teachers, new ideas and strategies for all teachers, and a forum for sharing expertise and tips with colleagues worldwide. The site features ideas and information in various subject and specialty areas, a comprehensive listing of educational resources (with links) on the Web, a question-and-answer forum, and more.

- **National Writing Project (NWP)**
  University of California
  2105 Bancroft Way #1042
  Berkeley, CA 94720-1042
  (510) 642-0963
  www.writingproject.org
  NWP is a national network of teachers of writing who wish to share tools, strategies, and resources to improve the teaching and learning of writing in grades K through 12. Members can participate in online discussion groups and conferences and receive an e-newsletter with links to related articles and announcements from the Writing Project.

ONE SMALL-SCALE CENTER

Teachers in one West Virginia school share their ideas and materials in a special teachers-only corner of a school media center. Teachers donate or suggest books and activities that they've found particularly useful and effective. For special whole-school themes or activities (such as Earth Day or Johnny Appleseed Day), the teachers pool their resources, centrally locating them for everyone's use. A resource specialist keeps track of the materials and offers suggestions to teachers looking for ideas.

Online Networks

Technology today has changed forever the character of teacher networks. The Internet is itself one mega-network, connecting individuals, businesses, governments, and organizations worldwide. E-mail, chat lines, and electronic bulletin boards are all ways to network or talk with colleagues who have the same interests as you. Some Internet networks are well known. Others you're likely to stumble upon as you use the Internet for other purposes.

❖ Teacher Centers

For practical solutions to teaching's daily problems and challenges, a teacher center is a sure bet. While many of your curricular and information needs can now be met through the Internet, a teacher center is someplace you can go for companionship and support.

There are many different types of centers. Some are organized and run by teachers for teachers; others are organized and run by school districts, agencies, or associations to support teacher development and improved practice. Check with your state, regional, or local education agencies for lists of centers in your area. Following are just a few examples:

1. **NASA Ames Educator Resource Centers** provide materials, lesson ideas, information, and support for science and astronomy instruction. Log on to www.nasa.gov/home/index.html. (Click on the appropriate grade level in the For Educators area and then go to Contacts for Educators for a listing of resource centers by state.)
2. More than 120 **Teacher Centers in New York,** including center, addresses, and directors are listed at www.nysed.gov/home/facmtg/teachctr.html. (Go to your state's Department of Education Web site to locate local networks.)
3. The **New Teacher Center** (NTC) at the University of California–Santa Cruz bills itself as a "national resource dedicated to teacher development and new teacher training, and the support of programs and practices that promote excellence and diversity in America's teaching force." Find it at www.newteachercenter.org.

No two centers look or function alike, but the best share certain characteristics:

✔ **A focus on individual and continuing needs, with local, practical solutions to specific problems**. A teacher who comes looking for help with a history unit, for example, might learn he or she can tap into a whole network of local resources, both human and material. There may be books, films, teaching aids, educational materials, and even local experts who can talk to a class.

✔ **Practical make-and-take programs**. Using center supplies and equipment, teachers can often make many types of classroom materials—from a customized worksheet to activities and manipulatives for a learning center.

✔ **Teachers teaching teachers**. Teachers with expertise in a certain area might demonstrate teaching techniques. Or they might help colleagues develop and plan a curriculum unit. The center director is often a resident mentor or adviser who, upon request, will coach teachers in their classrooms, demonstrate strategies, and even help teach lessons. Some set up informal networks of teachers sharing common interests.

Center directors and staff also arrange or conduct workshops and professional-development activities. In fact, so many professional-development activities take place in teacher centers that many are now officially called teacher-development centers. Teachers can often take in-service courses there or design their own course of study.

✔ **Opportunities for personal growth.** Centers frequently offer activities ranging from aerobic exercise and stress management to investment counseling. These informal opportunities to meet other teachers contribute to health and happiness.

✔ **A warm, friendly atmosphere and a spirit of collegiality.** Sound inviting? Teacher centers can be fantastic and fun places.

❖ Professional Associations

Another way to connect with colleagues and grow professionally is through professional associations. There are local, state, and national associations; content associations, such as the National Council of Teachers of Mathematics (www.nctm.org); special-interest associations, such as the Learning Disabilities Association of America (www.ldanatl.org); and many other types of education associations and organizations. Virtually all of them produce newsletters, magazines, and/or other publications; host conferences and special workshops; and provide communication forums and other vehicles for networking members. See page 298 for a list.

❖ Conferences and Conventions

Each year, teachers can interact with colleagues, sharpen their professional skills, and broaden their networks by attending local, state, or national conferences and conventions. Such professional meetings are held by subject-matter associations, special-interest groups (for example, educators of the learning disabled or gifted), county and state professional-development offices, educational publishers, the teachers' unions, and child and parent advocacy groups. Most feature papers and information formally presented by educators and other experts, exhibit areas set up by educational vendors, and hospitality suites or chat rooms sponsored by various associations.

Quality varies, to be sure. But any time teachers get together, the potential exists for a meaningful exchange of ideas and information. Here are some tips to make your conference experiences positive and productive.

✔ Ask your department head, principal, or staff-development specialist to send conference announcements your way. You can't attend meetings you don't know about.

✔ Watch for conference announcements in your professional magazines. Publications such as *Educational Leadership* (published by the Association for Supervision and Curriculum Development at www.ascd.org) feature entire issues describing conferences. Internet Web sites also list such meetings.

✔ Inquire about financial support for attending conferences. In my school district, mileage, registration, and hotel costs are often covered, provided teachers submit a written request far enough in advance to allow the school board to approve the meeting. We also are allotted substitutes for approved meetings.

✔ Take canvas tote bags (or an extra suitcase, if you are traveling by air) to bring home the written materials and free "goodies" you pick up. Many conventions also offer mailing facilities if you accumulate too much material to carry around.

✔ Carry along preprinted address labels for signing up for materials, information, mailing lists, or raffles.

✔ Take business cards to facilitate the process of exchanging names and addresses with new contacts you make.

✔ Study the conference program ahead of time, highlighting those sessions that sound most appropriate for you.

✔ Carry a pad and pens for taking notes.

✔ Team up with a colleague for concurrent sessions. Usually, conferences feature many more good sessions than you can attend. If you attend some and a colleague attends others, you can share the information and materials acquired. If that's not possible, inquire about handouts from sessions you are forced to miss or ask conference presenters for a copy of their papers.

❖ In Summary

As mentors and interns, peer coaches, partners, team teachers, members of professional associations or networks, colleagues meeting at a teacher center, or friends sharing advice and teaching tips, we're usually at our best when working together.

"Discuss things with colleagues and learn from their wisdom," advises Pennsylvania veteran Laurie Borger. "If you're not afraid to ask for help or take risks, you will make some great discoveries."

What options are available to you? How can you develop or improve a working relationship with colleagues? It's well worth the trouble to find out.

Professional Organizations

Through professional organizations, teachers can meet others sharing their particular interests. These organizations host meetings and offer professional-development opportunities in all fields of teaching. Many of their journals and magazines routinely include research-synthesis articles.

American Association of School Administrators (AASA)
801 N. Quincy St., Ste. 700
Arlington, VA 22203
(703) 528-0700
www.aasa.org

American Educational Research Association (AERA)
1230 17th St. NW
Washington, DC 20036
(202) 223-9485
www.aera.net

American Federation of Teachers (AFT)
555 New Jersey Ave. NW
Washington, DC 20001
(202) 879-4400
www.aft.org

Association for Childhood Education (ACE)
17904 Georgia Ave., Ste. 215
Wheaton, MD 20832
(800) 423-3563
www.udel.edu/bateman/acei

Association for Educational Communications and Technology (AECT)
1800 N. Stonelake Dr., Ste. 2
Bloomington, IN 47404
(877) 677-AECT
www.aect.org

Association for Supervision and Curriculum Development (ASCD)
1703 N. Beauregard St.
Alexandria, VA 22311
(800) 933-2723
www.ascd.org

Association of Science-Technology Centers (ASTC)
1025 Vermont Ave., NW, Ste. 500
Washington, DC 20005
(202) 783-7200
www.astc.org

Council for Exceptional Children (CEC)
1110 North Glebe Rd., Ste. 300
Arlington, VA 22201
(703) 620-3660
www.cec.sped.org

International Reading Association (IRA)
800 Barksdale Rd., P.O.B. 8139
Newark, DE 19714-8139
(302) 731-1600
www.reading.org

International Technology Education Association (ITEA)
1914 Association Dr., Ste. 201
Reston, VA 22091
(703) 860-2100
www.iteawww.org

Music Teachers National Association (MTNA)
441 Vine St., Ste. 505
Cincinnati, OH 45202
(513) 421-1420
www.mtna.org

National Alliance of Black School Educators (NABSE)
310 Pennsylvania Ave. SE
Washington, DC 20003
(202) 608-6310
www.nabse.org

National Art Education Association (NAEA)
1916 Association Dr.
Reston, VA 22091-1590
(703) 860-8000
www.naea-reston.org

National Association for Science, Technology & Society (NASTS)
University of Maryland, Baltimore County
1000 Hilltop Circle
Baltimore, MD 21250
(410) 455-2869
www.nasts.org

National Association of Elementary School Principals (NAESP)
1615 Duke St.
Arlington, VA 22314-3483
(703) 684-3345
www.naesp.org

National Association of Secondary School Principals (NASSP)
1904 Association Dr.
Reston, VA 22091
(703) 860-0200
www.nassp.org

National Council for Geographic Education (NCGE)
206A Martin Hall
Jacksonville, AL 36265-1602
(256) 782-5293
www.ncge.org

National Council for the Social Studies (NCSS)
8555 Sixteenth St., Ste. 500
Silver Spring, MD 20910
(301) 588-1800
www.socialstudies.org

National Council of Teachers of English (NCTE)
111 West Kenyon Rd.
Urbana, IL 61801
(217) 328-3870
www.ncte.org

National Council of Teachers of Mathematics (NCTM)
1906 Association Dr.
Reston, VA 20191-1502
(703) 620-9840
www.nctm.org

National Education Association (NEA)
1201 16th St. NW
Washington, DC 20036
(202) 833-4000
www.nea.org

National Middle School Association (NMSA)
4151 Executive Parkway, Ste. 300
Westerville, OH 43081
(800) 528-6672
www.nmsa.org

National School Boards Association (NSBA)
1680 Duke St.
Alexandria, VA 22314-3493
(703) 838-6722
www.nsba.org

National Science Teachers Association (NSTA)
1840 Wilson Blvd.
Arlington, VA 22201-3000
(703) 243-7100
www.nsta.org

National Staff Development Council (NSDC)
5995 Fairfield Rd., Ste. 4
Oxford, OH 45056
(513) 523-6029
www.nsdc.org

Phi Delta Kappa
408 N. Union St., P.O.B 789
Bloomington, IN 47402-0789
(800) 766-1156
www.pdkintl.org

❖ Works Cited

Acosta, Diana, Judith Shulman, and Joel Colbert. *The Mentor Teacher Casebook*. Eugene, OR: University of Oregon ERIC Clearinghouse, 1987.

Brandt, Ron. "On a New Direction for Teacher Evaluation: A Conversation with Tom McGreal." *Educational Leadership* 53, no. 6 (March 1996): 30–33.

Danielson, Charlotte. *Enhancing Professional Practice: A Framework for Teaching*. Alexandria, VA: Association for Supervision and Curriculum Development, 1996.

Devaney, Kathleen. *Building a Teachers' Center*. New York: Teachers College Press, 1979.

Joyce, Bruce, et al. *Student Achievement Through Staff Development*. 3rd ed. Alexandria, VA: Association for Supervision and Curriculum Development, 2002.

Katz, Lilian G. "Multiple Perspectives on the Quality of Early Childhood Programs." (ERIC Digest ED 355041). *ERIC Clearinghouse on Elementary and Early Childhood Education*, Urbana, IL, 1993. Available: http://ericadr.piccard.csc.com/extra/ericdigests/ed355041.html.

Little, Judith Warren, and Linda J. Nelson, eds. *A Leader's Guide to Mentor Training*. San Francisco, CA: WestEd, 1990.

Richardson, Joanna. "Networking." *Teacher Magazine* (August 1996): 40–44.

Shulman, Judith, and Joel Colbert eds. *The Intern Teacher Casebook*. 2nd ed. San Francisco: Far West Laboratory for Educational Research and Development, 1998.

Showers, Beverly, and Bruce Joyce. "The Evolution of Peer Coaching." *Educational Leadership* 53, no. 6 (March 1996): 12–16.

❖ Resources

Mentoring New Teachers

Feaster, Rebecca. "Mentoring the New Teacher." *Journal of School Improvement* 3, no.2 (Fall 2002).

Explains that mentoring programs that focus on training, support, and retention can help create an environment that fosters psychological and cognitive growth.

Feiman-Nemser, Sharon. "What New Teachers Need To Learn." *Educational Leadership* 60, no. 8 (May 2003): 25-29.
Examines the on-the-job learning needs of beginning teachers. Discusses research on teacher learning curve and enculturation process. Describes elements of a quality beginning-teacher induction program that involves mentoring and the use of standards.

Portner, Hal. *Mentoring New Teachers*. Thousand Oaks, CA: Corwin Press, 2002.

Scherer, Marge. *A Better Beginning: Supporting and Mentoring New Teachers*. Alexandria, VA: Association for Supervision and Curriculum Development, 1999.

Villani, Susan. *Mentoring Programs for New Teachers: Models of Induction and Support*. Thousand Oaks, CA: Corwin Press, 2001.

Wesley, Donald C. "Nurturing the Novices." *Phi Delta Kappan* 84, no. 6 (February 2003): 466–467, 470.
Describes how veteran and beginning teachers work together in a mutually beneficial nurturing relationship.

Wong, Harry K., and Christina Asquith. "Supporting New Teachers." *School Board Journal* 189, no. 12 (December 2002): 22–24.
Describes benefits of induction programs for beginning teachers. Profiles induction program called Framework for Inducting, Retaining, and

Supporting Teachers (FIRST) at Lafourche Parish Public School in Louisiana. Also includes brief descriptions of district programs and state support for new teacher inductions in several other states.

Peer Coaching

Allen, Dwight, and Alyce LeBlanc. *Collaborative Peer Coaching That Improves Instruction. The 2+2 Performance Appraisal Model.* Thousand Oaks, CA: Corwin Press, 2004.

Gottesman, Barbara. *Peer Coaching for Educators.* Lanham, MD: Scarecrow Press, 2000.

Robbins, Pam. *How to Plan and Implement a Peer Coaching Program.* Alexandria, VA: Association for Supervision and Curriculum Development, 1991.

Showers, Beverly, and Bruce Joyce. "The Evolution of Peer Coaching." *Educational Leadership,* 53(6), March 1996, pp. 12–16.

Staff Development

Brookfield, Stephen D. *Understanding and Facilitating Adult Learning: A Comprehensive Analysis of Principles and Effective Practices.* San Francisco: Jossey-Bass, 1986.

Jones, Elizabeth, ed. *Growing Teachers: Partnerships in Staff Development.* Washington, DC: National Association for the Education of Young Children, 1993. Available: www.clas.uiuc.edu. (Search CLAS Publications by author.) This excellent document features case studies, anecdotal records, and other sources of helpful information on all aspects of the mentoring process.

Rhodes, Christopher, et al. *A Practical Guide to Mentoring, Coaching, and Peer-Networking: Teacher Professional Development in Schools and Colleges.* New York: RoutledgeFalmer, 2004.

Chapter Eight

Reflective Teaching: Thinking and Growing Professionally

"Learning to teach is a bigger job than universities, schools, experience, or personal disposition alone can accomplish."

—*Sharon Feiman-Nemser, Brandeis University*

By now, it should be obvious that learning to teach is not just for beginners. It's a process that continues well beyond your first, third, or even twentieth year of teaching. But that's what keeps teaching interesting. Classrooms are places where both students and teachers learn.

"I think the most important idea for young teachers to grasp is that teaching is a constantly evolving process," stresses Pennsylvania veteran Laurie Borger. "We are constantly trying to perfect the art of instruction in our classrooms. You will never say, 'I am finally a master teacher,' but you will spend your career pursuing the science and art of instruction. You will always be learning and perfecting."

Author and educator David Hawkins recalls hearing a 35-year veteran tell a student teacher the reason she had stayed with teaching all those years was her constant awareness that there was still so much to learn.

Still so Much to Learn

"So much to learn." Why not adopt that as a personal motto to guide your professional teaching career? So much to learn . . . so much to explore . . . so many exciting challenges and opportunities. The hallmark of professionalism is a constant striving to refine and improve practice. And that's what this chapter is all about.

Professional development: Without it, we stagnate, wilt, burn out. Research surveys have revealed that professional development and expanded career opportunities mean more to teachers than increased salaries or improved working conditions. Professional development is the responsibility of professional teachers.

And what does it mean to be a professional? It means reflecting upon your practice making informed judgments in complex environments, supported by solid, research-based knowledge. Your professional development must revolve around thinking about what it is you do as a teacher. Professionals strive to improve their teaching by continually examining it and its effects on student learning.

It's the Thought That Counts

In teaching, it's the thought that counts. That doesn't mean that intentions are more important than actions. It means that teachers must be thinkers and decision makers who take full responsibility for their classrooms and students, as opposed to technicians merely applying a prescribed practice.

We often tell students, "Think about what you're doing!" The same advice applies to us. Reflecting on what one does in the classroom is the key to professional growth.

"The better you are at thinking and talking about teaching, the better you will be in practice," was a favorite piece of advice from the late Doris Dillon, a California teacher and professional development expert.

Many of the things teachers simply don't realize they are doing or not doing become obvious when they just stop and think. And just identifying a problem is taking a giant step toward solving it.

But systematic reflection is not as simple as it sounds. It takes time and concentrated effort—two things always in short supply. Fortunately, there are many strategies to help you stop and think. The activities and alternatives to one-shot in-services discussed in Chapter Seven—peer coaching, mentoring, networks and support groups, team teaching, and teacher centers—all facilitate reflective teaching. This chapter explores some other approaches.

Even if you don't have time to pursue many of these professional-development activities during your first years of teaching, you can still make the commitment to lifelong learning and professional excellence. After all, the very qualities that probably brought you to teaching—your own excitement and zest for life and learning and a desire to help young people develop into productive, whole, and happy persons—will keep you striving for excellence.

❖ Journal Keeping

Writing is thinking. Just ask any author. We don't really know what we think until we write about it. That is, our thinking evolves as we write. Even most fiction writers claim that characters and plot develop only through the actual writing.

When we ask students to write reader responses, we are really asking them to clarify their thinking through their writing. Writing-to-learn strategies allow students to examine and organize their thinking in any subject area, including math and science. The same idea can be applied to reflective teaching.

In their landmark studies of planning conducted at Michigan State University, researchers Christopher Clark and Robert Yinger asked teachers to describe their thinking and planning in a daily journal or diary.

"The process of journal keeping was a powerful experience for the teachers who undertook it," the researchers noted. "They reported that they learned a great deal about their thinking and teaching. Until asked to keep a detailed report of their planning, they did not realize how much thought and energy they put into planning for instruction. In a sense, they were newly appreciating themselves as professionals."

Two things happened to the teachers keeping journals.

"Their morale seemed to improve," said the researchers. "But more importantly, these teachers became researchers on their own teaching—alert to the many opportunities teachers have to take responsibility for their own continued professional development—and to gradually and systematically improve the effectiveness of their teaching and the quality of life in their classrooms."

These days, many student teaching, practicum, and professional-development programs require teachers to keep reflective journals. And journals are a large part of the National Board Certification process. (For information, see www.nbpts.org) It's a proven strategy that has made its way from research to practice.

❖ Writing for Others

When you write for an audience, the reflective process is much the same, because writing in any form requires thinking. There are many outlets for your thoughts and writings on your personal experiences, ideas, or innovations.

Class Newsletter

Test your wings (or pen) by developing your own class newsletter (see Chapter Six for some ideas on how to start). Parents are a captive audience who will enjoy the extra effort you put forth. Go beyond explanations of the rules and regulations in your classroom

---

TIPS ON JOURNAL KEEPING

Keeping a journal can be eye-opening, cathartic, and instructive. To make the experience as beneficial as possible, keep these tips in mind.

- **Make regular entries.** Get into the habit of writing often—every day, if possible.
- **Keep a permanent record** by writing in something durable—a spiral notebook, datebook, or diary.
- **Set aside a certain time** each day for journal writing. You might have your students keep daily journals, too, and work on yours at the same time. You'd be offering students a valuable experience, providing an effective model, and writing—all at the same time. Of course, give yourself the chance to write uninterrupted and in private sometimes.
- **Anything goes.** If all you can do at first is complain about how terrible everything is going, fine. Once that's off your chest, you'll be able to write more objectively and analyze what's going wrong. You'll probably even start noticing that a lot is going right.
- **Record your growth and look for those small successes.** "Take the time, every day, to pat yourself on the back for the risks you have dared to take and all the things you are learning to do well," suggests teacher and author Jane Bluestein. She offers these examples of entries made by beginners recording their growth each week:

  "My self-control seems to be improving. I kept my cool through a tough situation."

  "I don't cry every day."

  "I'm remembering to get each child's attention before talking."

  "I'm smiling more."

  "I am feeling comfortable with the faculty at my school. The teachers have become so supportive, and I am becoming more confident as a teacher."

- Occasionally try to **target different aspects of your teaching** to study in detail. Are you interested in offering equal time and attention to all students? Then keep track of your personal interactions each day. Make a list of the students you enjoy being around and those you don't. What are the characteristics you like or dislike? Write about it. Get it down in black and white where you can see it. Then try to assess where you can change.
- Daily journals are a good way to **keep track of your time allocations**—both academic and nonacademic.
- **Reread your journal entries occasionally.** It's instructive, sometimes amusing, and usually encouraging to see how your concerns have changed over time.
- **Store your journal in a safe place.** Your thoughts are private, and you need to be completely candid with yourself. Uninvited readers may misinterpret what you write.

and tell them about your general goals or teaching philosophy.

Describe the challenges of teaching fractions to your fourth graders or the joy of witnessing the students working out a problem on their own. Let readers know what teachers and teaching are all about. Give them some insight into the complex job you undertake every single day.

You could also invite parents to share their insights and responses to your articles. Or set up a question/answer format. Their questions and comments will stimulate your thinking even further. And just imagine the good will generated by such communications with parents!

Magazine Articles and Books

You can share your thoughts with other teachers by writing for a professional publication. *Instructor* regularly features articles written by practicing educators. So do most other professional publications. And many publications also have monthly columns that are forums for teachers' thoughts and ideas.

As more and more teachers engage in classroom research, they are publishing the results of their research in scholarly journals. (See the listing on page 306 of some of the more prominent journals and magazines). General-interest magazines such as *Parent* also frequently carry articles by teachers about teaching. Parents tend to be intensely interested in their children's education, and most publications reflect that interest.

Many veteran teachers land positions as columnists and regular contributors for magazines and even newspapers. Even if the writing you submit is not always accepted for publication, you still benefit from the process. And keep track of the things you write in your professional portfolio.

Teachers also constitute a large percentage of book authors. The book lists of large publishing houses such as Scholastic feature

WRITING FOR ONLINE JOURNALS

All major journals and magazines have Web sites and offerings online, but increasingly, new journals and magazines are published exclusively online. That is, the writing is submitted electronically, and subscribers read the finished product on a computer screen (or print it out). One of the best for teachers—and by teachers—is *Educational Insights*, produced by the University of British Columbia.

In the March 2004 issue, first-grade teacher Susan Pinsonneault and third-grade teacher Kara Malhi describe an action research project they undertook in Pinsonneault's classroom. As described in their article, "How Can Teachers Support Gender Equity in Their Classrooms," the teachers posed a basic question to guide their research: "Could we, by exposing our students to a variety of stories—in which both male and female characters play a variety of roles—help our students to become more open to different ideas or values with respect to the respective roles of the two genders?" The article goes on to describe how they investigated this issue by reading various stories to students and "examining what they preferred to read about and whom they identified with in the stories."

The online article is replete with children's drawings (part of the research data), discussions, and insights from the teacher researchers, and references to other studies of gender equity. Readers can even obtain a "printer-friendly" copy to examine away from the computer or share with colleagues.

The ease and accessibility of online journals represents what's best about technology these days. Check it out at www.ccfi.educ.ubc.ca. Click on publications, then *Educational Insights* and find the issue you want.

hundreds of teacher authors—teachers writing professional books for other teachers. That's not even counting the many teachers who use their professional knowledge of children and learning to write quality children's books, or the many teachers who are hired as textbook consultants and writers.

Write to the editors of the magazines, journals, or publishing houses that interest you and request a copy of their writers' guidelines. You can find addresses on publication mastheads or listed in the sourcebook *Writer's Market* (Cincinnati, OH: Writer's Digest Books, published annually).

Writing Online

From personal Web pages to e-mail, from chat lines to teaching tips on electronic bulletin boards, the Internet gives us an almost unlimited opportunity to write about teaching.

Virtually every Web site dedicated to teachers, and many of those that are educational in nature, include some forum for written responses. Just check your favorite sites. Following are a few good examples of online writing opportunities:

✔ **Instructor InterACTION** (http://teacher.scholastic.com) Among the choices at this site, teachers can participate in the Timely Topic area where the magazine solicits teacher input and ideas are shared.

✔ **Educational Insights** (www.ccfi.educ.ubc.ca. Click on publications, then *Educational Insights*, and follow the links from there.) This electronic journal offers several types of writing opportunities for teachers.

"Diary" is a space for readers to discuss "events, issues, theories, concepts, and challenges" in education. For each issue of the journal, a guest writer opens the

---

VIDEO CASE STUDIES

Viewing videos of other teachers teaching can be as instructive as viewing ourselves in action. Teacher educators James Rowley and Patricia Hart from the University of Dayton have developed two video series that feature expert teachers working with urban students. Each tape in each series includes eight to ten scenes of a teacher demonstrating a particular strategy. Viewers reflect on real teaching moments and share their reflections in group discussions.

Built into the video case studies are numerous "reflection points"—places where the video is paused for teachers to react to the actions taken in a problem situation and suggest what they might have done under similar circumstances. For example, in one scene, a teacher is confronted with a student who has put his head down on the desk to sleep during a presentation. Rowley and Hart explain that these reflection points enable viewers to participate in real teaching dilemmas in which often there is no one right answer.

Used extensively in the Dayton, Ohio, area for both preservice and in-service education, the video series (*Mentoring the New Teacher* and *Becoming a Star Urban Teacher*) are available from the Association for Supervision and Curriculum Development at (800) 933-ASCD or online at http://shop.ascd.org.

---

conversation with a short essay or reflection, and then readers are invited to respond. The editors compile readers' responses and publish the complete "Diary" in a related *Educational Insights* journal issue.

You can find a more formal writing opportunity in the "Notes From the Field" area. Here, *Educational Insights* invites practicing educators to "fill its virtual pages with the vibrancy and immediacy of their voices, sounded, as they are, in the midst of lived pedagogy." This section is dedicated to the reflections of teacher researchers.

In addition to articles, the journal also invites essays, works of poetic and/or artistic reflection, or book reviews.

✔ **Let's Talk!** (www.teachnet.org) This easy-to-use area is a bulletin board for ideas and input on specified topics. Topics vary and recently included educational technology, teacher-grant opportunities, and school reform through teacher leadership.

Journals and Other Educational Publications

Following is a list of educational journals and publications. This list is not all-inclusive, but it is a good starting point for teachers seeking the most current information on almost any education topic. Some of these publications are available via the Internet. Most sites include a limited amount of information or the table of contents for an issue. A few may contain full-text articles online, but typically, readers are required to purchase the magazine or journal.

Action Learning: Research and Practice

American Biology Teacher

American Educational Research Journal

American Journal of Education

American Journal on Mental Retardation

American Music Teacher

American School Board Journal

Arts Education Policy Review

Behavioral Disorders Journal

Book Links

British Journal of Special Education

Bulletin of the Council for Research in Music Education

Career Development Quarterly

Child Development

Child Welfare

Childhood Education

Chronicle of Higher Education

The Communication Education Journal

Comparative Education Review

Computers in Education

Creative Classroom

Current Issues in Education

Early Child Development and Care

Early Childhood Education

Educating Exceptional Children

Education

Education and Training in Mental Retardation and Developmental Disabilities

Education and Treatment of Children

Education Review

Education Week

Education Week on the Web

Educational Administration Quarterly

Educational Psychology

Educational Leadership

Educational Measurement: Issues and Practices

The Educational Record

Educational Research Quarterly

Educational Technology and Society

Educational Theory

Elementary School Journal

English Journal

Exceptional Children

Exceptional Parent

Focus on Exceptional Children

Gifted Child Quarterly

Harvard Educational Review

Health Education and Behavior (former title: Health Education Quarterly)

High School Journal

Highlights for Children

History of Education Quarterly

History Teacher

Horn Book Guide

Horn Book Magazine

Instructor

International Journal of Disability, Development, and Education

International Journal of Educational Management

International Journal of Instructional Media

International Review of Education

J.O.P.E.R.D. (former title: Journal of Physical Education, Recreation, & Dance)

Journal for Research in Mathematics Education

Journal for the Education of the Gifted

Journal of Adolescent and Adult Literacy (former title: Journal of Reading)

Journal of Art Education

Journal of Athletic Training

Journal of Blacks in Higher Education

Journal of Chemical Education

Journal of Child Language

Journal of Education

Journal of Education Policy

Journal of Educational Administration

Journal of Educational Measurement

Journal of Educational Psychology

Journal of Educational Research

Journal of Educational Thought

Journal of Environmental Education

Journal of Experimental Education

Journal of General Education

Journal of Health and Physical Education

Journal of Learning Disabilities

Journal of Literacy Research

Journal of Research and Development in Education

Journal of Research in Childhood Education

Journal of Research in Music Education

Journal of Research in Science Teaching

Journal of School Health

Journal of School Psychology

Journal of Special Education

Journal of Speech, Language, and Hearing Research

Journal of Teacher Education

Journal of the American Academy of Child and Adolescent Psychiatry

Journalism Educator

Language Arts

Language Learning

Leadership Learning Disability Quarterly

Library Administration Management

Library Journal

Library Resources and Technical Services

Library Trends

Mailbox

Mathematics Teacher

Media and Methods: Multimedia Products, Technologies, and Programs for K–12 School Districts

Mental Retardation

Middle School Journal

Music Educators Journal

NASSP Bulletin

National Forum: The Phi Kappa Phi Journal

NEA Today

New Library World

Parents

Peabody Journal of Education

Phi Delta Kappan

Physical Educator

Physics Teacher

Preventing School Failure

Principal

Principal Leadership

Professional School Counseling

Psychological Review

Psychology in the Schools

Public Administration Review

Quest (physical education)

Reading Improvement

Reading Research and Instruction

Reading Research Quarterly

Reading Teacher

Remedial and Special Education (RASE)

Research Quarterly for Exercise & Sport

Review of Educational Research

Scholastic Update

School and Community

School Arts

School Library Journal (SLT)

School Library Media Activities Monthly

School Science and Mathematics

Science and Children

Science Education

Science Teacher

Social Studies

Social Studies and the Young Learner

Sociology of Education

Sociology of Sport Journal

Studies in Art Education

Studies in Philosophy and Education

Teacher Education and Practice

Teacher Education Quarterly

Teaching and Teacher Education

Teaching Children Mathematics

Teaching English as a Second Language

Teaching Exceptional Children

Teaching History

Teaching Music

Teaching Pre-K–8

Teaching Tolerance

Techniques (former title: Vocational Education Journal)

TechDirections

T.H.E. Journal: Technological Horizons in Education

Theory Into Practice

Training

Young Children

❖ Viewing Videotapes

Reflection is a way of seeing. And nothing helps you see yourself more accurately than watching a videotape of your teaching. With recording equipment readily available in most schools, you can arrange for a colleague or parent volunteer to videotape your teaching. The tape allows you to look at the classroom as an outsider, analyze yourself in action, and see your practice in a new way.

For example, a tape might show when students are confused because you've failed to communicate the intent of a lesson or activity. Or it might reveal that when students gather in a circle, they tend to sit in the same configuration each time, leading you to consider whether you could improve the lesson or eliminate behavior problems by adjusting the seating arrangements.

For me, videotape revealed that I was consistently ignoring (unintentionally, of course) one quiet girl in my class whose more outgoing classmates dominated our literature discussions. I began to make a conscious effort to call on this student, even when she had not raised her hand, and was delighted to discover her deep insights about the novels we read. (Her classmates were impressed, too.) On a more personal note, videotapes also prompted me to improve my posture when I stood in front of the students.

West Virginia teacher Susie Davis had never seen a videotape of her own teaching until a parent volunteer taped a reading lesson. As she later viewed the tape, Davis immediately saw one behavior she wanted to change.

"I noticed that I never made eye contact with a student who responded correctly to a question," said Davis. "I was already looking ahead to my next question, so I'd say, 'That's right' and move on. Twenty years of teaching and I wasn't making eye contact!"

Just by seeing yourself in action, you can spot some easily remedied problems. And videotape affords us the chance to watch individual students, too—responding to a lesson, interacting with you or peers, and so on.

Teacher-educator Barbara Diamond gives the example of one child who persistently asked questions. After carefully studying him on videotape, she recognized two patterns to his questions. Some he asked to gain information, but others he asked to gain control.

Patterns and habits in speech, body language, interactions—all things teachers don't have time to analyze while they teach—reveal a lot when they're analyzed on videotape. So get those cameras rolling.

❖ The Search for Knowledge

In addition to reflecting on our own practices, we must also reach out to the profession at large. To grow professionally, teachers need information about teaching. And there's a lot of it out there. Just as lawyers or doctors or engineers need to

A RESOURCE FOR READERS

For busy teachers who need help sifting through vast amounts of printed information on education, the *Annual Editions* series might be the answer. The series features more than 70 annually updated volumes covering many different topics. Several are directly relevant for teachers: *Early Childhood Education, Educating Exceptional Children, Education, Educational Psychology, Teaching English as a Second Language,* and *Computers in Education.* (Many other volumes would be useful in various content areas.)

Series editors monitor more than 300 of the most important magazines, journals, and newspapers, selecting articles they feel are the most noteworthy. Thus, in one convenient source, the reader has inexpensive access to much of the most useful information. Each volume features topic guides, annotated tables of contents, unit overviews, and indexes.

For information, visit the Web site at www.dushkin.com/annualeditions.

keep current with what's happening in their professions, we teachers must keep pace with new knowledge about teaching—or create our own.

Read, Read, Read

There is extensive professional literature on teaching. It ranges from the practical to the scholarly, with books, publications, and Internet sources focusing on every aspect of teaching and all subject matters.

Practical publications offer ideas and activities teachers can implement immediately in the classroom. The more scholarly works— research reports and education journals— inform your thinking and provide information to help you make decisions and reflect on your own practice. Professional teachers need a healthy measure of both.

In a recent editorial Ron Brandt, former editor of *Educational Leadership*, discussed the importance of keeping informed:

"Professional practice is not just a matter of personal opinion. Our advanced civilization depends on shared knowledge. Progress comes through experimentation, documentation, and willingness to learn from the experiences of others. My perspective on school reform comes partly from personal experience but mostly from research findings and, even more convincing, from the testimony of practicing educators."

Professional Publications Many of the publications devoted to teaching and/or subject matter are listed in this chapter. Find these magazines in your library or teacher center, or write to the publishers for sample copies.

ONLINE PROFESSIONAL DEVELOPMENT

Increasingly, teachers are turning to online professional development. From courses for credit to online resource banks and mentoring support, there are a number of programs for the offering. Increasingly accessible, easy to use, and convenient (course participation takes place right at your home or school computer!), online PD courses can help you gain skills, deepen your practice, and meet district requirements. Here is a sampling of online programs.

COMPANY	WEB SITE	PROGRAM DESCRIPTION
Lesson Lab	www.skylightedu.com	Broad range of undergraduate and graduate courses online, including masters degree programs
University of Phoenix Online	http://online.phoenix.edu	Broad range of undergraduate and graduate courses online, including masters degree programs
Laureate Education	www.degrees4teachers.net	Broad range of online advanced degree programs and graduate courses for K–12 teachers
EdTech Leaders Online	www.edtechleaders.org	Train-the-trainer, online course design, and online course facilitator training
PBS TeacherLine	http://teacherline.pbs.org/teacherline	Online professional development through facilitated courses that target mathematics, reading/language arts, and technology integration
Scholastic Red	www.scholasticred.com	Online courses with site-based facilitators, designed to help raise student achievement in reading; courses available for individual teachers
The Distance Learning Project @Teachers College	http://dlp.tc.columbia.edu	Post-graduate courses in multiple disciplines
SchoolKiT International	www.schoolkit.com	Media-rich course offerings and supporting resource library
Educational Impact	www.educationalimpact.com	Extensive Web-based streaming video library, supported by Web-based teacher resource library
Classroom Connect	www.classroom.com	Online professional development across a wide range of subjects, with strong focus on integrating technology into classroom teaching

From "Take off With Online Learning" by Roberta Salvador, *Instructor*, October 2004.

Further, the National Education Association, the American Federation of Teachers, and their state affiliates have their own offerings of newsletters, publications, and curriculum materials. (For contact information, see Chapter Seven, page 298.)

ERIC Every educator needs to know about the Educational Resources Information Center (ERIC). Sponsored by the Institute of Education Sciences of the U.S. Department of Education, ERIC represents the world's premier database of journal and nonjournal education literature. The new ERIC online system, released in September 2004, offers a centralized ERIC Web site for searching the ERIC bibliographic database of more than 1.1 million citations going back to 1966. Further, more than 107,000 full-text nonjournal documents issued since 1993, previously available through fee-based services only, are now available for free.

The new site provides users with increased search capabilities and simple, streamlined retrieval methods. In addition, the Web site provides users with the capability to save and rerun searches using the My ERIC personalization feature. Newly indexed materials that are not available free of charge are made accessible through database links to commercial sources.

WRITING FOR GRANTS

Researching teaching can highlight instructional ideas and materials for which you may need additional funding. And there are a number of grants for educators available at the federal, state, and local levels.

One grant success story comes from West Virginia veteran Peggy Howry, who recognized her kindergartners' needs for multicultural experiences and hands-on learning. Howry wrote a proposal for one of her state's education mini-grants. She succeeded in securing enough funds to allow her to create and implement a curriculum featuring the customs, crafts, music, foods, games, and native dress of many different countries. Countries were studied one at a time, each with some culminating event involving parents and outside visitors; for example, the bagpipe player who entertained the children on the day they competed in their own Scottish Highland Games.

For a list of online sources for teacher grants, visit Teachers Network at www.teachnet.org and go to the Teacher Grants area. Also visit Education World at www.education-world.com (scroll down to more Resources on the home page and connect to The Grant Center).

ALTERNATIVE IN-SERVICES

Aside from the traditional seminars and one-shot workshops, professional development activities can include some diverse and stimulating nontraditional experiences, including (but certainly not limited to):

• curriculum development and textbook writing
• mentoring
• seeking National Board certification
• university classes and summer institutes
• advisory boards for professional publications and associations
• fellowships
• grant writing
• action research
• presenting papers at professional meetings
• school-based management

Visit the ERIC Web site at www.eric.ed.gov. To find an index and the full-text of documents issued after 1993, see http://ericadr.piccard.csc.com/extra/ericdigests/index.

Educational Laboratories and Research Centers

Some of the best repositories for information about teaching and learning are the educational laboratories and research centers located all around the country. Staff at these institutions study teaching and actively interpret and disseminate research results to teachers. Many are federally funded and offer information free or at a nominal cost.

Education Research & Development Centers

The Education Sciences Reform Act of 2002 established the Institute of Education Sciences as the research arm of the Department of Education. The act requires that the institute support at least eight national research and development centers, which contribute significantly to the solution of education problems in the United States by developing, testing, and disseminating new approaches to improve teaching and learning, and ultimately, student achievement. Each of the centers conducts research in its topic area, provides evidence and information to educators and policy makers, and guides research and development directions in the topic area. Below is a list of the research centers, their research topic area, and contact information.

Center for the Improvement of Early Reading Achievement (CIERA)

CIERA represents a consortium of researchers from five universities. The center's research addresses three areas: (1) characteristics of children and the texts they read; (2) home and school influences on early reading achievement; and (3) policy and teacher professional development effects on early reading achievement. The center ensures that the research on children's early reading acquisition is disseminated to teachers, teacher educators, parents, and policy makers.

Contact: Dr. Karen Wixson, Director
University of Michigan
Telephone: (734) 647-6940
E-mail: ciera@umich.edu
Web site: www.ciera.org

National Research & Development Center on English Learning & Achievement (CELA)

CELA conducts research designed to improve students' English and literacy achievement in schools across America. Researchers examine elements of curriculum, instruction, and assessment that are essential to developing high literacy achievement.

Contact: Dr. Judith Langer, Dr. Arthur Applebee, and Dr. Martin Nystrand, Co-Directors
State University of New York, Albany
Telephone: (518) 442-5026
Web site: http://cela.albany.edu

National Center for Improving Student Learning and Achievement in Mathematics and Science (NCISLA)

NCISLA's research focuses on developing ways of advancing K–12 students' learning of mathematics and science. The center's researchers work with teachers and diverse student populations to develop new math and science learning environments and professional development models for sustained student learning and achievement in math and science.

Contact: Dr. Thomas P. Carpenter, Director
University of Wisconsin, Wisconsin Center for Education Research
Telephone: (608) 265-6240
Web site:
www.wcer.wisc.edu/NCISLA

Center for Research on Education, Diversity & Excellence (CREDE)

CREDE researchers develop effective educational practices for linguistic and cultural minority students and evaluate their effectiveness on improving student learning. Research projects include evaluations of curriculum models in diverse settings and with student populations that range from Zuni-speaking students in New Mexico to Spanish-speaking children in California.

Contact: Dr. Roland Tharp, Director
University of California, Santa Cruz
Telephone: (831) 459-3500
E-mail: crede@cats.ucsc.edu
Web site: www.crede.ucsc.edu
or
Dr. Yolanda Padron, Co-Director
University of Houston
Telephone: (713) 743-0605
Web site: www.cal.org/crede

Center for Research on the Education of Students Placed at Risk (CRESPAR)

CRESPAR is a partnership between Johns Hopkins and Howard universities. CRESPAR conducts research related to the educational performance of poor and minority children. The center supports four programs of research: (1) early and elementary school studies; (2) middle and high school studies; (3) school and family partnerships; and (4) systematic supports for school reform efforts. The research projects are designed to improve the education of students at risk for educational failure by documenting determinants of school success, ensuring that successful educational reform programs and practices are widely implemented, and promoting intellectual achievement, motivation, socioemotional competence, and a positive school experience for students.

Contact: Dr. Robert E. Slavin, Co-Director
Johns Hopkins University
Telephone: (410) 516-8800
Web site:
www.csos.jhu.edu/CRESPAR/index.htm
or
Dr. A. Wade Boykin, Co-Director
Howard University
Telephone: (202) 806-8484
Web site:
http://crespar.law.howard.edu

National Center for Early Development & Learning (NCEDL)

The research at the NCEDL focuses on enhancing the cognitive, social, and emotional development of children from birth to age eight. Researchers examine early childhood practices related to children's development and education and ensure that the research is translated into educational practice and disseminated to practitioners and policy makers.

Contact: Dr. Don Bailey, Director
University of North Carolina–Chapel Hill
Frank Porter Graham Child Development Center
Telephone: (919) 966-4250
Web site: www.fpg.unc.edu/~ncedl

Education Research & Development Centers (continued)

National Center for the Study of Adult Learning and Literacy (NCSALL)

The mission of NCSALL is to improve practice in educational programs that serve adults with limited literacy and English-language skills and those without a high school diploma. They accomplish this by examining factors that contribute to program success and adult learning, such as adult development, adult reading, adult student persistence, literacy practices of adult learners, health and adult learning practices, and the impact of participation in adult education and literacy programs on students, families, and communities.

Contact: Dr. John P. Comings
Harvard Graduate School of Education
Telephone: (617) 495-4843
Web site:
http://gseweb.harvard.edu/~ncsall

National Center for Postsecondary Improvement (NCPI)

NCPI researchers examine postsecondary education issues such as effective teaching, learning, and assessment practices that contribute to student outcomes, professional development initiatives for educators, student transitions from school to work, and academic quality and productivity.

Contact: Dr. Patricia J. Gumport
Stanford University
Telephone: (650) 723-7724
Web site: http://ncpi.stanford.edu

Center for the Study of Teaching and Policy (CTP)

CTP researchers examine efforts to improve the quality of teachers, teaching, and learning. Their mission is to identify ways that leaders, policy makers, teacher developers, and the education reform community can support teachers' work and careers, improve teacher quality, and, ultimately, the quality of students' learning opportunities in elementary and secondary schools.

Contact: Dr. Michael Knapp, Director
University of Washington
Telephone: (206) 221-4114
Web site:
http://depts.washington.edu/ctpmail

National Center on Increasing the Effectiveness of State and Local Education Reform Efforts (CPRE)

CPRE researchers examine how educational reforms lead to improvement in instruction and how knowledge and experience influence school reform efforts. The research projects include looking at accountability and school reform, costs of school reform and effective resource use patterns, cost effectiveness of programs for students in high-poverty communities, knowledge- and skill-based teacher evaluation, teacher quality, and high school strategies for instructional improvement.

Contact: Dr. Susan Fuhrman, Director
University of Pennsylvania
Telephone: (215) 573-0700
Web site: www.cpre.org/index_js.htm

Center for Research on Evaluation, Standards, and Student Testing (CRESST)

CRESST has four programs of research that focus on assessing educational quality and addressing persistent problems in the design and use of assessment systems to serve multiple purposes.

Contact: Dr. Eva L. Baker and Dr. Robert L. Linn, Co-Directors
University of California, Los Angeles
Telephone: (310) 206-1532
Web site: http://cresst96.cse.ucla.edu

National Research Center on the Gifted and Talented (NRC/GT)

NRC/GT focuses on identifying and developing talent potentials in students and examining the role of school and community influences on the development of gifted and talented students.

Contact: Dr. Joseph S. Renzulli, Director
University of Connecticut
Telephone: (860) 486-2900
Web site:
www.gifted.uconn.edu/nrcgt.html

National Center for Restructuring Education, Schools, and Teaching (NCREST)

NCREST supports restructuring efforts by documenting successful initiatives, creating reform networks to share new research findings with practitioners, and linking policy to practice. Currently, NCREST is involved in a variety of projects including Professional Development Schools, teacher learning, assessment, the documentation of successful school reform efforts in elementary and secondary schools, educational technology in schools, and the development of local, state, and national policies based on practice.

Contact: Jacqueline Ancess and Thomas Hatch, Co-Directors
Teachers College, Columbia University
Telephone: (212) 678-3432
Web site:
www.tc.columbia.edu/NCREST

Federal Government Sites

Don't forget the U.S. Department of Education when you're seeking good information about teaching and learning. One great source is the Federal Government Internet Educational Resources site (www.ed.gov/EdRes/EdFed). This rich site provides direct links to ERIC database, the National Research Centers, Regional Educational Laboratories, Star Schools Program Sites, Regional Technology in Education Consortia, other Federal Agency Educational Resources, Federal Government Internet Library Resources, and much more. You can also access the Department of Education directly (www.ed.gov) and gain information on important resources, professional-development opportunities, and available grants.

Regional Educational Laboratories (REL) Network

The Regional Educational Laboratories are educational research and development organizations supported by contracts with the U.S. Department of Education, Office of Educational Research and Improvement (OERI). The ten regional educational laboratories work to help educators and policy makers solve education problems in their states and districts. The labs research education issues, print publications, and provide training programs to teachers and administrators. Each lab puts out a catalog of its publications, covering a wide range of topics such as teaching strategies, school improvement, and parental involvement. Catalogs and publications are available to anyone, regardless of region, and can be found online or requested directly from the labs; other services (training programs, etc.) are region-specific and must be acquired through district education officials. For direct links to any of these labs, go to www.relnetwork.org.

Northeast and Islands Regional Educational Laboratory at Brown University (LAB at Brown)

Region Served: Northeast and Islands (Connecticut, Maine, Massachusetts, New Hampshire, New York, Rhode Island, Vermont, Puerto Rico, and the Virgin Islands)
National Leadership Area:
Teaching Diverse Students
Executive Director: Dr. Mary-Beth Fafard
Address: The Education Alliance
Brown University
222 Richmond St., Ste. 300
Providence, RI 02903-4226
Telephone: (401) 274-9548
E-mail: info@alliance.brown.edu
Web site: www.alliance.brown.edu

Laboratory for Student Success (LSS)

Region Served: Mid-Atlantic
(Delaware, Maryland, New Jersey, Pennsylvania, and Washington, DC)
National Leadership Area:
Educational Leadership
Co-Directors: Marilyn Murphy and John Kovach

Address: Laboratory for Student Success
Mid-Atlantic Regional Educational Laboratory
Temple University
Center for Research in Human Development and Education
1301 Cecil B. Moore Ave.
Philadelphia, PA 19122-6091
Telephone: (215) 204-3030, (800) 892-5550
E-mail: lss@vm.temple.edu
Web site: www.temple.edu/lss

Regional Educational Laboratory at AEL

Region Served: Appalachian
(Kentucky, Tennessee, Virginia, and West Virginia)
National Leadership Area:
Educational Technology
Director: Dr. Doris Redfield
Address: P.O.B. 1348
Charleston, WV 25325-1348
Telephone: (304) 347-0400
E-mail: aelinfo@ael.org
Web site: www.ael.org

Regional Educational Laboratory at SERVE

Region Served: Southeastern
(Alabama, Florida, Georgia, Mississippi, North Carolina, and South Carolina)
National Leadership Area:
Expanded Learning Opportunities
Executive Director: Dr. John Sanders
Address: P.O.B. 5367
Greensboro, NC 27435-0367
Telephone: (336) 315-7400
E-mail: info@serve.org
Web site: www.serve.org

North Central Regional Educational Laboratory (NCREL)

Region Served: Midwestern
(Illinois, Indiana, Iowa, Michigan, Minnesota, Ohio, and Wisconsin)
National Leadership Area:
Educational Technology
Executive Director: Dr. Gina Burkhardt
Address: 1120 East Diehl Rd., Ste. 200
Naperville, IL 60563-1486
Telephone: (630) 649-6500, (800) 356-2735
E-mail: info@ncrel.org
Web site: www.ncrel.org

Regional Educational Laboratories Network (continued)

Southwest Educational Development Laboratory (SEDL)

Region Served: Southwestern (Arkansas, Louisiana, New Mexico, Oklahoma, and Texas)

National Leadership Area: Family and Community Involvement

Executive Director: Dr. Wesley A. Hoover

Address: 211 E. Seventh St. Austin, TX 78701-3281

Telephone: (512) 476-6861, (800) 476-6861

E-mail: info@sedl.org

Web site: www.sedl.org

Mid-continent Research for Education and Learning (McREL)

Region Served: Central (Colorado, Kansas, Missouri, Nebraska, North Dakota, South Dakota, and Wyoming)

National Leadership Area: Standards-Based Instructional Practice

Deputy Director and Executive VP: Dr. Louis F. Cicchinelli

Address: 2550 S. Parker Rd., Ste. 500 Aurora, CO 80014-1678

Telephone: (303) 337-0990

E-mail: info@mcrel.org

Web site: www.mcrel.org

WestEd

Region Served: Western (Arizona, California, Nevada, and Utah)

National Leadership Area: Assessment of Educational Achievement

Director: Dr. Gary Estes

Address: 730 Harrison St. San Francisco, CA 94107-1242

Telephone: (415) 565-3000, (877) 493-7833

E-mail: dtorres@wested.org

Web site: www.wested.org

Northwest Regional Educational Laboratory (NWREL)

Region Served: Northwestern (Alaska, Idaho, Montana, Oregon, and Washington)

National Leadership Area: Re-engineering Schools

Chief Executive Officer: Dr. Carol F. Thomas

Address: 101 S.W. Main St., Ste. 500 Portland, OR 97204-3297

Telephone: (503) 275-9500

E-mail: info@nwrel.org

Web site: www.nwrel.org

Pacific Resources for Education and Learning (PREL)

Region Served: Pacific (American Samoa, Commonwealth of the Northern Mariana Islands, Federated States of Micronesia, Guam, Hawaii, Republic of the Marshall Islands, and the Republic of Palau)

National Leadership Area: Curriculum and Instruction Related to Reading and Language Mastery

President and CEO: Dr. Tom W. Barlow

Address: 900 Fort St. Mall, Ste. 1300 Honolulu, HI 96813-4513

Telephone: (808) 441-1300

E-mail: askprel@prel.org

Web site: www.prel.org

Federal Government Sites

Don't forget the U.S. Department of Education when you're seeking good information about teaching and learning. One helpful source is the Federal Government Internet Educational Resources site (www.ed.gov/EdRes/EdFed). This site provides direct links to ERIC database, the National Research Centers, Regional Educational Laboratories, Star Schools Program Sites, Regional Technology in Education Consortia, other Federal Agency Educational Resources, Federal Government Internet Library Resources, and much more. You can also access the Department of Education directly (www.ed.gov) and gain information on important resources, professional-development opportunities, and available grants.

Most of the labs and centers publish at least one free newsletter or periodical. These publications highlight research results; offer practical suggestions for implementing research findings; announce conferences, workshops, and in-services; discuss national educational issues; and describe other products available.

Still one of the best-kept secrets in the profession, the educational laboratories and research centers offer teachers a wealth of information and services. And much of it is yours for the asking.

Write, call, or e-mail and ask to be placed on the newsletter mailing list or view the newsletter and the publication/products catalog online. (See pages 312 and 313.)

In-Services

We're lucky. Teacher in-services have come a long way since the days when university "experts" told teachers what was wrong with their teaching and how they should correct it.

Today, the more effective approach is for teachers to shape their own in-services. Frequently, teachers work on professional-development teams, such as those described in Chapter Seven. And while some in-services may be geared to individual needs and efforts, collaboration and teamwork seem to be the prevailing themes. Focusing on common problems, teachers share their experiences and work toward solutions—together. The source of new information may be an outside expert, but it doesn't need to be. More often these days, professionals right in the school or district share their expertise with colleagues.

Look for these features in the in-services you choose:

✔ opportunities to interact with colleagues— to discuss teaching and learning and share classroom experiences
✔ encouragement to adapt new teaching strategies to individual classrooms and situations and allowance for professional judgment calls (no "one-size-fits-all" approaches)
✔ opportunities to plan together for improved instruction
✔ the use of peer coaching to provide support and assistance when learning new teaching techniques
✔ sustained training, rather than one-shot in-services (except where the goal is to increase subject matter knowledge)

The American Federation of Teachers has developed its own list of Principles for Professional Development, available online at www.aft.org/pubs-reports (search for title). According to the AFT, professional development occurs "when there are clearly articulated, high standards for student achievement and when conversations take place about how to help students reach them." It doesn't matter whether this process is formal or informal. In fact, states the AFT, "The very organization of school should promote and provide for continuous and serious reflection about what students are learning and what needs to be done to continually improve."

Do the in-services you experience measure up? Weigh them against this AFT list of professional-development "shoulds":

✔ ensure depth of content knowledge
✔ provide a strong foundation in the pedagogy of particular disciplines
✔ provide more general knowledge about the teaching and learning processes and about school.
✔ be rooted in and reflect the best available research
✔ contribute to measurable improvement in student achievement
✔ expect teachers to be intellectually engaged with ideas and resources
✔ provide sufficient time, support, and resources to enable teachers to master new content and pedagogy and to integrate these into their practice
✔ be designed by representatives of those who participate in it, in cooperation with experts in the field
✔ take a variety of forms, including some not typically considered

❖ Researching Teaching

Certainly one way to gain new knowledge about teaching is to produce some of that new knowledge yourself—as a researcher in your classroom or some other.

Massachusetts teacher Jay Sugarman took a year's leave from his classroom to join a national research team. In professional-development centers and school districts nationwide, teachers design and conduct a variety of research projects. Teacher researchers Susan Pinsonneault and Kara Malhi, whose work on gender equity in the classroom is featured on page 304, conclude that, "Action research provides us with rich opportunities to examine what is happening in the world in which we function, and how different variables play out in real-life situations."

For these teachers, and many like them, *research* is more often a verb than a noun. They are active producers of knowledge about teaching, and they represent a rapidly growing segment of professionals who call themselves teacher researchers.

Consider the case of Helen Hait, a veteran teacher in Vancouver, British Columbia, whose roster one year included 27 fifth and sixth graders from many different ethnic backgrounds and ability levels. Hait viewed this challenge as an opportunity to build a true "classroom community."

"One of the most powerful factors contributing to community building is group work," writes Hait. "It is in the context of groups where social development can be most easily facilitated, encouraged, and taught."

With that in mind, she set about investigating "how four different types of grouping situations or activities, varied in their structural and teaching components, contributed to the building of community within our classroom." Specifically, she studied:

✔ changing table groups
✔ discrimination activity groups
✔ cooperative groups
✔ literature circles

Using student surveys, anecdotal observations, and students' comments and behaviors as evidence, Hait found that the factors in group work that most contribute to community building in a class were physical layout of the classroom, varied grouping opportunities, self-evaluation of group work, and curriculum issues. "All of these are connected to each other," writes Hait, "and revolve around what the children had made clear was the most important element in defining a community—respectful interactions."

Hait continues, "In my twenty-plus years of teaching, this research project proved to be one of the most helpful and effective tools for me to examine and improve my teaching practices. By taking the time to read about group processes and ideas, by implementing some of those ideas, and by closely observing and analyzing the resulting interactions and evidence of student growth, my understanding of the importance of group work in a classroom was greatly enhanced." (To read more about Hait's research, see the Works Cited at the end of this chapter.)

Some teacher researchers participate in formal university studies. Many more work on their own or as part of a school team. But no matter how or where they work, teacher researchers all engage in the same basic process—systematic inquiry. They ask questions and look for answers. In the process, they improve practice, grow intellectually and professionally, establish rewarding partnerships with colleagues, and sometimes create new career opportunities for themselves.

Action Research

The process of studying your own practice to gain insight into and improve your teaching can be traced back to John Dewey in the 1920s, according to author Beverly Johnson. But not until recently has it become a widely adapted strategy for professional development, school-based curriculum development, site-based management, and preservice and graduate teacher-education courses.

Cyclic in Nature As Johnson explains it, action research is cyclic in nature. It involves a teacher or groups of teachers identifying a problem, collecting data, reflecting on the process and analyzing the data, using their reflection and analysis to take some type of action in the classroom (a new strategy, for example), monitoring how well the action worked, and redefining the problem.

The essential features, says Johnson, are "trying out ideas in practice as a means of increasing knowledge about and/or improving curriculum, teaching, and learning."

Three Types There are three basic approaches to action research, says Emily Calhoun, who has studied action research in 76 schools across three states.

The first is **individual teacher research**. As its name implies, this type focuses on solving a problem in an individual classroom. The primary audience for the research results is the teacher himself or herself. Students can also be the target audience, if they have participated directly
in the study.

Helen Hait's research on group work, described on page 315, is one example. In my own seventh- and eighth-grade English class, my students helped me test the effects of giving out rubrics when I made writing assignments. They were as eager as I was for the results, and together, we discussed why rubrics seemed to be a good idea.

A second type of action research involves the **collaboration of a teacher with other teachers, administrators, or even university researchers.** The research team, which can consist of as few as two people, can focus on problems in a single classroom, in several classrooms, or in classrooms districtwide. It involves the same investigative and reflective cycle as the individual approach. Often, this approach involves school-university partnerships.

One such partnership developed between Massachusetts teacher Jay Sugarman and Stanford University researchers. "I'm someone who's always kept up with the literature, who's interested in continual learning and being exposed to new ideas," says Sugarman. So when members of the Teacher Assessment Project at Stanford University asked him to join their national research team, he jumped at the chance.

Taking a year's leave from his fourth-grade classroom, Sugarman moved across the country to participate in a major study identifying ways other than paper-and-pencil tests to assess teacher competence. It wasn't just token involvement.

Sugarman conducted a yearlong field test centered on teachers who developed portfolios of their language instruction. The goal was to find out whether teacher portfolios could contribute to a richer, more contextual assessment of teaching. He also managed an assessment center created by the research team.

"Teacher researchers were treated as equals by the university staff," Sugarman stresses. "They really listened to our voices. Even our teacher subjects—those developing the portfolios in their classrooms—were treated as co-researchers.

"Teachers in our study were encouraged to interact with other teachers at school, as well as with project staff, as they documented and reflected on their practice, " he continues. "They reported that this interaction was a wonderful growth opportunity. Perhaps one of the best ways for a teacher to grow is to get together with colleagues to talk about teaching," he concludes.

Sugarman's experience enabled him to develop new technical and intellectual skills. Since then, he has presented papers at professional meetings, written articles, edited a new professional journal for his district, and served on an advisory board for *Instructor* magazine.

"Perhaps most important," Sugarman notes, "research affords us the time and opportunity to think about what we do."

Schoolwide action research is the third type. Here, an entire faculty identifies a problem area, collects and interprets on-site data, sometimes uses data from other schools, and then decides what actions to take. One goal of this approach, in addition to improving instructional practices, is to help faculty members learn to work together to identify and solve problems, says Calhoun. To read more about Calhoun's strategies for action research, see the resources at the end of the chapter.

The Effects What are the benefits of action research? Both intuition and research results point to improved instruction and learning for students.

The process also has some equally powerful benefits for teachers. Teachers who conduct action research become more reflective of their teaching and their understanding of teaching. They become more critical and aware of their own practice and its effects on children. Also, action research reveals the "options and possibilities for change," says Johnson.

Action research gives teachers the avenues for collaborating and sharing with colleagues—both in conducting the research and disseminating the results. Results can be shared through presentations at workshops or professional meetings, in articles written for professional journals or district newsletters, or in face-to-face conversations.

The collaboration between school and university personnel pays big dividends, too. Stanford University professor Lee Shulman refers to "the fruitfulness of that shared activity in which researchers and practitioners jointly produce the wisdom that can guide future practice." Research on teaching *should* be a collaboration between teachers and educational researchers, Shulman stresses. Researchers know the research process, but teachers know schools.

Tips for Teacher Researchers
Whether you realize it or not, you are probably conducting research in your classroom already. Here's how you can make it even more beneficial—for yourself and others.

✔ **Clearly identify** a problem or topic of interest.
✔ **Take the initiative.** "Talk to others, do some reading on your topic. Make phone calls. Go to local and national conferences. Talk to people at the university level who can bring other resources to bear on your own investigations," suggests Jay Sugarman.
✔ **Solicit partners**—other teachers who could coach you, university staff, even student teachers.
✔ **Know the professional literature.** "Read, read, read," urges Pennsylvania teacher Laurie Borger.
✔ **Ask questions.** Research is a process of asking questions and "trying on" answers. "Keep asking questions and keep seeking answers until you get some satisfaction," advises Laura Fendel.
✔ **Use research tools at your disposal**—observe colleagues, videotape classes, keep a journal. "If you decide to use literature to teach reading, for example, you might try watching someone who already does this," says Sugarman. "This is valid, genuine research."
✔ **Share the results**—informally with colleagues in the building or on the Internet, or more formally with written articles, workshops, or conference presentations.

❖ The Professional Portfolio
Like other professionals, teachers need evidence of their growth and achievement over time. The professional portfolio is a vehicle for collecting and presenting that evidence. For many of us, it's just practicing what we preach. We encourage our students to select examples of their work over time to demonstrate how much they've learned, and we must do the same.

Portfolios allow us to become reflective about what it is we do. And they allow us to document the practices we'd like to preserve and even pass on to others.

"Portfolios have much to offer the teaching profession," writes Dr. Kenneth Wolf, University of Colorado. "When teachers carefully examine their own practices, those practices are likely to improve. The examples of accomplished practice that portfolios provide also can be studied and adapted for use in other classrooms."

And it's more than just a good idea. In many places, teachers and administrators must now develop portfolios to renew their professional licenses.

What to Include

A professional teaching portfolio is more than a hodgepodge of lesson plans and lists of professional activities. It is a careful record of specific accomplishments attained over an extended period of time. Wolf suggests that portfolios include the following:

1. **Background Information**
   - ✔ résumé (see pages 322 and 323 for a look at one veteran's résumé)
   - ✔ background information on teacher and teaching context
   - ✔ educational philosophy and teaching goals
2. **Teaching Artifacts and Reflections Documenting an Extended Teaching Activity**
   - ✔ overview of unit goals and instructional plan
   - ✔ list of resources used in unit
   - ✔ two consecutive lesson plans
   - ✔ videotape of teaching
   - ✔ student work samples
   - ✔ evaluation of student work
   - ✔ reflective commentary by the teacher
   - ✔ additional units/lessons/student work as appropriate
3. **Professional Information**
   - ✔ list of professional activities
   - ✔ letters of recommendation
   - ✔ formal evaluations

PORTFOLIO TIPS FROM VETERANS

Take it from teacher and professional-development expert Doris Dillon: The creation of a professional portfolio requires careful effort. Dillon, who served on the English/Language Arts Committee of the National Board for Professional Teaching Standards and presented workshops on developing a teaching portfolio, often compared a portfolio to a garden. "It takes planning and hard work, requires the weeding out of unnecessary elements, and promotes positive feelings. You're proud to show it off!"

First, make sure your résumé—that important "first impression" to those viewing your portfolio—is as good as it can be. Dillon recommended a number of categories or headings around which to format the résumé (see the Notes for a Résumé on page 320). To see how veteran teacher Alexis Ludewig has incorporated these suggestions in her own résumé, see pages 322 and 323.

Dillon also urged teachers to assess their personal strengths and highlight these strengths in their portfolios. Using a Strength Assessment Worksheet (see page 321), teachers can check which of ten important personal qualities pertain to them, then describe how they use these qualities in the work they do.

Ludewig advises teachers to update their portfolio annually or any time there is a change in credentials, awards, or affiliations.

"Something else that has helped me is I take a lot of pictures of my students working, showing finished products, or performing," says Ludewig, who is diligent about seeking permission to use student work. "I also take pictures of bulletin boards, files, and/or displays. Photos can give your portfolio a good backbone and provide a quick way for a prospective employer/hiring team to get a first impression of an applicant."

Although portfolios vary in form and content, depending upon their purpose, Wolf points out that "most contain some combination of teaching artifacts and written reflections. These are the heart of the portfolio."

Further, the artifacts, be they lesson plans, student work samples, or a parent newsletter, must be accompanied with written explanations. For example, what is the purpose of the parent newsletter? What did you and the students learn from the school survey you had them conduct? Be specific and be reflective. It's the intent and thoughtful planning and reflective evaluation that the artifacts should reveal. (Be sure to consider confidentiality and permissions from parents and students for the use of materials and pictures in a portfolio. Find out about your school district's policy.)

Wolf also suggests that each artifact be accompanied by a brief, identifying caption. Include, for example:

✔ title of the artifact
✔ date produced
✔ description of the context
✔ purpose, evaluation, or other types of comments

Additional Tips

A professional teaching portfolio can be created and presented in many ways. No matter which approach you take, however, the following tips from Kenneth Wolf should help:

✔ Explain your educational philosophy and teaching goals.
✔ Choose specific features of your instructional program to document.
✔ Collect a wide range of artifacts, and date and annotate them so you have the information you need when making your final selections.
✔ Keep a journal to draw upon for written reflections on your teaching.
✔ Collaborate with a mentor and other colleagues (preferably, those experienced in both teaching and portfolio construction). Meet regularly with colleagues to discuss your portfolio.
✔ Assemble the portfolio in an easily accessible form. The loose-leaf notebook works well, although electronic portfolios may be the wave of the future.
✔ Assess the portfolio. You and your colleagues can assess the portfolio informally, or you can have it formally scored by the National Board for Professional Teaching Standards.

The Benefits

Creating a professional portfolio involves considerable effort—good teaching, so you have something to showcase in the first place; careful planning; thorough record keeping; thoughtful selections of items to include; and certainly a fair measure of creativity. What are the payoffs?

One is the chance to reflect on our practice. And in that sense, portfolio development is an important growth experience. Also, the process allows us to collaborate with mentors and other colleagues. And it's an effective means of authentic assessment—both self-assessment and administrative assessment. But perhaps most important of all, portfolios preserve examples of good practice for other teachers.

"Too often," says Wolf, "good teaching vanishes without a trace because we have no structure or tradition for preserving the best of what teachers do. Portfolios allow teachers to retain examples of good teaching so they can examine them, talk about them, adapt them, and adopt them. The objective is not to create outstanding portfolios, but rather to cultivate outstanding teaching and learning."

For more information, try *Professional Portfolios*, online professional development content from Lessonlab Skylight, 1900 East Lake Ave., Glenville, IL 60025 (www.lessonlab.com).

❖ National Certification

Perhaps the biggest professional-development step a teacher can take these days is seeking certification from the National Board for Professional Teaching Standards. National Board Certification is a comprehensive, intensive, yearlong assessment of a teacher's knowledge and skills. To be certified, a teacher must demonstrate high and rigorous standards of teaching.

"These standards have been developed by teachers for teachers and capture the essence of what accomplished teachers should know and be able to do to improve student learning," according to the National Board's *Teacher to Teacher* newsletter (Spring 1996, p. 1).

And what should a professional teacher know and be able to do? The National Board has delineated **five general propositions about excellent teaching:**

✔ Teachers are committed to students and their learning.
✔ Teachers know the subjects they teach and how to teach those subjects to students.
✔ Teachers are responsible for managing and monitoring student learning.
✔ Teachers think systematically about their practice and learn from experience.
✔ Teachers are members of learning communities.

Notes for a Résumé

Jot down information about your background for each of the headings on this page. Use these notes to organize your professional résumé.

Name/Address

Goals

Career Objective

Qualification Summary

Certification(s)

Education

Professional Experience

Areas of Effectiveness

Professional Affiliations

Committees

Involvement

Awards and Accomplishments

Special Interests/Extracurricular

Skills

References

Strength Assessment Worksheet

Listed below are ten traits. Put a check next to each one that is true of you. Describe how you used each trait in some work, school, or other activity.

TRAIT	ACTIVITY
❏ Teamworker	_____
❏ Tactful	_____
❏ Able to change	_____
❏ Able to start things on my own	_____
❏ Self-disciplined	_____
❏ Follow through on work	_____
❏ Hard worker	_____
❏ Honest and sincere	_____
❏ Able to think	_____
❏ Get along well with others	_____

Sample Résumé

Alexis Ann Ludewig
1234 Main Street
Any Town, USA 10001
lexa@ateacher.net

QUALIFICATION SUMMARY: Innovative, resourceful facilitator/instructor with excellent teaching and skills. Proven results in motivating and instructing students and staff at a variety of levels. Enthusiasm, problem-solving abilities, and technology skills.

CERTIFICATION: Wisconsin–106, kindergarten through grade 6, Life License

EDUCATION: M.A., Education, Viterbo College, 1996. Thesis: "Identification of Character Values Through a Study of Heroes." B.S., Kindergarten and Elementary Education, University of Wisconsin–Stevens Point, 1973, Cum Laude.

PROFESSIONAL EXPERIENCE:

Third Grade Teacher **St. Germain Elementary School,** St. Germain, Wisconsin. Responsible for standard academic studies of third grade students in self-contained and teamed classrooms. Integrates technology. Modifies instruction to achieve optimal learning for all students. Uses a variety of community and personal resources and learning models to enhance student experiences. (1994–Present)

Chapter 1 Evaluator **Northland Pines School District,** Eagle River, Wisconsin. Responsible for the Chapter 1 evaluation report to D.P.I., which included directing district-wide evaluation, analysis, summary, and narrative of each component's characteristics/achievement data, basic and advanced skills outcomes, student and parent questionnaires, and sustained gains. (1975–94)

Chapter 1 Project Designer **Northland Pines School District,** Eagle River, Wisconsin. Responsible for the Chapter 1 Basic Grant application, instructional component design for preschool, K–5 language arts, and K–6 math phases, and development of the annual evaluation plan summary. At LEA level, designed components' basic and advanced skill record forms, student and parent questionnaires, parent handbook and involvement policy, and other record keeping forms. (1975–94)

Chapter 1 Head Teacher **Eagle River Grade School,** Eagle River, Wisconsin. Scheduled, developed educational plans, and taught approximately 85 K–5 Chapter 1 Language Arts and Math students each year. Coordinated program with district's Chapter 1 teachers and aides, classroom teachers, special services, AODA, gifted and talented, and at-risk staff. Organized Parents' Advisory Council. Processed Chapter 1 requisitions. (1975–94)

Title I Summer School Teacher **Oshkosh Area School District,** Oshkosh, Wisconsin. Provided introduction, participation, and follow-up activities for weekly field trips for first through third graders. Emphasized vocabulary development, writing and communication skills, and general fund of knowledge. (1977)

Third Grade Teacher **Phelps School District,** Phelps, Wisconsin. Taught students in a self-contained classroom. (1973–75)

Sample Résumé (continued)

Curriculum Vitae of Alexis Ludewig

RELATED EDUCATION EXPERIENCE: **Blue Ribbon Technology Panel, North Central Regional Educational Laboratory (NCREL)/Learning Point Associates** (2004)

TEACH Grant and Intel Master Teacher, CESA #9 Teach to the Future Training (2003). Instructed Intel classes (2004).

Teacher Advisory Council (TAC), North Central Regional Educational Laboratory (NCREL)/Learning Point Associates (2003–Present)

Technology Committee Member, Northland Pines Schools Wrote benchmarks, surveyed staff, designed, taught, and/or assisted with staff training, and acted as a consultant for district staff. (1989–Present)

Gifted and Talented Committee Member, Northland Pines Schools Assisted in the review and development of the Gifted and Talented program. (2000–Present)

Reading & Science Benchmark Committee Member, Northland Pines Schools Wrote curriculum benchmarks for elementary language arts and science. Assisted in the implementation design to meet state standards. (2000–Present)

Math Committee Member, Northland Pines Schools Analyzed district's math curriculum, evaluated textbooks and materials, disseminated information to staff, coordinated ordering. (1996–99)

PROFESSIONAL MEMBERSHIPS: **Phi Delta Kappa, Headwaters Chapter** Research Representative and Executive Board member. Former President, Vice President of Membership, Newsletter Editor, Secretary. (1978–Present)
P.T.A., St. Germain School, St. Germain, Wisconsin Teacher Representative, Enrichment Committee, Publicity. (1994–Present)

GRANTS: **Land O'Lakes Fish and Game Club Grant** "Extreme Eyes On." (2003)
Northland Pines Partners Inc. Grant "Welcome to Our World: Creating a Photo Record of Our Indoor and Outdoor School Environments." (1998)
Partnership 2000 Student Mini Grant "Good Choice Kids." (1997)

SCHOLARSHIP & AWARDS: **Scholastic Teacher Fellowship Recipient,** New York, New York. Participated in development of online professional development programs (Scholastic RED), reviewed professional books, wrote and recorded scripts. (2002)
2002 Wisconsin Teacher of the Year
2001–02 Wisconsin Elementary Teacher of the Year
2001 Kohl Teacher Fellowship Recipient
Herb Kohl Educational Foundation, Inc. (2001)
Gerald Howard Reed International Seminar Scholarship
Phi Delta Kappa International (1998)

Preparing for National Certification

If you intend to seek National Board Certification—or even if you are only toying with the idea at this point—here are some preliminary activities you might want to undertake. These are the activities suggested by teachers who have already completed the process. And whether you seek certification or not, they're just good professional practice. For guidelines, updates, and all National Board publications, call (800) 22TEACH or visit www.nbpts.org.

- **Become familiar with the standards for your field.** (For more information on standards for each content area, see Chapter Four.)
- **Think and write about your teaching philosophy.** Focus your writing by studying the National Board's guiding propositions in "What Teachers Should Know and Be Able to Do."
- **Keep a journal.**
- **Update your résumé** and expand it to describe your professional-development experiences, service to the community, and work with students' families.
- **Review research and ideas on teacher portfolios.**
- **Think and write about professional-development activities** and how they've affected your practice.
- **Establish networks of colleagues to work with** during the certification process, including online networks.
- **Review research on teaching,** including many different topics.
- **Read relevant professional journals.**
- **Review your curriculum** and think about units or lessons to improve or feature in your portfolio.
- **Strengthen your writing skills,** perhaps by taking a writing-process class.
- **Secure videotape equipment** and practice using it in the classroom to study your teaching.
- **Get involved with subject-matter professional-development activities,** as the National Board tests both the depth and breadth of your subject-matter knowledge and how you present it to students.

To demonstrate their skills and knowledge, the certification candidates first compile a portfolio documenting the effectiveness of their teaching. The portfolio includes videotapes of classroom teaching and interaction; student work samples; lesson plans; and journals or written commentaries that analyze and reflect upon the videos, work samples, and lesson plans. The portfolio process, which takes much of the year, encourages candidates to collaborate with colleagues and parents, and it allows them to examine their strengths and weaknesses, as well as their relationships with students, parents, other teachers, and administrators.

Toward the end of the yearlong process, the candidates spend a day at an assessment center, where they participate in classroom simulations and intensive writing exercises on both content knowledge and teaching strategies.

What are the payoffs for the huge mental, emotional, and physical demands of national certification?

"Nothing has forced me to examine teaching practices as the National Board Certification process did," writes nationally certified teacher Ann Sayas, from New Orleans. "Nothing else has offered me a vision of what education could be like and opportunities to participate in making the vision a reality."

Sayas's teaching styles and strategies today are very different from those she used before the certification process.

"Analysis and self-reflection about what I do has become automatic," she reports. "The result is amazing to me: I am more excited about teaching than I have ever been. I am more excited about the classroom experience and no longer dream of moving up the ladder away from daily contact with my students. Not enough time exists to try all the possible ideas that examination of my own classroom has produced."

Widely supported by educators, business leaders, and governors, National Board

Certification also provides other incentives to candidates, such as salary increases (determined on a state-by-state basis) and expanded roles. And like national board certification in the legal or medical professions, the ultimate goal of national teaching certification is improved performance for those we serve.

"The process is more than a 'test,'" says former North Carolina governor James B. Hunt, a founding chair of the National Board. "It's about making teaching a profession where teachers hold themselves to high standards and subsequently hold their students to higher standards . . . Ultimately, better teachers make better schools."

To find information on requirements and the certification process, visit www.nbpts.org.

❖ Technology

While technology is an integral part in all aspects of teaching and is featured throughout this book, it deserves special mention in this chapter on professional development. Technology, of course, is a wide umbrella. We're already familiar with and use such innovations as data projectors, calculators, VCRs, DVD players, digital cameras, and compact discs. But what about computers and the Internet? These most recent tools of the information age are the ones holding the greatest promise for improved teaching and learning.

Teacher Testimonial

Consider this e-mailed testimonial from Washington teacher Martine Wayman, who teaches sixth graders:

"For me, the very best professional development has been my involvement in telecommunications. Through that, I've met teachers all over the world. It's become a support group, training service, etc., right from my own home! I strongly believe that *all* the changes in my career directly result from this connection! My affiliations with *Instructor*, Scholastic, PBS, and NASA have all come from that. I'm just too tired to go to classes at night, and I've found that many classes are not relevant anyway. Teachers need to collaborate. Now, as I'm doing more and more training of other teachers, again, I'm finding that I learn as much as I teach!"

Support, affiliation, collaboration, lifelong learning—thanks to technology, teachers working in individual classrooms behind closed doors are no longer isolated. Technology is our link to colleagues and resources worldwide.

Seek Training and Information

The new technology won't do us any good, however, if we don't know how to use it. Unfortunately, the pace with which new computers reach the classroom far outstrips the pace with which teachers learn how to use those computers. Thus, a major focus of our professional development needs to be training in technology—how to use electronic networks and the Internet for our own growth, how to secure resources for teaching and learning, and how to teach students to use the technology effectively.

Thorough training in the use of the new technology is well beyond the scope of this book. But there are many good ways for teachers to get the help they need, and following are just a few.

Technology Conferences The National Education Association's Center for Education Technology hosts annual Technology and Learning Conferences. So do other national, state, or local associations. Plan to attend one near you.

> ## CENTER LINKS TEACHERS AND TECHNOLOGY
>
> The National Education Association's Center for Education Technology has many resources for teachers implementing technology in their classrooms and lives. For information, call the center at (202) 822-7354, or visit the NEA Web site at www.nea.org/cet.

Technology Magazines Periodicals are a great source of technology information, and there are a number of good ones. For example *MultiMedia & Internet @ Schools*, issued six times per year, offers how-to information on various forms of technology and reviews products. Contact the magazine at Information Today, 143 Old Marlton Pike, Medford, NJ 08055, call (609) 654-6266, or visit www.infotoday.com/MMschools.

Online Assistance What better way to learn about the Internet and its many advantages for teachers than through online programs and tutorials? You'll discover many good ones just by exploring various education Web sites and their links Here are several excellent and highly rated sites:

✔ **Online Internet Institute** (http://oii.org). This comprehensive site teaches participants about all phases of the Internet, and teachers develop online projects for their own classrooms. The focus is inquiry-based learning, enhanced by technology. One of the site's best features is the National Professional Development Library (http://oii.org/npdl.html). Here, teachers learn about the Internet, Internet research, and incorporating technology in their instruction. Various online projects and professional-development activities are also offered.

✔ **21st Century Teachers** (www.nekesc.k12.ks.uc/21tea.html). This large-scale volunteer effort encourages teachers to collaborate in developing the skills and knowledge to use technology in their teaching.

✔ **Professional Growth (LETSNet)** (http://commtechlab.msu.edu/sitesletsnet). This site, developed by New Jersey teacher Art Wolinsky, encourages teachers to integrate the Internet into classroom activities, to learn about new teaching strategies by connecting with other teachers, and to use these new learning experiences to stimulate personal and professional growth. It's part of a larger site sponsored by Michigan State University and Ameritech. The Professional Growth section is one of "10 Big Ideas" for using computer

technology. Others include electronic field trips, teamwork, global connection, research, visualization, publishing, home and community, individualizing, and kids corner.

✔ **Tech Learning** (www.techlearning.com). Sponsored by the National Science Foundation, this site facilitates teacher conversations about educational technology and aids teachers in learning what technologies work best in the classroom.

✔ **WWW 4 Teachers** (www.4teachers.org). Sponsored by the South Central Regional Technology Consortium, this site bills itself as "for teachers powering learning with technology." It includes testimonials from teachers and students, examples of how teachers are using technology, and various lessons for students.

✔ **U.S. Department of Education** (www.ed.gov). Among its plethora of offerings are numerous professional-development ideas and activities, and a listing of grants available.

❖ Personal Development

While working to improve your professional life, don't forget about the personal side. Here's how some teachers rejuvenate when teaching seems too tough. Their tips will help you make sure the "personal you" is nourished so the "professional you" can flourish.

Take Time for You

It's very important to acknowledge and nurture our personal lives apart from teaching. Obviously, we need to eat right, exercise, and get enough sleep. But we also need to pursue personal interests and hobbies.

"I believe that the more a teacher is, the more a teacher can do," says Cheryl Peden, first-grade teacher at Mountain View Elementary School in Colorado Springs and 1994 Disney Teacher of the Year. And that only makes sense. Expertise and enthusiasm that we develop for pursuits outside of teaching give us more to share with our students.

Take golf lessons, learn to scuba dive, or try making stained glass, suggests Alexis Ludewig. "Not only does this type of thing benefit you personally," she notes, "it also lets you meet people outside of the teaching world. And it reminds you of some of the frustrations of being a student."

Summer is the time many of us rejuvenate and nurture our personal selves. Here are some suggestions for summer or for any breaks during the year:

✔ **Read novels** or other books just because you want to, not because you feel obligated.

✔ **Call or e-mail** old friends you've been meaning to talk to all year long. Or do some detective work and try to re-establish contact with a long-lost friend.

✔ **Travel to new destinations.** Join the **Educators Bed and Breakfast Network** ($36 annual membership) and find inexpensive lodging in teachers' homes all over this country or in 40 other countries. For more information, call (800) 956-4822, or visit the Web site at www.edubabnet.com.

✔ **Exercise your social conscience** by using your vacation helping others or the earth. Not only will you work for a cause you believe in, you'll make new friends, explore a new environment, and develop new skills. (See the box at right for some meaningful options.)

✔ **Go to school.** Yes, you read it right. One of the most stimulating and rejuvenating activities a teacher on break can do is to become a student. When you attend classes, you interact with other adult learners. Even if you are not working on an advanced degree, take a class in photography, or music appreciation, or sculpting, or anything that engages your mind and stimulates a love of learning.

MEANINGFUL DESTINATIONS

Help to build a better world and enrich yourself in the process by spending some of your vacation time volunteering for one of these service agencies or others like them:

- **Habitat for Humanity** No skills are necessary to help build a house for a family in need. Call (800) 422-4828, or visit www.habitat.org.
- **Earthwatch** Worldwide projects in the areas of biology, archaeology, anthropology, geology, and more employ volunteer researchers for two-week stints. Expeditions cost between $600 and $2,200 and are tax deductible. Call (800) 776-0188, or visit www.earthwatch.org.
- **Fresh Air Fund** Adults with skills and expertise in many different areas are needed as paid staff members at a camp run for needy New York City teens in Fishkill, New York. Call (800) 367-0003, or visit www.freshair.org.
- **Passport in Time** Participate in projects such as excavating prehistoric sites or compiling oral histories with this program sponsored by the U.S. Forest Service. Projects are located all over the country. Call (800) 281-9176, or visit www.passportintime.com.
- **Global Citizens Network** Volunteers teach or help to build health clinics in Belize, Guatemala, Kenya, or Mexico. Costs vary. Call (800) 644-9292, or visit www.globalcitizens.org.

Give Yourself Some Credit

In striving for excellence, we teachers frequently are too hard on ourselves. It's too easy to lose sight of the many small successes achieved daily and become mired in frustrations and anxieties over problems beyond our control. Focusing on the negative can become a habit and can even lead to questioning our self-worth.

"It's an easy trap to fall into," warns Jane Schall, a former teacher who now writes about teaching. "Teachers, isolated in separate classrooms, don't receive enough pats on the back from colleagues observing their work," Schall says. "Often administrators, school boards, and even whole communities are busy examining 'the problems,' and the problems are what teachers hear about."

No wonder teachers get the blues."In a profession where it is often up to us to remind ourselves that the day wasn't so bleak, that we've given a child something lasting and special, and that teaching is really worth it, believing in ourselves is essential," Schall stresses.

ABC's for a Low-Stress School Year

Post this checklist on your refrigerator to remind yourself how to manage stress and keep your teaching batteries charged throughout the year.

A **Attitude** Nothing beats a positive attitude. If you think you'll have a great day, you will.

B **Balance** Equal parts of work and play make for a better day.

C **Calm** Count to ten before you act or speak. Take a slow, deep breath at the first sign of tension.

D **Discipline** Enforcing discipline doesn't mean you're a toughie. It means you care about all kids.

E **Escape** Take a five-minute "mental escape" to an exotic place.

F **Flexibility** Plan, but don't be so rigid that you can't change things if circumstances dictate.

G **Grow** Do something to expand your mind or tone your body.

H **Humor** Put something that makes you smile in your plan book or top desk drawer.

I **Inoculate** Protect yourself from "stress carriers"—people who gossip, breeding negativity.

J **Joy** Keep a joy journal by recording at least one good thing that happens every day.

K **Knowledge** Know yourself, the kids you teach, and most of all, your stress triggers.

L **Listen** Listen to yourself, to your body, and to others.

M **Meditate** Take a few minutes each day for quiet reflection.

N **Neutralize** If you can't change the situation, change how you view or respond to it.

O **Organize** Use a planning calendar to organize your activities.

P **Plan** . . . and have a backup plan for when your primary plan doesn't work out.

Q **Question** If you're not sure about school rules, procedures, or practices, ask someone who is.

R **Read** Take time to read for pleasure.

S **Socialize** All work and no play makes for a dull day.

T **Time** Make the most of the time you have. Ask colleagues to share timesaving tips.

U **Utilize** Take advantage of prepared forms and teaching aids.

V **Voice** Express your opinions. Pent-up thoughts and emotions create stress.

W **Walk** Get up and move. Walk around the playground or the building. Organize a walkers' club.

X **Exercise** Build in at least five minutes of exercise a day. Use stairs whenever possible.

Y **Yoga** Learn or practice relaxation techniques.

Z **ZZZs** Get plenty of rest. Know how much sleep your body needs and give it that much.

By Beblon Parks, former teacher and stress-management workshop leader for the Virginia Education Association. From *Instructor*, August 1977.

Denis Waitley, author of *The Winner's Edge: The Critical Attitude of Success*, endorses "positive self-talk as a way to build a stronger belief in yourself." As Waitley explains, repeatedly telling yourself things like "I can," "I look forward to . . .," or "Next time I'll do better" improves your self-image and builds more confidence. The result is a stronger, more positive you.

So don't wait for others to pat you on the back for a job well done. Do it yourself!

Handling Stress

Stress is a physiological state involving the fight-or-flight response. Whenever we face something threatening or unpleasant, our body naturally speeds up its heart rate, rushing blood to vital organs, pumping adrenaline, and allowing us the extra strength and energy to either fight or flee.

This fight-or-flight response worked well for our ancient ancestors, who faced deadly predators and other life-threatening situations. But today, we can't fight or flee from disruptive students, demanding parents, critical administrators, or any of a hundred teaching stresses we face daily. Instead, we must learn to deal with them. And perhaps even more important, we must learn how to relax afterward; if we don't, the tension and residual effects of the adrenaline start to accumulate in our bodies. When they do, illness and disease can result. Heed the warning signs of too much tension, including:

✔ racing heart
✔ headaches, including migraines
✔ persistent neck, jaw, shoulder, or back tension
✔ general irritability
✔ racing thoughts and the inability to concentrate
✔ insomnia
✔ fatigue
✔ digestive and bowel problems
✔ loss of appetite
✔ excessive or binge eating
✔ difficulty making decisions
✔ excessive worrying
✔ feeling weak or dizzy

Your personal well-being depends on how successfully you handle that inevitable job-related stress. Stress-management experts and veteran teachers offer these tips for releasing or reducing tension:

✔ Recognize that stress is a part of daily life and that you must learn to manage it.
✔ Monitor, think about, and try to improve the way you react to stressful situations. Instead of becoming angry or upset when a student is defiant, for example, try to stay calm. Or instead of becoming frustrated when an activity flops, try to laugh about it.
✔ Schedule your day to include something fun. (Even something as simple as watching a favorite sitcom will work.)
✔ Set realistic goals for yourself, just as you do for students. Take smaller steps and savor the successful completion of each one.
✔ Support your support system. Encourage your colleagues to share their ups and downs. And let others share yours.
✔ Pick your battles wisely. And don't waste time worrying about the little things.
✔ Be at least as tolerant, encouraging, and nonjudgmental of yourself as you are of students and colleagues. You have the most control over the stress you place on yourself.
✔ Unwind from school before facing your responsibilities at home. Take a walk, talk to a friend, or spend a few minutes alone.
✔ Write angry letters, but don't send them. Just the process of writing the letter can release tension.
✔ Let friends, family, and colleagues know when they've hurt your feelings. Tell them specifically what hurts.
✔ Make time during the school year for hobbies. Don't wait until summer break to relax and enjoy yourself.
✔ Apologize when you're wrong.
✔ Learn and use relaxation techniques, such as the five-minute relaxation break included on page 330.
✔ Don't forget to exercise regularly, eat a healthful diet, get enough sleep, and avoid too much caffeine or alcohol. Living a

A Five-Minute Relaxation Break

Got five minutes? That's all the time it takes to relax and de-stress. John O'Brien, a movement specialist and stress-management consultant, recommends these simple exercises. Pin up a copy of them where you will see them during the day. (You can practice some of these while you're teaching—no one will even notice!)

1. **For starters.** Sit upright in a chair on your "sit bones," with your spine straight but not rigid. Close your eyes if you wish.

2. **Try cleansing breaths.** Take a deep breath through the nose, filling your lungs from the bottom (your stomach will gently puff out), through the middle, and through the top. Exhale forcefully through the mouth, using your lips for resistance. As you inhale again, imagine gathering up all your tension and expelling it as you exhale. Repeat.

3. **Breathe deeply.** Continue to breathe through your nose, focusing on the continuous flow of the breath. If your mind wanders to the past or the future, acknowledge these thoughts and then put them aside. Remind yourself that you've committed this time to relaxing—you could be doing a million things, but you're not.

4. **Let go.** Systematically go through your body, tensing muscle groups as you inhale, holding the tension for a few seconds and releasing completely as you exhale. Tense and relax your face, neck, shoulders, and arms; then your stomach and entire back and buttocks; and finally your legs and feet. Make a point of memorizing how you feel when you release.

5. **Release neck tension.**
- Imagine that your head is a helium balloon being lifted off the top of your spine. Slowly reach your chin up to the ceiling, keeping the back of the neck relaxed. Reverse, lifting the base of the skull and softening your throat so your chin comes down to your chest. Repeat five times and then hold for five counts in each position. (Move smoothly at whatever speed feels right to you. Remember—no strain, no pain.)
- Keeping a sense of length in your spine, turn your head to look over your right shoulder. Then look over your left. Repeat five times and then hold for five counts on both sides.
- Reach your right ear up to the ceiling to stretch the right side of your neck. Reverse. Repeat five times and then hold for five counts on both sides.

6. **Roll your shoulders.** Imagine yourself as a puppet with strings attached to the tops of your shoulders with your arms relaxed. Begin to roll your shoulders up toward your ears; backward so you feel your shoulder blades gently squeeze together; downward; and then forward so your shoulder blades separate. You'll feel your shoulder blades massaging the muscles that surround them. Repeat five times and then reverse directions. Breathe.

7. **Stretch your arms.** As you inhale, interlace your fingers, raise your arms overhead (keep your shoulders relaxed; avoid arching your back), turn your palms toward the ceiling, and reach through the heels of your hands. Hold for five counts. Feel the stretch starting at the hips and moving through the ribs, under and through the arms. As you exhale, stretch to the right. Inhale as you come back to center, and exhale to the left. Repeat.

8. **Do the twist.** Put your hands on your legs or the arms of your chair and twist your trunk to the right as you exhale. (Initiate the movement from your body's center, and your head will follow.) Inhale and then twist to the left as you exhale. Repeat.

9. **Be a rag doll.** Inhale deeply, and as you exhale, hinge forward at the hip and let your head relax between your knees. As you hang over your chair, take five deep breaths. Then, keeping your neck and shoulders relaxed, round up your spine one vertebra at a time, starting at the bottom, until your head stacks up on top.

10. **Memorize how you feel.** Take one more ventilating breath. Consciously remind yourself that you want to maintain the peace that you've acquired during these exercises.

Reported by Meg Bozzone for *Instructor* online.

healthful life can keep your resistance and tolerance high.

✔ Just say no—to commitments and duties you can't handle comfortably with your present workload.

✔ Don't forget to laugh. Humor really is the best medicine, especially for situations we can't control.

✔ Stay home and take care of yourself when you don't feel well. Poor health lowers your emotional as well as physical stamina.

Avoiding Burnout

Stress left unmanaged for too long contributes to a debilitating condition known as teacher burnout. It's a condition resulting from too much effort with too little satisfaction and return. And it strikes most often among the most caring and committed of teachers—those who work so hard to do a good job but who become embittered, emotionally exhausted, cynical, callous, detached, frustrated, resentful.

Experts say that burnout is like battle fatigue. It occurs when our idealism and burning desire to be good teachers confront the harsh realities and struggles of teaching, and we simply become disillusioned.

The experts further point out that to feel emotionally satisfied, we need to identify with others, feel control over our lives, consider ourselves worthy of respect, and associate with people who are positive role models. Teachers suffering burnout don't do or feel any of these things.

Burnout is a recognized hazard in professions that are people-oriented, like teaching. "Even newcomers to the profession aren't immune," says Dr. Judy Downs Lombardi, who worked with teachers and student teachers at the University of Tampa.

There's even a test for determining burnout called the Maslach Burnout Inventory. Developed by Christina Maslach, professor of psychology at the University of California at Berkeley, the test identifies three primary indicators of burnout: emotional exhaustion (which often gives way to physical exhaustion); depersonalization (becoming negative about everyone around you); and lack of personal accomplishment.

How can we avoid burnout? By recognizing the warning signs and finding ways to rekindle the passion for teaching, Lombardi says. She describes ten symptoms of teacher burnout, noting that you may be headed toward burnout if you:

1. are bored with teaching and feel that there's nothing more to learn about it.
2. bristle at suggestions of new ways to teach.
3. dream of perfection and judge your professional performance without mercy.
4. are plagued by the feeling that you should be doing more at school, even though you're working hard.
5. are withdrawn and feel more comfortable doing paperwork than interacting with students, colleagues, or parents.
6. can't remember why you became a teacher, or find yourself wishing you weren't one.
7. find teaching isn't fun anymore, complain about it constantly, and take your frustrations home with you.
8. count the days until the next break or summer vacation.
9. worry excessively about students and their problems.
10. eat poorly, don't get enough sleep, let hobbies lapse, resort to unhealthy outlets for stress, and just generally don't take good care of yourself.

What can you do if you have several or all of these symptoms? Lombardi offers these suggestions:

✔ Overhaul your job. Come up with creative ways to handle even the most tedious teaching tasks.

✔ Try new instructional strategies.

✔ Challenge yourself to keep learning.

✔ Collaborate with colleagues. (See Chapter Seven for some good ideas.)

✔ Try changing grade levels or teaching assignments.

✔ Try not to wrap up your identity with your job. Cultivate outside interests and hobbies.

✔ Give yourself permission to be less than perfect. "Too many teachers believe that none of their successes count if they have one failure," says Lombardi. "Accept that teaching is difficult and challenging. Pain and failure will always be part of the profession, just as joy and success will be."

✔ Realize that you can help students, but you can't save them from society's ills.

✔ Learn to care for yourself. "As caretaker professionals, teachers often overcare for others and undercare for themselves," Lombardi notes. "Conserve and replenish your emotional and physiological resources—they're limited!"

✔ Practice techniques for stress reduction such as yoga.

✔ Evaluate your career goals. Is teaching still right for you? Do you need a break, or maybe some intensive training, before coming back to teaching? "Don't wait until you're completely disenchanted to assess where you are going and whether it's time for a change in professions," Lombardi advises.

Personal and professional growth are complementary processes. Neglect one, and the other will suffer. But by concentrating on both, you're assuring yourself of a healthy and happy teaching career.

❖ In Summary

Wanted: Bright, creative teachers who continually re-examine their beliefs about teaching and learning, who keep pace with new knowledge and technological developments, and who refine their strategies and approaches based on what they learn from experiences and research.

It sounds like a tall order. But this is what it takes to be an effective teaching professional in today's world. The profession needs individuals who are not just doers, but also are thinkers. Perhaps the National Board for Professional Teaching Standards states it best in its Proposition No. 4:

"**Teachers Think Systematically About Their Practice and Learn From Experience.** As with most professions, teaching requires an open-ended capacity that is not acquired once and for all. Because they work in a field marked by many unsolved puzzles and an expanding research base, teachers have a professional obligation to be lifelong students of their craft, seeking to expand their repertoire, deepen their knowledge and skill, and become wiser in rendering judgments. Accomplished teachers are inventive in their teaching and, recognizing the need to admit new findings and continue learning, stand ready to incorporate ideas and methods developed by others that fit their aims and their students. What exemplifies excellence, then, is a reverence for the craft, a recognition of its complexities, and a commitment to lifelong professional development."

❖ Works Cited (Chapter 8 and Conclusion)

American Federation of Teachers. *Principles for Professional Development.* 2002. Available: www.aft.org/pubs-reports/downloads/teachers/PRINCIPLES.pdf

Bluestein, Jane. *Beginning Teacher's Resource Book.* Parsippany, NJ: Globe-Fearon, 1988.

Brandt, Ron. "The Public vs. 'The Experts.'" *Educational Leadership* 52, no. 7 (April 1995): 5.

Clark, Christopher. *Thoughtful Teaching.* New York: Teachers College Press, 1996.

Clark, Christopher, and Robert Yinger. *The Hidden World of Teaching: Implications of Research on Teacher Planning.* East Lansing: Michigan State University, Institute for Research on Teaching, 1980.

Feiman-Nemser, Sharon. "Learning to Teach." In L. Shulman and G. Sykes, eds. *Handbook on Teaching and Policy.* Upper Saddle River, NJ: Longman/Pearson, 1983.

Hait, Helen. "Creating a Classroom Community: A Brief Study of Contributing Factors in Group Work." *Educational Insights* 8, no. 3 (March 2004). Available: www.ccfi.educ.ubc.ca. (Click on Publications, then *Educational Insights* and find the issue.)

Hawkins, David. "What It Means to Teach." *Teachers College Record* 75, no. 1 (1973): 7–16.

Hunt, James B. Editorial. *USA Today*, October 23, 1995, 13A.

Johnson, Beverly. "Teacher-as-Researcher." ERIC Digest, ED355205, March 1993. Available: http://ericadr.piccard.csc.com/extra/ericdigests/ed355205.html.

Pinsonneault, Susan, and Kara Malhi. "How Can Teachers Support Gender Equity in Their Classrooms?" *Educational Insights* 8, no. 3 (March 2004). Available: www.ccfi.educ.ubc.ca. (Click on Publications, then *Educational Insights* and find the issue.)

Salvador Roberta. "Take Off With Online Learning." *Instructor*, October 2004, 20.

Sayas, Ann. "To Grow a Teacher." *Teacher to Teacher* (Spring 1996): 1.

Waitley, Denis. *The Winner's Edge: The Critical Attitude of Success.* New York: Times Books, 1980.

Wolf, Kenneth. "Developing an Effective Teaching Portfolio." *Educational Leadership* 53, no. 6 (March 1996): 34–37.

❖ Resources

Researching Teaching and Action Research
Calhoun, Emily. *How to Use Action Research in the Self-Renewing School.* Alexandria, VA: Association for Supervision and Curriculum Development, 1994.

Dana, Nancy Fichtman, and Diane Yendol-Silva. *The Reflective Educator's Guide to Action Research: Learning to Teach and Teaching to Learn Through Practitioner Inquiry.* Thousand Oaks, CA: Corwin Press, 2003.

Joyce, Bruce, and Emily Calhoun. *Learning to Teach Inductively.* Boston: Allyn & Bacon, 1997.

Joyce, Bruce, Emily Calhoun, and David Hopkins. *The New Structure of School Improvement: Inquiring Schools and Achieving Students.* Berkshire, UK: Open University Press/McGraw-Hill, 1999.

Schmuck, Richard A. *Practical Action Research for Change.* Arlington Heights, IL: IRI/Skylight, 1997.

Sparks, Dennis. "The Singular Power of One Goal: An Interview with Emily Calhoun." (Action Researcher Narrows Focus to Broaden Effectiveness.) *Journal of Staff Development* 20, no. 1 (Winter 1999). Available: http://conference.nsdc.org/library/publications/jsd/calhoun201.cfm.

Stringer, Ernest. *Action Research in Education.* Upper Saddle River, NJ: Pearson/Merrill/Prentice Hall, 2004.

Professional Development
MyLearningPlan
(www.mylearningplan.com)
A Web-based service for tracking and managing professional-development activities. Includes tracking tools, substitute planning and feedback forms, calendars, financial forms, and more. (Fee and registration required.)

Professional Portfolios
Adams-Bullock, Ann, and Parmalee P. Hawk. *Developing a Teaching Portfolio: A Guide for Preservice and Practicing Teachers.* Upper Saddle River, NJ: Merrill/Prentice Hall, 2001.

Campbell, Dorothy M., et al. *How to Develop a Professional Portfolio: A Manual for Teachers.* Boston: Pearson/Allyn & Bacon, 2004.

National Board Certification

Hopkins, Martha A. *Navigating the National Board Certification Process: A Step-by-Step Workbook For Teachers*. Thousand Oaks, CA: Corwin Press, 2004.

Mack-Kirschner, Adrienne. *The Teacher's Guide to National Board Certification: Unpacking the Standards*. Portsmouth, NH: Heinemann, 2003.

Résumés

Enelow, Wendy S., and Louise M. Kursmark. *Expert Résumés for Teachers and Educators*. Indianapolis: Jist Works, 2002.

Conclusion

"In a completely rational society, the best of us would aspire to be teachers and the rest of us would have to settle for something less, because passing civilization along from one generation to the next ought to be the highest honor and the highest responsibility anyone could have."
—Lee Iacocca

Learning to teach is not just for beginners. It's a challenge that stimulates professionals throughout their careers. The best teachers are those who are always trying to become better.

Successful teaching is not a hit-or-miss proposition dependent on the right bag of tricks. There's a real "science of teaching" to guide our actions and decisions and a growing knowledge base gleaned from the practical wisdom of experienced teachers. We *do* know many of the factors contributing to effective practice. We *can* say that some practices are more effective than others in certain situations with certain students.

Yet there are no recipes for effective teaching. It all boils down to individual teachers making individual decisions for individual students. And the new information technology makes this more possible and more challenging than ever. Teaching, as other professions, relies on the judgments and commitment of its individual practitioners. Therein lies the "art of teaching."

You really matter! You are the most important factor in school learning. Your teaching is a unique product—the result of your individual endeavors. Protect it, nourish it, think about it, give it room to grow.

Describing his notion of a teacher as "an enlightened and passionate intellectual," Stanford professor emeritus Lee Shulman claims that teachers are "uniquely responsible for carrying on our cultural, intellectual and aesthetic achievements." They are "the mechanism by which our societies pass on knowledge and values."

As Dwight D. Eisenhower once noted: "In all our efforts for education—in providing adequate school research, and study—we must never lose sight of the very heart of education: good teaching itself. Good teachers do not just happen, they are the product of the highest of personal motivation."

Best wishes, teacher. And may your ongoing journey toward professional excellence be rewarding and filled with happy times.

Important Terms About Teaching and Learning

ability grouping: Grouping students of similar skill levels together. See *heterogeneous grouping* and *homogeneous grouping*.

acceleration: Having a student enter school early, skip a grade, or take advanced placement classes so that he or she can complete schooling in less time. Acceleration is often used with gifted students.

accountability: National, state, or local policies that schools, teachers, and students accountable to performance-related goals. For example, school and school district accountability might entail the structures in place to maintain high levels of student performance on standardized tests. This term also refers to the structures in place for schools, school districts, and teachers to ensure that each constituency is doing its part.

action research: The process of identifying a problem in a classroom, collecting and analyzing data on the problem, reflecting on the results of the research, and using the information to solve a teaching problem. Action research includes any of the following: an individual teacher focusing on solving a problem in his or her classroom; teachers collaborating with administrators or university researchers to solve a problem in a classroom or several classrooms; or a schoolwide effort with the entire faculty working together to solve a problem. Sometimes referred to as "teacher research."

active listening: A method in which the listener, in an attempt to fully understand what is being said, restates and clarifies what he or she has heard the person say.

ADD/ADHD: Attention deficit disorder and attention deficit hyperactivity disorder. A disorder marked by the inattention, impulsivity, and, in the case of ADHD, hyperactivity.

adequate yearly progress (AYP): An accountability provision in the No Child Left Behind Act that requires that all public schools, districts, and states receiving federal funding under Title 1 Part A make improvements in test scores from one year to the next and in either graduation rates (for high schools) or attendance rates (for elementary and middle/junior high school. See *No Child Left Behind (NCLB)*.

advanced organizer: Brief written text (in the form of ideas, facts, or questions) about a new book is presented to students before they read the book in an attempt to enhance their comprehension.

affective programs: Programs to address the social and emotional needs of students. For example, affective programs can be used with gifted students to focus on their special concerns and problems.

anticipation guide: (Readence, Bean, and Baldwin, 1985) Allows individual students to reflect on and express their opinions in response to written statements that challenge or confirm their beliefs about what they are reading. After responding to the statements, students can discuss their responses in small groups. Then all of the groups can meet together so that students can have the benefit of the collective knowledge of the larger group.

assertive discipline: A discipline system, developed by Lee and Marlene Canter (1976, 1982), that features a three-step method: 1) Teach the specific behaviors you want from students. 2) Use positive reinforcement to reinforce the behavior of students who follow directions and rules. 3) Use a negative consequence you have previously established to punish misbehavior.

assessment: The method of determining a student's progress. Assessments can include standardized tests and alternative (authentic) assessments such as student portfolios. See *authentic assessment*.

at risk: A general term referring to students whose economic, linguist, cognitive, sociological, or psychological factors might contribute to increased academic difficulties in school.

authentic assessment: Using a variety of methods, such as portfolios, exhibitions, performances, journals, projects, and experiments, to assess students' knowledge and achievement in order to fairly and accurately measure the learning of all students. Authentic assessment is used as an alternative to, or in addition to, formal assessments and standardized tests. See *assessment*, *formal assessment*, and *informal assessment*.

authentic learning: Students work on real problems, real tasks, or projects, and their academic growth is viewed in terms of not only the products and outcomes, but also in terms of the process they undertake.

author's chair: (Graves and Hansen, 1983) A way for students to share with each other the excitement of a particular moment in a book or their writing. The student in the author's chair reads aloud a selected piece of text or a piece of his or her own writing. Peers then have the opportunity to respond to what is read aloud.

automaticity: The ability to perform a skill, such as adding a set of numbers or reading a list of words, with high levels of fluency and rates of performance. A student has achieved automaticity when he or she has internalized and integrated the skills and strategies needed to do a task to the extent that the task can be accomplished with ease.

backward design: A process that helps teachers work "backward" from the standards to design assessment and instruction—first targeting the desired learning outcome, then designing the assessment to effectively demonstrate mastery of the outcome, and finally planning the instruction to meet the scope, content, and format of the assessment.

balanced literacy: Designed as an approach to mediate the "reading wars" between whole language and phonics, balanced literacy is a framework for teaching reading and writing that engages students in a variety of literacy experiences within the school day. There are numerous components to a balanced literacy framework, offering multiple opportunities to read and write through modeled, guided, and independent practice. For examples of components of a balanced literacy framework, see *guided reading, independent reading, interactive writing, reader's workshop, shared reading*, and *writer's workshop*.

basal reader: A book, organized by grade or reading levels, used to teach reading. In general, the texts are a part of a commercial curriculum and the student's text is used in unison with a teacher's guide.

basic skills: The minimal level of skills needed to accomplish a task with proficiency.

best practice: Teaching strategies that through research or experience have proved to work effectively with students.

big books: Enlarged reading books whose large size allows students to read together as they learn about concepts of print and various decoding and comprehension strategies. See *shared reading* for an example of an instructional strategy that can involve big books.

Bloom's taxonomy: A theory that describes the six levels of thinking skills, which include, from lowest to highest level, knowledge, comprehension, application, analysis, synthesis, and evaluation.

book talk: A strategy for discussing books. A book talk can be used to entice students to read a new book or to get them to think critically about a book they have just read. Book talks can be led by a teacher, a librarian, or the students themselves.

brain-based: Refers to learning theory and research that focuses exclusively on the functions of the brain.

bypass strategies: Strategies, frequently used with students who have learning disabilities, to help students circumvent their weak areas. An example is allowing a student who has difficulty taking notes to use a tape recorder to record a lesson.

character education: Curriculum designed to teach students specific values and behaviors, such as courage, loyalty, justice, hope, honesty, and love.

choral reading: A reading strategy involving students orally reading and rereading a text, in unison. Choral reading sometimes entails an interpretive reading of a text, such as poetry or songs.

classroom management: All the elements of organizing and managing a classroom, including classroom setup, class routines, discipline, and planning.

cloze: A variety of sentence-completion techniques in which words are strategically left out of a text so that readers supply the missing words using context, or sometimes limited graphophonic cues.

coaching: The teacher working alongside a student as the student receives and practices new information. See *guided practice*.

comprehension: The interpretation of print on the page into a meaningful message. Comprehension depends on readers' decoding abilities, prior knowledge and experiences, metacognition, and their ongoing comprehension strategies.

concepts about print or **concepts of print:** (Clay, 1982) Understandings about how written text works. Some of the basic concepts about print include the following: directionality (that readers and writers move from left to right and top to bottom); spacing (used to separate words); and recognition of words.

conference: An opportunity for a teacher to work one-on-one with a student to teach, reinforce, or coach him or her in a particular area of study. For example, a writing conference might involve teaching a writer one way to incorporate writer's craft into the text he or she is writing. Sometimes called *conferring*.

conflict-resolution education: Teaching students the skills and concepts they need to be able to resolve conflicts peacefully.

constructivism: A theory of learning that holds that students bring their experiences and knowledge to any new subject. Students learn by understanding from their prior knowledge and constructing meanings. In language acquisition, the constructivist theory suggests that a reader actively builds meaning from text.

content standards: Teaching and curriculum standards developed by professional organizations, such as the National Council of Teachers of English (NCTE), International Reading Association (IRA), and National Council of Teachers of Mathematics (NCTM), for individual curriculum areas. The standards outline what the curriculum should cover and what students should know in a particular subject area.

context clues: Clues to the meaning of a word that a reader can find in the surrounding text or in the pictures.

cooperative learning: Students work in small groups to help one another learn academic content.

criterion-referenced test: A test that compares a student's performance on certain skill objectives a performance standard.

critical period: A theory that proposes that during brain development there are "windows of opportunity" or critical periods when a person can best acquire specific skills and knowledge. An example is the idea that language development in children best occurs from birth to age 10.

critical thinking: Thinking process that involves the ability to acquire information and evaluate or analyze it before providing an answer or statement.

cross-age tutoring: Older students tutoring younger students.

cross-grouping: Grouping students from two to three classes together for a particular subject such as reading or math.

culturally relevant teaching: Teaching that incorporates students' backgrounds rather than attempting to override, ignore, or negate them. Principles and concepts are illustrated with examples that are relevant to a student's culture and history. Sometimes referred to as *multicultural education*.

curriculum compacting: Giving students credit for what they already know and modifying the curriculum to allow them to learn something new.

decoding: A series of strategies that readers use selectively to recognize written words. In decoding, the reader locates cues in a word that reveal enough about the word to help pronounce it and attach meaning to it.

developmental stages: (Piaget, 1954; Piaget & Inhelder, 1969) The different cognitive stages children move through as they grow, with each stage marked by specific characteristics. For example, preschool children tend to learn from concrete experiences; however, they do not acquire abstract thinking skills until later in their school years.

developmentally appropriate practice (DAP): (Bredekamp, 1987; Bredekamp & Copple, 1997) A term generally used in early childhood education, teaching, and curriculum that is adjusted to the physical, social, emotional, and cognitive level of the students. A developmentally appropriate curriculum takes into account what students are and are not capable of at varying developmental stages.

dialogue journal: A written dialogue between the journal "owner" and a selected "partner." The partner responds to what the owner has written. The responses should deal with what has been written and not just the conventions of writing. Journal partners can be students, teachers, or parents.

differentiated instruction: Providing students with tasks appropriate to their ability levels. Learning activities and lessons are designed to meet students where they are, maximizing their ability to learn new information most effectively. For example, differentiated leaning products are the different methods, besides paper-and-pencil tests, by which students can demonstrate their knowledge, including oral presentations, visual presentations, and written projects.

direct instruction: Teachers clearly lead learning activities. Academic tasks are carefully structured with teachers telling students how to accomplish a task and guiding them until they master the material. Sometimes direct instruction involves the use of a teacher's manual and/or teacher's script. Also called *systematic and explicit instruction* or *active teaching*.

double-entry journal: A double-entry record in which a student takes notes and adds reflections while reading a text. A two-column format is used. Typically, the left column is used to record specific statements from a text that are important to understanding the text; the right column is used to record responses and reactions to those statements.

dyslexia: A wide-encompassing term used to describe a genetic reading disability. In general, dyslexics have an average to above-average IQ and exhibit difficulties learning to read and write, noticeably in the area of phonological skills.

echo reading: A lead reader reads aloud a section of text, and a second reader's voice follows right after (or "echoes") the first reader.

ELL: English language learner. Any student whose primary language is not English. See *ESL*.

encoding: Transferring oral language into written language.

engaged time: The time when students are paying attention or busily involved in work.

enrichment: Extending classroom work for students by either using more in-depth material or adding topics/areas of study not usually covered in the curriculum. Enrichment is often used to enhance the education of gifted children.

environmental preferences: The lighting, noise, and temperature preferences students have for their surroundings.

environmental print: Any print that is found in the physical environment, such as street signs, billboards, labels, and business signs.

ESL: English as a second language. Refers to students for whom English is not the first or primary language. ESL also refers to the English as a Second Language programs, an instructional technique in which ESL students are taught English in a pull-out program with the aim of acquiring enough English to function in a mainstream classroom.

evidence-based learning: Learning that takes place as a result of teaching informed by data obtained from assessments. For example, a teacher might use informal assessments she has administered to help her select content for upcoming lessons and activities. An administrator might use a school's standardized test scores to identify areas of need for professional development and faculty focus. Sometimes described as *data-driven instruction*.

expository text: A form of writing intended to set forth or explain, and which employs a wide variety of structures. The five major types are: 1) enumeration (listing of facts); 2) time order (putting facts or events into a sequence using references to time); 3) comparison/contrast (pointing out likenesses and/or differences); 4) cause/effect (showing how facts or events affect other facts or events); 5) problem/
solution (showing the development of a problem and its solutions).

external motivation: Motivation that comes from anticipating an external reward for completing an activity or behaving in a certain way.

fluency: The ability to read with accuracy, with expression, and in a timely manner while still maintaining comprehension. See *prosody, oral reading rate, intonation,* and *phrasing.*

formal assessment: A systematized way of evaluating how a student is doing in a particular area of instruction. For example, an end-of-the-unit test is a formal assessment.

gender bias: Discriminatory behaviors that lead to girls and boys being treated differently. Examples of gender bias in the classroom include teachers giving boys more direct attention, expecting boys to be more assertive and girls to be more quiet and passive, and praising boys for the quality of their work and praising girls for neatness and matters of form.

genre: The different categories of literary work, such as novel, mystery, historical fiction, biography, short story, and poem.

gifted: The federal government, in the Education Consolidation and Improvement Act of 1981, offers the following definition of giftedness: "[Gifted children] give evidence of high performance capability in areas such as intellectual, creative, artistic, leadership capacity, or specific academic fields and . . . require services or activities not ordinarily provided by the school in order to fully develop such capabilities." In the broadest sense, children who are identified as gifted are able to think faster, identify and solve more complex problems, think in unusual and diverse ways, and exhibit profound insights.

grand conversation: (Eeds & Wells, 1989; Peterson & Eeds, 1990) A group leader encourages the group to participate in a discussion of a text that they have all just read. The discussion can be reflective and interpretive, leading students "into the text" in order to think about what the author has written and to encourage them to share what they think about it.

graphic organizer: Teaching tool designed to provide a visual representation of facts and concepts from a text and their relationships to each other. Examples of graphic organizers include Venn diagrams, story maps, and word webs. Graphic organizers are effective tools for thinking and learning, as they help teachers and students represent abstract or implicit information in more concrete form, depict the relationships between facts and concepts, organize and elaborate ideas, relate new information to prior knowledge, and effectively store and retrieve information.

group conferences: Meeting with parents in one large group, at an open house, for example, to discuss curriculum, grading policies, strategies, and goals for the year.

guided practice: Students practice a new concept; however, the teacher is still available to provide advice, feedback, assistance, or to reteach material. Whereas in independent practice a teacher might not be available to give immediate support, in guided practice a teacher is on hand to scaffold a student's knowledge and abilities. See *guided reading* and *scaffolding.*

guided reading: (Clay, 1991; Fountas & Pinnell, 1996) Students work in small groups to read as independently as possible a text the teacher has selected and introduced to them. This text should be at the group's instructional level. Students learn to self-monitor their own reading behaviors and use appropriate strategies to fully decode and comprehend a text. The teacher is available to support, assess, and use the text to teach concepts, if necessary. See *balanced literacy* and *guided practice*.

hemisphericity: Refers to left- and right-brain functions. People who are left-brain oriented are considered to think analytically and inductively, and to learn successively in small steps that lead to understanding. People who are right-brain oriented are considered to think more globally and deductively, and to learn broad concepts first and then the small details.

heterogeneous grouping: Placing students in groups with other students of varying ability levels.

Higher Order Thinking Skills (HOTS) Program: A program developed by Dr. Stanley Pogrow to teach low-achieving students how to think and reason. The program emphasizes modeling thinking processes through conversations.

homogeneous grouping: Placing students in groups with other students with the same ability level.

I-Chart: An organizer designed to foster critical thinking in which three to four questions that the teacher has prepared are listed across the top of a grid chart. Students list information they know or believe they know about each question underneath it on the chart. Then they discuss and list possible resources for finding out the information on the left side of the chart. As students find answers, they write them under the appropriate questions and next to the source. Columns are also created for "Other Interesting Facts" and "New Questions."

inclusion: Integrating exceptional children, including children with learning disabilities, behavior problems or physical disabilities, in regular education classrooms.

independent reading: Students read at an appropriate text level for a sustained period of time without support or guidance from a teacher or peer. In general, teachers are working in small groups or conferring when students are reading independently. Sometimes called *sustained silent reading* (SSR).

independent reading level: (Clay, 1991) The level of reading material that a student can easily read independently with high comprehension and few word-identification problems, and an accuracy rate of 95 to 100 percent. Independent reading levels can be determined by administering a running record. See *independent reading, instructional level,* and *running record.*

independent study: Students independently pursue and study a topic they are interested in.

Individualized Educational Plan (IEP): A legally binding document for a student with special needs. The document must be written by a multidisciplinary team of educators, discussed with families, and individualized to a student's unique set of needs.

Individuals with Disabilities Education Act (IDEA): Granted in 1975, IDEA guarantees that all individuals with disabilities, from birth to age 21, are guaranteed a free and appropriate public education.

informal assessment: Any unofficial assessment a teacher might incorporate or use to garner an understanding of students' abilities. See *formal assessment.*

inquiry-based learning: Students' questions and interests direct the study.

in-services: Professional development workshops and seminars designed to provide teachers with information about the latest educational research and the newest teaching strategies and techniques.

instructional reading level: (Clay, 1991) The level of reading material that a student can read successfully, with instruction and support, with 90 to 94 percent accuracy. An accuracy rate below 90 percent is frequently called the *frustration level*. Reading levels can be determined by administering a running record. *See guided reading, independent reading level,* and *running record.*

instructional time: The time a teacher actually has to teach.

intake preferences: Differences in students' needs to eat and/or drink while concentrating.

integrated curriculum: Combining different disciplines into multipurpose lessons to help students recognize connections between subjects and to make instruction more meaningful by giving students the opportunity to apply skills from one discipline in another. An integrated lesson might cover both science and social studies topics in a lesson on weather and climate.

interactive writing: A shared writing experience used to assist emergent readers in learning to read and write. With help from the teacher, students dictate sentences about a shared experience such as a story, movie, or event. The teacher verbally "stretches" each word so students can distinguish its sounds and letters as they write the word on chart paper while repeating the sounds. After each word is completed, the teacher and students reread it. Students take turns writing letters to complete the words and the sentence(s). The completed charts are put up on the wall so students can reread them or rely on them for standard spelling.

internal motivation: Motivation that is fueled by a person's curiosity or the desire for mastery and not based on any external rewards.

interrupted book report: Students take turns sharing the highlights of a self-selected text with the class in a brief time period (from 30 to 60 seconds). At the end of the time period, a student must stop and let the next student share his or her book. With the imposed time limit, students are forced to focus on the most important or interesting part of the text they've read.

intonation: The use of pitch to give meaning or importance to particular words in a text.

invented spelling: (Read, 1975) An emergent writer's attempt to spell a word phonetically when the spelling is unknown. Students' temporary spelling is a direct reflection of their own knowledge and understanding of how words are actually spelled. It can also be an invaluable medium for diagnosing difficulties and evaluating progress. By engaging students in thinking actively and reflectively about the sounds of words and their spellings, exercise in temporary spelling lays a strong cognitive foundation for both spelling and phonics. It does not, however, eliminate the need for learning to spell correctly. Support for temporary spelling should be combined with formal spelling instruction to move students toward rapid growth in word recognition and correct spelling. Also known as *temporary spelling* or *approximation*.

jigsaw: (Vogt) A collaborative learning technique in which individuals become experts on one portion of a text (usually informational text) and then share their knowledge with a small group, called their home group. Students can also work in small groups and then share the results with the class. This strategy is effective when a large piece of text must be covered in a short period of time.

KWHL: A spinoff of *KWL* (see definition below), with the H standing for *how* the students will find the information after they have determined what they want to find out.

KWL: (Ogle, 1986; Carr and Ogle, 1987) A flexible strategy for guiding students' thinking about a text before, during, and after reading. The letters stand for what students *know* about a particular topic, what they *want* to find out, and what they have *learned*. This strategy works especially well with informational texts.

learning center: Any part of the classroom designed for independent learning. Learning centers can be organized around any topic or theme and allow students to explore and apply newly learned skills independently. Centers should include a clear learning objective, simple directions, easily accessible materials, and, if possible, a way for students to self-evaluate their work. A center specific to literacy is referred to as a *literacy center*.

learning disabilities: Neurobiological disorders that interfere with a child's ability to sort, process, and retrieve information. Learning disabilities create a gap between a student's ability and performance. The major types of learning disabilities include apraxia (inability to motor-plan or make an appropriate body response), dysgraphia (difficulty writing), dyslexia (difficulty with literacy and language in its various uses), dyssemia (difficulty with social cues and signals), auditory discrimination (trouble perceiving the differences between sounds and sequence of sounds), and visual perception (difficulty understanding and putting meaning to what one sees).

learning styles: The different ways that people learn. Learning style is determined, in part, by a person's sensory preferences. For example, a visual learner acquires information through sight, an auditory learner acquires information by hearing it, and a tactile learner learns best by manipulating materials. Learning style is also influenced by a person's environmental preferences for sound and light levels, temperature, and group size.

LEP: Limited English Proficiency. Refers to people for whom English is not their primary language. See *ESL*.

leveled books: (Fountas & Pinnell, 1996) Organizing texts based on their increased difficulty. Factors such as word difficulty, number of words, size of the print, and nature of text determine how texts are leveled. See *guided reading*, *independent reading level*, and *instructional reading level*.

list-group-label: The teacher supplies students with a stimulus topic drawn from their experiences or from materials they are studying. Students contribute words they associate with the topic. When the list reaches 25 to 30 words, students are then directed to categorize the words and create labels for each group.

literacy center: See *learning center*.

literature circle: Students read a piece of literature and meet as a group to discuss it. The group can begin by discussing reactions to the book, sharing favorite parts, and raising questions about parts they did not understand or that surprised them. At the end of each discussion, the group decides what they want to talk about the next time they meet; this gives students time to reread certain sections of the book and to think about the topic or questions.

looping: A practice that allows a teacher to teach the same group of students for consecutive school years. The purpose is to encourage greater academic and social growth by extending the amount of time the class and teacher work together in the same class community. For example, Mr. Brown teaches the same group of students for fifth and sixth grade.

manipulatives: Materials used to facilitate a student's learning. Counters are an example of a math manipulative.

mentor teachers: Experienced and effective teachers who supervise, coach, and oversee the efforts of less experienced teachers or those in need of support.

metacognition: Reflection on one's own thinking and learning processes. For example, when reading, students need to learn to evaluate their own decoding and comprehension, plan sequences of actions, and regulate their reading behavior to changing conditions.

mini-lesson: Direct teaching on specific topics or skills that some members of the class seem ready to learn. This direct instruction can also be conducted for the benefit of students who need more information or further clarification of skills or topics that have already been taught. These lessons are presented succinctly, on the assumption that such information will be added to the set of ideas, strategies, and skills to be drawn upon as needed.

miscue analysis: Looking at a student's reading errors, omissions, or substitutions as a means for determining the particular strengths and weaknesses of a student's reading skills. See *three-cueing system*.

morning message: The teacher writes a meaningful morning message on the board to students about a specific event that is planned for the day, or an interesting thought or question for the day. The teacher uses the message as an instructional tool for discussing and reinforcing skills the students are learning or already know well (for example, the conventions of writing, the cueing systems, or a phonics lesson). Students point out the strategies used to help them read the message. Students may also have the opportunity to construct the morning message. Sometimes referred to as *daily news*.

morpheme: A linguistic unit of relatively stable meaning that cannot be divided into smaller meaningful parts; the smallest meaningful part of a word.

multiage classroom: Classroom in which students from different grades levels are grouped together. For example, a multiage classroom might include both first and second graders.

multicultural education: Incorporating a range of cultural perspectives throughout the curriculum. See *culturally relevant teaching*.

multiple intelligences: The theory of intelligence, developed by Howard Gardner, that states that people show intelligence in at least seven different ways: logical-mathematical intelligence, verbal-linguistic intelligence, musical-rhythmic intelligence, visual-spatial intelligence, bodily-kinesthetic intelligence, interpersonal-social intelligence, and intrapersonal-introspective intelligence.

multimedia: Incorporating any aspect of technology into classroom instruction.

multisensory instruction: Incorporating visual, auditory, tactile, and kinesthetic modalities into instructional activities.

narrative: A story or narrated account of actual or fictional events.

National Assessment of Educational Progress (NAEP): The "Nation's Report Card," a federal system for making objective information about student performance available to the public.

national certification: The teaching certification process developed and administered by the National Board for Professional Teaching Standards. To be certified, a teacher must demonstrate and meet the standards developed by the National Board. The certification process is a comprehensive, yearlong assessment of a teacher's knowledge and skills.

neural networks: The interconnected pathways of nerves in the brain.

No Child Left Behind (NCLB): The No Child Left Behind Act of 2001, signed into law by President George W. Bush, is a reauthorization of the Elementary and Secondary Education Act, the central federal law in precollegiate education. NCLB, designed to increase student achievement in public schools, outlines a series of measures to which the federal government holds local governments and school districts accountable. Measures outlined include policies on annual testing, reading instruction, academic progress, teacher qualifications, and funding regulations.

norm-referenced test: A test that compares a student's performance on certain skill objectives with that of other students at his or her grade level.

onset and rime: Intersyllabic units that are smaller than words and syllables but larger than phonemes. The onset is the portion of the syllable that precedes the vowel (for example, in the word *black* the onset is *bl*). The rime is the portion of the syllable including the vowel(s) and any consonant(s) that follow (for example, in the word *black* the rime is *ack*). Not all syllables or words have an onset, but they all have a rime (for example, the word or syllable *out* is a rime without an onset.)

oral reading rate: Number of words in a particular passage that a student can read orally in a minute. For example, if a text contains 50 words and a student reads the text orally in five minutes, then the student has an oral reading rate of 10 words per minute.

parent involvement: Involving parents to the fullest possible extent in their children's education.

pedagogy: The intended use of particular teaching methods to impart content-specific information. Direct instruction and project-based instruction are two different pedagogical approaches.

peer coaching: A reciprocal relationship between colleagues in which two teachers agree to observe and critique each other's teaching.

peer editing: Collaborative learning in which students work with peers editing a piece of writing.

peer tutors: Classmates tutoring one another.

performance assessment: In order to measure students' understanding of a concept or procedure, teachers ask students to perform a meaningful task in which they apply what they have learned. For example, a teacher might have students find the square footage of a classroom to assess their understanding of area.

performance-based teaching: Instruction guided by authentic tasks that can be performed or produced for evaluation, such as developing a portfolio, producing an exhibit, or conducting an experiment.

performance standards: The standards and criteria that students' work should meet or adhere to.

phoneme: The smallest units of speech that distinguish one utterance or word from another in a given language—for example, the /r/ in *rug* or the /b/ in *bug*.

phonemic awareness: The understanding that spoken words and syllables are themselves made up of sequences of elementary speech sounds, or phonemes. Phonemic awareness differs from phonics because it deals with sounds in the spoken word, whereas phonics is concerned with the printed word.

phonics: The understanding of the relationships between sounds and the spelling of letters and groups of letters. Phonics instruction refers to the method of teaching reading by teaching children the relationship between the sound and spelling of letters and/or groups of letters.

phrasing: Segmenting a text into phrases when reading aloud.

picture walk: The teacher guides students through the text by looking at and discussing the pictures before reading the story. This helps students to focus on illustrations instead of text and gives them a point of reference they can use when they actually read the story.

portfolio assessment: A form of authentic assessment in which students collect samples of their work in a portfolio to document their progress over time. Different types of portfolios include *showcase*, which celebrates a student's best work; *descriptive*, which demonstrates what a student can do; *evaluative*, which assesses the student's work against a standard; and *progress*, which documents a student's work over time.

positive discipline: A technique, similar to positive reinforcement (see definition below), which rewards and acknowledges appropriate behavior and disarms misbehavior by ignoring it or redirecting attention away from it.

positive reinforcement: A behavior-management technique that emphasizes rewarding or recognizing good behavior as well as, or instead of, punishing bad behavior.

predictable text: Text is predictable when it enables students to quickly and easily predict what the author is going to say and how he or she is going to say it based on their past experience with similar text patterns. Predictable text can contain rhythmical, repetitive, or cumulative patterns; familiar stories or story lines; familiar sequences; or a good match between illustrations and text. This type of reading material is especially valuable for readers who are not yet fluent or who do not yet use effective reading strategies.

primary and secondary behavior: When a student misbehaves, the primary behavior is what he or she did wrong, and the secondary behavior is any additional result of the primary behavior.

primary language: The first language a child learns to speak.

print-rich environment: An environment in which students are provided many opportunities to interact with print, and where an abundance and variety of printed materials are available and accessible. Students have many opportunities to read and be read to. In a print-rich environment, reading and writing are modeled by the teacher and are used for a wide variety of authentic, everyday purposes.

professional development: Professional support that helps teachers reflect on, develop, and improve their teaching practice.

professional portfolio: A collection of materials that reflect a teacher's experience, educational philosophy, and teaching practices. A professional portfolio might include a résumé, sample lesson plans, evaluations, student work samples, and a statement of educational philosophy.

project approach: Teachers and students select a topic that they would like to study in greater depth, determine the questions and subtopics for their study, investigate and research the topic, and finally report the results of their study.

prosody: The typical patterns of stress and intonation in a language.

pull-out programs: Programs in which students are removed from the classroom for special services or instruction.

quickwrite: Students write nonstop for a prescribed amount of time, usually for five to ten minutes. The quickwrite should be focused on one topic, generating as many ideas as possible. It may be used as a prewriting activity or as an opportunity for students to clarify their thoughts about the topic.

Reader's Theater: Bringing stories and characters to life through oral interpretation. Unlike a play, there is no costuming, movement, stage sets, or memorized lines. The focus is on the literature and on communicating with the audience through the use of facial expressions, voice, and gestures. To highlight multiple interpretations of texts, groups can try several different readings of the same story.

reader's workshop: A way to organize a balanced literacy curriculum. In general, reading workshop is divided into three parts: a mini-lesson, independent practice, and a group share. After a teacher completes a mini-lesson, students work independently while the teacher works with individual readers or in small groups. A reading workshop facilitates students' opportunities to read, explore, and respond to books from different genres and on a variety of topics, providing them with practice in using successful decoding and comprehension strategies. The term *reader's workshop* sometimes refers to any aspect of a balanced literacy framework that involves reading instruction. See *balanced literacy*, *conference*, *mini-lesson*, and *writer's workshop*.

Reading First: No Child Left Behind funding and policies for reading curriculum. A set of policies and practices in early reading instruction to help states and districts set up scientific, research-based reading programs for students in grades K through 3.

Reading Recovery: (Clay, 1979) A reading intervention program for first-grade students who are having difficulty learning to read and write. Designed as a pull-out program, Reading Recovery cycles students through the program as the reading specialist sets and administers short-term, individualized reading intervention plans to substantively improve the select students' reading abilities.

reading response log: Through writing in logs in response to texts read, students demonstrate their ability to synthesize and interpret information from silent reading and oral discussion in their writing. It is also an opportunity for students to write their opinions or questions about what was read or discussed.

reflective teaching: Systematically reflecting—through journal keeping, writing, interaction with other teachers, and reading professional literature—on one's practices as a teacher with the aim of growing professionally. See *action research*.

remedial education: Teaching students concepts and skills that they have not yet grasped from the previous year's schooling.

research-based instruction: Curriculum based on formal research findings. For example, constructivist math programs were designed based on many years of research findings that stated that young children learn best when they experience math in a hands-on fashion rather than by rote memorization.

retelling: A strategy for building and checking students' comprehension in relation to the plot, setting, characters, and any underlying inferences. A reader is invited to retell a story in detail in his or her own words. Sometimes the retelling can be followed by questions to elicit further information.

Ritalin: The brand name of the prescription drug methylphenidate, which is often prescribed to children with ADD or ADHD to stimulate the central nervous system and make them more responsive to feedback from the social and physical environment.

rote memorization: The memorization of facts or information without comprehension.

rubric: An assessment tool used to evaluate student performance on select tasks. Students are given a rubric, or may even help develop it, so they know in advance what they are expected to do. Rubrics communicate which skills and features will be evaluated in their work and are scaled (often on a scale of 1 to 4) so that the highest levels (3 and 4) are exemplars in the area being assessed.

running record: Assessment that involves a student reading to the teacher while the teacher takes notes and records miscues. With this data, the teacher performs a miscue analysis based on the three-cueing system. By taking a running record, a teacher is able to determine a student's independent and instructional reading level. See *independent reading level, instructional level, miscue analysis,* and *three-cueing system.*

scaffolding: What students can do with help, they can eventually do on their own. To facilitate this growth, students work with a more advanced peer or adult, who "scaffolds" a task by modeling it, or by assisting or instructing the student with the intention that the student will eventually work independently. See *guided practice* and *zone of proximal development.*

schema: A framework of information stored in the brain, unique to each individual. In learning, students attach new knowledge to their existing schema to build background knowledge.

scored discussions: Assessment in which groups of three to six students sit in front of the class to discuss and solve a problem in a certain amount of time. Scored discussions can be used to assess problem-solving skills.

seatwork: Tasks and assignments students complete independently at their desks, such as silent reading or worksheets.

self-assessment: Students develop their own list of characteristics or qualities by which they judge their own work.

self-determination: Giving students the opportunity to choose and direct their own learning experiences.

shared reading: Students read a text alongside a fluent reader, the teacher. In this activity all students can access the print visually, by using individual texts or reading enlarged formats such as a big books. Attention is paid to print skills, comprehension, and fluency; this is a widely used teaching strategy in elementary schools. See *balanced literacy, big books,* and *guided practice.*

shared writing: The teacher works as the students' scribe, demonstrating the writing process with the students' ideas.

sight vocabulary: Words that are automatically recalled on sight because they are familiar to the reader. See *word wall.*

skill and drill: Teaching and reinforcing specific skills by having students complete worksheets or practice problems.

special education: Education programs for students with disabilities. Teachers receive certification in this area and are trained to work with children with special needs, sometimes working in a general education classroom alongside these children or in a self-contained classroom for children with special needs.

spiraling: Revisiting a topic repeatedly across a range of time. For example, the topic of measurement in mathematics appears in different capacities in grades K through 5. This approach to curriculum does not assume that students will master the topic the first time it is presented to them.

standards or **standards of learning:** The criteria for what teachers should teach and what students should be able to learn and do. See *content standards* and *performance standards.*

standards-based assessment: Assessment derived from general academic standards and objectives developed by each state and used to explain the concepts and skills students are expected to master at each grade level.

storyboard: Students are asked to recall the major events of a story, usually between six and eight events. The teacher asks the students to illustrate each event, in order, on the squares of a storyboard form.

story map: A graphic organizer of major events and ideas from a story to help guide students' thinking and heighten their awareness of the structure of stories.

teachable moments: Times when students' learning potential is high because student motivation and interest are high.

teacher burnout: A teacher becomes disillusioned with teaching and feels embittered, cynical, detached, frustrated, and resentful. The primary indicators of burnout include emotional exhaustion, depersonalization (becoming negative about others in the environment), and lack of personal accomplishment.

teacher center: A resource center for teachers, run by a professional association or by teachers, organized to support teacher development and improve teaching practices.

team teaching: A partnership in which two colleagues teach together. Team teaching can involve a wide range of activities, including teaching a class together, teaming up to teach a unit, splitting curriculum between two teachers, or exchanging classes to take advantage of academic specialties.

test reliability: A test is considered reliable if a student scores the same on different versions of the test.

test validity: A valid test measures what the user wants the test to measure.

theme studies: Focusing studies on a particular theme, such as oceans or friendship, and teaching curriculum objectives by connecting them to the theme. Theme units are often student-directed, with students' questions and interests guiding the unit.

think aloud: The teacher models aloud for students the thinking processes used when reading or writing. After reading or writing and thinking aloud, the teacher leads a discussion about how certain conclusions were reached about what was read or about how something was written.

Think-Pair-Share: (Lyman, 1981) A cooperative learning strategy in which students listen to a question, think of a response, pair to discuss with a neighbor, and share their responses with the whole class.

three-cueing system: Three of the language systems that readers rely on for cues as they seek meaning from a text: syntactic (based on grammar), semantic (based on meaning), and graphophonic (based on letter-sound relationships or visual cues). Sometimes called *SMV* (syntactic, meaning, visual). See *miscue analysis*.

time on-task: The amount of time a student is actively engaged in the learning process.

time-out: A disruptive student spends a short amount of time, from 5 to 15 minutes, separated from the class in a time-out area or chair. The intention is to give the student a chance to cool down and think while allowing the rest of the class to continue working.

tracking: Placing students in groups or classes based on their ability levels. The criteria for placing students includes prior achievement, the results of standardized tests, and intelligence.

transition: The time spent moving between one activity and another.

Venn diagram: A graphic organizer with two overlapping circles, used to compare and contrast.

wait-time: The three to five seconds a teacher should wait for an answer after asking students questions. It gives them time to think about their responses. Observing wait-time is a common recommendation for teachers working with ELL students.

whole language: A teaching philosophy that asserts that language skills, including reading, writing, and speaking, are interconnected and should be taught as such, instead of teaching discrete subskills. In addition, the whole-language method advocates the use of real literature in the classroom instead of packaged materials designed to teach specific reading and writing skills.

word attack: The process used to decode words.

word play: A student's manipulation of sounds and words for purposes of language exploration and practice or for pleasure (for example, using alliteration, creating rhymes, singing songs, and clapping syllables).

word wall: (Cunningham, 1991) A wall or other surface in the classroom where words that students are learning or have mastered are posted. Word walls may be used for developing familiarity with word patterns and families, for remembering sight or high-frequency words, and for referencing content-area vocabulary. Word walls should include words students will need often in their reading and writing and words that are easily confused with other words. Strategies for remembering words, their spellings, and their meaning are discussed as words are added to the wall.

writer's notebook: A nonthreatening space where students can collect writing ideas and explore the craft of writing.

writer's workshop: A way for a teacher to organize his or her balanced literacy curriculum. In general, a writer's workshop is divided into three parts: a mini-lesson, independent practice, and a group share. After the teacher completes a mini-lesson, students write independently while the teacher works with individual writers or in small groups. A writer's workshop offers students a stable, predictable format for writing that balances instruction and modeling with adequate time for composing, sharing, and publishing. A constant sustained time for writing is set aside each day. The term *writer's workshop* sometimes refers to any aspect of a balanced literacy framework that involves writing instruction. Also called *writing workshop*. See *balanced literacy*, *conference*, *mini-lesson*, and *reader's workshop*.

writing process: The process by which a piece of writing is completed for "publication," involving prewriting, drafting, revising, editing, and "publishing."

zone of proximal development (ZPD): (Vygotsky, 1978) The "zone" between what a student can do with help and what he or she can do without guidance. Through an apprenticeship the student will, over time, learn to do the task independently.

Index

A

active listening, 225–27
ADD/ADHD, 72–75
age and developmental levels,
  51–55
arts assessment, 199
assessment and evaluation, 157–203
  authentic, 157–58, 162–66
  backward design, 161–62
  example—Measurement
    Matters, 161
  Model Developmental Reading
    Scale (resource pages),
    172–73
  rubrics (reproducible pages),
    167–70
  standard-based (defined), 158
  standardized tests, 174–77
  state standards and instruction,
    162
  subject, by, 178–99
  "traditional" assessment,
    166–73
  understanding assessment,
    160–61
assessment by subject
  arts, the, 199
  mathematics, 186–91
  quality vs. quantity, 178
  reading and language arts,
    178–86
  science, 191–94
  social studies, 194–98
authentic assessment
  defined, 157–58
  "differentiating the product,"
    163
  intent, 162
  portfolio assessment, 164–65
  rubrics, creating, 166, 169
  scoring, 165–66
  ways to assess (performance-
    based teaching), 163–64

B

backward design, 161–62
"Basic School," 121–22
beginning the school year
  before school starts, 13, 28, 35
  first day/weeks, 46–48
  note to teachers, 10
  parents—starting off right, 32
  see also *Home-School-
    Community*

behavior problems/consequences
  developmental considerations,
    215
  discipline (what it is), 208–209
  five persistent problems,
    211–13
  "I-messages," 209
  professional referrals, 210
  self esteem, 209, 227–28
  time out, 214
  tips on handling, 210–11,
    213–14
bibliotherapy, 230–32
Bloom's Taxonomy, 125

C

caring classroom climate, creating a
  activities, 218–20
  "care" projects, 221–22
  character education, 222
  classroom environments,
    218–19
  cooperation, 220–21
  group identity, 219–20
caring teachers, 205–208, 217
children as learners, 50–92
  age and developmental levels,
    51–55
  children in crisis, 87–88
  cultural differences, 66–68
  English Language Learners
    (ELL), 68–69, 234–35
  exceptionalities, 69–70
  gender differences, 79–87
  learning styles, 61–65
  multiple abilities/intelligences,
    56–61, 107–10
children in crisis, 87–88
choices, giving children, 110–12
classroom organization/
  management, 12–49
  first day/weeks, 46–48
  grouping, 22–25
  learning centers, 17–22
  paperwork, 31–32
  physical environment, 13–17
  planning, 33–42
  routines and procedures, 25–31
  seatwork, 38–42
  time management, 42–46
communication/interpersonal skills
  attitude, the right, 239
  deterrents to, 240
  listening, 240–41

open-door policy, 241–43
  parent interview, 241
  plain talk, 240
conferences and conventions,
  296–97
cooperative learning, 221
cultural differences
  biases, identifying, 67
  culturally relevant teaching,
    66–67
  diversity, 67–68
  resources (on diversity), 68
  uniformity, emphasis on, 66

D

discipline (what it is), 208–209
diversity, valuing, 232
  culturally responsible
    curriculum, 233
  ESL/ELL, 68–69, 234–35
  myths vs. facts, 233
dyslexia, 70–71

E

Educational Resources Information
  Center (ERIC), 275, 309
English Language Learners (ELL)
  language acquisition, 69
  resources, 234
  statistics, 68–69
  teaching strategies, 234–35
engaging students, 132–38
exceptionalities
  giftedness, 25, 75–79
  inclusion, 69–70
  learning disabilities, 70–75
  other types, 79
  organizations devoted to, 76
expectations, 104–105

F, G

Gardner, Dr. Howard, 56–57
gender differences
  Are Teachers Fair?
    (reproducible page), 82
  bias in children's books
    (resource pages), 84–85
  challenges of, 86–87
  discriminatory behavior, 79–86
  nonbiased teaching, 86
  subtle messages, 86

N

National Certification, 319–25
National Teacher of the Year, 297
networks
    examples, 293–94
    online, 293, 295
    professional development,
      293–94
No Child Left Behind (NCLB) Act,
    158–60, 174, 178–79, 182, 194

O, P

paperwork, 31–32
parent and community involvement
    advocates and decision makers
      (parents as), 254–55
    controlling unannounced visits,
      243
    curriculum enriching, 244
    family interview (reproducible
      pages), 256–57
    home, helping at, 258–61, 267
    homework, 150, 252–54
    parent instructors, 243–46
    parent resource center (resource
      page), 278
    parent volunteers, 247–52, 255
    parent-run writing club, 254
    parental involvement,
      improving (reproducible
      page), 276
    parents as children's teachers,
      243
    resource, 243
    Teachers Involve Parents in
      Schoolwork (TIPs), 253
    teacher's experience, 252
    teacher's do's and don'ts,
      248–52
    t.v. at home (resource page), 268
    your school's PPPQ
      (reproducible page), 277
parent conference
    cautions and considerations,
      269
    conducting/follow-up, 263–64
    conference form (reproducible
      page), 265
    group conference, 269–70
    home, at, 266
    planning/arranging setting,
      262–63
    rapport, establishing good, 264
    students, inviting, 264–66
partnerships/team teaching,
    284–86

peer coaching
    alternate approach, 290–91
    classroom observations,
      287–90
    framework (resource page), 288
    what it is, 286–87
performance-based teaching,
    163–64
phoning/writing home, 270–72
physical environment (classroom)
    arranging/designing space,
      13–15, 17
    desk placement, 15–17
    environmental preferences, 17
    special-use spaces, 15, 17
planning
    all-purpose chart (reproducible
      page), 34
    daily lesson plans, 37
    long-range plans, 36
    must-do list (reproducible
      page), 35
    process of, 33
    substitutes/unexpected,
      37–38, 40
    teachable moments, 33
    weekly schedule, 36
positive discipline, 215–218
professional associations/
    organizations, 296, 298
professional development
    see *reflective teaching*
project approach
    benefits of, 112
    example/resource pgs., 113–17
    phases of, distinct, 112–13
    student choice, 112

Q, R

reading
    computer program for, 96
    intelligence indicator, as, 105
    literature circles, 110
reading and language arts
    assessment
    domains, sampling of, 183
    guidelines, 181
    language arts resources, 179
    literacy framework, 180–81
    "Reading First," 178–79, 182
    running record, 182–83
    sample assessments, 181–82
    six skill areas, 179
    specific reading assessments,
      182–83
    spelling, 183–85
    word knowledge, 183–85
    writing, 185–86

reflective teaching—thinking and
    growing professionally, 301–32
    alternative in-services, 309
    burnout, 331–32
    education laboratories/research
      centers, 309–14
    grants, writing for, 309
    in-services, 314
    journals/publications, 306–309
    National Certification, 319–25
    personal development, 326–29
    professional development
      teams, 291
    professional portfolios, 317–23
    researching teaching, 315–17
    resources, 304, 307–308
    stress, handling, 328–31
    technology, 325–26
    videos, viewing, 305–307
    writing, 302–305
reproducible pages
    ABC's for Low-Stress School
      Year, 328
    All-Purpose Chart, 34
    Are Teachers Fair?, 82
    Assess Your School's PPPQ, 277
    Bridging the Home-School
      Divide, 274
    Checklist on Human Relations,
      216
    Creating a Rubric, 169
    Cycle of Ideas, 135
    Five-Minute Relaxation
      Break, 330
    Grouping ABC's and Animals,
      260–61
    Guidelines for Volunteers, 250
    "Hairy" Tales/Family
      Interview, 256–57
    Helping Your Child at Home,
      267
    Homework Hints for Parents,
      150
    How Raised Is Your
      Consciousness?, 80
    Idea Organizer, 134
    Idea Web, 133
    Ideas in Sequence, 136
    Improving Parental
      Involvement, 276
    Learning Styles Test/Scoring,
      62–63
    Materials to Save, 14
    Math Graphs, 258–59
    Must-Do List, 35
    Notes for a Résumé, 320
    Observing Teaching, 289,
    Oral Presentation Rubric, 168
    Parent Letter (test-taking), 177